Computer Arithmetic:
Key Insights

COMPUTER ARITHMETIC: KEY INSIGHTS

Jocelyn O. Padallan

ARCLER PRESS

www.arclerpress.com

Computer Arithmetic: Key Insights

Jocelyn O. Padallan

Arcler Press
224 Shoreacres Road
Burlington, ON L7L 2H2
Canada
www.arclerpress.com
Email: orders@arclereducation.com

ISBN: 978-1-77469-869-3 (Hardcover)

ABOUT THE AUTHOR

Jocelyn O. Padallan is Assistant Professor III from Laguna State Polytechnic University, Philippines and she is currently pursuing her Master in Information Technology and has Master of Arts in Education from the same University. She has passion for teaching been Instruction and College of Computer Studies - Student Council Adviser at Laguna State Polytechnic University.

TABLE OF CONTENTS

LIST OF FIGURES

LIST OF TABLES

PREFACE

In an era where computers have become an integral part of our daily lives, understanding the fundamental principles of computer arithmetic has never been more important. From simple calculations to complex algorithms, the accuracy and efficiency of numerical computations impact various domains, including scientific research, engineering, finance, and computer science.

"Computer arithmetic: Key insights" aims to provide readers with a comprehensive understanding of the underlying principles, techniques, and algorithms that form the foundation of computer arithmetic. This book serves as a guide for both students and professionals seeking to deepen their knowledge in this crucial field.

The field of computer arithmetic encompasses a broad range of topics, including number representation, arithmetic operations, error analysis, and optimization techniques. Each chapter of this book delves into these subjects, unraveling the intricacies of computer arithmetic while presenting clear explanations and practical examples.

Drawing upon the vast expertise of leading experts in the field, this book explores both classical and modern approaches to computer arithmetic. It covers topics such as fixed-point arithmetic, floating-point arithmetic, error analysis and propagation, numerical stability, and advanced optimization techniques. Additionally, it delves into emerging topics like approximate computing, parallel processing, and hardware accelerators.

The primary goal of "Computer Arithmetic: Key Insights" is to bridge the gap between theory and practice. While presenting theoretical concepts, this book emphasizes real-world applications, ensuring that readers understand the relevance and implications of the discussed principles. Numerous illustrative examples and exercises accompany the theoretical discussions to facilitate hands-on learning and reinforce comprehension.

Furthermore, this book acknowledges the rapid advancements in computer architecture and technology. It explores the impact of emerging hardware trends, such as multicore processors, graphics processing units (GPUs), and field-programmable gate arrays (FPGAs), on computer arithmetic. By considering both software and hardware aspects, this book equips readers with a holistic understanding of the subject.

—Author

CHAPTER

1 Introduction to Computer Arithmetic

Contents

1.1. INTRODUCTION

In common parlance, "digital computer" refers to an apparatus that processes information specifically that kept in binary numbers or bits. It is possible to use the bits in a computer to provide any physical thing. A user can instruct the system to do various operations on the data that has been stored. If the computer is working properly, its processing should be error-free. Because of this, people tend to believe that a computer that has been correctly programmed is an unfailing instrument. It is somewhat paradoxical that this opinion is frequently unjustified when the digital computer utilizes numerical processing. In mathematics, the real numbers are defined using two different approaches (Parhami, 2010).

The first method starts by creating natural numbers. One way is to take advantage of the famous Peano axiom. Then, rational numbers, irrational numbers, integrals, and complex numbers have their definitions, respectively. Integers, often called integers, are pairs of natural numbers while rational numbers are pairs of numbers. Subtraction between numbers is always possible.

The definition of a pair of real numbers includes complex numbers whose square root always exists. On the other hand, the evolution from the rational to the real is different from the previous one. This is not possible considering the relationship between pairs of rational numbers (Atkins, 1975).

Various methods are used to interpret real numbers. From an emotional point of view, they are interchangeable.

Dedekind's division of the set of numbers and prime numbers of significant numbers is the most famous genetic method for teaching real numbers. Both of these genetic techniques are based on a set of rational numbers. In either scenario, the definition of a real number requires an endlessly large number of rational numbers (Kulisch, 2013).

The second method involves the observation that the field of real numbers is linearly ordered. The similarity between all linearly ordered fields will then be proved. This means that there may be only one such field. The previously described genetic process proves that there is such a way, and that it is possible to achieve. Thus, the evolutionary method's specification of the real numbers represents the only possible realization of a conditionally complete and linearly ordered field. The axioms that govern this area serve as the foundation for the vast corpus of research and the applications of that analysis. In axiomatic geometry, it does not matter whether a line is a straight line or a point. The only significant thing is how points, straight lines, and other things are related following the axioms. Similarly, analysis is an abstract concept that does not matter what kind of real number is considered. The only thing that shows the axioms define the relationship between the real numbers (Garner, 1976).

Symbols such as the letter e and the sign tilde represent numbers with certain characteristics. The real numbers that are used in the evolutionary approach, as well as the decimal numbers that are used in everyday life, are only used as evidence that nontrivial models exist.

When it comes to applied mathematics, the situation is extremely different. Any competent programmer is aware that a number's name and value are two entirely different things (Swartzlander & Lemonds, 2015). Abstract methods can make advancements and evidence much easier to understand. They make it possible for work to concentrate on the core of a problem. When all other abstract methods have been tried and are no longer viable, only then should one use concrete number representations.

What is true for real numbers also holds for the floating point numbers used in computers. Even in this case, contrasting a general, axiomatic definition appropriate for theoretical research with specific representations appropriate for mathematical work is tremendously helpful. The decimal system is the most common "power" system used to express real numbers. Both the order relation and the equality can be easily defined in this context. Mathematical procedures, on the other hand, bring forth complications (Agrawal & Rao, 1983).

If a real number is irrational, then it can be represented by an infinite b-adic expansion, albeit in many cases, this is still true even if the number is rational. These kinds of infinite expansions are not amenable to exact addition or multiplication. On the other hand, easy methods can be used to perform the necessary operations for finite b-adic expansions. The definition of the operation is the maximum value of the sequence of results obtained when applying the operation to ever-increasing prefixes of infinite b-adic expansions. When performing operations on those expansions, this bound is what is left over. Theoretically, a computer might approximate this limiting procedure and achieve similar results (Goldberg, 1990).

The practice of numerical computing, as it is carried out now aims for appropriate approximations rather than accurate outcomes. On computers, real numbers are represented by an approximation that is based on a subset on which every operation can be performed quickly and easily. Floating-point numbers with a predetermined number of digits in the mantissa are by far the most popular option for this subset. The objective of numerical analysis is to create programs that use floating-point numbers and give results that are approximations of the precise result that are considered reasonably accurate. Quantifying the amount of error in the computed response is a key component of this endeavor. Controlling this rather common inaccuracy is the most important difficulty in computing. Hence, numerical computation is wholly unimportant to the kinds of commonplace uses of computers like the ones described in the first paragraph of this Introduction. Integer arithmetic, which can be relied on for its precision, is the method of choice—or at least it should be—whenever the application of mathematics is called for (Garzón et al., 2003).

The computer ought to be a mathematical instrument, with its numerical features being mathematically and accurately specified. The people who build computers and those who use them should have an easy time describing and comprehending these qualities and operations. This will allow both groups to work with a more comprehensive understanding of how computations are carried out. The computer arithmetic method explained in this book revolves heavily around the idea of semi-morphism as its guiding principle. The numerous models that are given in this article all lead straight to a comprehension of the characteristics of semi-morphism. These features embody an ordering principle that makes it possible for this book's arithmetic study to be comprehended in close approximation to geometry. Invariants are geometry features that remain the same regardless of whatever group of transformations it is subjected to. These attributes can be specified and deduced.

In a manner not dissimilar to that, the mathematical properties of a computer will be characterized here in terms of their invariance with regard to semi-morphisms. Semi-morphisms computer applications can be described by the programs performing arithmetic operations in various spaces. Consequently, arithmetic has been produced with many features, such as high speed, ideal accuracy, usefulness, applicability, and so on. Because of its striking similarities to geometry, computer arithmetic may be explained in this context exhaustively and comprehensively (Flynn & Oberman, 2001).

Implementing computer arithmetic algorithms and circuits is done in a way that is intuitive to someone who is not an expert in the field. When this is done, it prevents the confusion of the computer that is produced by its users having to deal with complicated implementations. A fundamental component of computer mathematics is the use of directed roundings and interval operations. The continuum is represented on the computer by intervals. The interval's two floating-point bounds express the continuous set of real numbers that is between two floating-point boundaries. The theoretical foundations of computer mathematics have been profoundly impacted by interval arithmetic. The outcome of a computation can be guaranteed by using interval arithmetic, which makes it possible to utilize a computer for verification and to solve decidable problems. Mathematical rounding done in the conventionally straightforward method cannot answer such issues (Omondi, 1994).

The foundation of the computer arithmetic that will be discussed here is provided by the spaces typically utilized in defining and analyzing numerical algorithms. Integers and real numbers are the foundation upon which all calculation is built. Therefore, numerical algorithms appear in space R and vectors V R or matrices M R that is defined over real numbers. Employing the related complex spaces C, V C, and M C is possible. The connection has been used to arrange all of these different spaces. The component-wise definition is used for C and the vector and matrix spaces. In numerical mathematics, methods for intervals in these spaces are also taken into consideration for the sake of decidability and error control. If we denote the set of intervals over a sequence M as IM, we obtain the regions IR, IV R, IM R, and IC, IV C, and IM C. This is due to the fact that IM is the set of ordered intervals over M.

A table of the available spaces may be found in Figure 1.1, which will serve as a point of reference throughout this discussion. The many contexts that were discussed before and contained definitions of arithmetic are enumerated in the second column of this image. On the other hand, algorithms that are derived and specified within these spaces are not usable on a computer because a computer can only represent finite subsets of data. For the set of real numbers expressed by R, the subset S typically consists of floating-point numbers, each with a predetermined number of digits in the mantissa. When computing within S is not precise enough, it is common practice to employ a bigger subset D of R, where R is greater than D and smaller than S (Koren, 2018).

1.2. APPLICATION OF ARITHMETIC

The applicability of arithmetic operations is necessary for the vector, matrix, and interval spaces, which are extensions of the sets S, D, and R. The result above produces a set of limited spaces, namely VS, MS, IS, IVS, IMS, CS, V CS, M CS, ICS, IV CS, and IM CS, along with their respective spaces over D. The areas mentioned above are delineated in the third and fourth columns of Figure 1.1. The set of all pairs of S and V can be denoted as CS. The set of all n-tuples consisting of pairs from CS can be represented as CS. In addition, we can write ICS to denote the set of all intervals over the ordered set CS, etc. Commonly used in real-world applications are single- and double-precision floating-point values, respectively, to implement S and D sets. Figure 1.1 and subsequent content utilize S and D as symbolic representations of generic subsets of R, the arithmetic properties of which will be subsequently explained (Kruskal, 1977).

Having established the sets of the third and fourth columns, the focus now shifts to the task of defining the operations that can be performed on these sets.

$$
\begin{array}{ccccccc}
\text{I} & & \text{II} & & \text{III} & & \text{IV} \\
 & & \mathbb{R} & \supset & D & \supset & S \\
 & & V\mathbb{R} & \supset & VD & \supset & VS \\
 & & M\mathbb{R} & \supset & MD & \supset & MS \\
\mathbb{PR} & \supset & \mathbb{IR} & \supset & \mathbb{I}D & \supset & \mathbb{I}S \\
\mathbb{P}V\mathbb{R} & \supset & \mathbb{I}V\mathbb{R} & \supset & \mathbb{I}VD & \supset & \mathbb{I}VS \\
\mathbb{P}M\mathbb{R} & \supset & \mathbb{I}M\mathbb{R} & \supset & \mathbb{I}MD & \supset & \mathbb{I}MS \\
 & & \mathbb{C} & \supset & \mathbb{C}D & \supset & \mathbb{C}S \\
 & & V\mathbb{C} & \supset & V\mathbb{C}D & \supset & V\mathbb{C}S \\
 & & M\mathbb{C} & \supset & M\mathbb{C}D & \supset & M\mathbb{C}S \\
\mathbb{PC} & \supset & \mathbb{IC} & \supset & \mathbb{IC}D & \supset & \mathbb{IC}S \\
\mathbb{P}V\mathbb{C} & \supset & \mathbb{I}V\mathbb{C} & \supset & \mathbb{I}V\mathbb{C}D & \supset & \mathbb{I}V\mathbb{C}S \\
\mathbb{P}M\mathbb{C} & \supset & \mathbb{I}M\mathbb{C} & \supset & \mathbb{I}M\mathbb{C}D & \supset & \mathbb{I}M\mathbb{C}S
\end{array}
$$

Figure 1.1. A group of spaces for numerical computations.

Additionally, it should be noted that the lines depicted in Figure 1.1 are not independent, meaning they are not mutually exclusive in their mathematical relationship. As an illustration, it is possible to perform scalar multiplication on a vector and matrix multiplication; similarly, interval multiplication can be carried out on an interval vector and an interval matrix. Consequently, the ensuing provisional and non-formal explanation of fundamental computer arithmetic is as follows (Roy & Roth, 2017):

The fundamental arithmetic operations in computing encompass all the requisite mathematical operations specified in the third and fourth columns of Figure 1.1 and all possible permutations of those sets.

S and D sets are floating-point numbers with single and double mantissa lengths, respectively. Within a programming system, various data types are associated with the spaces depicted in the third and fourth columns of the figure. A proficient programming system must provide operations for every potential combination of data types within each column for these spaces (Dahou et al., 2022).

The initial section of this literary work formulates precise explanations for the numerous operations and additionally designates uncomplicated frameworks as contexts for their implementation. The subsequent section pertains to the execution of said operations on computing systems. Specifically, it has been demonstrated that the operations can be systematically constructed from a limited number of fundamental algorithms. Rapid hardware circuits can be utilized to implement these.

Establishing arithmetic operations for all sets in the third and fourth columns is now possible. Consider the set M, for which certain operations have been defined. Moreover, let M denote the set of axioms provided for the constituents of M. One possible rule that could be considered is the commutative property of addition. The designation of the pair M, M as a structure, and its reference as the structure of the set M is a common practice. The well-known structures of the sets R, V R, M R, C, V C, and M C are established. Let M denote one of the sets mentioned above, and let the symbol represent one of the operations defined on M *. Let PM denote the power set of set M, defined as the collection of all possible subsets of M. The operation performed on set M can be expanded to include the power set PM through the subsequent definition:

$A \circ B := \{a \circ b \mid a \in A \wedge b \in B\}, B \in \mathrm{P}$

By generalizing this idea to all M operations, we gain the framework of the power set PM, PM, which can be inverted to produce the initial structure M, M. This program defines arithmetic operations and a related structure for the power sets of the spaces R, V R, M R, C, V C, and M C, as illustrated in the first column of Figure 1.1 (Lascoux, 2004).

Concisely stated, its structure and operations characterize the leftmost space of each row in Figure 1.1, denoted as {M, M}, which are consistently established. These structures can establish and infer the structures and operations of the remaining 30 spaces. It is unnecessary to perform this task for every individual subset space. The abstract mapping principle is utilized to perform the task above for all the rows of Figure 1.1 simultaneously. The above mentioned principle would be implemented if additional columns were situated to the right within the table depicted in Figure 1.1.

The cardinality of N, as a subset of M, may vary. An infinite number of elements characterizes the sets depicted in the first two columns of Figure 1.1. In contrast, those in the last two columns exhibit finite elements. Establishing a one-to-one correspondence or isomorphism between sets with distinct cardinalities is impossible. Homomorphisms are known to maintain the structural properties of groups, rings, and vector spaces. Using basic illustrations can demonstrate that realizing a logical homomorphism is unattainable in the context of floating-point values. Maintaining a high degree of proximity to the concept of homomorphism is advisable. It will be demonstrated subsequently that the set/subset pairs depicted in Figure 1.1 can achieve the following four properties.

For every arithmetic operation in M, a corresponding operation in N exists if M is a space and N is a subset to its right in Figure 1.1.

$a \circ b := \quad (a \circ b),\ a,b \in \mathrm{N} \qquad (RG)$

The given statement pertains to a mapping from M to N, referred to as a rounding. A rounding is characterized by possessing the following properties (Huang & Jou, 2004):

1. $a = a,\ a \in N \qquad (R1)$
2. $(a \leq b \Rightarrow a \leq b),\ a,b \in M \qquad (R2)$
3. $(-a) = -a,\ a \in M \qquad (R3)$

It can be demonstrated that the properties denoted as (RG), (R1), (R2), and (R4) are prerequisites for a homomorphism to exist between ordered algebraic structures {M, M}and {N, N }. Thus, a mapping that exhibits the above-mentioned properties is referred to as a semi-morphism. The subset N is equipped with approximating operations ∘, which are defined by (RG) for all operations ∘ in M in the context of a semimorphism. The property of being (R1) is highly inherent to the rounding process.

While (R1) and (R2) do not provide a unique definition for the rounding function from M to N, the semi-morphism is accountable for both the mapping of elements and the resultant structure {N, N}. The validity of the set of rules N within N is fundamentally contingent upon the characteristics of semimorphism. The set N can be precisely characterized as a collection of rules that exhibit invariance in relation to a semimorphism. Specifically, N is a subset of M, and the structural composition {N, N} represents a broader conceptualization of {M, M}. It is possible to draw the correct conclusion that N is a subset of M by analyzing the mapping between the second and third columns in any particular row, as shown in Figure 1.1. It can be observed that as one progresses from the third to the fourth column, and potentially beyond, the value of N is consistently equivalent to that of M. It will be demonstrated subsequently that the configurations of ringoids or vectoids that are ordered, weakly ordered, or isotonely ordered, embody the characteristics that remain unchanged in relation to semimorphism. The ringoid is a mathematical construct that extends the properties of a ring, and the vectoid expands upon the characteristics of a vector space (Fan, 2012). The preservation of sound mathematical structures by semi morphisms constitutes a compelling rationale for using semi-morphisms in the definition of arithmetic operations.

Figure 1.1 depicts a power set and an interval space, both of which can be sorted according to (R2), the subset relation. Properties (R1) and (R2), where the symbol is substituted for, and other relevant criteria can be utilized to characterize the act of mapping a power set or interval set M onto a subset N.

$a \subseteq a, a \in M.$ *(R3)*

The set and interval roundings exhibit anti-symmetry, as property (R4) indicates. When converting between the real numbers and floating-point numbers, there are two important monotone roundings: Q (downward) and (upward). The directed roundings in question are characterized by their unique adherence to the conditions outlined in (R1), (R2), and (R3) (Bertolini & Darmon, 1997). The roundings specified by (RG) also have arithmetic operations defined for them. The practicality of a definition of computer arithmetic is contingent upon its feasibility for implementation through efficient routines and circuitry. Later, we will present specialized hardware circuits that demonstrate the practicality of all semi-morphisms depicted in Figure 1.1. Additionally, we will showcase how all arithmetic operations can be executed with utmost precision. In product spaces, several operations differ significantly from those that rely on basic floating-point arithmetic (Elstrodt et al., 1983). It will be demonstrated subsequently that the arithmetic operations about floating-point numbers, as depicted in the third and fourth columns of Figure 1.1, can be expeditiously executed by utilizing a limited number of modular building blocks. The building mentioned above blocks have been designed to execute the fundamental mathematical operations. These operations are accompanied by three distinct rounding techniques: round-to-nearest, directed rounding, and round-up, as well as case selections essential for interval multiplication and division. It is noteworthy that an antisymmetric monotone rounding, similar to the rounding to the nearest method, characterizes the rounding process (Cascudo et al., 2011). The 15 operations denoted by ∘, Q∘, and Δ∘, where ∘ belongs to the set {+, –, ×, /, ·} as depicted in Figure 1.2, are established by (RG). Regarding the scalar product, the vectors a and b are defined as,

a = (a_i) and b = (b_i), each consisting of finite elements (Messine, 2002)

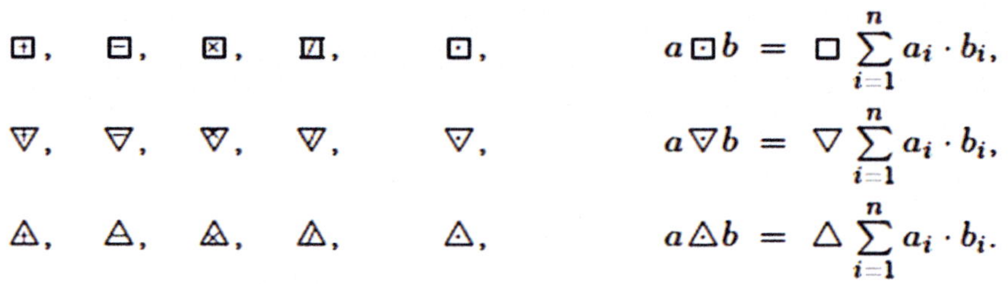

Figure 1.2. The 15 most fundamental steps in any computing program.

Part 2 of the study presents the development of high-speed hardware circuitry for the abovementioned operations. The mapping principle about a semi-morphismm can be obtained through a direct derivation from the distinctive models of the sets illustrated in Figure 1.2 (Kowalski et al., 2000). An example of interest is the function that maps the power set of the complex numbers onto the intervals of complex numbers. In complex numbers, an interval [a, b] is defined as a rectangular region in the complex plane, where a and b are two complex numbers and a ≤ b. The sides of this rectangle are parallel to the axes. When two complex intervals A and B, are operated upon as power set elements, the outcome is usually not an interval result. Instead, the outcome is more specific: AA ∘ B in the power set PC (White, 1989).

An interval operation always yields another interval in a computational environment. As a result, the rectangle in Figure 1.3 representing the minimal interval that contains the power set result A B must be assigned (Heath-Brown, 2000). If the set A B is already an interval, then (R1) holds, and the rounding has no effect. Growing the set A B increases the smallest interval that contains it, satisfying (R2). Because of symmetry, (R4) is always met. The result is a construction that, by definition, fulfills (RG) A B:= (A B) (De Figueiredo & Stolfi, 2004).

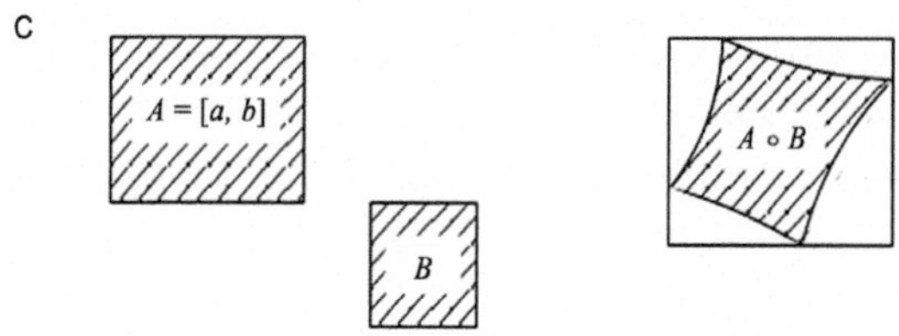

Figure 1.3. Operation for complex intervals.

An additional instance is represented by the fundamental set of spaces denoted as R and D in Figure 1.1 (Xu et al., 2019). Figure 1.4 shows that when adding two floating-point numbers, a and b in row 1, the result may not be an exact sum that is likewise a floating-point number within set D, which is relevant to the meaning of floating-point arithmetic. As a result, we must convert the outcome to a floating-point value within D and round it off (Colliot-Thélène et al., 1993). The conformity of the rounding process to (R1), (R2), and (R4) is demonstrated in Figure 1.4. The symbol ≤ denotes the order relation. As per RG, the definition of floating-point addition is given by the expression: a + b = (a + b), c = a + b

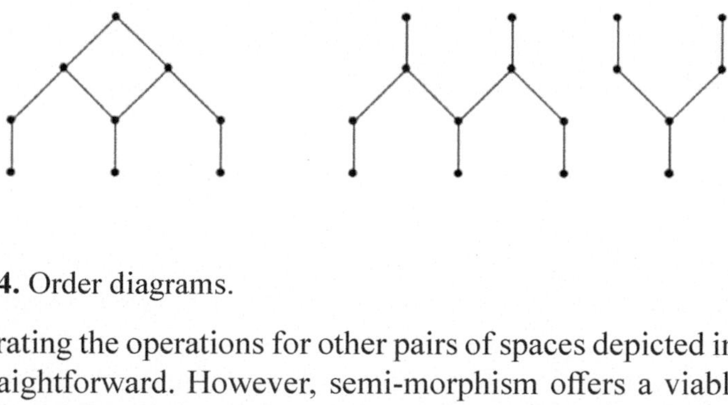

Figure 1.4. Order diagrams.

Illustrating the operations for other pairs of spaces depicted in Figure 1.1 is not straightforward. However, semi-morphism offers a viable approach for mapping these operations, which can be leveraged to develop highly efficient and precise algorithms and hardware circuits (Darmon, 2001) The property of a semi-morphism denoted as RG necessitates that each operation must yield an outcome equivalent to the result obtained by executing the mathematically accurate operation in the fundamental space M and then rounding off the outcome to the computer's representable subset N (Shoba & Nakkeeran, 2016). In contrast to the conventional approach of floating-point arithmetic, which involves approximating arithmetic operations in product spaces such as complex numbers, vectors, and matrices, semi-morphism defines the optimal operation. No computer-representable approximation of the true result can be improved about the required rounding. Stated differently, the computer-representable subset contains no intermediate value between a given computation's precise and calculated outcome (Aguirre-Hernandez & Linares-Aranda, 2010)

1.3. SEMI-MORPHIC COMPUTER OPERATIONS

It can be inferred that every semi-morphic-computer operation exhibits a precision level within 1 ulp (Ramaiah & Harkude, 2022). Rounding to the nearest value results in a half ulp accuracy. The rounding operation in product spaces is defined in a component-wise manner, thereby ensuring that this property applies to each individual component (Belavkin, 2012). Using semi-morphisms of Figure 1.1 to define arithmetic operations yields computer arithmetic that achieves optimal accuracy. Consequently, the analysis of numerical algorithms' errors is made simpler. Moreover, the subsequent compatibility properties are valid for the structures {M, M } and {N, N } concerning all operations ∘ in M (Kiesler, 1983):

$$(a \circ b \in N \Rightarrow a \circ b = a \circ b)\ a\ b \in N \qquad (RG1)$$

$$(a \circ b \leq c \circ d \Rightarrow a \circ b \leq c \circ d)\ a\ b,c,\ d \in N \quad (RG2)$$

1.4. COMPUTER ARITHMETIC

1.4.1. Initial Concepts

For the sets and subsets shown in Figure 11.1, this chapter provides an axiomatic account of their essential features (Ohlsson & Rees, 1991). The present study introduces the concept of rounding from a set M onto a subset N, then analyzes the fundamental characteristics of specific roundings and their interplay with basic arithmetic operations (Dodson & Shields, 1978). Several lattice theoretic concepts are utilized to achieve this objective, introduced earlier in this chapter (Walus et al., 2003).

1.4.2. Ordered Sets

In the second column of Figure 1.1, three distinct mathematical structures are identified: an arithmetic structure, a topographical or metric structure, and an organizational structure. Specific compatibility characteristics include the following link to the entities mentioned above (Mohd Syah et al., 2016). If an is less than or equal to b, then an incremented by c is less than or equal to b incremented by c. Their strength is significantly reduced when these structures are rounded and represented on subsets that computers can process (Teichroew & Hershey, 1977). Due to the monotonicity of rounding, the alterations to the order structure are negligible. The order structure is a crucial element that holds major significance for the arguments presented in this book. Consequently, the present chapter commences by enumerating several widely recognized notions and characteristics of ordered sets (Carrozzo et al., 2020).

1.5. SUMMARY

The computer can process the data through various operations, such as translation, searching, or sorting, as initiated by the user. Assuming proper functionality, the computer's processing is devoid of errors. A computer is commonly regarded as an impeccable instrument. Contemporary numerical computing endeavors to obtain practical and reasonable approximations rather than exact outcomes. In the realm of computing, the set of real numbers is subject to approximation. It is thus represented by a subset that facilitates efficient and straightforward execution of all mathematical operations. The prevalent option for this particular subset pertains to floating-point numbers. The objective of numerical analysis is to create and formulate computational procedures that utilize floating-point arithmetic to estimate the precise outcome accurately. Quantifying the error of the computed answer is a crucial aspect of this task. Rounding to the closest value results in an accuracy of half an ulp. The rounding operation in product spaces is defined component-wise, thereby ensuring that this property applies to each component.

REFERENCES

1. Agrawal, D. P., & Rao, T. R. N., (1983). Introduction: computer arithmetic. *IEEE Transactions on Computers, 100*(4), 329–330.
2. Aguirre-Hernandez, M., & Linares-Aranda, M., (2010). CMOS full-adders for energy-efficient arithmetic applications. *IEEE Transactions on Very Large-Scale Integration (VLSI) Systems, 19*(4), 718–721.
3. Atkins, D. E., (1975). Introduction to the role of redundancy in computer arithmetic. *Computer, 8*(6), 74–77.
4. Atsumi, K., (1966). On complete lattices having the Hausdorff interval topology. *Proceedings of the American Mathematical Society, 17*(1), 197–199.
5. Bancerek, G., & Endou, N., (2001). Compactness of Lim-inf topology. *Formalized Mathematics, 9*(4), 739–743.
6. Banon, G. J. F., & Barrera, J., (1993). Decomposition of mappings between complete lattices by mathematical morphology, Part I. general lattices. *Signal Processing, 30*(3), 299–327.
7. Belavkin, V. P., (2012). Quantum Lévy–Itô algebras and non-commutative stochastic analysis. *Stochastics An International Journal of Probability and Stochastic Processes, 84*(2–3), 393–405.
8. Bermúdez, A., Casado, R., Quiles, F. J., Pinkston, T. M., & Duato, J., (2003). Evaluation of a subnet management mechanism for InfiniBand networks. In: *Proceedings 2003 International Conference on Parallel Processing, 2003* (Vol. 1, pp. 117–124). IEEE.
9. Bertolini, M., & Darmon, H., (1997). A rigid analytic Gross-Zagier formula and arithmetic applications. *Annals of Mathematics, 146*(1), 111–147.
10. Brent, R. P., & Zimmermann, P., (2010). *Modern Computer Arithmetic* (Vol. 18, pp. 789–790). Cambridge University Press.
11. Carpi, S., Gaudio, T., & Hillier, R., (2019). Classification of unitary vertex subalgebras and conformal subnets for rank-one lattice chiral CFT models. *Journal of Mathematical Physics, 60*(9), 093505.
12. Carrozzo, G., Siddiqui, M. S., Betzler, A., Bonnet, J., Perez, G. M., Ramos, A., & Subramanya, T., (2020). AI-driven zero-touch operations, security, and trust in multi-operator 5G networks: A conceptual architecture. In: *2020 European Conference on Networks and Communications (EuCNC)* (Vol. 1, pp. 254–258). IEEE.
13. Carruth, P. W., (1942). Arithmetic of ordinals with applications to the theory of ordered Abelian groups. *Bulletin of the American Mathematical Society, 48*(4), 262–271.

14. Cascudo, I., Cramer, R., & Xing, C., (2011). The torsion-limit for algebraic function fields and its application to arithmetic secret sharing. In: *Proceedings Advances in Cryptology–CRYPTO 2011: 31st Annual Cryptology Conference, Santa Barbara, CA, USA* (Vol. 1, pp. 685–705). Springer Berlin Heidelberg.
15. Colliot-Thélène, J. L., Kato, K., Vojta, P., & Vojta, P., (1993). Applications of arithmetic algebraic geometry to Diophantine approximations. *Arithmetic Algebraic Geometry: Lectures Given at the 2nd Session of the Centro Internazionale Matematico Estivo (CIME) Held in Trento, Italy*, pp. 164–208.
16. Connor, W. S., & Clatworthy, W. H., (1954). Some theorems for partially balanced designs. *The Annals of Mathematical Statistics*, 100–112.
17. Dahou, A., Al-Qaness, M. A., Abd Elaziz, M., & Helmi, A., (2022). Human activity recognition in IoHT applications using arithmetic optimization algorithm and deep learning. *Measurement, 199*, 111445.
18. Darmon, H., (2001). Integration on Hp× H and arithmetic applications. *Annals of Mathematics*, *45*, 589–639.
19. Davis, A. C., (1955). A characterization of complete lattices. *Pacific J. Math*, *5*(2), 311–319.
20. De Figueiredo, L. H., & Stolfi, J., (2004). Affine arithmetic: concepts and applications. *Numerical Algorithms*, *37*, 147–158.
21. Dodson, D. W., & Shields Jr, N. L., (1978). Man/terminal interaction evaluation of computer operating system command and control service concepts. In: *Proceedings of the Human Factors Society Annual Meeting* (Vol. 22, pp. 388–392). Sage CA: Los Angeles, CA: SAGE Publications.
22. Eklund, P., Gutiérrez García, J., Höhle, U., & Kortelainen, J., (2018). Semigroups in complete lattices. *Quantales Modules and Related Topics*, *54*, 236–240.
23. Elstrodt, J., Grunewald, F., & Mennicke, J., (1983). Discontinuous groups on three-dimensional hyperbolic space: analytical theory and arithmetic applications. *Russian Mathematical Surveys*, *38*(1), 137.
24. Fan, L., (2012). Applications of arithmetic in US and Chinese textbooks: A comparative study. In: *International Comparisons in Mathematics Education* (Vol. 1, pp. 151–162). Routledge.
25. Flynn, M. J., & Oberman, S. F., (2001). *Advanced Computer Arithmetic Design* (Vol. 1, pp. 213–220).
26. Garner., (1976). A survey of some recent contributions to computer arithmetic. *IEEE Transactions on Computers*, *100*(12), 1277–1282.

27. Garzón, E. M., García, I., & Fernández, J. J., (2003). An approach to teaching computer arithmetic. In: *High Performance Computing for Computational Science—VECPAR 2002: 5th International Conference Porto, Portugal, Selected Papers and Invited Talks 5* (Vol. 1, pp. 269–283). Springer Berlin Heidelberg.
28. Georgiades, F., (2021). Augmented perpetual manifolds and perpetual mechanical systems—Part I: Definitions, theorem, and corollary for triggering perpetual manifolds, application in reduced-order modeling and particle-wave motion of flexible mechanical systems. *Journal of Computational and Nonlinear Dynamics*, *16*(7).
29. Gingras, A. R., (1976). Convergence lattices. *The Rocky Mountain Journal of Mathematics*, *10*, 85–104.
30. Goldberg, D., (1990). Computer arithmetic. In: David, P., & John, L. H., (eds.), *Computer Architecture: A Quantitative Approach* (Vol. 2, pp. 982–985). Morgan Kaufmann, Los Altos, Calif., Appendix A.
31. Graybill, F. A., & Hultquist, R. A., (1961). Theorems concerning Eisenhart's model II. *The Annals of Mathematical Statistics*, *32*(1), 261–269.
32. Grofman, B., Owen, G., & Feld, S. L., (1983). Thirteen theorems in search of the truth. *Theory and Decision*, *15*(3), 261–278.
33. Hansell, R. W., (1967). Monotone subnets in partially ordered sets. *Proceedings of the American Mathematical Society*, *18*(5), 854–858.
34. Hansell, R. W., (1968). On a conjecture of DeMarr on partially ordering topological spaces. *Proceedings of the American Mathematical Society*, *19*(3), 586–588.
35. Heath-Brown, D. R., (2000). Arithmetic applications of Kloosterman sums. *Nieuw Archief Voor Wiskunde*, *1*, 380–384.
36. Huang, S. J., & Jou, M. J., (2004). Application of arithmetic coding for electric power disturbance data compression with wavelet packet enhancement. *IEEE Transactions on Power Systems*, *19*(3), 1334–1341.
37. Insel, A. J., (1963). A compact topology for a lattice. *Proceedings of the American Mathematical Society*, *14*(3), 382–385.
38. Insel, A. J., (1964). A relationship between the complete topology and the order topology of a lattice. *Proceedings of the American Mathematical Society*, *15*(6), 847–850.
39. Jónsson, B., (1982). Arithmetic of ordered sets. In: *Ordered Sets: Proceedings of the NATO Advanced Study Institute Held at Banff, Canada* (Vol. 1, pp. 3–41). Springer Netherlands.

40. Kiesler, D. J., (1983). The 1982 interpersonal circle: A taxonomy for complementarity in human transactions. *Psychological Review, 90*(3), 185.

41. Klatte, R., & Ullrich, C., (1975). Consequences of a properly implemented computer arithmetic for periodicities of iterative methods. In: *1975 IEEE 3rd Symposium on Computer Arithmetic (ARITH)* (Vol. 1, pp. 24–32). IEEE.

42. Koren, I., (2018). *Computer Arithmetic Algorithms* (Vol. 45, No. 3, pp. 216–220). CRC Press.

43. Kowalski, E., Michel, P., & VanderKam, J., (2000). Mollification of the fourth moment of automorphic L-functions and arithmetic applications. *Inventiones Mathematicae, 142*, 95–151.

44. Kruskal, J. B., (1977). Three-way arrays: rank and uniqueness of trilinear decompositions, with application to arithmetic complexity and statistics. *Linear Algebra and its Applications, 18*(2), 95–138.

45. Kulisch, U., (2013). Computer arithmetic and validity. In: *Computer Arithmetic and Validity* (Vol. 85, p. 2365). de Gruyter.

46. Lascoux, A., (2004). Addition of application to arithmetic. *Séminaire Lotharingien de Combinatoire [electronic only], 52*, 8–9.

47. McKenzie, R., (2000). Arithmetic of finite ordered sets: Cancellation of exponents, II. *Order, 17*, 309–332.

48. Messine, F., (2002). Extensions of affine arithmetic: Application to unconstrained global optimization. *J. Univers. Comput. Sci., 8*(11), 992–1015.

49. Meyer, A. R., (1974). The inherent computational complexity of theories of ordered sets. In: *Proceedings of the International Congress of Mathematicians* (Vol. 2, pp. 477–482).

50. Mohd Syah, N. E., Hamzaid, N. A., Murphy, B. P., & Lim, E., (2016). Development of computer play pedagogy intervention for children with low conceptual understanding in basic mathematics operation using the dyscalculia feature approach. *Interactive Learning Environments, 24*(7), 1477–1496.

51. Möhring, R. H., (1989). Computationally tractable classes of ordered sets. *Algorithms and Order, 255*, 105–194.

52. Ohlsson, S., & Rees, E., (1991). The function of conceptual understanding in the learning of arithmetic procedures. *Cognition and Instruction, 8*(2), 103–179.

53. Omondi, A. R., (1994). *Computer Arithmetic Systems: Algorithms, Architecture, and Implementation* (Vol. 89, pp. 456–460). Prentice Hall International (UK) Ltd.
54. Parhami, B., (2010). *Computer Arithmetic* (Vols. 4, 20, No. 00, pp. 58–60). New York, NY: Oxford University Press.
55. Paulson, L. C., & Grabczewski, K., (1996). Mechanizing set theory: Cardinal arithmetic and the axiom of choice. *Journal of Automated Reasoning*, *17*, 291–323.
56. Ramaiah, G. K., & Harkude, S. A., (2022). Elliptic curve cryptography based homomorphic end-to-end encryption security in cloud computing. *Mathematical Statistician and Engineering Applications*, *71*(3s), 64–75.
57. Raney, G. N., (1952). Completely distributive complete lattices. *Proceedings of the American Mathematical Society*, *3*(5), 677–680.
58. Reisman, W. M., (1995). When are economic sanctions effective-selected theorems and corollaries. *ILSA J. Int'l & Comp. L.*, *2*, 587.
59. Rival, I. (Ed.)., (2012). *Ordered Sets: Proceedings of the NATO Advanced Study Institute Held at Banff, Canada* (Vol. 83, pp. 65–66). Springer Science & Business Media.
60. Roy, S., & Roth, D., (2017). Unit dependency graph and its application to arithmetic word problem solving. In: *Proceedings of the AAAI Conference on Artificial Intelligence* (Vol. 31, pp. 456–460).
61. Schröder, B. S., (2003). *Ordered Sets* (Vol. 29, p. 30). Springer.
62. Shoba, M., & Nakkeeran, R., (2016). GDI based full adders for energy efficient arithmetic applications. *Engineering Science and Technology, an International Journal*, *19*(1), 485–496.
63. Swartzlander, E. E., & Lemonds, C. E. (Eds.)., (2015). *Computer Arithmetic: Volume III* (Vol. 45, p. 256). World Scientific.
64. Teichroew, D., & Hershey, E. A., (1977). PSL/PSA: A computer-aided technique for structured documentation and analysis of information processing systems. *IEEE Transactions on Software Engineering*, (1), 41–48.
65. Tozal, M. E., & Sarac, K., (2012). Estimating network layer subnet characteristics via statistical sampling. In: *Networking 2012: 11th International IFIP TC 6 Networking Conference, Prague, Czech Republic, Proceedings, Part I 11* (Vol. 1, pp. 274–288). Springer Berlin Heidelberg.
66. Trotter, W. T., & Winkler, P., (1987). Arithmetic progressions in partially ordered sets. *Order*, *4*(1), 37–42.

67. Van den Bulcke, T., Van Leemput, K., Naudts, B., van Remortel, P., Ma, H., Verschoren, A., & Marchal, K., (2006). SynTReN: A generator of synthetic gene expression data for design and analysis of structure learning algorithms. *BMC Bioinformatics*, *7*, 1–12.
68. Vishnu, A., Mamidala, A. R., Jin, H. W., & Panda, D. K., (2005). Performance modeling of subnet management on fat tree InfiniBand networks using opensm. In: *19th IEEE International Parallel and Distributed Processing Symposium* (Vol. 2, p. 8). IEEE.
69. Walus, K., Jullien, G. A., & Dimitrov, V. S., (2003). Computer arithmetic structures for quantum cellular automata. In: *The 37th Asilomar Conference on Signals, Systems & Computers, 2003* (Vol. 2, pp. 1435–1439). IEEE.
70. White, S. A., (1989). Applications of distributed arithmetic to digital signal processing: A tutorial review. *IEEE ASSP Magazine*, *6*(3), 4–19.
71. Xu, L., Yuan, R., Zhu, Z., Liu, K., Jing, Z., Cai, Y., & Huang, R., (2019). Memristor - based efficient in - memory logic for cryptologic and arithmetic applications. *Advanced Materials Technologies*, *4*(7), 1900212.
72. Zhao, B., & Zhao, D., (2005). Lim-inf convergence in partially ordered sets. *Journal of Mathematical Analysis and Applications*, *309*(2), 701–708.
73. Zherui, M., & Wangming, W., (1991). Logical operators on complete lattices. *Information Sciences*, *55*(1–3), 77–97.

CHAPTER

2 Implementation of Arithmetic in Computers

Contents

2.1. INTRODUCTION

This chapter pertains to the execution of arithmetic operations on a computer, specifically through the utilization of a floating-point display, denoted as S. This report will describe the implementation for all operations and rows depicted in Figure 2.1. The principles of floating-point arithmetic are founded upon those of integer arithmetic. The book does not prioritize the topic of integer arithmetic. In the following sections, we will examine the concept of floating-point arithmetic. The execution was bifurcated into two distinct phases, with the specifications of the second tier being contingent upon the first tier. The initial procedure tier encompasses various floating-point computations about the topmost row depicted in Figure 2.1. The operations mentioned above are formally defined by the (RG) formula, which applies to all possible roundings of Q, Δ, μ,μ = 0(1)b. The second-degree phase delineates the procedures specified in the remaining rows depicted in Figure 2.1 (Omondi, 1994).

In contemporary times, computer hardware is equipped with highly potent technology, thereby rendering arithmetic operations predominantly facilitated by computer hardware, including floating-point arithmetic. Vendors have devised sophisticated concepts to facilitate arithmetic operations.

The examination and analysis of these techniques are outside the purview of this literary work. Instead of a brief explanation, we present a comprehensive algorithmic depiction of the execution of floating-point arithmetic. The present study demonstrates that the process above can be decomposed into multiple autonomous procedures, encompassing the approximation of arithmetic operations, normalization, and diverse rounding techniques. The present discourse pertains to delineating routines for two distinct types of accumulators, namely the long and the short. The latter denotes the minimal prerequisite. The eighth chapter of this literary work is dedicated to calculating the scalar product (Kulisch & Miranker, 1986).

The final segment of this chapter presents a concise discourse on the level 2 procedures. The present analysis provides a concise overview of the operations outlined in Figure 2.1, highlighting their feasibility using level 1 operations. The concepts mentioned above have been thoroughly examined in the preceding sections. The algorithms for these operations are not derived due to their inherent simplicity and lack of difficulty, provided that the level 1 routines are accessible (Parhami, 2020).

2.2. A QUICK REVIEW OF INTEGER ARITHMETIC REALIZATION

This section of the literature pertains to the concept of floating-point arithmetic. The principles of floating-point arithmetic are founded on those of integer arithmetic. The secondary significance of computer-based integer arithmetic implementation is the focus of this discussion. There are various high-quality books available on the subject matter. A fundamental comprehension of integer arithmetic in computer systems is necessary to grasp this comprehensively and the subsequent two sections. The information is made available in this particular section. Our objective is not to achieve comprehensiveness. We are not currently engaging in a discussion regarding cutting-edge technologies. The rudimentary logical operators serve as the fundamental constituents for integer arithmetic. Gates are electrical circuits that are capable of implementing these operators. The set of three logical operators, namely and, or, and not, constitutes a comprehensive system of operators. The operators mentioned above are formally defined in the subsequent table (Vincent, 1992).

Table 2.1. Logical Operators AND, OR, and NOT

		a ^ b	a V b	-a
a	*b*	(and)	(or)	(not)
0	0	0	0	1
0	1	0	1	1
1	0	0	1	0
1	1	1	1	0

On certain occasions, there may be utilization of the operators that encompass a greater number of input entities. When a switch is utilized as a fundamental bi-stable component, it can exhibit a state of 0 when open and 1 when closed. The logical operation of "or" can be achieved by placing two switches in parallel, while placing two switches in series can result in the logical operation of "and" (Palchaudhuri & Chakraborty, 2016) (Table 2.1).

In his Treatise on the Laws of Human Thought, published in 1854, George Boole, a prominent British mathematician, demonstrated that any logical function f that involves n logical variables $v_1, v_2, \ldots, v_n$ can be exhaustively characterized by an expression that incorporates the logical values true and false, as well as the three logical operators and, or, and not. Therefore, this set of three logical operators is called a comprehensive operator system (Krasnobayev et al., 2014).

Arithmetic operations for binary numbers can be constructed using logical operators such as "and," "or," and "not." The fundamental components for arithmetic operations consist of the full and half adder. The half adder is a digital circuit that receives two binary inputs and generates two binary outputs, namely the sum digit (s) and the carry digit (c) (Dietzfelbinger, 1996).

Up to this point, our analysis has been based on the overarching presumption that the set R depicted in Figure 2.1 conforms to the characteristics of a linearly ordered ringoid. The present discourse shall henceforth adopt a more precise approach by considering R as a linearly directed field of real numbers and D and S as distinct subsets that possess unique characteristics, called floating-point systems. The topic of floating-point numbers and systems is addressed in Section 2.3. The paper also analyses various fundamental approximations of the set of real numbers in the context of a floating-point framework. Additionally, the study establishes the limits of accuracy for these approximations (Tzou & Hsu, 1997).

The present study delves into floating-point operations as defined by semi-morphisms in Section 2.3. Subsequently, we examine the operations that have been defined in the product sets as enumerated in S and D. We then proceed to deduce error and limits as well. These actions are executed based on the premise that semi-morphisms define the operations. Error formulas and bounds are derived to define scalar product and matrix multiplication operations. Error formulas are simplified when semi-morphisms are used to define operations, and the error bounds are decreased by at least a factor of n when compared to the bounds determined from the description of the operations themselves (Leibowitz, 1976).

2.3. INTRODUCTION AND FEATURES OF REAL NUMBERS

The real numbers are typically demonstrated through two predominant methods. The two methods under consideration are commonly known as the axiomatic method and the constructive method. The concepts explained above have been previously introduced in the introductory section of this literary work. In order to enhance clarity, we will provide a brief overview of the axiomatic method. The set of real numbers {R, +, ·, ≤} can be formally defined as a linearly ordered field that is conditionally complete.

The R order structure and the algebraic structure share the following properties of compatibility (González-Martín et al., 2013):

- a, b, c∈R (a ≤ b ⇒ a + c ≤ b + c).
- a, b, c∈R (a ≤ b ∧ c ≥ 0 ⇒ a • c ≤ b • c).

The algebraic structure {R, +, •} exhibits commutative group properties for both multiplication and addition operations. The elements 0 and 1 are considered neutral with respect to multiplication and addition in the field of real numbers, denoted as R, respectively. It is important to note that 0 is not equal to 1. The distributive law serves as a connection between both groups. The distributive property of multiplication over addition states that the product of a number 'a' with the addition of two other numbers 'b' and 'c' is equal to the addition of the products of 'a' with 'b' and 'a' with 'c.' In mathematical notation, this can be expressed as a • (b + c) = a • b + a • c. All subsequent characteristics of the real numbers are deduced from their fundamental characteristics. The theorem presented here is of significant importance in this context (Hunter, 2014).

- **Theorem 2.1:** R and RJ are two linearly ordered isomorphic fields, subject to certain conditions.

The assertion made by Theorem 2.1 is that a conditionally complete, linearly ordered field can exist at most once due to the possibility of identifying corresponding elements of isomorphic structures. Indeed, a structure of this nature does exist, as the constructive approach outlined in the introductory section of this publication yields such a result. The method used to define the real numbers in this context represents the sole manifestation of a linearly ordered field that is conditionally complete (Bartle & Sherbert, 2000).

The implication of Theorem 2.1 is that the addition of further elements to the real numbers is not feasible without compromising or diminishing one or more of the properties mentioned above. The acquisition of complex numbers can be achieved by partially abandoning the order structure. The real number system is occasionally augmented by including the two elements –∞ and +∞, which possess the property that –∞ < a < +∞ for all a ∈ R. The set {R ∪ {–∞} ∪ {+∞}, ≤} forms a complete lattice. Nevertheless, the field is no more linearly ordered. For example, it is true that a + ∞ = b + ∞, regardless of whether an is less than b. The absolute value function is a mapping denoted by $|\bullet|: R \rightarrow R+:= \{x \in R \mid x \geq 0\}$, defined for real numbers. It possesses the property that for any real number a∈R, the absolute value of an is non-negative (Kantor et al., 1989).

$$|a| := \sup(a, -a) = a \quad \text{for } a \geq 0, -a \quad \text{for } a \leq 0.$$

A series {an} ∈RN:= {α | α: N → R} of real numbers is said to converge to a real number a ∈ R if and only if the absolute difference between each element of the sequence and an is less than a given positive number ε, denoted as |an – a| < ε. In this case, we write lim a = a. Moreover, for any given ε > 0, there exists a natural number N(ε) ∈ N such that for all n > N(ε), |an – a| < ε.

Alternatively, if the sequence does not converge, it is referred to as divergent. A sequence {an} can be utilized to define an associated sequence {sn} (Lam, 1984).

$$\bigwedge_{\varepsilon>0} \bigvee_{N(\varepsilon)>N} \bigwedge_{n>N(\varepsilon)} |a_n - a| < \varepsilon.$$

If the sequence {sn} approaches a finite value s, then we refer to the infinite sum of the terms in the sequence as a convergent series.

$$s_n : \sum_{v=1}^{n} a_v$$

$$s = \lim_{x \to \infty} s_n = \sum_{v=1}^{\infty} a_v$$

The variable 's' is denoted as the summation of the given series. The series of numbers represented by sn are called partial sums. In the event that {sn} exhibits divergence, the series in question is classified as divergent. It is vital to remember that while abstract theories are highly valuable, the field of analysis has been primarily created for its practical use in the natural world.

In the field of applied mathematics, the significance of real numbers extends beyond their abstract theory and symbolic representation, as their numerical value holds considerable weight. Real numbers are typically denoted in specialized number systems. Applied mathematics must take into account specific representations of real numbers. The investigation of the portrayal of actual numbers commences with the subsequent widely recognized theorem concerning b-adic systems. It is possible to demonstrate that this theorem can be derived from the axioms I-III (Rosenlicht, 1986).

2.4. FLOATING-POINT NUMBERS

The discussion commences by invoking Theorem 2.2, which states that any real number x can be written distinctly by a b-adic expansion of a particular form (Muller et al., 2018).

$$x = od_n d_{n-1} \ldots\ldots d_1 d_0 . d_{-1} d_{-2} \ldots = o \sum_{v=n}^{-\infty} d^v b^v \qquad (2.1)$$

with $\circ \in \{+,-\}, b \in N, b > 1$, and

$0 \le d_i \le b-1$ for all $i = n(-1)-\infty$, (2.2)

$d_i \le b-2$ for infinitely many i. (2.3)

It can be assumed that dn is not equal to zero.

The (b-ary) point in equation (2.1) can be translated to a different position by applying a multiplication with appropriate power of b to account for the translation. The real number zero is the sole entity that lacks a distinct representation. The symbol Rb is utilized to represent all of these numerical values, which encompasses the value of zero (Clenshaw & Olver, 1984):

$$\mathbb{R}:\{0\} \cup \left\{ x = om.b^e \mid o \in \{+,\_\}, b \in \mathbb{N}, b > 1, e \in \mathbb{Z}, m = \sum_{i=1}^{\infty} x_i b^{-i}, x_i \varepsilon \{0,1,\ldots,b-1\}, 1(1)\infty, x \neq_1 0\ x_i \le b-2 \text{ for infinitely many } i \right\}.$$

Z is the set of integers, while b is referred to as the base. The symbol represents the sign of x ∘, whereas m denotes the mantissa of x, and e represents the exponent. The nomenclature employed in scholarly works designates "m" as the fraction part. The sign $\circ \in \{+, -\}$ is commonly regarded as a constituent of the mantissa. Typically, the constituents of b are not computable on a computing device. The representation of these elements is limited to truncated versions (Morris, 1971).

A floating point is a real number that belongs to the set $S = S(b, r, e_1, e_2)$:

$$S = S(b,r,e1,e2) := \left\{ x \varepsilon \mathbb{R}_b \mid m = \sum_{i=1}^{r} x_i b^{-i}, e1 \le e \le e2, e1, e2 \varepsilon \mathbb{Z} \right\}$$

Typically, the value of e_1 is negative, while the value of e_2 is positive. In order to establish a distinct depiction of zero within the set S, it is postulated that sgn(0) = +, mant(0) = 0.00… 0, and exp(0) = 0. The nomenclature $S(b, r, e_1, e_2)$ denotes a floating-point system. S imposes limitations on the length of the mantissa, which is finite and has a maximum length of r, as well as on the range of the exponent, which is bounded by e_1 and e_2 (Dekker, 1971).

The distribution of floating-point numbers within S is non-uniform. The relationship between density and exponent is inversely proportional, as density decreases with an increase in exponent. We employ a case study of a 33-element floating-point system to exemplify this. b = 2, r = 3, $e_1 = -1$, and $e_2 = 2$.

The floating-point system denoted as S(2, 3, 1, 2). A floating-point system can be expressed as S(b, r, e_1, e_2) (Demmel & Nguyen, 2013).

$R:=R \cup \{-\infty\} \cup \{+\infty\}$,

$S:=S(b,r,e_1,e_2):=S(b,r,e_1,e_2) \cup \{-\infty\} \cup \{+\infty\}, S^j:=[-B,+B] \subset R.$

The screen of R can be represented as S(b, r, e_1, e_2). The screen of SJ is represented by Further S(b, r, e_1, e_2). All of the screens above exhibit symmetry, specifically possessing the property denoted as (S3).

The present discourse examines roundings originating from R and directed towards S(b, r, e_1, e_2). It is possible to define analogous roundings from SJ to S(b, r, e_1, e_2) (Goldberg, 1991).

Arounding, R→Sis defined by the property

(R1) $x=x, x \in S$

(R2)$(x \leq y \Rightarrow x \leq y)$ (monotonicity),

The present discourse primarily focuses on the monotonic directed roundings Q and Δ, alongside the monotonic and antisymmetric roundings. The subsequent roundings will be taken into consideration:

$$\bigwedge_{x \varepsilon \bar{R}} \nabla x := \max\left\{y \varepsilon \bar{S} \mid y \leq x\right\},$$

$$\bigwedge_{x \varepsilon \bar{R}} \nabla x := \min\left\{y \varepsilon \bar{S} \mid y \geq x\right\},$$

$$\bigwedge_{x \varepsilon \bar{R}} \square bx : \begin{cases} \nabla x \text{ if } x \geq 0 \\ \Delta x \text{ if } x < 0 \end{cases},$$

$$\bigwedge_{x \varepsilon \bar{R}} \square ox : \begin{cases} \nabla x \text{ if } x \geq 0 \\ \Delta x \text{ if } x < 0 \end{cases},$$

Using the notation,

$$\bigwedge_{x \varepsilon \bar{R}, x \geq 0} s_\mu(x) := \nabla x + (\Delta x - \nabla x).\mu / b, \mu = 1(1)b-1,$$

qx for$x \in [qx, s_\mu(x))$,

Δx for$x \in [s_\mu(x), \Delta x]$

$x<0$

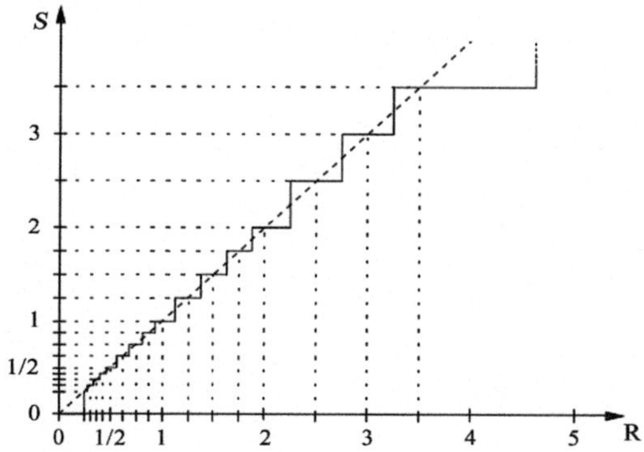

Figure 2.1. Floating-point arithmetic rounding.

The preceding roundings share several common characteristics. Here's an example:

$qx{=}{-}\Delta(-x) \wedge \Delta x{=}{-}q(-x),$ (2.7)

${}_{b}x{=}\mathrm{sgn}(x)\cdot q|x| \wedge {}_{0}x{=}\mathrm{sgn}(x)\cdot \Delta|x|.$ (2.8)

All roundings above exhibit monotonicity, specifically in the second order (R2). The roundings mentioned above, denoted as μ,μ = 0(1)b, exhibit anti-symmetric properties per the R4 criterion.

It is important to note that within a linearly ordered set, any monotone rounding, including all roundings μ, μ = 0(1)b, can be represented using Q or Δ, as discussed. As the relationship between Δ and Q is reciprocal, we precisely depict the rounding function Q: R → S. In the subsequent exposition of Q, the abbreviation B = 0 is employed. (b–1)The expression (b–1)... (b–1) · be2 pertains to the computation of the maximum positive floating-point value.

Subsequently, we derive the value of x (Clinger, 1990):

$$\nabla x = \begin{cases} +\infty & \text{for } x = +\infty \\ +B & \text{for } +B \le x < +\infty \\ +0.x_1x_2\ldots\ldots x_r.b^{e} & \text{for } b^{e1-1} \le x < +B \\ +0.000\ldots\ldots 0.b^{e1} & \text{for } 0 \le x < b^{e1-1} \\ -0.100\ldots\ldots 0.b^{e1} & \text{for } -b^{e1-1} \le x < 0 \\ -0x_1x_2\ldots\ldots x_r.b^{e} & \text{for } -B \le x < -b^{e1-1} \\ & \\ -0.100\ldots\ldots 0.b^{e+1} & \text{for } -B \le x < -b^{e1-1} \\ -(0.x_1x_2\ldots\ldots x_r + b^{-r}).b^{e} & \text{for } -B \le x < -b^{e1-1} \\ -\infty & \text{for } -\infty \le x < -B \end{cases}$$

By utilizing the floor function [x], it is possible to abbreviate the depiction of x.

$$\overset{Q}{\nabla x} = \begin{cases} +\infty & \text{for } x = +\infty \\ +B & \text{for } +B \leq x < +\infty \\ [m.b^{r}].b^{e-r} & \text{for } b^{e1-1} \leq | \mathbf{x} | \leq +B \\ +0.000.....0.b^{e1} & \text{for } 0 \leq x < b^{e1-1} \\ -0.100.....0.b^{e1} & \text{for } -b^{e1-1} \leq x < 0 \\ -\infty & \text{for } -\infty \leq x < -B. \end{cases}$$

The elaboration provided above regarding Qx indicates that a normalization process may still be required.

Several comparable cases arise when the exponent e is assigned the value of e_1 and unnormalized mantissa are allowed, provided that $e < e_1$ (Michel et al., 2001). The simplification of implementing rounding Q on a computer can be achieved through the availability of the function [x]. The assumed representations for Qx involve the utilization of the signed-magnitude representation to represent the mantissa of a floating-point number when dealing with real numbers x where x is greater than 0, the rounded value Qx can be achieved by truncating x after the rth digit of the normalized mantissa m of x. If the truncation process is denoted by t(x), then the following holds (Steele Jr & White, 1990).

$qx = t(x)$ for $x \geq 0$.

The implementation of this task is relatively straightforward. Using truncation can also facilitate rounding Qx for negative values of $x < 0$, provided that negative numbers are denoted by their b-complement. The rounded value Qx can be derived through the truncation of the b-complement x + an of x, utilizing the process mentioned above (Aliasgari et al., 2012):

$qx = t(x+a) - a$ for $x < 0$ (2.9)

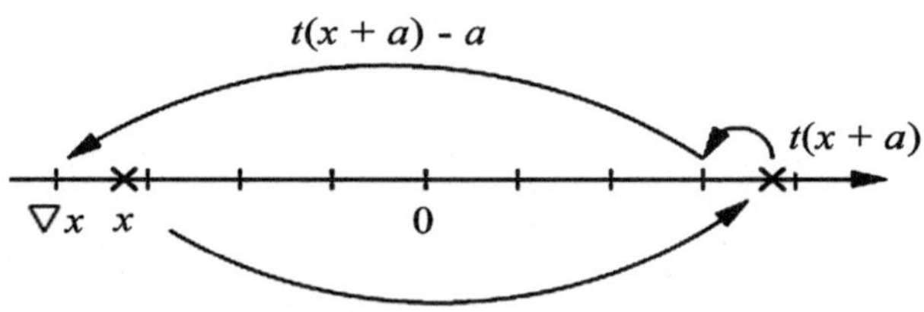

Figure 2.2. The rounding operation x = 0 is used to express negative values as b-complements.

- **Example 2.1:** It is assumed that the numerical system in use is decimal and that the mantissa comprises 3 decimal digits. Subsequently, we derive the value of x as a positive real number, specifically 0.354672 · 103, belonging to the set of real numbers.

$qx = t(x) = 0.354 \cdot 10^3$.

For the negative number $x = -0.354672 \cdot 10^3$,

Hence,

$qx = -0.355 \cdot 10^3$.

This value is obtained by application of equation, where $a = 1.00...0 \cdot 10^3$

$x + a = 0.645328 \cdot 10^3$,

$t(x + a) = 0.645 \cdot 10^3$,

$qx = t(x + a) - a = -0.355 \cdot 10^3$.

Here, the (b–1)-complement representation is intriguing because the function t(x) cannot perform the monotone downwardly directed rounding Qx. The representation mentioned above exhibits isomorphism with the sign-magnitude representation. The $R \rightarrow S(b, r, e_1, e_2)$ roundings constitute merely a subset of the various rounding methods employed in computer arithmetic and numerical analysis. In the context of error analysis in numerical procedures, it is customary to assume that rounding possesses a certain property (Daumas et al., 2001).

$x = x(1 - \epsilon) \text{with} |\epsilon| \leq \epsilon^* = \text{const.}$ (2.10)

The property of rounding is depicted in Figure 2.3. The graph associated with those mentioned above must remain confined within a cone near the identity mapping. The function in question may not exhibit monotonicity or antisymmetry (Blinn, 1997).

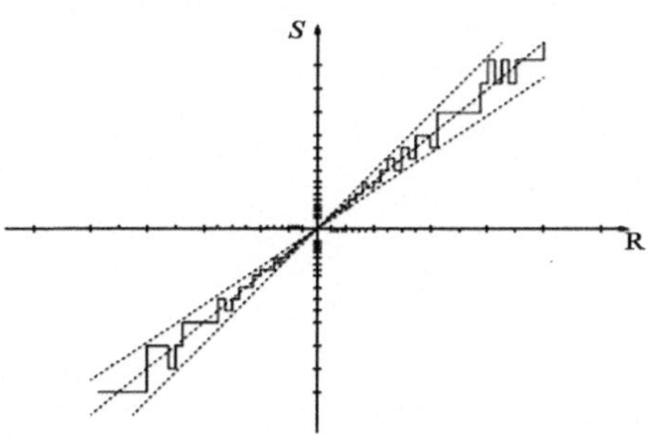

Figure 2.3. A rounding.

The presence of (R1) implies that each instance of rounding is associated with a step function that intersects with the graph of the unique mapping for every value within the set S(b, r, e_1, e_2). This suggests that equation (2.2.10) cannot explain the rounding phenomenon within a certain range near zero. Conduct a comparative analysis of Figures 2.1 and 2.3. While equation may not inherently depict a monotonic mapping, it is demonstrated in the ensuing theorem that any monotonic rounding within the range of be1–1 ≤ |x| ≤ B will possess the property mentioned above (Cowlishaw, 2003).

According to Theorem, if S is a floating-point system with parameters b, r, e1, and e2, and if: R → S is a monotone rounding function, then... Let δ(x) be defined as the difference between x and x, representing the rounding error. The relative rounding errors can be expressed as ∈1 = δ(x)/x and ∈2 = δ(x)/x. Then,

$$\underset{\varepsilon>R}{\wedge}(b^{e1-1} \le |x| \le B) \Rightarrow \square x = x(1-\varepsilon_1) \text{ with} |\varepsilon_1| \le \varepsilon^*$$

$$\wedge x = \square x(1-\varepsilon_2) \text{ with } |\varepsilon_2| \le \varepsilon^*$$

$$\wedge |\mathbf{x}-\square x| < \varepsilon^* |\mathbf{x}| \wedge |x-\square x| < \varepsilon^* |\square x|).$$

Here ∈*is independent of x, and

$$\varepsilon^* = \begin{cases} \frac{1}{2} b^{1-r} & \text{for} \square = o \\ b^{1-r} & \text{for} \square \ne 0 \end{cases}$$

The term "denotes" refers to the process of rounding S to the closest floating-point number, where B equals 0.(b – 1)(b – 1)... (b – 1) · be2.

- **Proof:** The formula under consideration incorporates the variable $\in_1$. The formula containing the variable $\in_2$ can be approached similarly. We have

$x{=}x{+}\delta(x){=}x{+}\in_1 x{\Rightarrow}x{=}x(1{-}\in_1)$.

With $x= \circ m{\cdot}b^e$ we obtain using that $b^{-1}{\cdot}b^e{\le}|x|{<}b^e$. Since $|\delta(x)|{\le}b^{-r}{\cdot}b^e$, we get,

$|\in_1|{=}|\delta(x)|/|x|{\le}(b \quad {\cdot}b)/(b \quad {\cdot}b){=}b$

$|\in_1|{<}b^{1-r}$:If$x{=}b^{-1}{\cdot}b^e$,

where, (R1),$\delta(x){=}0$.

If

$\delta(x){=}b^{-r}{\cdot}b^e$, then $|x|{>}b^{-1}{\cdot}b^e$.

Theorem furnishes error bounds for a rounding only for x $[b^{e1-1}, B]$. When the absolute value of x is less than b, the relative error ϵ_1 can be equal to one or approach infinity, depending on how the rounding function is defined. As x approaches infinity for values of |x| greater than B, the relative error ϵ_1 converges to unity (Higham, 1993). The relative error of the rounding depicted in Figure 2.1 is presented in Figure 2.4. When considering the range of values for x that satisfy the inequality be1–1 ≤ |x| ≤ B, it can be observed that the absolute value of ϵ_1 is less than a predetermined value of ϵ*, which is calculated as 1 multiplied by b1–r. In this area, relative error reduction is achievable by increasing the number of digits, denoted as r, in the mantissa (Marre et al., 2017). As depicted in Figure 2.4, the accurate approximation of real numbers on a computer is challenging or unfeasible when they are positioned to the left or right of the area above. When the absolute value of x is less than b multiplied by e to the power of negative one, the relative error is equal to one. As the absolute value of x becomes greater than or equal to B, the limit of the expression approaches 1 as x approaches infinity. The sole method to reduce the magnitude of said peripheral areas is to diminish e_1 while augmenting e_2. Expanding the range utilized for the exponent's representation is necessary (Janikow & Michalewicz, 1991).

The findings are synthesized into two rules as follows:

1. To achieve greater accuracy within the region of be1–1 ≤ |x| ≤ B, it is necessary to utilize a higher number of numbers.
2. More digits are required to express the exponent to expand the interval be1–1 ≤ |x|≤ B with a higher degree of accuracy (Goubault, 2001).

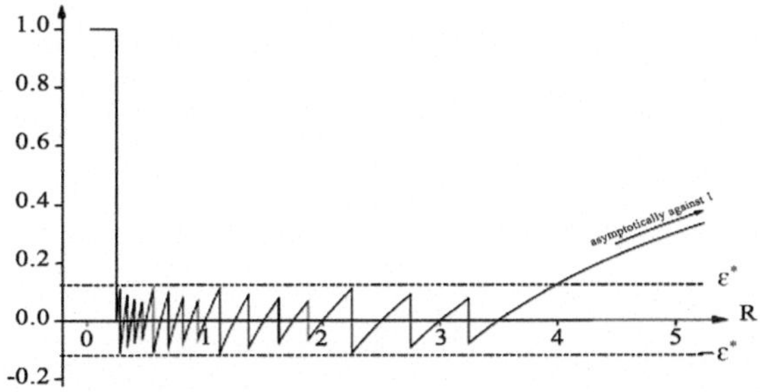

Figure 2.4. Relative rounding error.

If a numerical value |x| falls within the interval (0, be1–1) and is encountered in a virtual capacity within a computer system, the technical terminology utilized to describe this phenomenon is exponent underflow or, alternatively, underflow. Similarly, the term "exponent overflow" or "overflow" is used when the absolute value of x exceeds B. The condition of be1–1 ≤ |x| ≤ B is commonly articulated as follows (Johnson, 2018):

2.5. SUBNORMAL FLOATING-POINT NUMBERS

In a normalized floating-point system denoted as S = S(b, r, e_1, e_2), an element a ∈S can possess multiple additive inverses. Illustrations of this phenomenon have been provided in Section 3.6. Specifically, it has been demonstrated that the multiplicative identity element, denoted as 1, can possess multiple additive inverses. The theorem presents a condition that is both necessary and sufficient for the existence of a unique additive inverse within a discrete subset of the real number system R. The outcome mentioned above is expanded to encompass more comprehensive structures in Theorem 3.13 (Andrysco et al., 2015).

The condition for meeting the requirements of a floating-point system S(b, r, e_1, e_2) has been demonstrated to include the admission of unnormalized mantissas for e = e_1, along with the standardized floating-point numbers of S(b, r, e_1, e_2) (Dooley & Kale, 2006).

2.6. IEEE FLOATING-POINT STANDARD

Konrad Zuse's early computer models, namely the Z3 (1941) and the Z4 (1945), pioneered the floating-point and binary number system for numerical representation. The normalization of floating-point numbers was observed. The mantissa was represented in the format "1." with a numerical value ranging from 1 to 2. The digit "1" at the beginning of the memory was not retained. The term "hidden bit" was employed to refer to its usage. Both machines performed the fundamental arithmetic operations through hardware implementation. The Z4 computer system utilized a 32-bit representation for floating-point numbers. The exponent was represented using 8 bits, the sign using 1 bit, and the mantissa using 24 bits. In performing arithmetic operations, utilizing two supplementary bits to enhance precision and facilitate proper rounding was necessary (Overton, 2001).

Special encoding schemes and corresponding circuitry were developed to manage the three exceptional quantities: zero, infinity, and indeterminate (pertaining to expressions such as 0/0 or infinity minus infinity, among others). An extra bit was employed for the purpose of discriminating between numerical values and the aforementioned exceptional values. In the event that the value equated to zero, the term denoted a standard floating-point numeral. If the numerical value of the word was one, it denoted a unique significance, and the encoding of the word determined whether it was equivalent to zero, infinity, or indeterminate. The representation of zero was achieved through the utilization of the least exponent, while the representation of infinity was accomplished through the utilization of the greatest exponent. The initial computing machines constructed by Konrad Zuse were equipped with all the fundamental functionalities presently deemed necessary by the IEEE floating-point arithmetic criterion (Gal, 1991; Lin et al., 2022).

The IEEE 754 standard outlines the prescribed formats for binary floating-point numbers. The statement delineates atypical circumstances and designates the standard protocol for addressing said circumstances. The primary objective of the standard is to significantly streamline the process of transferring software applications from one system to another. As prescribed by the standard, the numerical outcomes and exceptional operations cases are exclusively ascertained by the input data value, the order of operations, and the destination formats. Consequently, in the event of a program's relocation from one machine to another, the fundamental operations' outcomes will be identical in all bits, provided that both machines adhere to the established norm. The IEEE 754 standard utilizes a binary base of b = 2. It is recommended that the single extended format possess a minimum of 44 bits, while the double expanded format should possess a minimum of 80 bits. In the single precision format, the mantissa takes up 24 bits and the exponent takes up 8 bits (Kahan, 1996; Sohn & Swartzlander, 2012).

In contrast, in the double precision format, the mantissa occupies 53 bits and the exponent 11 bits. The formats have been devised to optimize the amount of data that can be accommodated within 32 and 64 bits. In the binary number system context, it is a common practice to normalize floating-point numbers such that the leading digit is always 1. As a result, this particular bit is not retained while storing these numbers. The concealed bit is maintained in a latent state. This makes the utilization of a single bit for the mantissa sign in both double and single precision format possible. When compared to their 32-bit and 64-bit counterparts, the mantissa and coefficient in the two extended forms use more bits. The IEEE 854 standard allows for either a binary or decimal base to be used (Beaumont-Smith et al., 1999; Cody, 1981).

In contrast to IEEE 754, the encoding of floating-point numbers into bits is not specified. The specification outlines limitations on the permissible quantity of bits to portray the mantissa in single and double-precision configurations. The IEEE binary standard employs a characteristic or bias, denoted as c, to circumvent the need for a significant digit in representing the exponent e. The selection of c is such that the biased exponent E is an unofficial integer (Rajaraman, 2016; Thompson et al., 2004).

$E{:=}c{+}e.$

The exponent of the floating-point number is e = E c if the biased exponent is E. For single precision and double precision, the bias in the IEEE binary standard is 127 and 1023, respectively. According to Figure 2.5, which codes the two data forms, M denotes the mantissa. The floating-point number f has the value 0 (Goldberg, 1991; Cowlishaw, 2003).

$f = (-1)^{S} \cdot M \cdot 2^{E-c}.$

The integer has a negative sign if S is 1 and a positive sign if S is 0. Nonnegative floating-point numbers can be used as integers for comparisons, which is a benefit of the specific coding of floating-point numbers with a skewed exponent (Seidel & Even, 2004; Tang, 1989).

According to IEEE 754, each of the four fundamental arithmetic operations—addition, subtraction, multiplication, and division—must be offered with one of four rounding options: either rounding to the closest floating-point integer, rounding upwards, rounding downwards, or rounding toward 0. In the latter scenario, it is also necessary to round the midpoint between two neighboring floating-point integers such that the output has an even least significant digit. Round-to-nearest-even is the term for this rounding technique? When the value of the exponent is e_{min}, the IEEE 754 standard utilizes denormalized numbers, allowing denormalized mantissas. One possible explanation for this is that denormalized numbers ensure the distinctiveness of additive inverses (Fagin & Renard, 1994; Whitehead & Fit-Florea, 2011).

$x - y = 0 \Leftrightarrow x = y.$

In 854 and 754, denormalized numbers are referred to as subnormal and denormal. Another term for underflow is elegant underflow or progressive underflow. A lot of IEEE-compliant arithmetic units don't directly support denormalized integers; instead, they leave their treatment to software. Programmers can choose not to use denormalized integers even in hardware architectures that support them if they want their programs to run more quickly (Brain et al., 2015; Havaldar & Gurumurthy, 2016). A computation may experience uncommon occurrences like division by zero. The IEEE standard has specific bit patterns to express unique quantities for such events. The special representations for +, +0, 0 are specified. Historically, the computation would be stopped due to an overrun or division by zero. However, there are some instances where continuing the computation makes sense. The standard procedure in IEEE arithmetic is to provide an outcome and resume the computation in the event of an extraordinary event. This necessitates the definition of the outcome of operations on or leading to exceptional values. Examples include (Miner, 1995; Salehi & DeMara, 2015).

$4/0=\infty, -4/0=-\infty, 0/0=\mathrm{NaN}, \infty-\infty=\mathrm{NaN}, 0\cdot\infty=\mathrm{NaN}, \infty/\infty=\mathrm{NaN},$

$1/(-\infty)=-0, 3/(+\infty)=-0, \log 0=-\infty, \log x=\mathrm{NaN}\ \mathrm{when}\ x<0, 4-\infty=\mathrm{NaN}$

These unique operations and results are designed to give programmers the flexibility to move some tests and choices to a more convenient location in the program later. The user must be made aware of the situation when an extraordinary event occurs during a program operation, and the calculation is resumed. Status flags are used for this. The IEEE standard distinguishes Five categories of exceptions: overflow, underflow, division by zero, invalid operation and inexact. For every one of the five exceptions, a status flag is present. Any exception that occurs sets the relevant status flag. The IEEE standard suggests installing so-called trap handlers to assist users in analyzing exceptions in a program (Rao et al., 2018; Taylor & Patterson, 1981).

The present iteration of the Draft Standard for Floating-Point Arithmetic P 754 does not impose an explicit mandate for the provision of individual operation codes for each of the operations involving directed roundings, namely Q+, Q-, Qx, Q/, and Δ+, Δ-, Δx, Δ/, on upcoming processors. Regarding rounded operations, the present draft explicitly stipulates that each operation must be executed as if it initially generated an intermediate outcome that is accurate to an infinite degree of precision and has an unbounded range and subsequently rounded that outcome by one of the available rounding modes. The determination of the mode is contingent upon the value of a designated mode variable, which is presumed to have been established prior to the execution of the operation. It can be inferred that forthcoming processors that comply with the IEEE P 754 floating-point arithmetic standard will continue segregating rounding from arithmetic operations. This raises concerns that interval arithmetic performance may once again be sluggish and fail to align with the rapid floating-point arithmetic on upcoming processors (Hauser,

1996; Burgess, 2005). The current iteration of the IEEE P 754 standard does not necessitate the inclusion of a precise multiply and accumulate instruction or a corresponding precise scalar product (Carreño & Miner, 1995; Liang et al., 2023).

2.7. ADDITIONAL ARITHMETIC FEATURES

Two supplementary mathematical characteristics are essential and indispensable (Imbo et al., 2007):

1. Providing efficient hardware assistance for extended interval arithmetic is a crucial aspect that warrants academic attention (Roy & Roth, 2016).
2. The requirement is for a rapid and precise operation that combines multiplication and addition (Kulisch & Miranker, 1986).

The utilization of interval arithmetic appears to be supported by the IEEE standards. The fundamental arithmetic operations must incorporate the functionality of rounding to the nearest, towards zero, as well as downwards and upwards. The latter two components are deemed indispensable for the field of interval arithmetic. Most processors that offer IEEE arithmetic exhibit a distinct separation between the rounding and fundamental operation, resulting in a significant disadvantage. This does not pose any challenges in a typical floating-point calculation. The configuration of the rounding method is established as a singular event. Subsequently, many operations are executed utilizing this rounding mode, occurring once per cycle. Nevertheless, in the execution of interval arithmetic, it is necessary to alternate the rounding mode frequently (Misra et al., 2018).

It is necessary to round down the lower and upper bound for the result of each interval operation. Consequently, it is necessary to reset the rounding mode for each arithmetic operation. When the setting of the rounding mode and the arithmetic operation are similarly efficient, the computation of each bound is needlessly slowed down by a factor of two compared to conventional floating-point arithmetic. On most commercial processors, establishing the rounding mode requires a duration that is a multiple of the time required for the arithmetic operation, typically 3, 5, or 10 times longer. It can be observed that the execution of an interval operation is significantly slower, at a minimum of eight times, and potentially up to 20 or more times slower than the corresponding floating-point operation. This is without taking into account the requisite case distinctions that are necessary for interval multiplication and interval division. This phenomenon has a detrimental impact on the field of interval arithmetic. Incorporating rounding into arithmetic operations is imperative. All of the rounded arithmetic operations, including rounding to the nearest, rounding downwards, and rounding upwards, should exhibit equal speed (Bohlender et al., 1993).

In the context of interval arithmetic, it is imperative to have the capability of invoking each of the operations Q+, Q-, Q×, Q/, Δ+, Δ-, Δ×, and Δ/ as a unified instruction, whereby the rounding is intrinsically embedded within each operation. Hence, programming languages must furnish notations for arithmetic operations that accommodate diverse rounding methods. Possible academic rewrite: Various rounding modes can be applied to arithmetic operations in computer programs. For instance, basic operations can be performed by rounding to the closest floating-point number using the symbols +, –, *, and /, respectively. Alternatively, rounding upwards can be achieved with the symbols + >, – >, *>, and />, while rounding downwards can be obtained with + <, – <, * <, and / <. Finally, rounding toward zero, also known as chopping, can be implemented with +|, –|, *|, and /| (Marklof, 2006).

There is a need for the development of new operation codes. It is unfortunate that commonly utilized programming languages do not offer arithmetic operators for floating-point numbers, specifically those for addition, subtraction, multiplication, and division. However, this does not provide justification for the general separation of rounding from arithmetic. A prospective standard for floating-point arithmetic ought to mandate that all forthcoming processors furnish the 16 operations enumerated previously. A forthcoming standard is recommended to prescribe names for the associated assembler instructions, such as addp, subp, mulp, divp, addn, subn, muln, divn, addz, subz, mulz, and divz. In the given context, the symbol 'p' denotes the process of rounding towards positive values, 'n' denotes rounding towards negative values, and 'z' denotes rounding towards zero. Interval operations can be conveniently programmed using these operators. The proposed system exhibits high speed and complete portability across different processors (Rahimpour et al., 2017).

The C++ class library C-XSC has been utilized for over 15 years and offers interval arithmetic in a manner consistent with the description mentioned above. C-XSC does not provide operations with directed roundings, as C++ only allows operator overloading. The utilization of these operations is infrequent in various applications. In cases where they are deemed necessary, interval operations are executed in lieu of other methods. Subsequently, the resultant upper or lower bound is utilized to derive the intended solution (Landerl et al., 2009). The utilization of the traditional approach in which the rounding mode is established prior to the execution of the arithmetic operation is imperative in certain scenarios, particularly in instances where the selection of the rounding mode is arbitrary. In this instance, the status register ought to furnish an additional option for selecting the rounding mode in a stochastic manner facilitated by a hardware-based random number generator. Subsequently, all conventional rounding procedures would be executed utilizing random alterations in rounding. The specified rounding for arithmetic operations would remain unaffected by this (Barwell, 2005).

In order to achieve precise limits for a solution, it is necessary to integrate interval arithmetic with either defect revision or iterative refinement methodologies. In order to achieve efficacy, these techniques necessitate a precise instruction for multiplication and accumulation or alternatively, a precise scalar product. Accumulating entire double-length products into a large fixed-point register is the first step. Truncation errors do not occur during the fixed-point accumulation process (Fagin & Renard, 1994).

The seamless integration of the multiply and gather instruction results in expeditious and uncomplicated circuitry. The pipeline executes a sequence of stages, namely data loading, computation, shifting, and buildup of products, in a unified manner. In addition, it is noteworthy that the process of accumulating products in fixed-point arithmetic is less complex compared to buildup in floating-point arithmetic. Instead of performing several intermediate steps required by the floating-point accumulation method, such as normalization and rounding of products and sums, and disintegration into mantissa and exponent for the next operation, the fixed-point accumulation method simply proceeds directly to the next operation (Ashenhurst, 1962). The procedure is implemented by doing a simple addition of entire double-length products in an extensive fixed-point register after a shift. The utilization of this method results in a significant enhancement in speed as opposed to the potential inaccuracy that may arise from the accumulation of the scalar product through traditional floating-point arithmetic. It's hardware cost is similar to that of a high-speed multiplier featuring an adder tree, which was widely acknowledged several years ago. A minimalistic local memory of approximately 1 kilobyte is sufficient for the arithmetic unit to function effectively. In light of the current era where computer memory is quantified in gigabytes, it is feasible and imperative to allocate resources towards this endeavor. The arithmetic operations involved do not significantly deviate from those that are accessible on a traditional central processing unit. The process of fixed-point accumulation is devoid of errors (Kulisch & Bohlender, 1983).

The provision of fast multiple precision calculation can be facilitated through the utilization of a swift and precise multiply and accumulate instruction. A multiple-precision number is represented as a list of floating-point digits. The numerical magnitude of this quantity is equivalent to the aggregate total of its constituent parts. The representation can be expressed within a broad fixed-point register. This register can conveniently execute subtraction and addition operations on numbers with multiple precision. Multiplying two numbers involves calculating the sum of the products of floating-point numbers (Braithwaite et al., 2017).

The utilization of interval arithmetic can provide a level of certainty in computational processes, whereas implementing an exact multiply and gathering instruction can yield a high degree of precision through defect correction techniques and at a rapid pace. Incorporating prompt and precise hardware assistance for both primary and secondary operations is imperative to enhance conventional floating-point arithmetic. Both of these extensions are deemed necessary. Rather than functioning solely as a rapid computational device, the computer would be transformed into a scientific apparatus for mathematical purposes. The accelerated pace of computing necessitates the adoption of this step, which in turn raises doubts about the efficacy of traditional computing methods. Undoubtedly, the computational system would frequently necessitate additional effort to acquire validated outcomes. However, the mathematical security aspect should be deemed valuable. The transition from assembler to higher-level programming languages entails a significant computational overhead, which is generally accepted without objection. Computers with high processing speeds are frequently employed in safety-critical domains. Miscalculating the eigenfrequencies of a large electrical generator might lead to disastrous outcomes (Neumann et al., 2006).

The IEEE standards 754 and 854 and the anticipated forthcoming standard P 754 exhibit a highly cautious approach. The sole operation surpasses Zuse's basic floating-point arithmetic is the combination of multiplication and addition, also known as fused multiply-add. Otherwise, the standards solely increase the size of the word. Nevertheless, this phenomenon is insufficient to cope with the significant increase in computational velocity. Shortly, it is anticipated that computations will require a minimum of

1020 arithmetic operations, if not more. The remarkable advancements in technology and the significant enhancement in processing speed necessitate a corresponding expansion of the mathematical capabilities of the computer. The book's development of advanced computer arithmetic represents a significant advancement. The software offers a plethora of supplementary arithmetic operations of superior quality (Förstner & Gülch, 1987).

Additionally, it furnishes expeditious tools for scrutinizing intermediate outcomes' caliber and dynamically augmenting precision in difficult circumstances. Fundamental instruments for validating computed outcomes must be universally integrated into all computer systems in the current era. The scope of computer arithmetic ought to extend beyond basic floating-point arithmetic limited to a small number of fixed precisions (Applebaum et al., 2017; Chiarulli et al., 1985).

2.8. SUMMARY

The veracity of a statement is often found in its simplicity. The forthcoming computer arithmetic standard ought to encompass the subsequent prerequisites:

i. A precisely defined arithmetic system that utilizes double-precision floating-point numbers.

ii. The provision of efficient and immediate hardware assistance for double precision interval arithmetic.

The requirement is for multiplying and accumulating rapid and precise operation or a precise scalar product for the double precision format. The tool above is the fundamental instrument for attaining rapid and dynamic precision arithmetic for both real and interval data. The implementation of pipe lining in computing systems results in increased speed, while the incorporation of exactitude ensures a high degree of accuracy in computations. Please refer to Chapters 8 and 9 of the aforementioned book. Undoubtedly, computer arithmetic necessitates the inclusion of elementary functions that possess established and dependable a priori error bounds. The C-XSC software package provides elementary functions that support multiple precision computations.

The utilization of the 128-bit arithmetics may prove advantageous for addressing issues that necessitate an extensive exponent range. Greater flexibility is a highly coveted attribute for forthcoming computing systems. The complexity of implementing a full 128-bit floating-point arithmetic is not significantly higher than that needed to generate an exact scalar product for the double precision format in a fast transmitted hardware approach. The completion of multiple precision computation is aided by the use of a fast, accurate scalar product. Multiple precision computations are not limited by the exponent range of the double precision format. The use of an exponent as a scaling factor is a practical mathematical tool.

REFERENCES

1. Aliasgari, M., Blanton, M., Zhang, Y., & Steele, A., (2012). Secure computation on floating point numbers. *Cryptology ePrint Archive*.
2. Andrysco, M., Kohlbrenner, D., Mowery, K., Jhala, R., Lerner, S., & Shacham, H., (2015). On subnormal floating point and abnormal timing. In: *2015 IEEE Symposium on Security and Privacy* (pp. 623–639). IEEE.
3. Applebaum, B., Damgård, I., Ishai, Y., Nielsen, M., & Zichron, L., (2017). Secure arithmetic computation with constant computational overhead. In: *Advances in Cryptology–CRYPTO 2017: 37th Annual International Cryptology Conference, Santa Barbara, CA, USA, August 20–24, 2017, Proceedings, Part I* (pp. 223–254). Cham: Springer International Publishing.
4. Ashenhurst, R. L., (1962). The Maniac III arithmetic system. In: *Proceedings of the May 1–3, 1962, Spring Joint Computer Conference* (pp. 195–202).
5. Bartle, R. G., & Sherbert, D. R., (2000). *Introduction to Real Analysis* (Vol. 2, p. 2). New York: Wiley.
6. Barwell, R., (2005). Working on arithmetic word problems when English is an additional language. *British Educational Research Journal*, *31*(3), 329–348.
7. Beaumont-Smith, A., Burgess, N., Lefrere, S., & Lim, C. C., (1999). Reduced latency IEEE floating-point standard adder architectures. In: *Proceedings 14th IEEE Symposium on Computer Arithmetic (Cat. No. 99CB36336)* (pp. 35–42). IEEE.
8. Blinn, J. F., (1997). Floating-point tricks. *IEEE Computer Graphics and Applications*, *17*(4), 80–84.
9. Bohlender, G., Cordes, D., Knöfel, A., Kulisch, U., Lohner, R., & Walter, W. V., (1993). Proposal for accurate floating-point vector arithmetic. In: *Mathematics in Science and Engineering* (Vol. 189, pp. 87–102). Elsevier.
10. Bohlender, G., Walter, W., Kornerup, P., Matula, D. W., Kornerup, P., & Matula, D. W., (1991). Semantics for exact floating-point operations. In: *IEEE Symposium on Computer Arithmetic* (Vol. 91, pp. 22–26).
11. Brain, M., Tinelli, C., Rümmer, P., & Wahl, T., (2015). An automatable formal semantics for IEEE-754 floating-point arithmetic. In: *2015 IEEE 22nd Symposium on Computer Arithmetic* (pp. 160–167). IEEE.
12. Braithwaite, D. W., Pyke, A. A., & Siegler, R. S., (2017). A computational model of fraction arithmetic. *Psychological Review*, *124*(5), 603.

13. Burgess, N., (2005). Prenormalization rounding in IEEE floating-point operations using a flagged prefix adder. *IEEE Transactions on Very Large Scale Integration (VLSI) Systems, 13*(2), 266–277.
14. Carr, S., & Kennedy, K., (1994). Improving the ratio of memory operations to floating-point operations in loops. *ACM Transactions on Programming Languages and Systems (TOPLAS), 16*(6), 1768–1810.
15. Carreño, V. A., & Miner, P. S., (1995). Specification of the IEEE-854 floating-point standard in HOL and PVS. *High Order Logic Theorem Proving and its Applications, 16*.
16. Chiarulli, D. M., Rudd, W. G., & Buell, D. A., (1985). Draft: A dynamically reconfigurable processor for integer arithmetic. In: *1985 IEEE 7th Symposium on Computer Arithmetic (ARITH)* (pp. 309–317). IEEE.
17. Clenshaw, C. W., & Olver, F. W., (1984). Beyond floating point. *Journal of the ACM (JACM), 31*(2), 319–328.
18. Clinger, W. D., (1990). How to read floating point numbers accurately. *ACM SIGPLAN Notices, 25*(6), 92–101.
19. Cody, W. J., (1981). Analysis of proposals for the floating-point standard. *Computer, 14*(03), 63–68.
20. Cowlishaw, M. F., (2003). Decimal floating-point: Algorism for computers. In: *Proceedings 2003 16th IEEE Symposium on Computer Arithmetic* (pp. 104–111). IEEE.
21. Cowlishaw, M. F., (2003). Decimal floating-point: Algorism for computers. In: *Proceedings 2003 16th IEEE Symposium on Computer Arithmetic* (pp. 104–111). IEEE.
22. Daumas, M., Rideau, L., & Théry, L., (2001). A generic library for floating-point numbers and its application to exact computing. In: *Theorem Proving in Higher Order Logics: Proceedings 14th International Conference, TPHOLs 2001 Edinburgh, Scotland, UK* (pp. 169–184). Springer Berlin Heidelberg.
23. Dekker, T. J., (1971). A floating-point technique for extending the available precision. *Numerische Mathematik, 18*(3), 224–242.
24. Demmel, J., & Nguyen, H. D., (2013). Fast reproducible floating-point summation. In: *2013 IEEE 21st Symposium on Computer Arithmetic* (pp. 163–172). IEEE.
25. Dietzfelbinger, M., (1996). Universal hashing and k-wise independent random variables via integer arithmetic without primes. In: *STACS 96: Proceedings 13th Annual Symposium on Theoretical Aspects of Computer Science Grenoble, France* (pp. 567–580). Springer Berlin Heidelberg.

26. Dooley, I., & Kale, L., (2006). Quantifying the interference caused by subnormal floating-point values. In: *Proceedings of the Workshop on Operating System Interference in High Performance Applications.*
27. Fagin, B., & Renard, C., (1994). Field programmable gate arrays and floating-point arithmetic. *IEEE Transactions on Very Large-Scale Integration (VLSI) Systems*, *2*(3), 365–367.
28. Förstner, W., & Gülch, E., (1987). A fast operator for detection and precise location of distinct points, corners and centers of circular features. In: *Proc. ISPRS Intercommission Conference on Fast Processing of Photogrammetric Data* (Vol. 6, pp. 281–305).
29. Gal, S., (1991). An accurate elementary mathematical library for the IEEE floating point standard. *ACM Transactions on Mathematical Software (TOMS)*, *17*(1), 26–45.
30. Goldberg, D., (1991). What every computer scientist should know about floating-point arithmetic. *ACM Computing Surveys (CSUR)*, *23*(1), 5–48.
31. González-Martín, A. S., Giraldo, V., & Souto, A. M., (2013). The introduction of real numbers in secondary education: An institutional analysis of textbooks. *Research in Mathematics Education*, *15*(3), 230–248.
32. Goubault, E., (2001). Static analyses of the precision of floating-point operations. In: *Proceedings Static Analysis: 8th International Symposium, SAS 2001 Paris, France* (pp. 234–259). Berlin, Heidelberg: Springer Berlin Heidelberg.
33. Hauser, J. R., (1996). Handling floating-point exceptions in numeric programs. *ACM Transactions on Programming Languages and Systems (TOPLAS)*, *18*(2), 139–174.
34. Havaldar, S., & Gurumurthy, K. S., (2016). Design of Vedic IEEE 754 floating point multiplier. In: *2016 IEEE International Conference on Recent Trends in Electronics, Information & Communication Technology (RTEICT)* (pp. 1131–1135). IEEE.
35. Higham, N. J., (1993). The accuracy of floating-point summation. *SIAM Journal on Scientific Computing*, *14*(4), 783–799.
36. Hunter, J. K., (2014). An introduction to real analysis. *Department of Mathematics, University of California at Davis.*
37. Imbo, I., Vandierendonck, A., & Rosseel, Y., (2007). The influence of problem features and individual differences on strategic performance in simple arithmetic. *Memory & Cognition*, *35*, 454–463.
38. Janikow, C. Z., & Michalewicz, Z., (1991). An experimental comparison of binary and floating-point representations in genetic algorithms. In:

ICGA (Vol. 1991, pp. 31–36).

39. Johnson, J., (2018). Rethinking floating point for deep learning. *arXiv preprint arXiv:1811.01721*.
40. Kahan, W., (1996). IEEE standard 754 for binary floating-point arithmetic. *Lecture Notes on the Status of IEEE, 754*(94720–1776), 11.
41. Kantor, I. L., Solodovnikov, A. S., & Shenitzer, A., (1989). *Hypercomplex Numbers: An Elementary Introduction to Algebras* (Vol. 302). New York: Springer-Verlag.
42. Krasnobayev, V. A., Tyrtyshnikov, O. I., Sliusar, I. I., Kurchanov, V. N., & Koshman, S. A., (2014). The model and the method of implementation of integer arithmetic operations within the RSA crypto algorithms. *Системи Обробки Інформації*, (1), 117–122.
43. Kulisch, U. W., & Miranker, W. L., (1986). The arithmetic of the digital computer: A new approach. *Siam Review*, *28*(1), 1–40.
44. Kulisch, U., & Bohlender, G., (1983). Features of a hardware implementation of an optimal arithmetic. In: *A New Approach to Scientific Computation* (pp. 269–290). Academic Press.
45. Lam, T. Y., (1984). An introduction to real algebra. *The Rocky Mountain Journal of Mathematics*, *14*(4), 767–814.
46. Landerl, K., Fussenegger, B., Moll, K., & Willburger, E., (2009). Dyslexia and dyscalculia: Two learning disorders with different cognitive profiles. *Journal of Experimental Child Psychology*, *103*(3), 309–324.
47. Lee, B., & Burgess, N., (2002). Parameterizable floating-point operations on FPGA. In: *Conference Record of the 36th Asilomar Conference on Signals, Systems and Computers, 2002* (Vol. 2, pp. 1064–1068). IEEE.
48. Leibowitz, L., (1976). A simplified binary arithmetic for the Fermat number transform. *IEEE Transactions on Acoustics, Speech, and Signal Processing*, *24*(5), 356–359.
49. Liang, J., Tessier, R., & Mencer, O., (2003). Floating point unit generation and evaluation for FPGAs. In: *11th Annual IEEE Symposium on Field-Programmable Custom Computing Machines, 2003* (pp. 185–194). IEEE.
50. Lin, C. C., Pu, H. C., Su, S. J., & Lee, M. S., (2020). A concept map-based remedial learning system with applications to the IEEE floating-point standard and MIPS encoding. *IEEE Transactions on Education*, *64*(2), 147–154.
51. Marklof, J., (2006). Arithmetic quantum chaos. *Encyclopedia of Mathematical Physics*, *1*, 212–220.
52. Marre, B., Bobot, F., & Chihani, Z., (2017). Real behavior of floating-point numbers. In: *The SMT Workshop*.

53. Michel, C., Rueher, M., & Lebbah, Y., (2001). Solving constraints over floating-point numbers. In: *Principles and Practice of Constraint Programming—CP 2001: Proceedings 7th International Conference, CP 2001 Paphos, Cyprus* (pp. 524–538). Springer Berlin Heidelberg.
54. Miner, P. S., (1995). *Defining the IEEE-854 Floating-Point Standard in PVS* (No. NASA-TM-110167).
55. Misra, S., Singha, J., & Laskar, R. H., (2018). Vision-based hand gesture recognition of alphabets, numbers, arithmetic operators, and ASCII characters in order to develop a virtual text-entry interface system. *Neural Computing and Applications*, *29*, 117–135.
56. Morris, R., (1971). Tapered floating point: A new floating-point representation. *IEEE Transactions on Computers*, *100*(12), 1578–1579.
57. Muller, J. M., Brisebarre, N., De Dinechin, F., Jeannerod, C. P., Lefevre, V., Melquiond, G., & Torres, S., (2018). *Handbook of Floating-Point Arithmetic* (pp. 44–91). Basel, Switzerland: Birkhäuser.
58. Neumann, B., Von Sydow, T., Blume, H., & Noll, T. G., (2006). Design and quantitative analysis of parametrizable eFPGA-architectures for arithmetic. *Advances in Radio Science*, *4*, 251–257.
59. Oberman, S. F., & Flynn, M. J., (1997). Design issues in division and other floating-point operations. *IEEE Transactions on Computers*, *46*(2), 154–161.
60. Omondi, A. R., (1994). *Computer Arithmetic Systems: Algorithms, Architecture, and Implementation*. Prentice Hall International (UK) Ltd.
61. Overton, M. L., (2001). *Numerical Computing with IEEE Floating Point Arithmetic*. Society for Industrial and Applied Mathematics.
62. Palchaudhuri, A., & Chakraborty, R. S., (2016). High performance integer arithmetic circuit design on FPGA. *Springer India, India. DOI*, *10*, 978–81.
63. Parhami, B., (2020). Computing with logarithmic number system arithmetic: Implementation methods and performance benefits. *Computers & Electrical Engineering*, *87*, 106800.
64. Rahimpour, A., Dadashi, A., Soltanian-Zadeh, H., & Setarehdan, S. K., (2017). Classification of fNIRS based brain hemodynamic response to mental arithmetic tasks. In: *2017 3rd International Conference on Pattern Recognition and Image Analysis (IPRIA)* (pp. 113–117). IEEE.
65. Rajaraman, V., (2016). IEEE standard for floating point numbers. *Resonance*, *21*, 11–30.
66. Rao, R. P., Rao, N. D., Naveen, K., & Ramya, P., (2018). Implementation of the standard floating point MAC using IEEE 754 floating point adder.

In: *2018 Second International Conference on Computing Methodologies and Communication (ICCMC)* (pp. 717–722). IEEE.

67. Rosenlicht, M., (1986). *Introduction to Analysis*. Courier Corporation.
68. Roy, S., & Roth, D., (2016). Solving general arithmetic word problems. *arXiv Preprint arXiv:1608.01413*.
69. Salehi, S., & DeMara, R. F., (2015). Energy and area analysis of a floating-point unit in 15 nm CMOs process technology. In: *SoutheastCon 2015* (pp. 1–5). IEEE.
70. Seidel, P. M., & Even, G., (2004). Delay-optimized implementation of IEEE floating-point addition. *IEEE Transactions on Computers, 53*(2), 97–113.
71. Sohn, J., & Swartzlander, E. E., (2012). Improved architectures for a fused floating-point add-subtract unit. *IEEE Transactions on Circuits and Systems I: Regular Papers, 59*(10), 2285–2291.
72. Steele Jr, G. L., & White, J. L., (1990). How to print floating-point numbers accurately. In: *Proceedings of the ACM SIGPLAN 1990 Conference on Programming Language Design and Implementation* (pp. 112–126).
73. Swartzlander, E. E., & Saleh, H. H., (2010). FFT implementation with fused floating-point operations. *IEEE Transactions on Computers, 61*(2), 284–288.
74. Tang, P. T. P., (1989). Table-driven implementation of the exponential function in IEEE floating-point arithmetic. *ACM Transactions on Mathematical Software (TOMS), 15*(2), 144–157.
75. Taylor, G. S., & Patterson, D. A., (1981). VAX hardware for the proposed IEEE floating-point standard. In: *1981 IEEE 5th Symposium on Computer Arithmetic (ARITH)* (pp. 190–196). IEEE.
76. Thompson, J., Karra, N., & Schulte, M. J., (2004). A 64-bit decimal floating-point adder. In: *IEEE Computer Society Annual Symposium on VLSI* (pp. 297–298). IEEE.
77. Tzou, Y. Y., & Hsu, H. J., (1997). FPGA realization of space-vector PWM control IC for three-phase PWM inverters. *IEEE Transactions on Power Electronics, 12*(6), 953–963.
78. Vincent, J. M., (1992). Finite word length, integer arithmetic multilayer perceptron modelling for hardware realization. *Neural Networks for Vision, Speech, and Natural Language*, 293–311.
79. Whitehead, N., & Fit-Florea, A., (2011). Precision & performance: Floating point and IEEE 754 compliance for NVIDIA GPUs. *rn (A+ B), 21*(1), 18749–19424.

CHAPTER 3

Decimal Arithmetic

Contents

3.1. INTRODUCTION

This chapter defines decimal arithmetic that may be used for general purposes. Correctly implementing this specification would support integer and unrounded floating-point arithmetic and the decimal arithmetic required by IEEE standard 854-1987, 1. This is the correct way to implement this specification. As part of the ongoing revision, IEEE 854 will be integrated with the IEEE 754-1985 standard 2, and this section will chronicle that revision as it happens. This chapter is aimed primarily at implementers who will benefit from including examples and other illustrative and explanatory content (Lortie-Forgues et al., 2015; Lortie-Forgues & Siegler, 2017).

The decimal floating-point arithmetic defined by ANSI standard X3.274-1996 is described in this chapter, along with a simplified subset of the whole arithmetic that implements it. This model serves as the basis for the unrounded floating-point rules. This chapter defines decimal arithmetic that may be used for general purposes (Busaba et al., 2001; Tian et al., 2021).

3.1.1. Inclusions

The following terms will be defined in this chapter:

- Limits are placed on the values that decimal numerals can take
- Methods for working with decimal numbers, including
- The conversions between text and internal representations of numbers that are required
- Arithmetic operations on numbers expressed as decimals (such as addition, subtraction, etc.)
- Information about the context can change the results of an operation, as well as the contexts used by default.
- Conditions considered extraordinary, such as overflow, underflow, undefined results, and other unusual scenarios, may arise during calculations.

3.2. THE ARITHMETIC MODEL

The present chapter is founded on a decimal arithmetic model that formally represents the decimal numeration system. The model comprises three distinct components.

1. The numerical values are utilized as operands or outcomes of the fundamental operations specified in this section.

2. The fundamental mathematical processes that can be performed on numerical values are referred to as operations, including but not limited to addition, multiplication, and other similar procedures.
3. The context refers to the parameters and rules chosen by the user and dictates the outcomes of arithmetic operations, such as the level of precision to be employed (Schmookler & Weinberger, 1971; Hiebert & Wearne, 1985).

The abstract of this chapter delineates the components above. The specification in question does not encompass the expression of operations, which may differ based on the utilized computer language or interface. Additionally, it does not outline the tangible representation of numbers or context, such as their specific storage layout or placement in a processor's register. The subsequent section delineates the theoretical framework for every constituent (Wang et al., 2007; Duale et al., 2007).

3.2.1. Abstract Representation of Numbers

The numerical quantities denote the values subject to manipulation by, or can be, the outcomes of, the fundamental operations delineated in this section. Numeric values can be classified as finite numbers, precisely represented, or as special values, such as infinities and other non-finite numbers (Kadosh, 2008; Naccache & Dehaene, 2001).

3.2.2. Finite Numbers

The definition of finite numbers entails the utilization of three integer parameters:

1. The sign of a number is a binary value that can only be either 0 or 1. A value of 1 denotes that the number is negative, while 0 denotes that the number is either 0 or positive.
2. A coefficient is a mathematical term that refers to an integer that can either be zero or positive. The abstract section does not impose any constraint on the upper bound of the coefficient's maximum magnitude. In practical applications, it may be necessary to establish a precise upper boundary, such as the maximum coefficient length that is accommodated by the particular concrete representation utilized in the implementation. The constraint above must be represented as a whole number integral to denote decimal digits.

3. An exponent is a numerical value with a sign that denotes the degree to which the coefficient is multiplied by 10 (Talenti, 1987; Smith et al., 1973).

The adjusted exponent refers to the exponent of a number represented in scientific notation with one non-zero digit preceding any decimal point. The expression above is determined by the sum of the exponent and the length of the coefficient minus one, where the c length refers to the number of decimal digits in the coefficient. When a limit is imposed on the exponent, it is necessary to ensure that the resulting range of numbers is balanced between positive and negative values while also considering the coefficient's magnitude. To attain a well-proportioned scope, the adjusted exponent (E_{min} and E_{max}) must be set in such a way that the absolute values of their magnitudes do not deviate by more than one. It can be observed that E max is equivalent to the E limit, which represents the highest possible value of the exponent. On the other hand, E min can be expressed as $-E_{max}\pm1$. Thus, in the case where the coefficient has a length of c length digits, the exponent has the potential to assume any value within the range of $-\infty$ to $+\infty$. Eliminate the character at index $-E_{limit}$clength–1 up to the character at index E_{limit}clength–1. In the given scenario, assuming the coefficient to be 123456789 with a total of 9 digits and the exponent having an E limit of 999 with 3 digits, it can be inferred that the range of the exponent would be from –1007 to +991. The above range permits the inclusion of favorable numerical values, spanning from 1.23456789E –999 to 1.23456789E+999. The finite numerical quantity can be expressed as (–1)*sign coefficient* 10*exponent*.

The value of a finite quantity is expressed as 1 multiplied by 10, raised to the power of an exponent (John et al., 2007; Miller et al., 1971).

3.2.3. Special Values

Along with the finite set of numerical values, numbers must possess the capacity to express one of three designated special values (Kadosh et al., 2008).

1. **Infinity:** It is a numerical concept that denotes a value with an infinitely large magnitude, represented by the symbol "∞" as per the IEEE 854 §6.1 standard.
2. **Quiet NaN:** The term "Quiet NaN" refers to a numerical value that denotes undefined outcomes, commonly known as "Not a Number." According to IEEE 854, it is recommended to associate supplementary diagnostic information with NaNs.

3. **Signaling NaN:** This concept pertains to a numerical value that signifies undefined outcomes, commonly called "Not a Number." Its utilization in any operation outlined in this chapter will result in an Invalid operation condition (Martí & Müller, 2003; Yule, 1927).

When a numerical value assumes one of these distinctive values, the coefficient and exponent cannot be determined. 16 A NaN, nevertheless, may possess correlated diagnostic data, commonly referred to as its payload. This is considered to be representable as a positive integer with a coefficient that is not greater than the maximum representable value. Finite numbers can possess a sign, which also applies to all special values. The significance of infinity lies in its sign, which can be either positive or negative. On the other hand, NaN does not possess any inherent meaning in its sign, although it can be regarded as a component of diagnostic data (Weir, 1949; Fjelstad, 1986).

3.3. SUBNORMAL NUMBERS AND UNDERFLOW

Subnormal numbers are a class of non-zero numerical values with adjusted exponents lower than the minimum exponent value (E_{min}) (Higham et al., 2019; Kahan, 1996). Subnormal numbers are considered valid operands for all mathematical operations and can be produced from any operation. If a given outcome falls below the normal range, the Subnormal condition will be triggered prior to any rounding procedures. When the outcome is below the normal range, the exponent's minimum value is denoted as E_{min} and is calculated as E_{min}–(precision–1). The working precision is defined as precision and is further elaborated on page 10. The outcome will be rounded as needed if the exponent is less than E_{min}. If the outcome of the rounding process is imprecise, the Underflow condition is triggered. The occurrence of a subnormal result does not inevitably trigger Underflow. However, it is consistently denoted by the Subnormal condition, irrespective of whether its value is 0 or 10 to the power of E_{min} after rounding. In the event that a numerical value undergoes a calculation resulting in a value of zero, the corresponding exponent will assume the value of E_{min}. The upper limit of the exponent remains unaltered. It should be noted that the exponent's minimum value for subnormal numbers is equivalent to the bare minimum value of the exponent that may arise during non-subnormal number operations. This situation occurs when the clength is equal to the precision (Higham et al., 2019; Kahan, 1996).

3.3.1. Notation

Subsequent sections within this chapter illustrate a distinct finite quantity, denoted by its abstract representation through the triad notation: [sign, coefficient, exponent]. It is noteworthy that each value within this notation is an integer. Solely the power can possess a negative value. Likewise, duplexes or triads are employed to denote distinct values. The entities mentioned above are represented in either of the two formats: [sign, special-value] or [sign, special-value, diagnostic]. The sign is denoted in the same manner as previously mentioned, while the special value can take on one of three values: inf, qNaN, or sNaN, representing infinity, quiet NaN, or signaling NaN. The optional diagnostic component is a positive integer (Chrisomalis, 2010; Chrisomalis, 2004).

As an illustration, consider the triad [0,2708,–2], which denotes the numerical value 27.08, while the triad [1,1953,0] represents the integer –1953. Similarly, the duple [1,inf] signifies negative infinity, and the duple [0,qNaN] denotes a quiet NaN. This phrase refers to the depiction of operations conceptually or symbolically without necessarily representing them in a concrete or physical form. It is a common approach in various fields.

The subsequent sections delineate the essential functions that an implementation must furnish, namely Conversion and Arithmetic Operations. Each computational process is assigned a theoretical designation, such as "addition," and its meaning is precisely specified. This section does not define the execution of each operation or the method by which each operation is carried out (Lang, 1956; Ganor-Stern & Tzelgov, 2008).

As an illustration, within an object-oriented programming language, the execution of the addition operation could be facilitated by means of a method denominated "add." Conversely, the addition operation could be executed in calculator software by pressing a button icon. In alternative contexts, the infix symbol " + " could denote the arithmetic operation of addition. In all instances, the execution of the task may be performed utilizing software, hardware, or a hybrid of both (Libertus et al., 2007; Khain et al., 2000).

Analogously, unique operations in the chapter don't need to correspond to separate operations in the implementation as long as all fundamental operations are present. A possible approach is to implement a unified method for converting to a string, which can be adapted based on the context or by providing supplementary arguments (Sinclair et al., 1992; Doedel, 2007).

3.4. CONTEXTUAL INFORMATION REPRESENTED ABSTRACTLY

The context refers to the set of parameters that can be chosen by the user and the corresponding rules that dictate the outcomes of arithmetic operations. These parameters may include, for instance, the level of precision to be employed. The parameters outlined below serve to define it:

3.4.1. Precision

A positive integer is defined as an integer greater than zero. This establishes the upper limit for the number of significant digits that may arise due to a mathematical operation. The abstract does not limit the precision level, albeit a particular degree of precision must be furnished. In practical applications, it may be necessary to establish an upper limit (such as the maximum coefficient length supported by a specific representation) for the variable mentioned above. The abovementioned constraint must be represented as an integer value of decimal digits using integration (Yan, 2016; Gupta et al., 2015). Likewise, a minimum threshold can exist for precision settings, which may coincide with the maximum threshold (e.g., if it is inferred from the highest coefficient length that a particular representation can accommodate). The aforementioned constraint needs to be represented in the form of a whole number of digits in the decimal system. It is imperative for an implementation to specify a precision that is commonly referred to as single precision. The value in question must exceed a minimum threshold of 5 and fall within the bounds of the implemented levels of precision. The minimum value should be 9. It is possible for an implementation to specify a precision referred to as "double precision," which must fall within the spectrum of precisions that have been implemented (Pena-Marin & Yan, 2021; Xie & Kronrod, 2012). When a double precision is specified, certain limitations must be adhered to:

- If we denote the value of single precision as Ps and the value of double precision as Pd, it follows that Pd must satisfy the inequality $Pd \geq 2Ps + 1$.
- The designated single precision must have a maximum exponent (E_{limit}), no less than one unit lower than the E limit at double precision, divided by eight.

In cases where such constraints cannot be realized, such as when an implementation can accommodate exceedingly large exponents but cannot establish distinct exponent limits for varying precisions, double precision mustn't be specified (Hoehfeld & Fahlman, 1991; Martel, 2009).

3.4.2. Arithmetic Operations

This segment delineates the arithmetic operations and additional functions pertaining to numerical values, encompassing subnormal numbers, negative zeros, and distinct values (Ershov, 1958).

3.4.3. Arithmetic Operation Notation

Within this part, a simplified notation is employed to exemplify arithmetic operations. Specifically, a numerical value is represented as the sequence of characters that would be produced by applying the to-scientific-string function. The utilization of single quotation marks indicates the implication of a number that has been switched from an abstract representation (Xu et al., 2022; Panyukov & Golodov, 2015).

In addition, operations are denoted as functions, which can take one or two operands. Moreover, the symbol ==> signifies "results in." Therefore, the operation of adding ('12,' '7.00') to obtain '19.00' refers to the computation of the sum between the operands [0,12,0] and [0,700,–2], which yields a result of [0,1900,–2] (Bribiesca, 1981).

The present example and subsequent instances presume a context with a precision value of 9, a rounding mechanism of round-half-up, and all trap-enablers set to 0 (Zhou et al., 2009; Hong, 2006).

3.4.4. Arithmetic Operation Rules

The arithmetic operations are subject to certain overarching principles. Specifically, all operations performed on finite numbers are executed per the procedures outlined for each operation. In such cases, the computation is conducted as if an exact mathematical outcome is obtained, utilizing integer arithmetic on the coefficient wherever feasible (Liu et al., 2015; Guo, & Zhang, 2008).

If the coefficient of the exact conceptual outcome possesses precision digits or fewer, and there is no occurrence of underflow or overflow, the outcome is utilized without any alterations. In cases where the number of digits exceeds the precision limit, it is truncated to the specified number of digits using the prevailing rounding method. The count of removed digits concurrently increments the exponent. In cases where the adjusted exponent of the outcome is lower than E_{min}, indicating that the result is either zero or subnormal, the outcome is determined by the calculated coefficient and exponent. However, if the exponent value is less than E tiny, the exponent will be assigned a value of E_{min}, the coefficient will be rounded to align with the exponent adjustment, and the sign will remain unchanged. In the event that the outcome (prior to rounding) is both non-zero and subnormal, the exceptional condition of Subnormal is triggered. In cases where the rounding of a subnormal outcome results in an imprecise outcome, the Underflow exceptional condition is likewise triggered (Irion, 1998; Guo, P & Chen, 2008).

In the event that the adjusted exponent of a non-zero outcome exceeds E_{max}, an exceptional circumstance, commonly referred to as overflow, arises. The outcome in this scenario conforms to the Overflow exceptional circumstance, which has the potential to be boundless. The resultant sign will be identical to the theoretical outcome (Wang et al., 2018; Gong et al., 2018). The application of arithmetic operations involving the special value of infinity adheres to the conventional rules, whereby the interval [1,inf] is considered to be less than any finite number, while the interval [0,inf] is deemed greater than any finite number. According to these regulations, an outcome that is infinite in nature is invariably precise. Some applications of infinity can result in an Invalid operation error (Tatsuoka et al., 1989; Chen et al., 2014).

- The utilization of signaling NaNs as an operand in an arithmetic operation invariably triggers the Invalid operation condition.
- The condition of invalid operation can be triggered when an operation's operand is deemed invalid, such as when it surpasses the limits of what an implementation can accommodate or when the operation involves a logarithm and the operand is negative (Bohlender & Kulisch, 2011).
- The outcome of any arithmetic computation involving an operand categorized as a NaN, whether a quiet NaN or a signaling NaN, is [s,qNaN] or [s,qNaN,d]. The diagnostic data and sign are replicated from the initial operand, which could either be a signaling NaN or, if both operands are non-signaling, then from the first NaN operand. In instances where the outcome of a calculation is classified as NaN (Not a Number), the polarity of said outcome is solely determined by the copied operand. It is not subject to the application of the subsequent rules.

- The signum of the outcome of a multiplication or division operation will be a positive one solely when the factors exhibit opposite signs (Dong et al., 2023).
- The sign of the outcome of an arithmetic operation involving addition or subtraction will be positive if and only if the outcome is greater than zero. However, there are certain exceptional cases where the outcome is a negative zero, yielding a negative sign.
- The occurrence of a negative zero result ([1,0,n]) is conditional upon rounding a value to zero, provided that the value possessed a sign of 1 prior to the rounding process.
- The operation mentioned above involves the addition of [1,0,n] to [1,0,n] (Guo et al., 2015).
- When performing an operation that involves adding operands with opposite signs or subtracting operands with the same sign, the resulting coefficient is 0, and the rounding method used is round-floor.
- If the signs of the operands are different, and the operation performed is either multiplication or division, then the resulting coefficient would be 0 (Dagenbach & McCloskey, 1992).
- The mathematical operation being performed is exponentiation, where the base is a list of elements 1, 0, and n. The exponent, or right-hand operand, is a positive integer that is also odd.
- The mathematical operation referred to is exponentiation, where the base is a positive real number greater than or equal to 1, and the exponent is a negative integer integral and odd.
- In the scenario where the operation being performed is to quantize or round-to-integral-value, and the left-hand operand holds a negative value, the outcome of the operation would yield a result of zero magnitudes. In either scenario, the ultimate exponent has the potential to be non-zero (Kutter et al., 2022).
- The mathematical operation is the square root, with the operand being a numerical array consisting of 1, 0, and n values (Zeng et al., 2012).
- **Examples Involving Special Values:**

add('Infinity,"1')	==>	'Infinity'
add('NaN,"1')	==>	'NaN'

add('NaN,"Infinity')	==>	'NaN'
subtract('1,"Infinity')	==>	'–Infinity'
multiply('–1,"Infinity')	==>	'–Infinity'
subtract('–0,"0')	==>	'–0'
multiply('–1,"0')	==>	'–0'
divide('1,"0')	==>	'Infinity'
divide('1,"–0')	==>	'–Infinity'
divide('–1,"0')	==>	'–Infinity'

3.4.5. Abs

The abs function requires a single operand. In cases where the operand is negative, the outcome is equivalent to applying the minus operation, as outlined on page 32, to the operand. If not, the outcome is identical to employing the addition operation (refer to page 32) on the operand (Johnsen et al., 2010; Hafner, 2008).

- **Examples:**

abs('2.1') ==> '2.1'

abs('–100')==> '100'

abs('101.5') ==> '101.5'

abs('–101.5') ==> '101.5'

3.5. ADD AND SUBTRACT

Both addition and subtraction operations require two operands. If either of the operands is a special value, the standard regulations are to be followed.

If the operation is not a subtraction, the operands are combined through addition, with the second operand's sign being inverted beforehand (Carpenter & Moser, 2020; Vergnaud, 2020).

- The computation of the coefficient of the outcome involves the addition or subtraction of the aligned coefficients of the two operands. The computation of the aligned coefficients involves a comparison of the exponents of the operands (McCrink & Wynn, 2004).
- When the exponent is identical, the aligned coefficient values remain unchanged from their original values (Fuson et al., 1997).

- Alternatively, in cases where two numbers with different exponents are being aligned, the coefficient of the number with the larger exponent is obtained by multiplying its real coefficient by 10, raised to the absolute difference between the exponents (Navarrete-Benlloch et al., 2012).
- In cases where the signs of the operands are not the same, the larger coefficient is subtracted from, the smaller ones after aligning them. Conversely, if the signs are the same, the coefficients are added (Nesher, 1982).
- The minimum exponent of the two operands determines the exponent of the resulting value.
- The determination of the sign of the result is based on the following criterion. If the outcome is not equal to zero, then the sign corresponds to the sign of the operand that possesses the greater absolute value (Kara & Incikabi, 2018).
- In the absence of any other circumstance, a zero outcome is indicated by the numerical symbol 0, except in cases where both operands were negative (Brush, 1978).
- **Examples:**

add('12,"7.00') ==>'19.00'

add('1E+2,"1E+4') ==>'1.01E+4'

subtract('1.3,"1.07')==>'0.23'

subtract('1.3,"1.30')==>'0.00'

subtract('1.3,"2.07')==>'–0.77'

3.5.1. Comparison

The comparison operation involves evaluating two operands to determine whether they possess equal or unequal numerical values. In cases where one of the operands is a special value, the standard rules are to be followed. Alternatively, the operands are contrasted in the following manner (Agrawal, 2004).

In cases where the signs of the operands are not the same, comparing them is performed using a value that represents each operand. Specifically, the value used is '–1' if the operand is less than zero, '0' if the operand is zero or negative zero, or '1' if the operand is greater than zero. This value is substituted for the actual operand during the comparison process. The comparison process involves the subtraction of the second operand from the first operand. The resulting value determines the comparison output: a value of '–1' is returned if the result is negative, '0' is returned if the result is zero or negative zero, and '1' is returned if the result is positive. This operation can be used in an implementation to implement a closed set of comparison operations, such as greater than, equal, and others if deemed necessary (Cheon et al., 2019; Robertson et al., 1995).

- **Examples:**

compare('2.1,"3') ==>'–1'

compare('2.1,"2.1') ==>'0'

compare('2.1,"2.10')==>'0'

compare('3,"2.1') ==>'1'

compare('2.1,"–3') ==>'1'

compare('–3,"2.1') ==>'–1'

3.6. DIVISION

The mathematical operation of division requires the utilization of two operands. In case either of the operands is a special value, the standard regulations are enforced. In the event that the divisor is equal to zero, one of two conditions may arise. If the dividend is also zero, the Division undefined condition is triggered, resulting in a NaN value. Alternatively, if the dividend is non-zero, the Division by zero condition is triggered, resulting in an Infinity value (Isik & Kar, 2012).

Alternatively, a process of "long division" is carried out in the following manner:

- A variable of integer data type, named 'adjust,' is initialized with a value 0.
- If the dividend is not equal to zero, the coefficient of the outcome is determined through the following process, utilizing operational duplicates of the operand coefficients as required (Nuari et al., 2019):
  - First, the coefficients of the operands are changed so that the dividend's coefficient is more than or equal to the divisor's and less than 10 times the divisor's. If the dividend's coefficient is less than the divisor's, the adjustment is multiplied by 10, and the dividend's coefficient is multiplied by 1 (Prahmana & Suwasti, 2014).

- The coefficient of the divisor is multiplied by 10 when the dividend's coefficient is equal to or greater than 10 times the divisor's, and the adjustment is reduced by one.
- The coefficient of the result is initialized to zero (Prahmana, 2013).
- The subsequent procedures are iterated until the division process is finalized.
- When the divisor's coefficient is less than or equal to the dividend's, the divisor is subtracted from the dividend, and the quotient's coefficient is raised by 1 (Erdem et al., 2015).
- The division process is considered complete if either of the following conditions is met: the coefficient of the dividend is reduced to 0, the adjusted value is greater than or equal to 0, or the coefficient of the result attains precision digits (Toro et al., 2016).
- If the coefficient s of the quotient and the dividend are incompatible, a multiplication by a factor of 10 is performed, and the adjustment value is increased by 1.
- The residual value, which denotes the ultimate coefficient of the dividend, is duly noted and factored in for the purpose of rounding (Koichu et al., 2013).
- In the event that the dividend is zero, the resulting coefficient is also zero, and the adjusted value remains unaltered at zero (Koichu et al., 2013).
- The exclusive disjunction of the signs of the operands determines the sign of the outcome.
- As required, the outcome is subsequently rounded to a specified number of precision digits, utilizing the rounding algorithm and considering the remainder from the division (Askey, 1999).

- **Examples:**

divide('1,"3')	==>	'0.333333333'
divide('2,"3')	==>	'0.666666667'
divide('5,"2')	==>	'2.5'
divide('1,"10')	==>	'0.1'

divide('12,"12')	==>	'1'
divide('8.00,"2')	==>	'4.00'
divide('2.400,"2.0')	==>	'1.20'
divide('1000,"100')	==>	'10'
divide('1000,"1')	==>	'1000'
divide('2.40E+6,"2')	==>	'1.20E+6'

It is important to note that the outcomes as mentioned earlier can be articulated alternatively. Specifically, the most optimal exponent for the outcome of a division can be determined by subtracting the divisor's exponent from the dividend's exponent. In the event of a division operation, if the outcome is precise, the coefficient and exponent that yield the accurate value and have the exponent closest to the optimal exponent are returned. In case of an imprecise outcome, the coefficient shall possess a precise number of digits, equivalent to the precision, except in the event of a subnormal result. Moreover, the exponent shall be adjusted accordingly (Resnick, 2020).

3.7. DIVIDE-INTEGER

The divide-integer function is a binary operation that requires two operands to perform division on two numerical values and outputs the integer component of the quotient. In the event that one of the operands is a special value, the standard rules are applicable. In the absence of other conditions, the outcome obtained is deemed to be the outcome that would arise from iteratively deducting the divisor from the dividend as long as the dividend remains greater than the divisor. In the subtraction process, the absolute values of both the dividend and the divisor are employed, and the resultant sign of the outcome is consistent with that which would ensue if the conventional division were implemented. Stated differently, the identity mentioned above is satisfied when the divide-integer and remainder operations are performed on operands x and y, yielding i and r as outputs (Nurnberger-Haag, 2007).

$$x = i'y + r$$

The resultant exponent is required to be zero. Consequently, in cases where the outcome cannot be precisely articulated within the designated number of digits of accuracy, the operation will be deemed erroneous and unsuccessful. This implies that the outcome cannot surpass the number of digits specified for precision during the operation and will not be subject to rounding. An instance of divide-integer operation involving the operands '10000000000' and '3' necessitates a 10-digit expression to represent the outcome as '3333333333 accurately.' This operation would not be successful if the precision were confined within the range of 1 to 9 (Khalid & Embong, 2019).

- **Notes:**

1. The operation of dividing integers may yield dissimilar outcomes as compared to the truncation of regular division, which may be influenced by rounding.
2. The operations of divide-integer and remainder are established in such a way that they can be computed as a secondary outcome of the conventional division operation, as explained previously. The division process is terminated upon the attainment of the integer quotient, with the remaining portion of the dividend being referred to as the residue or remainder.
3. The division and integer division operations yield identical numerical values for a given set of operands, provided there are no errors and no remainder is generated during the integer division operation (Bloom, 2001).

- **Examples:**

divide–integer('2,"3')	==>	'0'
divide–integer('10,"3')	==>	'3'
divide–integer('1,"0.3')	==>	'3'

3.7.1. Fundamental Concepts

During arithmetic operations, individuals frequently utilize decimal arithmetic, in which the decimal point adjusts as necessary. The outcome that is ultimately recorded is determined by three factors. These factors include:

1. The particular procedure executed.
2. The explicit information contained within the operand or operands utilized in the operation.
3. The precision required and other contextual factors play a crucial role in the calculation process (Snyder & Mitchell, 1999).

More precisely,

- The aforementioned item encompasses an elective symbol, which holds significance solely in instances where it denotes negativity.
- The numeric component comprises digits, which may incorporate a decimal point. The decimal point holds significance only if any digits succeed it.
- The presence of an exponent is discretionary and indicates the magnitude of the power of 10 by which the numeric value is multiplied. This is particularly significant when the numeric value and the exponent are non-zero (Hilbert, 1905).

The conventional floating-point representations, such as ANSI/IEEE 754-1985, do not incorporate the magnitude of the numeric and initial position of the decimal point. However, these details are crucial for achieving the desired outcome.

As an illustration, it is commonly anticipated that trailing zeros will be conventionally denoted in a given outcome. For instance, when adding 1.57 and 2.03, the anticipated result is 3.60 instead of 3.6. Nevertheless, if the positional information is lost during the operation, it becomes unfeasible to exhibit the expected outcome. In certain contexts, the omission of trailing zeros holds significant material implications (Resnick, 1991).

Fortunately, the subsequent ANSI/IEEE 854-1987 standard, designed for decimal and binary floating-point arithmetic, does not prohibit using representations that maintain the desired information. Thus, a viable internal representation for decimal numbers encompasses three components: a sign, an integer (referred to as the coefficient in this particular context), and an exponent (which denotes an integral power of ten).

In scientific or engineering applications, decimal arithmetic is commonly founded on a floating-point model as opposed to a fixed-point or fixed-scale model. It is worth noting that this approach was initially the foundation for the principles that underlie binary floating points. Fixed-point decimal arithmetic packages, such as the Big Decimal class in Java 1.1, have limited applicability and are only suitable for a specific subset of arithmetic problems. The significance of the data encompassed within a computation framework holds considerable weight. Typically, it pertains to a complete series of actions instead of a solitary action and is not linked to specific operands. In practical applications, it is reasonable to assume the existence of appropriate default settings. However, it is imperative to provide users with the ability to exercise control over various aspects of the application in numerous scenarios

(White, 1989). The primary contextual factor of significance pertains to the level of precision sought for the computation. The range of values for certain problems in Mathematics and Physics can vary from relatively small values, typically in the order of six digits, to significantly larger values, often in the hundreds or thousands of digits. Certain decimal arithmetics, such as the decimal arithmetic utilized in the Atari Operating System, provide limited options for precision, often with no clear rationale for the chosen alternatives. The aforementioned statement is incongruent with the decimal arithmetic user model. A user-oriented decimal arithmetic system must offer a diverse selection of precision options. The establishment of a contextual framework for arithmetic operations is an essential prerequisite for attaining the intended outcomes, akin to the requirement of a designated setting for text-based operations (Jones, 1950).

This particular segment offers explicit management over various elements of the context, such as the necessary level of precision at which rounding is implemented, the algorithm for rounding that is to be employed when digits need to be discarded, the scope of regular numbers that establishes the limits for overflow and underflow, and lastly, a collection of flags and trap-enablers that indicate exceptional conditional and regulate how they are managed.

The complete segment within the main body of this chapter outlines a decimal floating-point computation that yields precise outcomes and conserves exponents whenever feasible.

In cases where precision is inadequate, numerical values are processed in accordance with the guidelines outlined in IEEE 854. Incorporating IEEE 854 regulations involves the inclusion of exceptional values such as infinities and NaNs, as well as subnormal values and the value of negative zero.

In certain contexts and programming paradigms, particularly those aimed at individuals lacking mathematical expertise, it may be suitable to furnish an arithmetic system that consistently regards infinite, NaN, or subnormal outcomes as erroneous, conceals –0 results, and introduces other primarily superficial modifications to facilitate the acceptance of results. The arithmetic delineated in ANSI X3.274 is of such a nature; the present section explicates the distinctions between this arithmetic and the comprehensive specification. Implementations that explicitly support this particular subset may offer the subset behavior through a parameter in the context 38 or through a distinct interface that includes additional or parameterized methods (Demirci, 2002).

3.7.2. Simplified Number Set

Subset arithmetic is a mathematical operation that involves a limited set of numerical values. In this operation, numbers with positive exponents are reduced to zero, if applicable. Specifically:

- If the coefficient of a finite number is zero during the to-number conversion process, then both the sign and exponent are assigned a value of 0.
- In the event that the coefficient in a given outcome holds a numerical value of zero, the corresponding sign shall be assigned a value of 0. Additionally, unless the operation being performed is quantization, the exponent shall also be assigned a value of 0.39
- Special value strings are not allowed in the to-number conversion process. Namely, solely numbers that are finite in nature are deemed acceptable.

Numbers that fall below a certain threshold of magnitude, commonly referred to as subnormal numbers, are deemed unacceptable. In the event that a transformation or operation yields a value that is below the normal range, it will trigger an Underflow error. Upon completion of an operation and subsequent rounding of its result (excluding the quantize operation), any outcome with a positive exponent will be transformed into an integer, given that the resulting coefficient does not exceed the precision digits. To clarify, it can be observed that a positive exponent is nullified by multiplying the coefficient with 10 raised to the power of the exponent, resulting in the addition of exponentiated zeros to the end of the number.40(Geary et al., 2009).

3.8. OPERATION DIFFERENCES

Specifically, in the event that the coefficient of an operand in operation contains a greater number of decimal digits than the current precision within the given context, the operand will be subject to rounding to precision significant digits through the utilization of the context's specified rounding algorithm prior to its use in computation. Stated differently, a pre-existing algorithm for automatic conversion to a condensed format is implemented prior to the execution of the task.

In the context of addition or subtraction, in the event that one of the operands is zero, the other operand is utilized as the outcome, rounded to the required level of precision, with appropriate sign modification (Raghubar et al., 2010).

The abstract context is supplemented with the inclusion of the Lost Digits condition, which ought to be initialized to a value of zero in standard contexts (DeMars, 1998).

The aforementioned condition is triggered in instances where digits that hold a non-zero value are omitted prior to the execution of an operation. This phenomenon may arise when an operator with a coefficient containing a greater number of significant digits in its leading digits than the precision value is truncated to the precision digits prior to its utilization (Raghubar et al., 2010).

It should be noted that the lost digits test does not consider trailing decimal zeros in the coefficient to be significant. In the event that the value of precision is 5, the occurrence of an exception due to the operands would be avoided. However, if the operands were [0,123451,–1] or [0,1234500001,0], an exception would be triggered (Else-Quest et al., 2010).

[0,12345,–5]

[0,12345,–2]

[0,12345,0]

[1,12345,0]

[0,123450000,–4]

[0,1234500000,0]

Following the completion of a division or exponentiation operation and subsequent rounding, any trailing zeros that are deemed insignificant are eliminated. In the event that the exponent is non-zero and the coefficient is a positive power of ten's multiple, the coefficient is divided by said power of ten, and the exponent is correspondingly incremented. In the event that the exponent is negative, it will not be elevated beyond zero.

If more precision is needed, the sum is rounded to the requested number of digits after the addition is performed. The procedure takes into account the presence of a leading zero or a carry digit on the left side of a sum. Instead of starting with the most significant digit of the sum or difference, it begins counting from the place corresponding to the most significant digit of the operands.

In the context of mathematical operations, when faced with numerically equal operands, the first operand on the left-hand side is selected for both the maximum and minimum operations. In the case of a power operation where both operands are zero, the resulting value is 1 rather than an error. However, it is important to note that if the left-hand operand is zero, the right-hand operand cannot be negative.

The power operation allows for an integer to be used as the right-hand operand, and subset implementations must furnish the power function solely for integer powers. The algorithm delineated below can be employed to compute the outcome in this instance (Beller & Gafni, 2000).

3.8.1. Rules for Rounding and Special Cases

In subset arithmetic, it is imperative to treat exceptional conditions, beyond the scope of informational conditions, such as Lost digits, Inexact, Rounded, and Subnormal, as errors. Any results obtained after encountering such errors are deemed undefined. Consequently, the inclusion of special values and subnormal numbers is not considered a component of the arithmetic. The Lost digits trap enabler is the sole requirement within the subset. The optional trap enablers include Inexact, Rounded, and Sub-normal, while the remaining ones are effectively pre-set. Likewise, the optional nature of the status bits within the context is evident. The exclusive rounding mode mandated is round-half-up (Ziv, 1991).

3.8.2. Calculating an Integer Power

Subset implementations must furnish the power function solely for integer powers. To perform this calculation, it is necessary to multiply the left-hand operand by itself a number of times equivalent to the power that has been expressed. In the event that the right-hand operand bears a negative value, the left-hand operand is utilized without modification, the absolute value of the right-hand operand is employed, and the outcome is reversed. The process of left-to-right binary reduction is frequently utilized in calculating power in practical applications, as outlined in the note below, for contextual reasons. The function power(x, n) involves the conversion of the exponent "n" into binary form, followed by the initialization of a temporary accumulator to a value of 1. Once the value of "n" is determined to be 0, the initial computation is considered finished. Alternatively, each bit is examined from left to right, commencing from the initial non-zero bit. In the event that the present bit holds a value of 1, the accumulator undergoes multiplication by a factor of "x." Upon completion of the inspection of all bits, the initial calculation is deemed concluded. However, if not all bits have been inspected, the accumulator undergoes a squaring operation through multiplication, and the subsequent bit is subjected to inspection. The arithmetic operations of multiplication and division are executed according to standard arithmetic rules, utilizing the precision provided for the operation. However, it should be noted that these operations are performed with an augmented accuracy of precision+elength+1 digits. The variable "e" represents the number of decimal digits in the integer part or coefficient of the whole number "n." This excludes any sign, decimal point, decimal part, or insignificant leading zeros (Mackiw, 2000).

- ***Notes:***

1. In the event of an underflow during the division into 1 when raising to a negative power, the operation persists rather than being terminated.
2. The text outlines a specific algorithm for computing integer powers that are deemed efficient, albeit not optimal, as it significantly minimizes the number of multiplicative operations executed. Consequently, it yields superior performance compared to the more basic approach of iteratively multiplying. The algorithm presented in this context is designed to ensure consistency in the power operation results across various implementations. This is necessary due to the possibility of discrepancies arising from repeated multiplication. By adhering to this algorithm, different implementations can produce identical results for the same input values, thereby enabling the use of identical test cases. Alternative algorithms for the power operation may be employed, provided that the outcome is within a range of 1 ulp (unit in last place) from the accurate result.
3. It is recommended that implementations include a power operator that can handle a non-integral right-hand operand, provided that the left-hand operand is non-negative, as outlined in the specifications (Beiranvand & Kamalvand, 2022).

3.9. DESIGN CONCEPTS

The present section provides an overview of the fundamental principles that form the basis of the arithmetic discussed in this chapter, serving as contextual information. This element is not included in the designated specifications.

The floating-point model utilized in this chapter for decimal arithmetic is predicated on a human-centric design philosophy and is underpinned by a fundamental tenet that computers must furnish an arithmetic system that aligns with the arithmetic principles taught in educational institutions.

It is worth noting that there exists a lack of awareness among a significant portion of the population regarding the variations in algorithms utilized for manual decimal arithmetic across different countries. However, it is reassuring to observe that the ultimate outcomes are distinguishable only by nuances of rounding and formatting, which is not unexpected. The selection of the specific model was informed by a comprehensive examination of decimal arithmetic and subsequently refined over a period of four years (1979–1982) through the incorporation of input from numerous users across over 40 nations. Since 1982, many implementations have been authored, and minor adjustments to the definition were introduced throughout the ANSI standardization process from 1991 to 1996.

The fundamental floating-point model has demonstrated its appropriateness for expansion to fulfill the supplementary criteria and amenities as stipulated in ANSI/IEEE 854-1987, 48. Essentially, the comprehensive specification is the amalgamation of the floating-point specifications of both standards.

The aforementioned statement implies that a uniform numerical system and arithmetic facilitate precise unrounded decimal arithmetic, also known as "fixed-point" arithmetic, and approximated floating-point arithmetic without bias. The former encompasses the features and numerical quantities presently prevalent in binary floating-point executions (Lo et al., 2017).

3.9.1. Fundamental Concepts

In performing arithmetic operations, such as adding or multiplying two numerical values, individuals frequently employ decimal arithmetic, wherein the decimal point is allowed to shift as necessary. The outcome that is ultimately recorded is contingent upon three distinct factors.

- The precise procedure was executed.
- The operand or operands involved in the operation contain explicit information.
- The precision required and other contextual factors are crucial in the calculation process.
- The written representation of an operand contains more information

than what is typically encoded for floating-point arithmetic. More precisely, the feature mentioned above comprises an elective symbol that holds importance solely in cases of negativity.

- The conventional floating-point representations, such as ANSI/IEEE 754-1985, do not incorporate the magnitude of the numeric and the initial position of the decimal point. However, these details are crucial for achieving the intended outcome.

As an illustration, it is customary for individuals to anticipate the conventional representation of trailing zeros in a given outcome. For instance, when adding 1.57 and 2.03, the expected result is 3.60 instead of 3.6. Nevertheless, if the positional information is lost during the operation, it becomes unfeasible to exhibit the anticipated outcome. In certain contexts, the omission of trailing zeros can have a significant impact (Hutto et al., 2015).

Fortunately, the subsequent ANSI/IEEE 854-1987 standard, designed for both decimal and binary floating-point arithmetic, does not prohibit representations that maintain the intended information. An appropriate internal depiction of decimal numbers involves a sign, an integer, and an exponent.

In scientific or engineering applications, decimal arithmetic relies on a floating-point model rather than a fixed-point or fixed-scale model. It is worth noting that this approach is the fundamental basis for the principles underlying binary floating-point. The utility of fixed-point decimal arithmetic packages, such as the Big Decimal class in Java 1.1, is limited to a specific subset of arithmetic-related issues.

The significance of the data encompassed within the framework of a computation holds considerable weight. Typically, it pertains to a complete series of procedures, as opposed to a solitary procedure, and is not linked to specific operands. In practical applications, it is reasonable to assume the existence of sensible defaults, although it is imperative to provide users with control options in numerous scenarios.

The primary contextual factor of significance pertains to the level of accuracy sought in the computation. The range of values for certain problems in Mathematics and Physics can vary from relatively small values. Certain decimal arithmetic systems, such as the one utilized in the Atari Operating System, provide limited options for precision, often without clear justification. The current implementation does not align with the decimal arithmetic user model, which necessitates a diverse array of precision options to cater to user needs.

This segment allows the user to choose the level of precision. The representation may have a predetermined maximum precision while adhering to the IEEE above 854-1987 standard. However, the programmer can select the precision used for operations within the maximum limit allowed by the representation.

Establishing a contextual framework for arithmetic operations is an essential prerequisite for attaining the intended outcomes, akin to the requirement of a designated setting for text-based operations (Subramanya & Farahani, 2012).

3.10. SUMMARY

The present chapter is grounded on a decimal arithmetic model that constitutes a formal representation of the decimal numeration system (Algorism), as well as its corresponding standards that provide further definitions and limitations.

The model comprises three distinct components.

1. The numerical values are utilized as operands or outcomes of the fundamental operations specified in this section.
2. The fundamental mathematical procedures, including addition, multiplication, and other related operations that can be performed on numerical values are referred to as operations.
3 .The context refers to the parameters and rules that are chosen by the user and dictates the outcomes of arithmetic operations, such as the level of precision to be employed.

The abstract of this chapter delineates the components mentioned above. The specification in question does not define the expression of operations, as this can differ based on the computer language or interface employed. Additionally, it does not define the concrete representation of numbers or context, such as their specific layout in storage. The subsequent section delineates the abstract model for every constituent.

REFERENCES

1. Agrawal, R., Kiernan, J., Srikant, R., & Xu, Y., (2004). Order preserving encryption for numeric data. In: *Proceedings of the 2004 ACM SIGMOD International Conference on Management of Data* (pp. 563–574).
2. Askey, R., (1999). Knowing and teaching elementary mathematics. *American Educator*, *23*, 6–13.
3. Beiranvand, M., & Kamalvand, M. G., (2022). Positive integer powers of certain tridiagonal matrices and corresponding anti-tridiagonal matrices. *Advances in Mathematical Physics*, *2022*.
4. Beller, M., & Gafni, N., (2000). Can item format (multiple choice vs. open-ended) account for gender differences in mathematics achievement? *Sex Roles*, *42*, 1–21.
5. Bloom, I., (2001). *Curriculum Reforms That Increase the Mathematical Understanding of Prospective Elementary Teachers* (Vol.1., pp.1-10)
6. Bohlender, G., & Kulisch, U., (2011). Definition of the arithmetic operations and comparison relations for an interval arithmetic standard. *Reliable Computing*, *15*, 37.
7. Bribiesca, E., (1981). Arithmetic operations among shapes using shape numbers. *Pattern Recognition*, *13*(2), 123–137.
8. Brush, L. R., (1978). Preschool children's knowledge of addition and subtraction. *Journal for Research in Mathematics Education*, *9*(1), 44–54.
9. Busaba, F. Y., Krygowski, C. A., Li, W. H., Schwarz, E. M., & Carlough, S. R., (2001). The IBM z900 decimal arithmetic unit. In: *Conference Record of 35th Asilomar Conference on Signals, Systems and Computers (Cat. No. 01CH37256)* (Vol. 2, pp. 1335–1339). IEEE.
10. Carpenter, T. P., & Moser, J. M., (2020). The development of addition and subtraction problem-solving skills. In: *Addition and Subtraction* (pp. 9–24). Routledge.
11. Chen, Y., Zhang, G., Wang, T., & Huang, X., (2014). Automatic design of P systems for five basic arithmetic operations within one framework. *Chinese Journal of Electronics*, *23*(2), 302–304.
12. Cheon, J. H., Kim, D., Kim, D., Lee, H. H., & Lee, K., (2019). Numerical method for comparison on homomorphically encrypted numbers. In: *Advances in Cryptology–ASIACRYPT 2019: 25th International Conference on the Theory and Application of Cryptology and Information Security, Kobe, Japan, Proceedings, Part II* (pp. 415–445). Cham: Springer International Publishing.
13. Chrisomalis, S., (2004). A cognitive typology for numerical notation. *Cambridge Archaeological Journal*, *14*(1), 37–52.

14. Chrisomalis, S., (2010). *Numerical Notation: A Comparative History.* Cambridge University Press.
15. Dagenbach, D., & McCloskey, M., (1992). The organization of arithmetic facts in memory: Evidence from a brain-damaged patient. *Brain and Cognition, 20*(2), 345–366.
16. DeMars, C. E., (1998). Gender differences in mathematics and science on a high school proficiency exam: The role of response format. *Applied Measurement in Education, 11*(3), 279–299.
17. Demirci, M., (2002). Fundamentals of M-vague algebra and M-vague arithmetic operations. *International Journal of Uncertainty, Fuzziness and Knowledge-Based Systems, 10*(01), 25–75.
18. Doedel, E. J., (2007). Lecture notes on numerical analysis of nonlinear equations. *Numerical Continuation Methods for Dynamical Systems: Path Following and Boundary Value Problems*, 1–49.
19. Dong, J., Luo, B., & Zhang, G., (2023). Automatic design of arithmetic operation spiking neural P systems. *Natural Computing, 22*(1), 55–67.
20. Duale, A. Y., Decker, M. H., Zipperer, H. G., Aharoni, M., & Bohizic, T. J., (2007). Decimal floating-point in z9: An implementation and testing perspective. *IBM Journal of Research and Development, 51*(1.2), 217–227.
21. Else-Quest, N. M., Hyde, J. S., & Linn, M. C., (2010). Cross-national patterns of gender differences in mathematics: A meta-analysis. *Psychological Bulletin, 136*(1), 103.
22. Erdem, E., Gökkurt, B., Şahin, Ö., Başibüyük, K., & Soylu, Y., (2015). Examining prospective middle school mathematics teachers' modelling skills of multiplication and division in fractions. *Croatian Journal Educational/Hrvatski Casopis za Odgoj I Obrazovanje, 17*(1).
23. Ershov, A. P., (1958). On programming of arithmetic operations. *Communications of the ACM, 1*(8), 3–6.
24. Fjelstad, P., (1986). Extending special relativity via the perplex numbers. *American Journal of Physics, 54*(5), 416–422.
25. Fuson, K. C., Wearne, D., Hiebert, J. C., Murray, H. G., Human, P. G., Olivier, A. I., & Fennema, E., (1997). Children's conceptual structures for multidigit numbers and methods of multidigit addition and subtraction. *Journal for Research in Mathematics Education, 28*(2), 130–162.
26. Ganor-Stern, D., & Tzelgov, J., (2008). Across-notation automatic numerical processing. *Journal of Experimental Psychology: Learning, Memory, and Cognition, 34*(2), 430.

27. Geary, D. C., Bailey, D. H., & Hoard, M. K., (2009). Predicting mathematical achievement and mathematical learning disability with a simple screening tool: The number sets test. *Journal of Psychoeducational Assessment*, *27*(3), 265–279.
28. Gong, C., Li, M., Zhao, L., Guo, Z., & Han, G., (2018). Homomorphic evaluation of the integer arithmetic operations for mobile edge computing. *Wireless Communications and Mobile Computing*, *2018*, 1–13.
29. Guo, P., & Chen, J., (2008). Arithmetic operation in membrane system. In: *2008 International Conference on BioMedical Engineering and Informatics* (Vol. 1, pp. 231–234). IEEE.
30. Guo, P., & Zhang, H., (2008). Arithmetic operation in single membrane. In: *2008 International Conference on Computer Science and Software Engineering* (Vol. 3, pp. 532–535). IEEE.
31. Guo, P., Chen, H., & Zhang, H., (2015). An integrated P system for arithmetic operations. *Journal of Computational and Theoretical Nanoscience*, *12*(10), 3346–3356.
32. Gupta, S., Agrawal, A., Gopalakrishnan, K., & Narayanan, P., (2015). Deep learning with limited numerical precision. In: *International Conference on Machine Learning* (pp. 1737–1746). PMLR.
33. Hafner, J., (2008). Ab - initio simulations of materials using VASP: Density - functional theory and beyond. *Journal of Computational Chemistry*, *29*(13), 2044–2078.
34. Hiebert, J., & Wearne, D., (1985). A model of students' decimal computation procedures. *Cognition and Instruction*, *2*(3–4), 175–205.
35. Higham, N. J., Pranesh, S., & Zounon, M., (2019). Squeezing a matrix into half precision, with an application to solving linear systems. *SIAM Journal on Scientific Computing*, *41*(4), A2536–A2551.
36. Hilbert, D., (1905). On the foundations of logic and arithmetic. *The Monist*, 338–352.
37. Hoehfeld, M., & Fahlman, S. E., (1991). *Learning with Limited Numerical Precision Using the Cascade-Correlation Algorithm* (pp. 602–611). Carnegie-Mellon University. Department of Computer Science.
38. Hong, D. H., (2006). Fuzzy measures for a correlation coefficient of fuzzy numbers under TW (the weakest t-norm)-based fuzzy arithmetic operations. *Information Sciences*, *176*(2), 150–160.
39. Hutto, D. D., Kirchhoff, M. D., & Abrahamson, D., (2015). The enactive roots of STEM: Rethinking educational design in mathematics. *Educational Psychology Review*, *27*, 371–389.

40. Irion, A., (1998). Fuzzy rules and fuzzy functions: A combination of logic and arithmetic operations for fuzzy numbers. *Fuzzy Sets and Systems, 99*(1), 49–56.
41. Isik, C., & Kar, T., (2012). An error analysis in division problems in fractions posed by pre-service elementary mathematics teachers. *Educational Sciences: Theory and Practice, 12*(3), 2303–2309.
42. John, V., Angelov, I., Öncül, A. A., & Thévenin, D., (2007). Techniques for the reconstruction of a distribution from a finite number of its moments. *Chemical Engineering Science, 62*(11), 2890–2904.
43. Johnsen, E. B., Hähnle, R., Schäfer, J., Schlatte, R., & Steffen, M., (2010). ABS: A core language for abstract behavioral specification. In: *International Symposium on Formal Methods for Components and Objects* (pp. 142–164). Berlin, Heidelberg: Springer Berlin Heidelberg.
44. Jones, B. W., (1950). *The Arithmetic Theory of Quadratic Forms* (Vol. 10). American Mathematical Soc.
45. Kadosh, R. C., (2008). Numerical representation: Abstract or nonabstract? *Quarterly Journal of Experimental Psychology, 61*(8), 1160–1168.
46. Kadosh, R. C., Lammertyn, J., & Izard, V., (2008). Are numbers special? An overview of chronometric, neuroimaging, developmental and comparative studies of magnitude representation. *Progress in Neurobiology, 84*(2), 132–147.
47. Kahan, W., (1996). IEEE standard 754 for binary floating-point arithmetic. *Lecture Notes on the Status of IEEE, 754*(94720–1776), 11.
48. Kara, F., & Incikabi, L., (2018). Sixth grade students' skills of using multiple representations in addition and subtraction operations in fractions. *International Electronic Journal of Elementary Education, 10*(4), 463–474.
49. Khain, A., Ovtchinnikov, M., Pinsky, M., Pokrovsky, A., & Krugliak, H., (2000). Notes on the state-of-the-art numerical modeling of cloud microphysics. *Atmospheric Research, 55*(3–4), 159–224.
50. Khalid, M., & Embong, Z., (2019). Sources and possible causes of errors and misconceptions in operations of integers. *International Electronic Journal of Mathematics Education, 15*(2), em0568.
51. Koichu, B., Harel, G., & Manaster, A., (2013). Ways of thinking associated with mathematics teachers' problem posing in the context of division of fractions. *Instructional Science, 41*, 681–698.
52. Kutter, E. F., Boström, J., Elger, C. E., Nieder, A., & Mormann, F., (2022). Neuronal codes for arithmetic rule processing in the human brain. *Current Biology, 32*(6), 1275–1284.

53. Lang, M., (1956). Numerical notation on Greek vases. *Hesperia: The Journal of the American School of Classical Studies at Athens*, *25*(1), 1–24.

54. Libertus, M. E., Woldorff, M. G., & Brannon, E. M., (2007). Electrophysiological evidence for notation independence in numerical processing. *Behavioral and Brain Functions*, *3*, 1–15.

55. Liu, X., Li, Z., Liu, J., Liu, L., & Zeng, X., (2015). Implementation of arithmetic operations with time-free spiking neural P systems. *IEEE Transactions on Nanobioscience*, *14*(6), 617–624.

56. Lo, C. K., Hew, K. F., & Chen, G., (2017). Toward a set of design principles for mathematics flipped classrooms: A synthesis of research in mathematics education. *Educational Research Review*, *22*, 50–73.

57. Lortie-Forgues, H., & Siegler, R. S., (2017). Conceptual knowledge of decimal arithmetic. *Journal of Educational Psychology*, *109*(3), 374.

58. Lortie-Forgues, H., Tian, J., & Siegler, R. S., (2015). Why is learning fraction and decimal arithmetic so difficult? *Developmental Review*, *38*, 201–221.

59. Mackiw, G., (2000). A combinatorial approach to sums of integer powers. *Mathematics Magazine*, *73*(1), 44–46.

60. Martel, M., (2009). Program transformation for numerical precision. In: *Proceedings of the 2009 ACM SIGPLAN workshop on Partial Evaluation and Program Manipulation* (pp. 101–110).

61. Martí, J. M., & Müller, E., (2003). Numerical hydrodynamics in special relativity. *Living Reviews in Relativity*, *6*, 1–100.

62. McCrink, K., & Wynn, K., (2004). Large-number addition and subtraction by 9-month-old infants. *Psychological Science*, *15*(11), 776–781.

63. Miller, E. R., MoCurry, E. M., & Hruska, B., (1971). An infinite number of laminagrams from a finite number of radiographs. *Radiology*, *98*(2), 249–255.

64. Naccache, L., & Dehaene, S., (2001). The priming method: imaging unconscious repetition priming reveals an abstract representation of number in the parietal lobes. *Cerebral Cortex*, *11*(10), 966–974.

65. Navarrete-Benlloch, C., García-Patrón, R., Shapiro, J. H., & Cerf, N. J., (2012). Enhancing quantum entanglement by photon addition and subtraction. *Physical Review A*, *86*(1), 012328.

66. Nesher, P., Greeno, J. G., & Riley, M. S., (1982). The development of semantic categories for addition and subtraction. *Educational Studies in Mathematics*, *13*(4), 373–394.

67. Nuari, L. F., Prahmana, C. I., & Fatmawati, I., (2019). Learning of division operation for mental retardations' student through math GASING. *Journal on Mathematics Education, 10*(1), 127–142.

68. Nurnberger-Haag, J., (2007). Quick reads: Another good idea: Integers made easy: Just walk it off. *MatheMatics Teaching in the Middle School, 13*(2), 118–121.

69. Panyukov, A. V., & Golodov, V. A., (2015). Scalability of algorithms for arithmetic operations in radix notation. *Reliable Computing, 19*(4), 417.

70. Pena-Marin, J., & Yan, D., (2021). Reliance on numerical precision: Compatibility between accuracy versus efficiency goals and numerical precision level influence attribute weighting in two-stage decisions. *Journal of Consumer Psychology, 31*(1), 22–36.

71. Prahmana, R. C. I., & Suwasti, P., (2014). Local instruction theory on division in mathematics GASING. *Journal on Mathematics Education, 5*(1), 17–26.

72. Prahmana, R. C. I., (2013). Designing division operation learning in the mathematics of gazing. In: *The First South East Asia Design/Development Research (SEADR) Conference* (pp. 391–398).

73. Raghubar, K. P., Barnes, M. A., & Hecht, S. A., (2010). Working memory and mathematics: A review of developmental, individual difference, and cognitive approaches. *Learning and Individual Differences, 20*(2), 110–122.

74. Resnick, L. B., (1991). Thinking in arithmetic class. *SPONS Agency Department of Education, Washington, DC. Office of Planning, Budget, and Evaluation. PUB DATE Mar 91 CONTRACT LC89089001*, 136.

75. Resnick, L. B., (2020). From protoquantities to operators: Building mathematical competence on a foundation of everyday knowledge. In: *Analysis of Arithmetic for Mathematics Teaching* (pp. 373–429). Routledge.

76. Robertson, P., Villebrun, E., & Hoeher, P., (1995). A comparison of optimal and sub-optimal MAP decoding algorithms operating in the log domain. In: *Proceedings IEEE International Conference on Communications ICC'95* (Vol. 2, pp. 1009–1013). IEEE.

77. Schmookler, M. S., & Weinberger, A., (1971). High speed decimal addition. *IEEE Transactions on Computers, 100*(8), 862–866.

78. Sinclair, A., Garin, A., & Tièche-Christinat, C., (1992). Constructing and understanding of place value in numerical notation. *European Journal of Psychology of Education, 7*, 191–207.

79. Smith, P. R., Peters, T. M., & Bates, R. H. T., (1973). Image reconstruction from finite numbers of projections. *Journal of Physics A: Mathematical, Nuclear and General*, *6*(3), 361.
80. Snyder, A. W., & Mitchell, D. J., (1999). Is integer arithmetic fundamental to mental processing?: The mind's secret arithmetic. *Proceedings of the Royal Society of London. Series B: Biological Sciences*, *266*(1419), 587–592.
81. Subramanya, S., & Farahani, A., (2012). Point-of-view article on: Design of a smartphone app for learning concepts in mathematics and engineering. *International Journal of Innovation Science*.
82. Talenti, G., (1987). Recovering a function from a finite number of moments. *Inverse Problems*, *3*(3), 501.
83. Tatsuoka, K. K., Birenbaum, M., & Arnold, J., (1989). On the stability of students' rules of operation for solving arithmetic problems. *Journal of Educational Measurement*, *26*(4), 351–361.
84. Tian, J., Braithwaite, D. W., & Siegler, R. S., (2021). Distributions of textbook problems predict student learning: Data from decimal arithmetic. *Journal of Educational Psychology*, *113*(3), 516.
85. Toro, S., Patil, A., Chavan, Y. V., Patil, S. C., Bormane, D. S., & Wadar, S., (2016). Division operation based on Vedic mathematics. In: *2016 IEEE International Conference on Advances in Electronics, Communication and Computer Technology (ICAECCT)* (pp. 450–454). IEEE.
86. Vergnaud, G., (2020). A classification of cognitive tasks and operations of thought involved in addition and subtraction problems. In: *Addition and Subtraction* (pp. 39–59). Routledge.
87. Wang, H., Zhou, K., & Zhang, G., (2018). Arithmetic operations with spiking neural P systems with rules and weights on synapses. *International Journal of Computers Communications & Control*, *13*(4), 574–589.
88. Wang, L. K., Tsen, C., Schulte, M. J., & Jhalani, D., (2007). Benchmarks and performance analysis of decimal floating-point applications. In: *2007 25th International Conference on Computer Design* (pp. 164–170). IEEE.
89. Weir, J. D. V., (1949). New methods for calculating metabolic rate with special reference to protein metabolism. *The Journal of Physiology*, *109*(1–2), 1.
90. White, S. A., (1989). Applications of distributed arithmetic to digital signal processing: A tutorial review. *IEEE ASSP Magazine*, *6*(3), 4–19.
91. Xie, G. X., & Kronrod, A., (2012). Is the devil in the details? The signaling effect of numerical precision in environmental advertising claims. *Journal*

of Advertising, 41(4), 103–117.

92. Xu, C., Li, H., Burr, S. D. L., Si, J., LeFevre, J. A., & Huang, B., (2022). Divide and conquer: Relations among arithmetic operations and emerging knowledge of fraction notation for Chinese students in Grade 4. *Journal of Experimental Child Psychology, 217*, 105371.
93. Yan, D., (2016). Numbers are gendered: The role of numerical precision. *Journal of Consumer Research, 43*(2), 303–316.
94. Yule, G. U., (1927). VII. On a method of investigating periodicities disturbed series, with special reference to Wolfer's sunspot numbers. *Philosophical Transactions of the Royal Society of London. Series A, Containing Papers of a Mathematical or Physical Character, 226*(636–646), 267–298.
95. Zeng, X., Song, T., Zhang, X., & Pan, L., (2012). Performing four basic arithmetic operations with spiking neural P systems. *IEEE Transactions on Nanobioscience, 11*(4), 366–374.
96. Zhou, X., Chen, C., Qiao, S., Chen, C., Chen, L., Lu, N., & Dong, Q., (2009). Event-related potentials for simple arithmetic in Arabic digits and Chinese number words: A study of the mental representation of arithmetic facts through notation and operation effects. *Brain Research, 1302*, 212–224.
97. Ziv, A., (1991). Fast evaluation of elementary mathematical functions with correctly rounded last bit. *ACM Transactions on Mathematical Software (TOMS), 17*(3), 410–423.

CHAPTER

4 Real Arithmetic: Floating Operations

Contents

Efficient representation and manipulation of real numbers is a prerequisite in numerous domains such as engineering, science, banking, and other fields. Numerous methods for approximating real numbers have been established since the inception of electronic computing (Panchekha et al., 2015).

A floating-point number of radix-β and precision-p can be expressed as a number in the following format (Rümmer & Wahl, 2010):

$\pm m_0.m_1m_2 \cdots m_{p-1} \times \beta,$

The given expression denotes that the significand, denoted as m_0, m_1, m_2, m_{p-1}, is represented in radix β, while e, also known as the exponent, is an integer. The primary objective of this literary work is to explain the efficient and secure manipulation of these numerical values (Cody, 1973).

4.1. HISTORY

While the floating-point arithmetic's execution on processors is a modern innovation, such arithmetic has existed for quite some time. Donald Knuth provides a brief historical account of floating-point arithmetic in his work, The Art of Computer Programming. The author perceives the radix-60 numerical system utilized by the Babylonian civilization as an antecedent to the contemporary floating-point system. The absence of zero in the Babylonian numerical system is a well-known fact. Consequently, it follows that when two numbers are in a ratio that is a power of 60, their representation remains identical (Tziantzioulis et al., 2015).

YBC 7289, a renowned tablet housed in the Yale Babylonian Collection, provides a four-sexagesimal place estimation of 2, as denoted by the digits 1, 24, 51, and 10 inscribed on the tablet. The tablet in question has been visually documented, and a comprehensive examination of the Babylonian mathematical concepts pertaining to YBC 7289 has been conducted by Fowler and Robson, yielding intriguing insights. The slide rule's mathematical operations, devised circa 1630 by William Oughtred, may be regarded as a variant of floating-point arithmetic. Similar to the Babylonian numerical system, the manipulation of numbers is limited to their significands, specifically radix-10 significands (Goldberg, 1991).

Quevedo and Zuse are widely regarded as the contemporary co-inventors of floating-point arithmetic. However, it is noteworthy that the initial practical application of floating-point arithmetic in a contemporary context was observed in the Z3 computer constructed by Konrad Zuse in 1941. The system employed a radix-2 floating-point numerical representation featuring a 14-bit significand, a 7-bit exponent, and a 1-bit sign. The Z3 computing machine was equipped with distinct notations to denote infinite values and outcomes that are indeterminate. The attributes mentioned above rendered the arithmetic of real numbers in the Z3 machine significantly advanced for its era. Recently, the Z3 underwent a reconstruction process. Individuals inclined toward the historical background of computing devices are advised to peruse the exceptional literary work authored by Aspray et al. The decimal numeral system, also known as radix 10, is commonly utilized by humans in their daily lives to represent numerical values and carry out manual calculations using writing instruments. Hence, in order to circumvent the need for conversions between input and output radices, a plausible approach for the automation of calculations is to employ a uniform radix (Barr et al., 2013).

Despite the existence of alternative numeral systems, the prevalent use of binary logic in computing renders radix 2, and other power-of-2 radices, the most straightforward to execute. Therefore, the selection of an appropriate radix was not a straightforward task. Various solutions were investigated during the initial stages of automated computing. The decimal numeral system, also known as radix 10, has been widely employed in financial computations and handheld electronic calculators. Developing an effective implementation of radix-10 floating-point arithmetic remains an important area of investigation. Maple, a computer algebra system, employs radix 10 as its internal numerical representation. Hence, it appears that the radix values utilized in the existing floating-point arithmetic systems have predominantly been either 10 or a power of 2 (Backus, 1978).

The SETUN computer, which originated from Moscow University in 1958, utilized a radix-3 numerical system that employed 1, 0, and 1 digits. The utilization of the "balanced ternary" system presents various benefits. One of the notable observations is that the process of rounding off to the nearest value is equivalent to truncation. Another example is as follows. Suppose a radix-β fixed-point system is utilized, where the system comprises p-digit numbers. A high magnitude of β results in intricacy in the execution process, as the system necessitates the capability to discern and operate β distinct symbols. A diminutive value of β necessitates an increased quantity of digits to express a specific numerical value. In the event that β is of a reduced magnitude, the value of p must be augmented. To reach a compromise, one may attempt to reduce the value of βp while maintaining a relatively constant maximum representable number of βp–1. In most cases, the ideal solution would be when β equals 3. Several researchers have demonstrated that radix

2, utilizing the unspoken leading bit convention, provides superior worst-case accuracy compared to alternative radices. The present prevalence of Radix 2 can be attributed to its simplicity of implementation (Horprasert et al., 1999).

In 1985, the release of the IEEE 754-1985 Standard for Binary Floating-Point Arithmetic brought about significant changes to the realm of numerical computation. The present standard delineates diverse formats, the conduct of fundamental operations and conversions, and exceptional circumstances. The Intel 8087 mathematics co-processor, designed to be used in conjunction with the Intel 8088 and 8086 processors, was developed in 1980 and remarkably similar to the subsequent IEEE 754-1985 standard. Currently, a majority of commercially significant systems provide support for IEEE 754-1985 compatibility. Arithmetic in the radix-2 system was the sole focus of the IEEE 754-1985 standard. Binary and decimal arithmetic are both covered under the IEEE 854-1987 Standard for Radix Independent Floating-Point Arithmetic. Since 2001, updates to the IEEE 754-1985 and 854-1987 standards have been in the works. In this literature, the revised standards are referred to as IEEE 754 and include several important updates. In June of 2008, those mentioned above was officially adopted (Zeljić et al., 2018).

4.2. DESIRABLE PROPERTIES

The specification of floating-point arithmetic, including formats and operator behavior, necessitates the identification of trade-offs between often-incompatible requirements. Several desirable properties can be identified, including:

- The computation of tomorrow's weather forecast must be completed within a 24-hour, prioritizing speed and accuracy (Flegar et al., 2019).
- While speed is crucial, an incorrect result is more detrimental than a correct one obtained immediately. Additionally, it may be necessary to represent both large and small numerical values in the forecast.
- Two important considerations in software development are portability and ease of implementation and use. Portability refers to the ability of programs to run on several systems. Ease of implementation and use is crucial, as complex or obscure arithmetic may discourage usage.

In terms of precision, contemporary physical measurements exhibit a high degree of accuracy, enabling the verification of certain projections of quantum. Consequently, it is imperative to accurately represent numerical data in certain instances, which can be achieved effortlessly by utilizing universally implemented formats across contemporary platforms. This implies that there are instances where computations must result in a relative error of 10^{-15} or less, which can be considerably challenging. Occasionally, utilizing a notably expanded floating-point format or employing clever techniques may be necessary. Laskar's team at the Paris observatory conducted a meticulous computation, exemplifying the magnitude of calculations that demand great attention. The researchers calculated extended numerical solutions for the Earth's insolation variables over a significant temporal span, encompassing a range of 250 million years in both the past and future.

In certain fields, such as the study of numbers, computations involving multiple precision are executed utilizing an exceedingly high degree of precision (Harrison, 1999).

4.3. FLOATING-POINT NUMBERS

The floating-point numbers' definition is primarily derived from the diverse IEEE standards (Morris, 1971).

4.3.1. Primary Definitions

Any finite floating-point number that is portrayed by at least one pair of values (M, e) within the given format is said to be in the "floating-point" format, which is defined by four integers: a radix greater than or equal to 2, a precision p greater than or equal to 2, two exponents e_{min} and e_{max} such that e_{min} is less than e_{max}, and a radix greater than or equal to 2. In practical cases, e_{min} is less than 0, and e_{max} is greater than 0.

$$x = M \cdot \beta^{e-p+1}, \qquad (4.1)$$

The variable M is an integer with an absolute value that is either less than or equal to βp–1. The representation of x is characterized by its integral significand. In contrast, the exponent of the representation of x is denoted by e, an integer that satisfies the $e_{min} \leq e \leq e_{max}$.

The uniqueness of a floating-point number's representation (M, e) cannot be guaranteed. An illustration of this concept can be observed when β is equal to 10, and p is equal to 3. In this scenario, the numerical value 17 can be denoted as either 17 multiplied by 10 to the power of 2 or 170 multiplied by 10 to the power of negative 1. This is because both 17 and 170 are smaller than the product of β and p, which is equal to 1000. The collection of these comparable depictions is referred to as a cohort. The number

βe–p+1

from Expression (4.1) is referred to as x's Quantum Representation. We refer to this factor—the quantum exponent—as

q=e-p+1

The concept of quantum is intricately linked to the concept of ulp, which can be found expounded upon in Section 2.6.1 (Guralnik et al., 2010).

An alternative method of representing a floating-point value, x, is through the use of a triplet (s, m, e).

$x = (-1)^s \cdot m \cdot \beta^e$,

where;

- The variable "e" remains unchanged (Janikow & Michalewicz, 1991).
- The normal significand, denoted as "m = M β^{1-p}," is referred to as the significand of the representation. The numerical value denoted by x is characterized by a single digit preceding the radix point and a maximum of p–1 digits following it, with the caveat that m, being a non-negative integer, must satisfy the condition $0 \leq m < \beta$.
- Additionally, the sign of x is represented by the binary variable s, which can take on the values of either 0 or 1 (Gal, 1991).

In academic literature, it is common to refer to the significand as the mantissa, although this terminology is not entirely accurate. The present study adopts the radix β of 2, precision p of 4, e_{min} of 7, and e_{max} of +8. The aforementioned numerical value, 341610, can be represented as a binary floating-point number, specifically in the form of 1101000002. The given numerical value can be expressed in a unique form with an integral significand of 1310 and an exponent of 810 (Kumar & Raj, 2020).

$416 = 13 \cdot 2^{8-4+1}$

The smallest unit in this representation is 2^5, which equals 32. It's important to note that any representation exceeding 2^{p+1} (where p = 15) is excluded. Similarly, in a toy system, the number 4.25_{10} is not considered a floating-point number as it cannot be expressed exactly as M β^{e-p+1}, where M

$\leq 2^4$ and p = 1. When x represents any nonzero real number, we denote the infinitely precise significand of x as follows:

$\beta\lfloor \log_\beta |x| \rfloor$

where; $\beta\lfloor \log\beta\ |x| \rfloor$ is the largest integer power of β smaller than $|x|$ (Daumas et al., 2001).

4.3.2. Normalized Representations

As previously elucidated, certain floating-point values possess multiple representations in the form of (M, e). However, it is often advantageous to mandate distinctive depictions. To ensure a distinct depiction, it may be desirable to standardize the finite non-zero floating-point values by electing the representation that possesses the smallest exponent. The representation that has been acquired will be referred to as a normalized representation. The imposition of normalized representations facilitates the articulation of error bounds, streamlines implementation to some extent, and enables a reduction of one bit in radix 2.4 (Kalliojarvi & Astola, 1996).

Given the uniqueness of the representation of a finite nonzero number x, the values of M, q, m, and e are solely determined by the value of x, indicating a high degree of normalization. The nomenclature used in this context designates e as the exponent of x, q as its quantum exponent (where q is equal to e raised to the power of p plus one), M as its integer significand, and m as its significand.

In the radix 2 numeral system, it is customary for the initial digit of the significand of a normal number to be represented by the value 1, while the initial digit of the significand of a subnormal number is conventionally denoted by the value 0. If a distinctive encoding, typically in the exponent, is utilized to indicate whether a number is normal or subnormal, retaining the initial bit of its significand becomes unnecessary. Utilizing a leading bit, also known as implicit bit or hidden bit convention, is commonly employed. Therefore, it can be observed that in radix 2, the significand of a normal number is consistently represented in a particular format (Shirazi et al., 1995).

$1.m_1m_2m_3\ldots\ldots m_{p-1}$

In contrast, the significand of a subnormal number is always of the type:

$0.m_1m_2m_3\ldots\ldots\ldots m_{p-1}$

The digit sequence $m_1m_2m_3\ldots m_{p-1}$ is called the *trailing-significand* of the number (Dido et al., 2002).

4.3.3. A Note on Subnormal Numbers

The topic of subnormal numbers has been a contentious aspect of IEEE 754-1985. According to Schwarz et al., implementing these numbers in floating-point units is highly challenging. Consequently, there are instances where these numbers are executed in software instead of hardware, leading to prolonged execution times during calculations (Andrysco et al., 2015).

It is possible to establish floating-point systems without incorporating subnormal numbers. Notwithstanding, the aforementioned numerical values facilitate a phenomenon referred to as gradual underflow by Kahan, whereby the reduction in accuracy occurs gradually as opposed to suddenly. The presence of subnormal numbers entails a noteworthy characteristic: if a and b are equivalent, then the resultant value of b divided by an is inevitably non-zero. The phenomenon of gradual underflow is occasionally referred to as graceful underflow within academic discourse (Gellar & Wallen, 1970).

Several mathematical properties, including Sterbenz's lemma, hold true solely in the presence of subnormal numbers. In the absence of subnormal numbers, an additional condition must be included in these properties, namely, "if no underflow occurs" (Jung & Li, 2001).

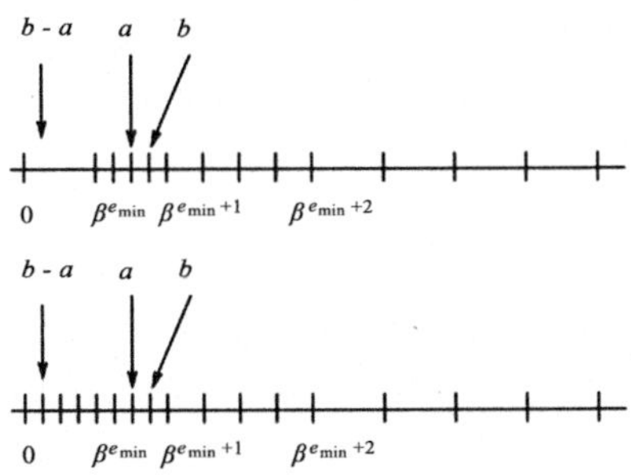

Figure 4.1. The present study concerns the set of positive floating-point numbers within the framework of the toy system characterized by β = 2 and p = 3. The scope of consideration is limited to regular floating-point numbers. The set in question lacks the ability to represent b a, resulting in a computation of 0 when b and is calculated in round-to-nearest mode.

4.3.4. Special Floating-Point Data

Certain data cannot be represented in the form of either normal or subnormal numbers. A conspicuous illustration pertains to the numerical digit zero, necessitating a distinct encoding. There exist additional instances that are not entirely numerical (Higbie, 1976).

In general, the implementation of a closed system is considered highly advantageous as it allows for precise specification of machine operations without the occurrence of any trap7 errors, even when such operations involve invalid manipulations of real numbers. Introducing a distinct value known as NaN and its subsequent versions serves as a means to address this particular issue. The occurrence of an invalid operation will result in the return of a NaN (Burtscher & Ratanaworabhan, 2007).

Furthermore, as a result of the restricted range of exponents, it becomes necessary to incorporate additional exceptional values. In order to address the issue of values exceeding the maximum representable magnitude, the floating-point system can incorporate either two signed infinities or an unsigned infinity. The inclusion of signed zeros, denoted as +0 and 0, may be desired for the sake of symmetry if one opts for the utilization of signed infinities. The IEEE standards encompass the provision of signed zeros and infinities in floating-point arithmetic. Kahan [204] has observed that the utilization of signed zeros is advantageous in effectively managing branch cuts of complex elementary functions (Anderson & Gregg, 2016).

Nonetheless, unless an additional unsigned zero is introduced, this selection creates a disparity between the precise zero and the outcome of (+0) + (0). The Texas Instruments pocket calculators possess a system that comprises three zeros and three infinities, namely positive, negative, and indeterminate signs. The Z3 computer, constructed by Konrad Zuse in 1941, was equipped with mechanisms to handle floating-point exceptions (Ratanaworabhan & Burtscher, 2006).

4.4. ROUNDING

4.4.1. Rounding Modes

Typically, the outcome of a computation or function performed on floating-point numbers cannot be precisely represented within the utilized floating-point framework, necessitating the need for rounding. The rounding method employed in early floating-point systems was not consistently specified. The IEEE 754-1985 standard introduces a compelling notion regarding the rounding mode, which pertains to the process of rounding a numerical value to a finite or infinite floating-point number. Specifically, a rounding mode, also known as a rounding direction attribute, prescribes a rounding function that determines how the numerical value should be rounded appropriately.

In the context of computing, it can be observed that the operation of adding two floating-point numbers, denoted as a and b, yields a resultant value of (a + b). There exist various conceivable rounding modes that can be defined. As an example, the IEEE 754-2008 standard encompasses four distinct rounding modes (Kuck & Sameh, 1977):

1. **Round Toward –∞:** The function RD(x) denotes the maximum value of a floating-point number that is less than or equal to x, and this value may be negative infinity. The rounding is done in the direction of positive infinity. The function RU(x) denotes the minimum floating-point value that is greater than or equal to x, which may potentially be positive infinity (Defour et al., 2004);
2. **Round Toward Zero:** The function RZ(x) denotes the floating-point number that is nearest to x while not exceeding its magnitude. Specifically, when x is non-negative, RZ(x) is equivalent to RD(x), and when x is non-positive, RZ(x) is equivalent to RU(x).
3. **Round to Nearest:** The RN(x) value corresponds to the floating-point number that exhibits the shortest distance to x. A tie-breaking rule must be selected when x is equidistant between two consecutive floating-point numbers. The commonly employed method for resolving ties is referred to as "round to nearest even." This approach entails rounding the value of x to the nearest floating-point number that is one of two consecutive options and whose integral significand is even. The IEEE 754-2008 Standard incorporates a default mode (Rump et al., 2009).
4. **Round Ties to Away:** Typically, the desirable characteristics of a tie-breaking mechanism include sign symmetry, wherein RN(x) = RN(x) holds true, absence of statistical bias, simplicity of implementation, and consistency (Boldo & Melquiond, 2011).

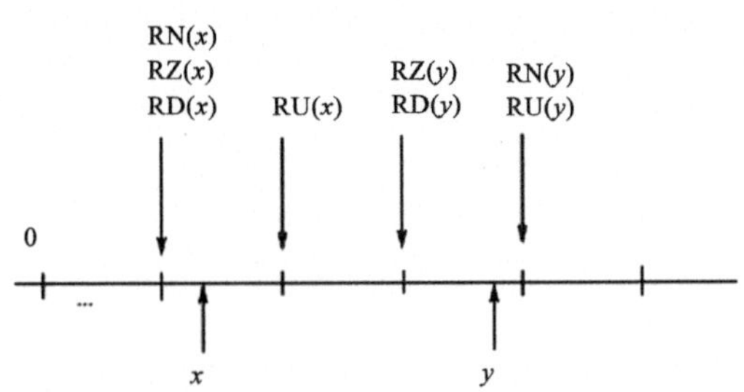

Figure 4.2. The four rounding modes.

The rounding process of a positive real value x in radix 2 and precision p, with an infinitely precise significand of $m_1m_2m_3$..., can be mathematically represented as a function that takes into account the values of the round bit (mp) and the sticky bit (m_{p+1}, m_{p+2},...). In the subsequent discussion, the term "rounding breakpoint" will refer to a numerical value at which the rounding function undergoes a transition. When operating in the round-to-nearest mode, the points at which rounding occurs are precisely located at the midpoint between two consecutive floating-point numbers. The floating-point numbers themselves serve as the directed rounding modes, distinct from the other rounding modes (Clinger, 1990).

Table 4.1 illustrates the process of rounding a radix-2 infinitely accurate significand, which is contingent upon the presence of both "round" and "sticky" bits. Consider the rounding mode ∘, where ∘ is an element of the set {RN, RD, RU}, which we aim to implement. In the table, the symbol "-" indicates that the significand of ∘(x) is m_1, m_2, m_3,..., m_{p-1}, which denotes the exact significand that has been truncated. In the given table, the symbol "+" denotes the requirement of adding 2_{-p+1} to the truncated significand. This addition may change the exponent if all the mi's up to mp–1 are equal to 1. The symbol "/+" denotes the intermediate scenarios for the round-to-nearest (RN) mode, where the final outcome is contingent on the specific convention employed.

Table 4.1. The Process of Rounding a Radix-2

Round/sticky	RD	RU	RN
0 / 0	-	-	-
0 / 1	-	+	-
1 / 0	-	+	—/ +
1 / 1	-	+	+

Achieving a correct rounding outcome can be accomplished with relative ease for arithmetic operations such as addition, subtraction, multiplication, and division, and also for the square root function. The IEEE 754-1985 standard mandates the accurate rounding of said functions in floating-point arithmetic. However, certain functions may pose significant challenges.11 In the event that an exact outcome y is consistently mapped to either RD(y) or RU(y), it is deemed that the value returned is a dedicated lead and that the arithmetic involved is also faithful. Caution should be exercised as the term "faithful rounding" is occasionally used in literature. However, it does not qualify as a rounding mode as per the aforementioned definition (Wang & Schulte, 2004).

4.4.2. Useful Features

Accurate rounding is a valuable tool in algorithm design and verification and in determining precise and validated error margins. A significant and beneficial characteristic is that the rounding function exhibits non-decreasing behavior for all four rounding modes delineated previously. In other words, if x is less than y, then the result of rounding x is less than or equal to the result of rounding y (Whitehead & Fit-Florea, 2011). Additionally, in the event that y is a floating-point value, it can be inferred that (y) is equivalent to y. This implies that in cases where a function is correctly rounded and produces an exact result in floating-point format, the outcome will be precisely as expected. Moreover, in the event that the rounding mode is symmetric, specifically when it is RZ or RN with a symmetrical selection in the event of a tie, a precisely rounded implementation maintains the symmetries of a given function. When considering other rounding modes, certain characteristics, such as properties, may come into play (De Dinechin et al., 2010).

$$\mathrm{RU}\ (a + b) = -\mathrm{RD}\ (-a - b)$$

or

$$\mathrm{RD}\ (a \times b) = -\mathrm{RU}((-a) \times b)$$

Notably, the rounding modes of the IEEE standards exhibit a particular behavior in instances where the values are either extremely small or large. This behavior is characterized by the property outlined below. This attribute proves to be advantageous, especially in the process of enhancing the execution of accurately rounded arithmetic operators (Steele & White, 1990).

4.5. PROPERTIES OF ARITHMETIC ON REAL NUMBERS

A number of established properties characterizes real number arithmetic.

- Within the set of mathematical operations, it is noteworthy that addition and multiplication exhibit commutativity:

$a + b = b + a$
and $a \times b = b \times a$ for all a and b;

- Addition and multiplication are the associative operations:

  $a + (b + c) = (a + b) + c$ and

  $a \times (b \times c) = (a \times b) \times c$ for all a, b, and c;

- Distributivity applies as follows (Tent, 2006):

$a \times (b + c) = a \times b + a \times c.$

When arithmetic operations are accurately rounded in any of the four rounding modes, the commutativity of floating-point addition and multiplication is preserved. If the active rounding mode is 14, then it can be observed that the commutative property holds true for addition and multiplication operations on all floating-point numbers a and b, such that (a + b) = (b + a) and (a * b) = (b * a). The properties of associativity and distributivity are not preserved. With regards to associativity, the subsequent events may transpire (Cartwright & Boehm, 1990).

- In some cases, $\circ(a + \circ(b + c))$ can be different from $(\circ(a+b)+c)$. A simple example, in radix-β, precision-p arithmetic with round-to-nearest mode is $a = \beta^{p+1}$, $b = -\beta^{p+1}$, and $c = 1$, since

  $$\mathrm{RN}\,(a + \mathrm{RN}\,(b + c)) = \mathrm{RN}\,(\beta^{p+1} - \beta^{p+1}) = 0,$$

Whereas

$$\mathrm{RN}\,(\mathrm{RN}\,(a + b) + c) = \mathrm{RN}\,(0 + 1) = 1.$$

Many studies have focused on discovering effective ways to rearrange the operands when evaluating the sum of many floating-point values.

P_1 = (a b) c) and P_2 = (a (b) c) can be slightly distinct if there is no overflow or underflow. To be more specific, while using round-to-nearest mode in radix-, precision-p arithmetic (Bux & Wortman, 2007):

$$RN(a \times b) = a \times b \times (1+\varepsilon_1)$$

$$|\varepsilon_1| \le \frac{1}{2}\beta^{1-p}, \text{so that}$$

$$P_1 = RN(RN(a \times b) \times c = a \times b \times c \times (1+\varepsilon_1)(1+\varepsilon_2)$$

$$|\varepsilon_1| \le \frac{1}{2}\beta^{1-p} \text{ Similarly;}$$

$$P_2 = RN(a \times RN(b \times c)) = a \times b \times c \times (1+\varepsilon_3)(1+\varepsilon_4)$$

$$|\varepsilon_3|, |\varepsilon_4| \le \frac{1}{2}\beta^{1-p}. \text{Therefore}$$

$$\left(\frac{1-\frac{1}{2}\beta^{1-p}}{1+\frac{1}{2}\beta^{1-p}}\right)^2 \le \frac{P_1}{P_2} \le \left(\frac{1+\frac{1}{2}\beta^{1-p}}{1-\frac{1}{2}\beta^{1-p}}\right)^2$$

$$\frac{P_1}{P_2} = 1+\varepsilon,$$

$$|\varepsilon| \le 2\beta^{1-p} + 2(\beta^{1-p}) + 3/2(\beta^{1-p})^3 + \ldots\ldots$$

It is noteworthy that this constraint is considerably stringent. As an illustration, consider the binary32 arithmetic system of the IEEE 754-2008 standard with parameters β= 2, p = 24, e_{min} = 126, and e_{max} = 127 (refer to Section 3.4, page 79). According to equation (2.2), the limit on the error term ∈ is 4.00000048 2–24. The following holds in the scenario where a = 8622645, b = 16404663, and c = 8647279.

$\underline{P\,1} = 3.86 \cdots \times 2^{-24}$.

In case of overflow or underflow, ◦(*a* × ◦(*b* × *c*)) can be *drastically* different from ◦(◦(*a* × *b*) × *c*). For instance, in binary64 arithmetic (β = 2, *p* = 53, e_{min} = –1022, e_{max} = 1023; see Section 3.4 page 79), with *a* = *b* = 2513 and *c* = 2–1022, RN(RN(*a* × *b*) × *c*) will be +∞, whereas RN(*a* × RN(*b* × *c*)) will be 16 (Kulisch, 2009).

4.6. FLOATING-POINT ADDITION AND SUBTRACTION

When *x* or *y* is nonzero, the addition of *x* = (1)*sx x* and *y* = (1)*sy y* is based on the identity

$$x + y = (-1)^{sx} \,|x| + (-1)^{sz}\, y| \qquad s_z = s_x \text{ XOR } s_y \in \{0, 1\}.$$

Therefore, in the subsequent discussion, we will solely focus on the addition operation. The complete specification for floating-point addition can be derived from the IEEE 754-2008 standard in conjunction with equations, provided that either x or y is non-zero. In instances where x and y hold values of zero, the established convention dictates that the outcome should be either +0 or 0, contingent upon the specific operation being performed (addition or subtraction) and the attribute of the rounding direction. The arithmetic operation of addition or subtraction (x ± y) between two finite positive floating-point values (Marre & Michel, 2010).

$$|x| = m_x \beta^{ex} \text{ and } |y| = m_y \beta^{ey}$$

is given by

$$|x| \pm |y| = m_x \beta^{ex} \pm m_y \beta^{ey} \tag{4.2}$$

The subsequent segment elaborates on the calculation of the right-hand side of the equation mentioned above. It should be noted that in the context of floating-point arithmetic, solely invalid operation, overflow, underflow, and inexact are feasible exceptions. In greater depth, the customary sequence of procedures employed for implementation is as follows. Initially, a comparison is made between the two exponents e_x and e_y, and subsequently, the inputs x and y may be interchanged to guarantee that e_x is greater than or equal to e_y (Feldstein & Turner, 1986).

Table 4.2. Addition/Subtraction Parameters when both x and y are Null

x op *y*	(*x* op *y*) for ∈{RN, RZ, RU}	RD(*x* op *y*)
(+0) + (+0)	+0	+0
(+0) + (−0)	+0	−0
(−0) + (+0)	+0	−0
(−0) + (−0)	−0	−0
(+0) −(+0)	+0	−0
(+0) −(−0)	+0	+0
(−0) −(+0)	−0	−0
(−0) −(−0)	+0	−0

Table 4.3. Specification of Addition for Positive Floating-Point Data

$\lvert x\rvert + \lvert y\rvert$ +0		$\lvert y\rvert$			
		(Sub) normal	$+\infty$	**NaN**	
$\lvert x\rvert$	+0 (sub)normal $+\infty$ NaN	+0 $\lvert x\rvert$ $+\infty$	$\lvert y\rvert$ $(\lvert x\rvert + \lvert y\rvert)$ $+\infty$	$+\infty$ $+\infty$ $+\infty$	qNaN qNaN qNaN qNaN
		qNaN	qNaN	qNaN	

Table 4.4. Floating-Point Values with a Positive Sign Require a Subtraction Specification

$\lvert x\rvert - \lvert y\rvert$		$\lvert y\rvert$			
	+0 (sub)normal $+\infty$ NaN				
$\lvert x\rvert$	+0 (sub)normal $+\infty$ NaN	± 0	$-\lvert y\rvert$	$-\infty$	qNaN qNaN qNaN qNaN
		$\lvert x\rvert$	∘ $(\lvert x\rvert - \lvert y\rvert)$	$-\infty$	
		$+\infty$	$+\infty$	qNaN	
		qNaN	qNaN	qNaN	

- The subsequent procedure involves the calculation of $\beta^{-(ex-ey)}$ by displacing the right by e_x e_y digits, which is commonly referred to as significand alignment. The value of the exponent outcome, denoted as e_r, is provisionally established as e_x (Seidel & Even, 2004).
- The summation in question may not be normalized, as defined in Section 8.2. Normalization may be required in two instances.

1. A carry-out occurred during the process of significand addition, specifically in the mr β component. It should be noted that the value of "mr" is always kept strictly below 2β, ensuring that any resulting carry will not exceed a value of 1 (Saleh & Swartzlander, 2008).
2. A cancellation occurred during the addition of the significands when the magnitude of the result was less than 1. Typically, when

the count of leading zeros in mr is denoted by λ, the leftward shift of mr is executed by λ digit positions while simultaneously setting er to er λ. In the event that λ is less than e_{min}, signifying that the intermediate result has been reduced to the underflow range due to cancellation, the exponent will be assigned the value of e_{min} (Sohn & Swartzlander, 2012).

3. It should be noted that in the case of decimals, the recommended exponent rule specifies that imprecise outcomes should be normalized as previously described. In contrast, precise outcomes need not be normalized. This case will be revisited at a later time. Ultimately, the summation is normalized, ensuring that it is perpetually finite and subsequently rounded. Let us proceed to scrutinize this algorithm in greater detail. Significant observations can be made.
4. The algorithm in question has the property of never necessitating an effective addition of more than p digits for the significands. The observation is readily apparent when considering the addition operation: the digits with the least significance in the outcome correspond to those of the initial operand "my," as they are combined with zeroes. This assertion holds valid even in the case of y's subtraction, given that the computation of the sticky bit is suitably adjusted (Bommana et al., 2023).
5. The realignment adjustment is always limited to a maximum of p + 1 digits. If the difference between exponents exceeds p + 1, the variable y will solely compute the sticky bit. Its failure to shift to its designated position becomes inconsequential (Swartzlander & Saleh, 2010).
6. The utilization of leading-zero count and variable shifting shall solely be necessary in the event of a cancellation, specifically when the significands are subjected to subtraction and the disparity between the exponents is either 0 or 1. However, in this particular scenario, multiple aspects are less complex. The value of the sticky bit is equivalent to zero and therefore does not necessitate computation. Of greater significance, the realignment displacement is limited to a maximum of one digit (Dekker, 1971).
7. Stated differently, the algorithm previously discussed entails two significant shifts, namely one to align the significand and another

for normalization in the event of a cancellation. It is important to note that these shifts are not concurrent and cannot occur simultaneously. In academic literature, the two distinct scenarios are identified as the close case, which occurs when the exponents are in close proximity, and the far case, which arises when the difference between the exponents exceeds 1 (Coleman & Ismail, 2015).

8. The normalization process must precede rounding in our algorithm. This is because rounding necessitates awareness of the location of the round and sticky bits, or a normalized infinite significand. Nonetheless, the differentiation between the proximate and remote instances renders the matter more straightforward. In the event of a close case, the value of the sticky bit remains zero regardless of any shifts that may occur during normalization. If normalization is required, it will involve a maximum shift of one digit. Traditionally, the initial sticky bit computation involves the digits located to the right of the (p +2)-nd digit, specifically the lower digits of the lesser addend. The digit in the (p+2) position is commonly referred to as the guard digit. In the event of a 1-digit shift, the digit in question will assume a rounded value, or alternatively, it will be consolidated with the preceding sticky bit if no such shift occurred. It can be concluded that a significant portion of the computation involved in determining the sticky bit can be executed concurrently with the addition of the significand (Hunt & Swords, 2009).

4.6.1. Decimal Addition

The exponent rule that is commonly favored, as outlined in Section 3.4.7 on page 97, dictates that precise outcomes ought not to be standardized. The concept of exactness is intricately linked to that of normalization, whereby a result is deemed exact if it possesses a normalized illustration that can be accommodated within p digits. Consequently, the conventional approach to verifying exactness entails the normalization of X, followed by the application of the algorithm outlined earlier. The precision of the intermediary outcome is established through combinatorial means based on the carry-out and sticky bits, as well as the round and guard digits (Schmookler & Weinberger, 1971). In the context of addition, it is recommended to utilize the lesser of the two input exponents, specifically ey, as opposed to ex. In the event that the outcome is precise, it is necessary to shift "mr" to the right and reduce "er" to "ey." Thus, the exponent rule that is preferred involves two significant shifts. In the event of a carry, the outcome can be precise, however, the group of results may not contain a member with the desired exponent. An illustrative instance involves the expression 9.999e0 + 0.0001e0 within a p = 4-digit framework. Despite both input numbers sharing the same quantum exponent, the outcome of the calculation yields the value of 10, which cannot be expressed using the identical quantum exponent. As a result, the value is represented as 1.000e1.

The precise scenario of decimal applications, particularly in accounting, frequently involves the exact case. Hardware implementations of decimal floating-point addition also prioritize this common case by distinguishing it and striving to enhance its speed. The IBM POWER 6 identifies three distinct scenarios, ranging from the least intricate to the most intricate (Erle & Schulte, 2003).

Case 1 The exponents exhibit equality. The most prevalent scenario in accounting involves the summation of monetary values that share a common decimal point placement. This represents the most basic scenario, as there is no requirement for any adjustment in alignment. Moreover, the outcome is acquired directly by utilizing the desired exponent. In the context of decimal64 accounting applications, it is possible that a one-digit normalization shift and one-digit rounding may be necessary for the event of an overflow. However, it is important to note that such an occurrence is uncommon and would only arise in situations involving extremely large sums of money.

In Case 2, it is recommended to align the operand with the smaller exponent by shifting the operand with the larger exponent leftwards. Following normalization and rounding procedures, the optimal exponent can be readily derived.

In the third case, both operands are shifted. The aforementioned scenario represents the overall situation that has been previously examined. A comprehensive account of the operations executed in each instance within the POWER6 processor can be found in the provided details. The process of decimal addition results in a fluctuating quantity of cycles, ranging from 9 to 17 when dealing with decimal 64 (Kenney & Schulte, 2004).

4.6.2. Abnormal Binary Addition with Inputs and Outputs

The biased exponents of the inputs, E_x and E_y, are calculated as follows: $e_x = E_x - \text{bias} + 1 - n_x$, and $e_y = E_y - \text{bias} + 1 - n_y$. The alignment shifting exponent difference is now calculated as $E_x - n_x - E_y + n_y$. Two abnormal inputs are naturally in phase with one another (Jin et al., 2000).

4.7. FLOATING-POINT MULTIPLICATION

Given $x = (-1)^{s_x} \lvert x\rvert$ and $y = (-1)^{s_y} \lvert y\rvert$, the exact product $x \times y$ satisfies

$$x \times y = (-1)^{s_r} \cdot \lvert x\rvert \times \lvert y\rvert, \qquad s_r = s_x \text{ XOR } s_y \in \{0, 1\}.$$

Table 4.5. Multiplication Norm for Positive-Sign Floating-Point Data (Even & Seidel, 2000)

$\lvert x\rvert \times \lvert y\rvert$		$\lvert y\rvert$		
	+0 (sub)normal +∞ NaN			
$\lvert x\rvert$	+0	+0	+0	qNaN qNaN
	(sub)normal	+0	$\circ(\lvert x\rvert \times \lvert y\rvert)$ +∞	qNaN qNaN
	+∞	qNaN	+∞ +∞	qNaN
	NaN	qNaN	qNaN qNaN	

4.7.1. Handling Subnormal Numbers in Binary Multiplication

The algorithm is being extended to accommodate subnormal inputs and generate subnormal outputs as required, building upon the previous version. Let us proceed to redefine the "is normal" bits n_x and n_y for the given inputs x and y. The computation of n_x can be achieved by performing a logical OR operation on the individual bits of the exponent field E_x. The fragment above may serve as the implicit component to augment the significand, and concurrently function as the bias correction for subnormal numbers. It is now apparent that e_x equals E_x bias plus one multiplied by n_x, and e_y is equivalent to E_y bias plus one multiplied by n_y (Gerwig et al., 2003).

It is important to acknowledge that in the event that both operands are subnormal, with n_x and n_y being equal to zero, the outcome will either be zero or one of the smallest subnormals, contingent upon the rounding mode. Thus, this particular case is being dealt with directly and uncomplicatedly. Let us assume that solely one of the operands possesses subnormal characteristics. The most straightforward approach initially involves normalizing it, returning us to the standard scenario. In order to accomplish this objective, it is necessary to determine the quantity of zeros that precede the given value. The variable "l" shall denote the quantity of leading zeros present in the significand, which has been extended by "n_x." A value of l = 0 is assigned to a number considered normal, while a value of l = 1 is assigned to a number classified as subnormal. The significance of the subnormal is shifted to the left by l bit positions, while its exponent is adjusted to e_{min} + l. A broader range of exponents is necessary beyond the limitations of the standard format. In practical applications, the exponent data is only extended by a single bit (Zhang et al., 2019).

A viable option to preprocess subnormal input before conducting a regular computation is to instead standardize the product following the multiplication process. Specifically, the identical multiplication procedure utilized to determine the product of two p-bit figures will yield an exact product outcome in the event that either input contains l leading zeros. Subsequently, the resultant product shall exhibit either l or l+1 leading zeros, necessitating normalization through a leftward shift. Nevertheless, the benefit of employing this methodology is that the computation of subnormal leading zeros can be executed concurrently with the process of multiplication. To enhance clarity, we adopt the perspective that both inputs have undergone normalization with a 1-bit wider exponent range. Our attention is directed toward generating subnormal outputs. It should be noted that these occurrences may manifest even in cases of typical inputs. The standard normalization process outlined in Section 8.2 can be utilized to manage them. In order to round a significand, an arbitrary shift to the right is performed. This shift is determined by the condition that if the sum of e_x and e_y is less than e_{min}, then the shift is equal to e_{min} minus the sum of e_x and e_y (Venishetti & Akoglu, 2007). In brief, the expenses associated with managing subnormal numbers include expanding the range of exponents for internal exponent calculations, executing a step to count leading zeros, performing a left shift operation on either the subnormal input or the product, and carrying out a right shift operation prior to rounding. The forthcoming Section 9.4.4 will demonstrate how these supplementary measures can be arranged in a hardware realization with the aim of mitigating their influence on latency (He et al., 2005).

4.7.2. Decimal Specifics

The exponent rule for multiplication, as stated in Section 3.4.7 on page 97, specifies that in order to obtain precise outcomes, the recommended quantum exponent to be utilized is Q(x) + Q(y). The given relation is Q(x)

$= e_x\ p + 1$. The precision of a computation can be determined by initially standardizing the two inputs, subsequently calculating and standardizing the product, and finally examining its rounded digit and sticky bit. It is possible to anticipate precision when the number of leading zeros in the multiplicands exceeds p, which is a frequently occurring scenario (Breunesse et al., 2002). To gain comprehension, reconsider the field of accounting. The operation of multiplication is predominantly utilized for the purpose of applying a rate to an account, such as a tax rate, an interest rate, or a currency conversion rate. Upon applying the rate, the output is subjected to rounding to the nearest cent before undergoing subsequent processing. The IEEE 754-2008 standard specifies the quantize operation to perform rounding to the nearest cent (Lancashire et al., 1991). The rates above are numerical values ranging from three to six digits. Notably, the official conversion rates of the euro in relation to the currencies it supersedes were established as six-digit numerical values. Assuming utilization of the 16-digit format decimal64, the resultant value of the multiplication between the aforementioned rate and your bank account will be precise, except in cases where your financial assets surpass 10^{10} cents (equivalent to 100 million dollars). In such instances, your financial institution will be content to allocate additional computational resources toward its management. Typically, when the product is precise, the quantum exponent is established as Q(x) + Q(y) in order to ensure that the rate has a quantum exponent of zero, thereby enabling the direct expression of the product in cents. Consequently, normalization of the product is unnecessary. The output significand is determined by extracting the final p digits of the resulting product. The computation of leading zeros in the input values is a computationally intensive task, however, it can be executed concurrently with the multiplication process (Erle et al., 2005).

4.8. FLOATING-POINT FUSED MULTIPLY-ADD

In the computation of (ab + c), it is required that the 2p-digit number ab be added to the p-digit number c. The process of sign manipulation is simple, as the crucial factor lies in determining whether the operation will result in an effective addition or subtraction. The subsequent analysis is founded upon the factual exponent of the input values, which is represented as e_a, e_b, and e_c. The computation of ab + c necessitates the initial alignment of the product ab, followed by the utilization of the exponent difference in conjunction with the summand c (Bruguera & Lang, 2005).

$$d = e_c - (e_a + e_b)$$

4.8.1. Normal Inputs Case Study

If both a and b are natural integers, then the product ab contains no more than two digits in front of the point that corresponds to a = $m_a \beta^e a$ and b = $m_b \beta^e b$.

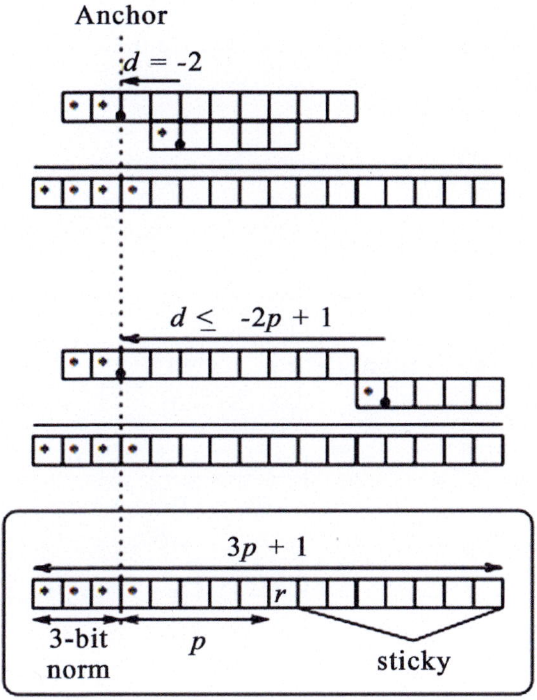

Figure 4.3. Computation of the FMA with a product anchor for typical inputs.

It may be suggested to initially consider a 1-digit normalization of the product ab.

However, this additional step can be circumvented, and its exclusion only slightly reduces the quantity of cases that require handling. Consequently, we have opted to center our case analysis solely on the three input exponents, as is customary in the majority of implementations.

A review of the potential alignment scenarios is now presented. These cases are considered to be mutually exclusive. Subsequent to any of the aforementioned steps, it is necessary to execute a rounding procedure following Section 8.2. This action has the potential to increase the exponent of the outcome once more (Liew et al., 2017).

4.9. FLOATING-POINT DIVISION

4.9.1. Overview and Special Cases

Given $x = (-1)^{s}x \cdot |x|$ and $y = (-1)^{s}y \cdot |y|$, we want to compute:

$x/y = (-1)^{s}r \cdot |x|/|y|,\ s_r = s_x$ XOR $s_y \in \{0, 1\}$

We now address the computation of the quotient of $|x| = m_x \cdot \beta^{e}x$ and $|y| = m_y \cdot \beta^{e}y$

We obtain,

$|x|/|y| = m_x/m_y \cdot \beta^{e}x{-}ey$

Table 4.6. Special Values for |x|/|y|

$\lvert x\rvert/\lvert y\rvert$		$\lvert y\rvert$		
	+0 (sub)normal	**+∞**	**NaN**	
$\lvert x\rvert$	+0 (sub)normal +∞ NaN	qNaN	+0 +0	qNaN qNaN qNaN qNaN
		+∞	∘($\lvert x\rvert/\lvert y\rvert$)+0	
		+∞ +∞	qNaN qNaN	
		qNaN qNaN		

Let's pretend that m_x and m_y are both real integers with the notation $m_x = (m_{x,0}, m_{x,1} \ldots, m_{x,p-1})_\beta$ and $m_y = (m_{y,0} \cdot m_{y,1}, \ldots, m_{y,p-1})_\beta$, respectively, $m_{x,0}$ /= 0 and $m_{y,0}$= 0. If both inputs are sub-normals or decimal values with leading zeroes, an implementation may first normalize them using an expanded exponent range. After applying this transformation, we obtain $m_x = [1, \beta)$ and $m_y = [1, \beta)$, therefore, m_x/m_y $(\frac{1}{\beta}, \beta)$.). This suggests that normalization to a single digit may be required before rounding (Duale et al., 2007).

4.9.2. Managing Subnormal Numbers

The optimal approach for handling subnormal inputs involves initial normalization through a broader exponent range. The discrepancy in exponents can be used to anticipate a suboptimal outcome. Due to its lower number of significand digits, the computation necessitates less precision than a typical calculation. In the context of functional iteration, it is adequate to round the intermediate result with high precision to the appropriate digit position. In the context of digit-recurrence implementation, a viable approach to address the rounding of subnormal numbers is to terminate the iteration process once the requisite number of digits has been generated. Subsequently, these digits can be appropriately shifted to their designated position. The rounding logic remains consistent with the standard scenario (Seal et al., 2002).

4.9.3. The Inexact Exception

Typically, the imprecise exception is derived from accurate rounding. The detection of exactness and half-ulp exactness is necessary for directed rounding modes and round to nearest even in the "even" case. Alternatively, it can be argued that the imprecise exception can be derived directly from the sticky bit. The property of exactness in digit-recurrence algorithms is derived from the absence of a remainder. Polynomial approximation techniques necessitate the computation of the remainder for rounding purposes, and the inclusion of the inexact flag does not incur any additional expenses. Functional iterations based on FMA exhibit a slight deviation from conventional methods in that they do not explicitly compute a sticky bit. Nevertheless, they can be structured in a manner that causes the ultimate FMA operation to trigger the inexact flag exclusively when the quotient is deemed imprecise (Fousse et al., 2007).

4.9.4. Decimal Specifics

The preferred exponent rule specifies that Q(x) Q(y) is to be used for accurate results in division.

4.10. FLOATING-POINT SQUARE ROOT

As we near the end of this chapter, we perform the fifth basic arithmetic operation, the square root operation sqrt. While both square root and division share some commonalities, the square root is easier to implement in a way compliant with IEEE 754. In particular, the input must be + for it to overflow, and it is univariate and never underflows.

4.10.1. Overview and Special Cases

If x is positive (sub) normal, then the correctly rounded value ($\sqrt{x}$) must be returned. Otherwise, a special value must be returned conformally with Table 4.7.

Table 4.7. Special Values for sqrt(x)

Operand x	+0	+∞	−0	less	than zero	NaN
Result r	+0	+∞	−0	qNaN		qNaN

$$m_x \cdot \beta^{ex} = \begin{cases} m_x \cdot \beta^{ex} & \text{if } e_x \text{ is even,} \\ (\beta \cdot m_x).\beta^{ex-1} & \text{if } e_x \text{is odd.} \end{cases}$$

Consequently, for $c \in \{0, 1\}$ depending on the parity of e_x, we have:

$$\sqrt{m_x \cdot \beta^{ex}} = \sqrt{\beta^c \cdot m_x} \cdot \beta^{\frac{e_x - c}{2}}$$

where; $(e_x\ c)/2 = e_x/2$ is an integer. Since $\beta^c\ m_x\ [1, \beta^2)$, the significand square root satisfies (Jeannerod & Rump, 2013).

$$\sqrt{\beta^c \cdot m_x} \varepsilon(1 \cdot \beta)$$

4.10.2. Computing the Significand Square Root

Montuschi and Mezzalama comprehensively survey the most popular algorithm families for multiplication and division.

1. **Algorithms with Recursive Digits:** These methods are discussed at length with an eye toward practical hardware implementations. In this context, it is sufficient to remark that the recurrence is often somewhat more complicated than for division; for instance, the software implementation of the restoration method given in Section 10.5.3 on page 366.
2. **Algorithms based on Functional Iteration:** For the positive real solution y = x to the equation y2 x = 0, those techniques again generalize Newton's iteration. It is common practice to employ such procedures for division when an FMA operator is available.
3. **Approximation Quality Assessment Using Polynomials:** These techniques involve determining whether or not a certain polynomial approximation of the function x is "good enough" to use for division (Viitanen et al., 2013).

4.10.3. Managing Subnormal Numbers

While dealing with atypical input, it is preferable first to normalize using a larger exponent range, much as one would while dividing. Since it is impossible to generate a subnormal output, the situation is substantially less complex than in the case of division. This practical result is a natural consequence of the next property.

Property 17: *For $x = m_x \beta$, a positive, finite floating-point number, the real $\sqrt{x}$ satisfies*

$\sqrt{x} \in [\beta e_{min}, \beta 1 e_{max})$

- Proof:

$\beta(1-p+e_{min})/2 \leq \sqrt{x} < \beta e_{max}/2,$

The upper bound follows immediately. Using p 1$e_{min,}$ we get further $\sqrt{x} \geq \beta e_{min}$.

Because of this characteristic, we know that:

- The square root of a floating-point number never underflows. If the input is +, then the result will overflow.
- Only invalid and imprecise exceptions should be taken into account (Jeavons & Clark, 1974).

4.10.4. The Inexact Exception

As in division, a null residual is used to infer exactness in digit recurrence algorithms and polynomial-based methods; in this case, the remainder is x r^2. The final FMA operation in a sequence of FMA-based functional repetitions can be programmed to raise the inexact flag if the square root is inexact (Stevenson, 1981).

4.11. SUMMARY

The implementation of radix 2 is the simplest among the radices that are a power of 2, because most of our computers operate on two-state logic. Therefore, selecting an appropriate radix for the internal representation of floating-point numbers was not a straightforward task. Various solutions were investigated during the initial stages of automated computing. Several early computing machines employed radix-8 floating-point arithmetic, including the PDP-10, as well as the Burroughs 570 and 6700. The IBM 360 was equipped with a radix-16 floating-point arithmetic system. The decimal numeral system, known as radix 10, has widespread application in financial computations and handheld electronic calculators. The development of a successful implementation of radix-10 floating-point arithmetic remains an area of active research. Maple, a computer algebra system, employs radix 10 as its internal numerical representation. Hence, it appears that most floating-point arithmetic systems executed to date have utilized radices of either 10 or a power of 2. In the context of addition, utilizing the lesser of the two input exponents, denoted as "e_y" rather than "e_x" is recommended. If the outcome is precise, it is necessary to shift towards the right and decrease "e_r" to "e_y." Thus, the exponent rule that is preferred involves two significant shifts. In the event of a carry-out operation, it is possible for the outcome to be precise, yet the group of results may not encompass an element with the desired exponent. An illustrative instance entails the expression 9.999e0 + 0.0001e0 in a p = 4-digit numerical system. Despite both input numbers sharing the same quantum exponent, the outcome of 10 cannot be expressed with an identical quantum exponent and necessitates representation as 1.000e1.

REFERENCES

1. Anderson, A., & Gregg, D., (2016). Vectorization of multibyte floating point data formats. In: *Proceedings of the 2016 International Conference on Parallel Architectures and Compilation* (Vol. 1. pp. 363–372).
2. Andrysco, M., Kohlbrenner, D., Mowery, K., Jhala, R., Lerner, S., & Shacham, H., (2015). On subnormal floating point and abnormal timing. In: *2015 IEEE Symposium on Security and Privacy* (Vol. 3, pp. 623–639). IEEE.
3. Backus, J., (1978). The history of Fortran I, II, and III. *ACM Sigplan Notices*, *13*(8), 165–180.
4. Barr, E. T., Vo, T., Le, V., & Su, Z., (2013). Automatic detection of floating-point exceptions. *ACM Sigplan Notices*, *48*(1), 549–560.
5. Boldo, S., & Melquiond, G., (2011). Flocq: A unified library for proving floating-point algorithms in Coq. In: *2011 IEEE 20th Symposium on Computer Arithmetic* (Vol. 2, pp. 243–252). IEEE.
6. Bommana, A. R., Siddamshetty, S. U., Pudi, D., Thumatti KR, A., Boppu, S., Sabarimalai Manikandan, M., & Cenkeramaddi, L. R., (2023). Design of synthesis-time vectorized arithmetic hardware for tapered floating-point addition and subtraction. *ACM Transactions on Design Automation of Electronic Systems*, *28*(3), 1–35.
7. Breunesse, C. B., Jacobs, B., & van den Berg, J., (2002). Specifying and verifying a decimal representation in Java for smart cards. In: *AMAST* (Vol. 2, pp. 304–318).
8. Bruguera, J. D., & Lang, T., (2005). Floating-point fused multiply-add: Reduced latency for floating-point addition. In: *17th IEEE Symposium on Computer Arithmetic (ARITH'05)* (Vol. 1, pp. 42–51). IEEE.
9. Burtscher, M., & Ratanaworabhan, P., (2007). High throughput compression of double-precision floating-point data. In: *2007 Data Compression Conference (DCC'07)* (Vol. 2, pp. 293–302). IEEE.
10. Bux, K. U., & Wortman, K., (2007). Finiteness properties of arithmetic groups over function fields. *Inventiones Mathematicae*, *167*(2), 355–378.
11. Cartwright, R., & Boehm, B., (1990). Exact real arithmetic, formulating real numbers as functions. *Research Topics in Functional Programming. University of Texas at Austin Year of Programming Series*, 4, 43–64.
12. Clinger, W. D., (1990). How to read floating point numbers accurately. *ACM SIGPLAN Notices*, *25*(6), 92–101.
13. Cody, W. J., (1973). Static and dynamic numerical characteristics of floating-point arithmetic. *IEEE Transactions on Computers*, *100*(6), 598–601.

14. Coleman, J. N., & Ismail, R. C., (2015). LNS with co-transformation competes with floating-point. *IEEE Transactions on Computers, 65*(1), 136–146.

15. Cornea, M., Harrison, J., Anderson, C., Tang, P. T. P., Schneider, E., & Gvozdev, E., (2008). A software implementation of the IEEE 754R decimal floating-point arithmetic using the binary encoding format. *IEEE Transactions on Computers, 58*(2), 148–162.

16. Daumas, M., Rideau, L., & Théry, L., (2001). A generic library for floating-point numbers and its application to exact computing. In: *Theorem Proving in Higher Order Logics: Proceedings 14th International Conference, TPHOLs 2001 Edinburgh, Scotland, UK* (Vol. 2, pp. 169–184). Springer Berlin Heidelberg.

17. De Dinechin, F., Lauter, C., & Melquiond, G., (2010). Certifying the floating-point implementation of an elementary function using Gappa. *IEEE Transactions on Computers, 60*(2), 242–253.

18. Defour, D., Hanrot, G., Lefevre, V., Muller, J. M., Revol, N., & Zimmermann, P., (2004). Proposal for a standardization of mathematical function implementation in floating-point arithmetic. *Numerical Algorithms, 37*, 367–375.

19. Dekker, T. J., (1971). A floating-point technique for extending the available precision. *Numerische Mathematik, 18*(3), 224–242.

20. Dido, J., Geraudie, N., Loiseau, L., Payeur, O., Savaria, Y., & Poirier, D., (2002). A flexible floating-point format for optimizing data-paths and operators in FPGA based DSPs. In: *Proceedings of the 2002 ACM/SIGDA 10th International Symposium on Field-Programmable Gate Arrays* (Vol. 3, pp. 50–55).

21. Duale, A. Y., Decker, M. H., Zipperer, H. G., Aharoni, M., & Bohizic, T. J., (2007). Decimal floating-point in z9: An implementation and testing perspective. *IBM Journal of Research and Development, 51*(1.2), 217–227.

22. Erle, M. A., & Schulte, M. J., (2003). Decimal multiplication via carry-save addition. In: *Proceedings IEEE International Conference on Application-Specific Systems, Architectures, and Processors. ASAP 2003* (Vol. 3, pp. 348–358). IEEE.

23. Erle, M. A., Schwarz, E. M., & Schulte, M. J., (2005). Decimal multiplication with efficient partial product generation. In: *17th IEEE Symposium on Computer Arithmetic (ARITH'05)* (Vol. 2, pp. 21–28). IEEE.

24. Even, G., & Seidel, P. M., (2000). A comparison of three rounding algorithms for IEEE floating-point multiplication. *IEEE Transactions on Computers, 49*(7), 638–650.

25. Feldstein, A., & Turner, P., (1986). Overflow, underflow, and severe loss of significance in floating-point addition and subtraction. *IMA Journal of Numerical Analysis*, *6*(2), 241–251.
26. Flegar, G., Scheidegger, F., Novaković, V., Mariani, G., Tomás, A. E., Malossi, A. C. I., & Quintana-Ortí, E. S., (2019). Floatx: Ac++ library for customized floating-point arithmetic. *ACM Transactions on Mathematical Software (TOMS)*, *45*(4), 1–23.
27. Fousse, L., Hanrot, G., Lefèvre, V., Pélissier, P., & Zimmermann, P., (2007). MPFR: A multiple-precision binary floating-point library with correct rounding. *ACM Transactions on Mathematical Software (TOMS)*, *33*(2), 13–15.
28. Gal, S., (1991). An accurate elementary mathematical library for the IEEE floating point standard. *ACM Transactions on Mathematical Software (TOMS)*, *17*(1), 26–45.
29. Gellar, R., & Wallen, L. J., (1970). Subnormal weighted shifts and the Halmos-Bram criterion. *Proceedings of the Japan Academy*, *46*(4), 375–378.
30. Gerwig, G., Wetter, H., Schwarz, E. M., & Haess, J., (2003). High performance floating-point unit with 116 bit wide divider. In: *Proceedings 2003 16th IEEE Symposium on Computer Arithmetic* (Vol. 2, pp. 87–94). IEEE.
31. Goldberg, D., (1991). What every computer scientist should know about floating-point arithmetic. *ACM Computing Surveys (CSUR)*, *23*(1), 5–48.
32. Guralnik, E., Aharoni, M., Birnbaum, A. J., & Koyfman, A., (2010). Simulation-based verification of floating-point division. *IEEE Transactions on Computers*, *60*(2), 176–188.
33. Harrison, J., (1999). A machine-checked theory of floating-point arithmetic. In: *Theorem Proving in Higher Order Logics: Proceedings 12th International Conference, TPHOLs'99 Nice, France* (Vol. 1, pp. 113–130). Springer Berlin Heidelberg.
34. He, H., Li, Z., & Sun, Y., (2005). Multiply-add fused float point unit with on-fly denormalized number processing. In: *48th Midwest Symposium on Circuits and Systems, 2005* (Vol. 4, pp. 1466–1468). IEEE.
35. Higbie, L. C., (1976). Vector floating-point data format. *IEEE Transactions on Computers*, *100*(1), 25–32.
36. Horprasert, T., Harwood, D., & Davis, L. S., (1999). A statistical approach for real-time robust background subtraction and shadow detection. In: *IEEE ICCV* (Vol. 99, pp. 1–19). Citeseer.

37. Hunt, W. A., & Swords, S., (2009). Centaur technology media unit verification: Case study: Floating-point addition. In: *Computer Aided Verification: Proceedings 21st International Conference, CAV 2009, Grenoble, France* (Vol. 3, pp. 353–367). Springer Berlin Heidelberg.
38. Janikow, C. Z., & Michalewicz, Z., (1991). An experimental comparison of binary and floating-point representations in genetic algorithms. In: *ICGA* (Vol. 1991, pp. 31–36).
39. Jeannerod, C. P., & Rump, S. M., (2013). Improved error bounds for inner products in floating-point arithmetic. *SIAM Journal on Matrix Analysis and Applications*, *34*(2), 338–344.
40. Jeavons, P. M., & Clark, J. E., (1974). Sodium valproate in treatment of epilepsy. *Br. Med. J.*, *2*(5919), 584–586.
41. Jin, H., Khandekar, A., & McEliece, R., (2000). Irregular repeat-accumulate codes. In: *Proc. 2nd Int. Symp. Turbo Codes and Related Topics* (Vol. 2. pp. 1–8).
42. Jung, I., & Li, C., (2001). A formula for □-hyponormality of backstep extensions of subnormal weighted shifts. *Proceedings of the American Mathematical Society*, *129*(8), 2343–2351.
43. Kalliojarvi, K., & Astola, J., (1996). Roundoff errors in block-floating-point systems. *IEEE Transactions on Signal Processing*, *44*(4), 783–790.
44. Kenney, R. D., & Schulte, M. J., (2004). Multioperand decimal addition. In: *IEEE Computer Society Annual Symposium on VLSI* (Vol. 2, pp. 251–253). IEEE.
45. Kuck, & Sameh., (1977). Analysis of rounding methods in floating-point arithmetic. *IEEE Transactions on Computers*, *100*(7), 643–650.
46. Kulisch, U. W., (2009). Complete interval arithmetic and its implementation on the computer. In: *Numerical Validation in Current Hardware Architectures: International Dagstuhl Seminar, Dagstuhl Castle, Germany, Revised Papers* (Vol. 2, pp. 7–26). Springer Berlin Heidelberg.
47. Kumar, R., & Raj, A. A. B., (2020). Customized floating-point algorithm for the ranging system. In: *2020 International Conference on System, Computation, Automation and Networking (ICSCAN)* (Vol. 1, pp. 1–7). IEEE.
48. Lancashire, P. D., Bleiholder, H., Boom, T. V. D., Langelüddeke, P., Stauss, R., Weber, E., & Witzenberger, A., (1991). A uniform decimal code for growth stages of crops and weeds. *Annals of Applied Biology*, *119*(3), 561–601.

49. Liew, D., Schemmel, D., Cadar, C., Donaldson, A. F., Zahl, R., & Wehrle, K., (2017). Floating-point symbolic execution: A case study in N-version programming. In: *2017 32nd IEEE/ACM International Conference on Automated Software Engineering (ASE)* (Vol. 1, pp. 601–612). IEEE.
50. Marre, B., & Michel, C., (2010). Improving the floating-point addition and subtraction constraints. In: *Principles and Practice of Constraint Programming–CP 2010: Proceedings 16th International Conference, CP 2010, St. Andrews, Scotland* (Vol. 2, pp. 360–367). Springer Berlin Heidelberg.
51. Morris, R., (1971). Tapered floating point: A new floating-point representation. *IEEE Transactions on Computers, 100*(12), 1578–1579.
52. Panchekha, P., Sanchez-Stern, A., Wilcox, J. R., & Tatlock, Z., (2015). Automatically improving accuracy for floating point expressions. *ACM SIGPLAN Notices, 50*(6), 1–11.
53. Ratanaworabhan, P., Ke, J., & Burtscher, M., (2006). Fast lossless compression of scientific floating-point data. In: *Data Compression Conference (DCC'06)*. IEEE. (Vol. 2, pp. 133–142).
54. Rümmer, P., & Wahl, T., (2010). An SMT-LIB theory of binary floating-point arithmetic. In: *International Workshop on Satisfiability Modulo Theories (SMT)* (Vol. 2, pp. 151).
55. Rump, S. M., Ogita, T., & Oishi, S. I., (2009). Accurate floating-point summation part II: Sign, K-fold faithful and rounding to nearest. *SIAM Journal on Scientific Computing, 31*(2), 1269–1302.
56. Saleh, H., & Swartzlander, E. E., (2008). A floating-point fused add-subtract unit. In: *2008 51st Midwest Symposium on Circuits and Systems* (Vol. 2, pp. 519–522). IEEE.
57. Schmookler, M. S., & Weinberger, A., (1971). High speed decimal addition. *IEEE Transactions on Computers, 100*(8), 862–866.
58. Seal, E. C., Metz, J., Flicker, L., & Melny, J., (2002). A randomized, double - blind, placebo - controlled study of oral vitamin B12 supplementation in older patients with subnormal or borderline serum vitamin B12 concentrations. *Journal of the American Geriatrics Society, 50*(1), 146–151.
59. Seidel, P. M., & Even, G., (2004). Delay-optimized implementation of IEEE floating-point addition. *IEEE Transactions on Computers, 53*(2), 97–113.
60. Shirazi, N., Walters, A., & Athanas, P., (1995). Quantitative analysis of floating-point arithmetic on FPGA based custom computing machines. In: *Proceedings IEEE Symposium on FPGAs for Custom Computing Machines*. IEEE. (Vol. 3, pp. 155–162).

61. Sohn, J., & Swartzlander, E. E., (2012). Improved architectures for a fused floating-point add-subtract unit. *IEEE Transactions on Circuits and Systems I: Regular Papers*, *59*(10), 2285–2291.
62. Steele Jr, G. L., & White, J. L., (1990). How to print floating-point numbers accurately. In: *Proceedings of the ACM SIGPLAN 1990 Conference on Programming Language Design and Implementation* (Vol. 3, pp. 112–126).
63. Stevenson, D., (1981). A proposed standard for binary floating-point arithmetic. *Computer*, *14*(03), 51–62.
64. Swartzlander, E. E., & Saleh, H. H., (2010). FFT implementation with fused floating-point operations. *IEEE Transactions on Computers*, *61*(2), 284–288.
65. Tent, M. W., (2006). Understanding the properties of arithmetic: A prerequisite for success in algebra. *Mathematics Teaching in the Middle School*, *12*(1), 22–25.
66. Tziantzioulis, G., Gok, A. M., Faisal, S. M., Hardavellas, N., Ogrenci-Memik, S., & Parthasarathy, S., (2015). b-HiVE: A bit-level history-based error model with value correlation for voltage-scaled integer and floating-point units. In: *Proceedings of the 52nd Annual Design Automation Conference* (Vol. 2. pp. 1–6).
67. Venishetti, S. K., & Akoglu, A., (2007). A highly parallel FPGA based IEEE-754 compliant double-precision binary floating-point multiplication algorithm. In: *2007 International Conference on Field-Programmable Technology* (Vol. 1, pp. 145–152). IEEE.
68. Viitanen, T., Jääskeläinen, P., & Takala, J., (2013). Inexpensive correctly rounded floating-point division and square root with input scaling. In: *SiPS 2013 Proceedings* (Vol. 3, pp. 159–164). IEEE.
69. Wang, L. K., & Schulte, M. J., (2004). Decimal floating-point division using Newton-Raphson iteration. In: *Proceedings 15th IEEE International Conference on Application-Specific Systems, Architectures and Processors* (Vol. 3, pp. 84–95). IEEE.
70. Whitehead, N., & Fit-Florea, A., (2011). Precision & performance: Floating point and IEEE 754 compliance for NVIDIA GPUs. *rn (A+ B)*, *21*(1), 18749–19424.
71. Zeljić, A., Backeman, P., Wintersteiger, C. M., & Rümmer, P., (2018). Exploring approximations for floating-point arithmetic using UppSAT. In: *Automated Reasoning: Proceedings 9th International Joint Conference, IJCAR 2018, Held as Part of the Federated Logic Conference, FloC 2018, Oxford, UK* (Vol. 2, pp. 246–262). Springer International Publishing.

72. Zhang, H., Chen, D., & Ko, S. B., (2019). New flexible multiple-precision multiply-accumulate unit for deep neural network training and inference. *IEEE Transactions on Computers*, *69*(1), 26–38.

CHAPTER

5 Addition and Subtraction

Contents

Addition and subtraction are primary operations in arithmetics. The multiplication and division operations are founded on the principles of subtraction and addition.

Using fast adders and subtractors is advantageous in expediting basic arithmetic operations such as addition and subtraction and hastening the processes of division and multiplication, which necessitate extensive addition and subtraction. This chapter pertains to the analysis of two-operand adders. The following types of adders will be presented: carry-completion adders, ripple carry-adding machines, conditional-sum adders, and carry-look-ahead adders (Hwang et al., 2021).

5.1. SINGLE-BIT ADDERS

5.1.1. Logical Devices

The ALU is built with two goals in mind: maximizing throughput at low cost and minimizing footprint for maximum efficiency. The scope of our discourse in this literary work is confined to the design of the logic level. The swift progression of diverse logic families has resulted in the need for further examination of electronic implementation, considering the trade-offs between density and cost, as well as speed and power dispersion.

The time complexity shall be represented as ΔT, while the area complexity shall be denoted as AT. Table 5.1 presents the AT and AT values for different logic gates that function as essential components in the design of Arithmetic Logic Units (ALUs). The logic gates are restricted to n-input gates, where n ranges from 1 to 10. The metric denoting AT is represented by lA, which corresponds to the duration of signal propagation through either a NAND gate or a NOR gate. The quantity denoting AT is represented by the A, which signifies the surface area necessary to implement a single NAND or NOR gate (Andréasson et al., 2011).

Table 5.1. Area and Delay Time of Logic Gates

NAND	$1\Delta_g$	$1A_g$
NOR	$1\Delta_g$	$1A_g$
NOT	$1\Delta_g$	$2A_g$
AND	$2\Delta_g$	$2A_g$
OR	$2\Delta_g$	$2\Delta_g$

XOR	$2\Delta_g$	$3\Delta_g$
XNOR	$2\Delta_g$	$3\Delta_g$
AOI	$1\Delta_g$	$2\Delta_g$

Connecting the high-impedance outputs of two NAND gates together creates a hard-wired circuit that can perform an AND-OR-Invert operation. The mathematical expression for the product of vectors A and B is F = AB. The equation presented is CD = A B + CD. In the context of a limited RC load, it can be observed that the current, denoted as AT, attains a value of 1 A for one input and 2 A for two inputs. The decoder under consideration comprises n address lines and 2^m output lines. Specifically, it is a 71-to-2^m decoder. There are two available AND gates, each offering an output line. These gates are equipped with n inputs linked to the variables on the address lines or their complements. Based on the logical values in the address lines, a singular 2" output line is expected to be activated with a "high" signal (Nesher & Katriel, 1977).

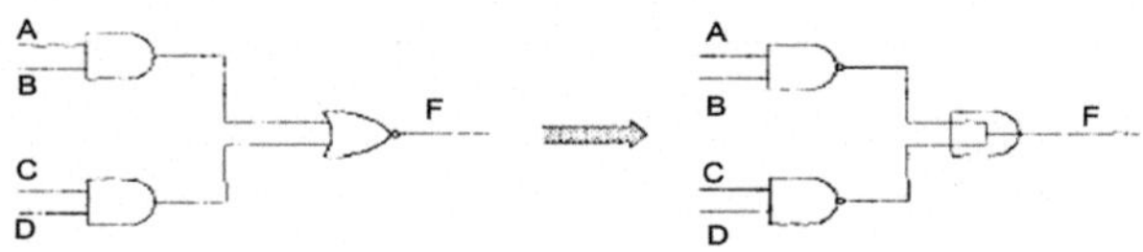

Figure 5.1. A01 function.

The diagram in Figure 5.2(a) depicts a 2-to-4 decoder incorporating an enable line. The Decoder exhibits a delay time of 3Ag and a high area complexity. A multiplexer, commonly abbreviated as MUX, is a functional unit that performs a many-to-one operation. It is designed to accommodate multiple inputs and produce a single output. A multiplexer with a 2-to-1 ratio is characterized by n control input lines and 2 raised to the power of n data input lines. The system is founded upon an n-to-2 decoder. Data input is assigned to each of the 2" AND gates. The decoder's address lines are utilized to select the gate. The data can only be routed to the output by the gate that has been specifically chosen (Bogoni et al., 2008).

The diagram depicted in Figure 5.2(b) illustrates the utilization of a 2-to-4 decoder to construct a 4-to-1 multiplexer, which serves the purpose of selecting a single data input from a set of four and transmitting it to the output.

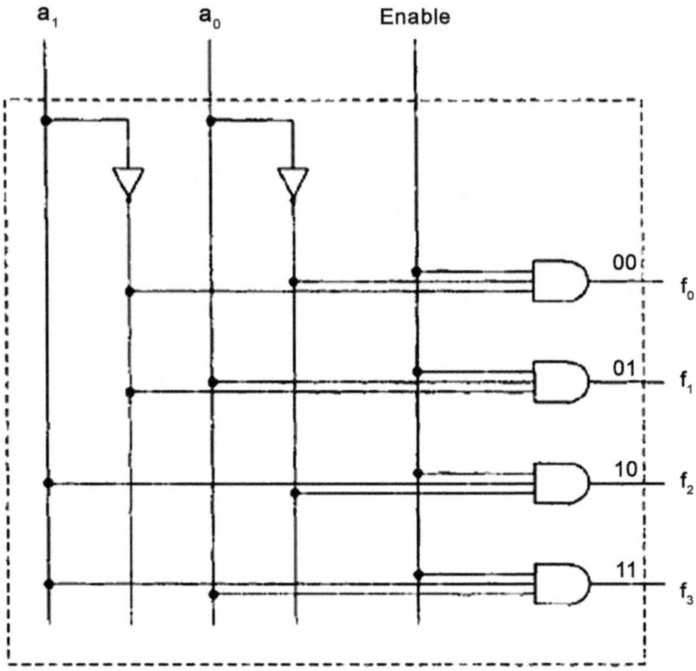

Figure 5.2(a). 2-to-4 decoder.

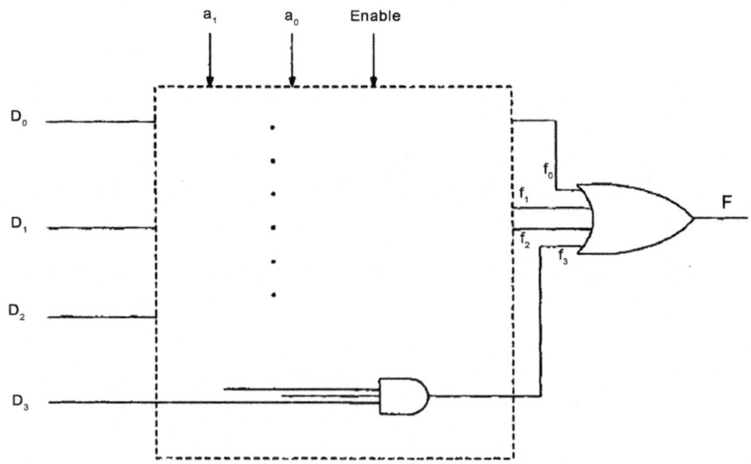

Figure 5.2(b). 4-to-1 multiplexer.

The implementation of the hardware can be achieved through the utilization of a wired A01 and an inverter. Consequently, the Quad 2-to-1 Multiplexers, Dual 4-to-1 Multiplexers, Dual 8-to-1 Multiplexers, and Single 16-to-1 Multiplexer exhibit a delay time of 30 g for the 4-to-1 Multiplexer, while the area complexity is 7Ag. Multiplexer (MUX) components can be found on Integrated Circuit (IC) chips (Li et al., 1999).

5.1.2 Single-Bit Half and Full-Adders

A half-adder with a single-bit capacity can execute the addition operation for two bits. Table 5.2 enumerates the logic function that is required to be executed by the HA.

Table 5.2. Logic Function of a Half-Adder

a_i	b_i	c_{i+1}	s_i
0	0	0	0
0	1	0	1
1	0	0	1
1	1	1	0

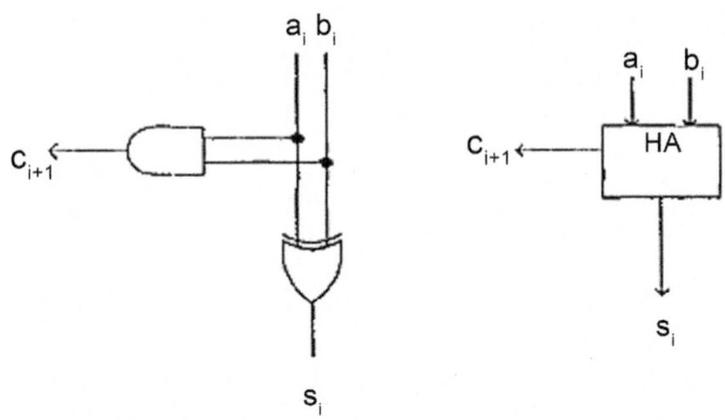

Figure 5.3. Single-bit half-adder.

The logical expression for the sum bit can be observed as follows:

si = *ai* + *h i,*

and that of the carry-out bit is

ci+l = *aibi* (5.1.)

ci+l = *aibi* + *bici* + *aici* (5.2)

The outputs can be considered a two-bit number which equals the number of 1s in the input. *ci+lsi+l* equals 01 if there is just one 1. *ci+lsi+l* equals 10 if there are two Is. When there are three ones, *ci+lsi+l* equals 11. The logic symbol and circuit diagram for a single-bit full-adder (FA) with three inputs and two outputs are depicted in Figure 2.4 (Mak et al., 2022).

ci+l = aibi + (ai + bi)ci

aibi + iiibici + aibici

aibi + bici + aici,

Upon applying Equation (5.1), the resulting expression is obtained.

si = ABC + ABC + ABC + ABC."

The area complexity is:

AT = lOA

Table 5.3. Single-Bit Subtractor

a_i	b_i	l_i	l_{i+1}	d_i
0	0	0	0	0
0	0	1	1	1
0	1	0	1	1
0	1	1	1	0
1	0	0	0	1
1	0	1	0	0
1	1	0	0	0
1	1	1	1	1

The resulting difference is expressed as bit di when conducting a subtraction operation with a single bit, denoted as ai – bi. Furthermore, there is an inclusion of a borrow bit. In the context of binary arithmetic, a request for borrowing from bit position i can be represented as a borrow-in signal, denoted as li, which indicates the receipt of a loan from position i. The concept of borrow-out in binary arithmetic involves a request for borrowing from bit position i + 1 or a loan from bit position i + 1.

5.2. CONTRADICTIONS

The negation operation involves determining the complement number of a given value A by finding its additive inverse, –A. Given a positive number

A, the negation of A results in a negative number (Miller, 1922). On the contrary, if A is a negative numerical value, the process of negation will yield a positive numerical value. In this section, we present the concept of negation operation within the frameworks of 1's and 2's complement systems (Rysin et al., 2021).

5.2.1. Contradiction in One's Complement System

In the 1's complement system, the negation of a given number is achieved through a bit-wise NOT function, wherein 0 is replaced with 1, and 1 is replaced with 0.

The diagram depicted in Figure facilitates the conduction of the negation of an n-bit numerical value within the 1's complement system. The most basic negation operation is facilitated by provisioning n NOT gates in scenario (a). Frequently, the online platform enables the function of negation. In the calculation of A + B, negation is not required. Negating B and executing A + (–B) is necessary in the A – B computation. The circuit depicted in (b) can perform two operations on the n-bit input number, namely, forwarding it to the output without any alteration or computing its 1's complement prior to transmission. The presence of a control line enables this functionality (Samuel & Herbert, 2020).

It should be noted that in the case of an exclusive OR gate if one of the inputs is set to a value of 1, the other input will be subjected to negation prior to the output. The circuits depicted in figure is commonly known as 1's complementors. The truth table pertaining to the enable signal E, input ai, and output u is presented below (Tsang, 2004).

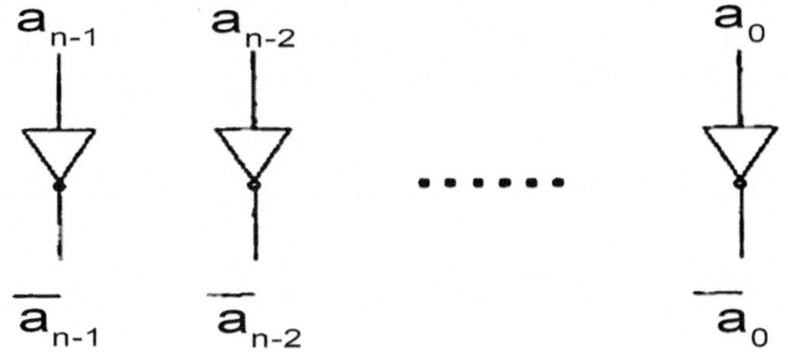

Figure 5.4(a). Realizing negation by NOT gates.

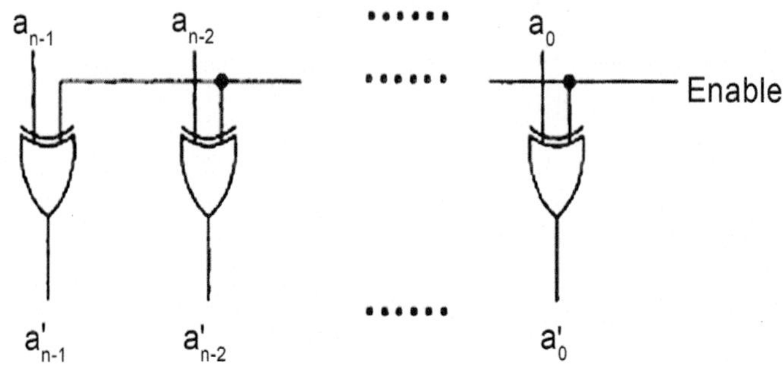

Figure 5.4(b). Negation by XOR gates.

5.2.2. Contradiction in Two's Complement System

In the Two's complement system, to perform negation on a given number:

a, –1... ai +. a0 7

Two distinct approaches exist for determining the 2's complement representation of a given number. The initial technique in the manual depiction utilizing writing utensils is delineated as follows:

It should be noted that there is an absence of carry-in for the least significant bit (LSB) position, but rather a value of "1" is added. Conversely, there is no value to be added for the remaining bit positions; instead, a carry-in is present. Figure 2.7(a) depicts the logic circuit. The delay duration of an n-bit 2's complement can be determined as follows (Maweu, 2011):

AT = A l n v e r t e r + ~ (A A N D) = (1 +2n)Ag.

The delay time of the XOR component within the half-adder circuit is observed to overlap with the delay time of the AND gate.

The computation of the area additional complexity of this complementor is determined subsequently:

AT = n (A 1 n v e r t e r + AAND + AXOR)

= n (l + 2 + 3) A g

= 6nAg.

The second approach for negating a number in the 2's complement system can be executed using the traditional pencil-and-paper method. Perform a binary operation whereby the value of 0 is replaced with 1, and the value of

1 is replaced with 0, starting from the leftmost digit and proceeding towards the rightmost digit until the rightmost 1 is reached. Subsequently, replicate the rightmost 1 along with any subsequent 0s that may follow. Assuming a numerical value of 101 10100, the following is observed (Lorenz et al., 2019):

1 0 1 1 0 1 0 0

I I I I I

O 1 O O 1 ~ Q Q

In the instance mentioned above, the sub-string 10110 is transformed into 01001 in a left-to-right manner, while the bit string 100 that is underlined is replicated. This method is, in fact, consistent with the initial approach. After performing the 1's complement operation, the binary digit that is situated on the rightmost end of the sequence of 1s, followed by a series of 0s, is transformed into the binary digit that is situated on the rightmost end of the sequence of 0s, followed by a series of 1s. During the increment by 1 operation, the contiguous sequence of 1s can transmit the carry bit by bit. The sole factor that can impede the carry propagation is the presence of the "rightmost 0." The resultant string obtained by adding 1 to the given string "01... 1" is "10... 0." It is noteworthy that this resultant string is identical to a substring of the original string (Sterling, 2014).

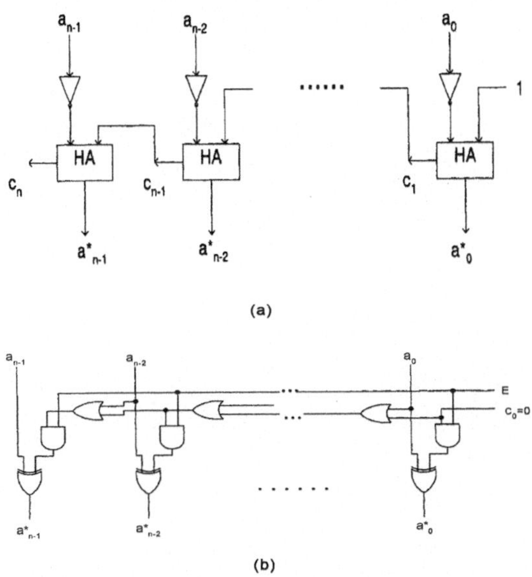

Figure 5.5. Negation in two's complement system.

Therefore, the increment operation is not executed, and this substring is directly copied. Referencing the circuit depicted in Figure 2.7(b). In the event that E is assigned a value of 1, the series of OR gates will govern the selection of the subset of input bits that will undergo modification and those that will remain unaltered.

The variable "Co" is initialized to a value of 0. If a_0 is equal to 0, the OR gate will transmit a value of 0 towards the left, and the same applies to al. Whenever the rightmost digit with a value of 1 is impacted, a binary digit with a value of 1 will be transmitted toward the leftmost position (Hoffmann & Houle, 1995).

Adjacent to the numeral "1," where the sequence of OR gates produces a binary zero digit, the resultant output bit shall correspond to the input bit ai. The output bit a on the left side of the "1" in the OR gate chain will be the complement of ai as a result of the XOR gate's function. The aforementioned occurrence takes place. In the context where E is assigned a value of 1, the anticipated outcome is the negation in the 2's complement system. If E is assigned a value of 0, the value of a; will invariably be equivalent to ai, resulting in the input number retaining its original value (Fisher et al., 2005).

$$\begin{aligned}\Delta_T &= (n-1)\Delta_{OR} + \Delta_{XOR} \\ &= [(n-1)\times 2 + 2]\Delta_g \\ &= 2n\Delta_g.\end{aligned}$$

$$\begin{aligned}A_T &= n(A_{OR} + A_{XOR}) - A_{OR} \\ &= [n(2+3) - 2]A_g \\ &= (5n-2)A_g.\end{aligned}$$

5.3. SUBTRACTION THROUGH ADDITION

Let A = (*un-l* 1. + also) and B = (bnPl… blbo) be two signed numbers. *S* =A + *B* is also a signed number represented as *sn-l*. In mathematical terms, the value denoted by the A is commonly known as the augend. At the same time, the value represented by the letter B is also referred to as the addend. Alternatively, both A and B can be collectively referred to as summands. The mathematical term that refers to the result of adding A and B is S (Thompson, 1999).

A + (–B) = A + B

A single-bit full-adder has been developed to execute two operand addition. Devising a distinct and novel hardware component for subtraction is unnecessary, as computer arithmetic achieves subtraction using addition. The hardware unit that is utilized for addition can also be employed to execute subtraction (Carpenter & Moser, 1984).

Contemplate the act of adjusting the position of the hand on a timepiece. The clockwise movement can be likened to the mathematical operation of addition, while the counter-clockwise movement can be likened to the mathematical operation of subtraction. As an illustration, let us consider a scenario where a pointer initially points towards the 12 o'clock position. Rotating the object in a counterclockwise direction for three hours will yield a resultant value of 9, which is obtained by subtracting 3 from 12. Conversely, if the clock is rotated in a clockwise direction for a duration of 9 hours, it will return to its original position because (12+9) mod 12 is equivalent to 9. (Refer to Figure 2.8.) The numbers 3 and 9 are complementary to one another, specifically serving as the 12's complement numbers. The arithmetic operation of subtracting 3 from 12 can be equivalently expressed as the addition of 12 and the additive inverse of 3, denoted as (–3) (Lewandowski & Bizzoco, 2007).

In the realm of computer systems, a comparable concept is employed, albeit with the utilization of the 1's or 2's complement system as opposed to the 12's complement system. The negation function and its corresponding hardware can determine a given numerical input B's negative value (-B) (González et al., 2015).

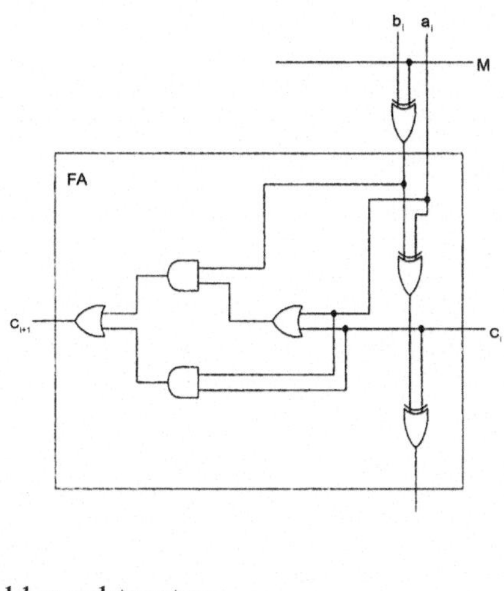

Figure 5.6. One-bit adder subtractor.

A unit that can perform addition and subtraction can be devised by integrating an adder and a complementor. Figure depicts the output of a single-bit full-adder, which corresponds to the logic presented in Equation (2.2) (Zaranis, 2017).

In the case where M equals 1, the input supplied to the adder is 6i, which represents 1's complement of bi. The operation ai + ($-b_i$) is then executed, resulting in $a_i - b_i$. Therefore, equations (5.1) and (5.7) are transformed (Woranetsudathip et al., 2021).

$$c_{i+1} = (a_i + c_i)(b_i \oplus M) + a_i c_i,$$

5.4. OVERFLOW

Assume that A = ($a_{n-1,}$ $a_{n-2\ldots}$ a_0),= ($b_{n-1,}$ $b_{n-2\ldots}$ b_0) and s ums = ($S_{n-1,}$ $S_{n-2\ldots}$ S_0) and that S = A + B. The formula S = A + B denotes

$$\begin{array}{rllll} & a_{n-1} & a_{n-2} & \cdots & a_0 \\ +) & b_{n-1} & b_{n-2} & \cdots & b_0 \\ \hline & \nwarrow c_{n-1} \; s_{n-1} & \nwarrow c_{n-2} \; s_{n-2} & \cdots & s_0. \end{array}$$

The subscript in the notation for carry is modified in this section. The variable S_{n-1} represents the carry-in value of the bit position a, while ci denotes the corresponding carry-out value (Pai & Tran, 1992).

Subsequently, we will delve into the concept of "overflow" concerning the 2's complement system. This situation applies to other systems as well. Three potential scenarios exist in addition based on the polarity of the augend and addend.

When both A and B are positive, the values of a,-l and b,-l are equal to zero. It is imperative that c_{n-1} be present, which is equivalent to 0 + 0 = 0, indicating that the outcome is a favorable value. In the event that s_{n-1} equals 1, an overflow situation arises. Arithmetic errors may occur due to overflow, whereby the result of an operation exceeds the maximum value that the system can represent. For instance, the addition of two positive numbers may lead to a negative number, which is not mathematically feasible. The error above can be attributed to generating a carry-in bit c_{n-2} = 1 by the lower order bits. Due to insufficient bits to represent the addition result, a carry-out was introduced into the sign bit (MSB) position, resulting in an incorrect sign for the outcome (Garner, 1978). In other words,

$$\text{if } |A| + |B| < 2^{n-1}, \quad \text{no overflow.}$$
$$\text{if } |A| + |B| \geq 2^{n-1}, \quad \text{overflow occurs.}$$

The present discourse pertains to the scenario where A exhibits positivity while B manifests negativity. The scenario in which B is positive while A is negative can be perceived symmetrically. The equations A = IAl and B = 2" – IBI are given. By adding A and B, we obtain the expression A + B = IAl+ (2" – IBI) = 2" + 1Al – (B ((mod 2") (Qingkun et al., 2016).

$$\text{if } |A| < |B|, \quad A + B = 2^n - (|B| - |A|).$$

$$\text{if } |A| \geq |B|, \quad A + B = |A| - |B|.$$

Following the modulo operation. The absence of overflow is observed, and an accurate outcome is achieved. In order to delve deeper into the circumstances that give rise to overflow, an examination is conducted on the carry-in, c,-z, and carry-out, cn-l, with respect to the most significant bit position. In the scenario where both A and B are positive (case 1), there is invariably a value of c, represented by —~ = 0. In order to achieve a positive sum when snP1 equals zero, it is anticipated that c,-~ will also equal zero. When both A and B are negative (case 2), the value of cnwl invariably equals 1. Hence,

$$Overflow = c_{n-1} \oplus c_{n-2}.$$

5.5. RIPPLE CARRY ADDERS

5.5.1. Two's Complement Addition

Figure illustrates a 2's complement adder-subtractor consisting of n negation units and n-one-bit full adders. Additionally, an algorithm for detecting overflow has been incorporated.

The execution of either addition or subtraction is contingent upon the configuration of the mode control M. When M equals zero, numerical values denoted as A and B are supplied as input to the full adder (FA), which then executes the operation of adding A and B. If M equals 1, the full-adder will receive the 2's complement of B as input and execute a subtraction operation.

It should be noted that the negation module, as described earlier, can solely invert the input bit and execute the function of 1's complement. In the context of 2's complement operation, it is essential to perform an additional increment. It is evident from the diagram that the carry-in of the least significant bit position is linked to mode M (Blair, 1998). The 1's complement of B and a value of 1 are added to A. The operation involves the addition of the 2's complement of B to A, which can be interpreted as an A – B operation.

As depicted in Figure 5.10, the carry is propagated in a ripple fashion toward the left through the Full Adders (FAs) (Cilardo, 2009).

The readiness of the carry-in at bit position i is contingent upon completing the addition at bit position *i – 1*. The time complexity associated with the 2's complement adder is under consideration (Salomon et al., 1995).

$$\begin{aligned} \Delta_T &= \Delta_{XOR} + n(\Delta_{FA}) + \Delta_{XOR} \\ &= (2 + 2n + 2)\Delta_g \\ &= (2n + 4)\Delta_g. \end{aligned}$$

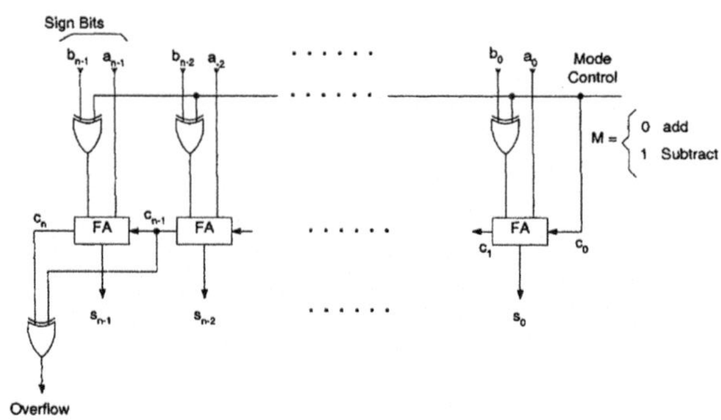

Figure 5.7. Two's complement addition subtraction.

$$\begin{aligned} A_T &= n(A_{XOR} + A_{FA}) + A_{XOR} \\ &= (n(3 + 10) + 3)A_g \\ &= (13n + 3)A_g. \end{aligned}$$

5.5.2. One's Complement Addition

This section pertains to the development of an adder that is capable of computing the sum of two 1's complement numbers, denoted as A and B, and producing an output, denoted as S, that is expressed in the 1's complement format. Particular emphasis will be placed on a technique referred to as the "end-around carry" scheme.

The end-around carry scheme repurposes the carry-out signal originally intended for the most significant bit position c as the carry-in signal *co* for the least significant bit position l. The implementation of a 1's complement addition can be achieved by utilizing a 2's complement adder, specifically employing the end-around carry method as previously outlined. In the following discourse, we examine the accuracy of integrating said scheme into a 1's complement adder on a case-by-case basis (Hoover, 1990).

When both variables A and B hold positive values, the process of performing 1's complement addition can be executed in a manner that is analogous to that of 2's complement addition. Routing the carry-out signal c to the least significant bit while maintaining its value at 0 will not impact the addition operation's outcome.

When the values of A and B are negative, the value of c equals 1. By comparing the output produced by a circuit that lacks end-around carry with the anticipated correct output, it can be determined whether the carry (c) ought to be directed to the least significant bit. The circuit's performance is impacted in the absence of an end-around carry (Pekmestzi & Efstathiou, 2016).

$$\begin{array}{rc} & 2^n - 1 - |A| \\ +) & 2^n - 1 - |B| \\ \hline \text{(after } mod\text{)} & 2^n - 1 - (|A| + |B|) - 1. \end{array}$$

The anticipated accurate outcome is 2 inches minus one minus the sum of cell A1 and cell IBI. The circuit's output can be incremented by adding a "1" without end-around carry, which can be facilitated by the variable c.

In instances where A is negative and B is positive, it is possible for two distinct scenarios to arise. It should be noted that the case where A is positive, and B is negative can be seen in a manner that is symmetrical to the scenario above (Warren, 1977).

a. 1-41 > IBI.

$$\begin{array}{rll} & 2^n - 1 & -|A| + |B| \\ = & 2^n - 1 & -(|A| - |B|) \\ < & 2^n - 1. & \end{array}$$

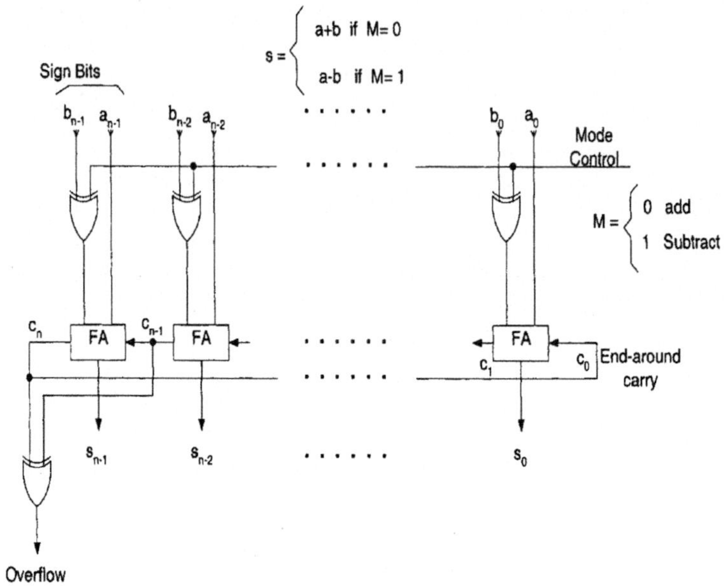

Figure 5.8. One's complement addition subtraction.

The anticipated right outcome is identical to the one mentioned before. Given that the output of the circuit is less than two and c equals zero, directing c to the least significant bit (LSB) will not have any impact on the outcome of the addition operation. The inequality IAI < IBI holds.

In the absence of the end-around carry, the circuit executes its function (Lyon, 1976).

$$\begin{aligned} & 2^n - 1 \quad -|A| + |B| \\ = \; & 2^n - 1 \quad +(|B| - |A|) \\ > \; & 2^n - 1. \end{aligned}$$

Thus, the value of c is equal to 1. Following the application of the mod 2 function, the circuit outputted IB(–[A1–1), whereas the anticipated accurate outcome is (BI-[A). To achieve an accurate outcome, it is recommended to include a value of "1." This can be accomplished by assigning the variable c a value of 1. The proper interconnection of the carry-out of the most significant bit position to the carry-in of the least significant bit position results in accurate functionality across all scenarios. When an addition operation involving the value "1" is required in the least significant bit position, carrying out the most significant bit is equivalent to 1. Otherwise, it is equivalent to zero (Wang & Tull, 2004).

Regarding the time complexity, the subsequent computation is presented as:

$$
\begin{aligned}
\triangle_T &= \triangle_{XOR} + n\triangle_{FA} \\
&\quad + n\triangle_{FA} \text{ (for end-around carry)} \\
&= (2 + 2n + 2n)\triangle_g
\end{aligned}
$$

The stability of the first carry in the 1's complement adder and subtractor is contingent upon the rippling of the carry through all the full adders. Subsequently, the value of c will be redirected to the least significant bit position, initiating the second carry propagation phase. The 1's complement adder and subtractor exhibit a delay time that is twice as long as that of the 2's complement adder and subtractor, which accounts for its comparatively lower prevalence in usage (Hashemian, 1996).

5.5.3. Sign-Magnitude Addition

Both addends must be expressed in sign-magnitude form for the sign-magnitude addition to be performed. The resultant sum must be expressed in the sign-magnitude format after performing the addition operation. The block diagram of a sign-magnitude adder/subtractor is presented in Figure 5.9. A comprehensive introduction will be presented, emphasizing the pre-complement and post-complement arrangements. The addition operation is executed using a 1's complement adder in the diagram. To furnish the adder with operands in the appropriate representation, it may be necessary to perform a pre-complement operation. Let us thoroughly examine the following cases comprehensively. Assuming that A is a positive value (Vassiliadis et al., 1989).

Given that the subtraction of a number can be achieved by adding its negation, the classification can be reduced to two cases. In the scenario where two summands of the same sign, IAI, and IBI, are added, we have Case 1. In Case 2, we consider the addition of two summands of different signs, specifically IAI + (–(BI) (An et al., 2023).

If A is negative, two scenarios are taken into account. In Case 1, the sum of the magnitudes of A and B is required to calculate –(IAI + IBI), which is analogous to Case above 1. In Case 2, the expression –(IAI + (-IBI)) demonstrates the cancellation of the magnitudes of A and B, resembling the Case above 2. In instances where the magnitudes of A and B are equal in magnitude but opposite in sign, it is necessary to execute a 1's complement operation on the magnitude of B before performing the addition. The linguistic phenomenon being referred to is commonly known as pre-complement. The expression P is defined as a_{n-1}. The variable M denotes the mode, which takes on a value of either 0 or 1, corresponding to addition or subtraction, respectively. Based on the preceding analysis, it can be inferred that the execution of pre-complement is necessary when P equals 1 (Zhakatayev et al., 2018). Therefore, the signal P serves as the enabling factor for pre-complementation.

It is noteworthy that in the case of adding two numbers with opposite signs, the outcome will be negative if the absolute value of the negative number is larger. Furthermore, the addition of two negative integers yields a negative integer. Given that the output of the 1's complement adder is expressed in 1's complement notation, it is necessary to perform a conversion to obtain a sign-magnitude representation. Consequently, it is necessary to have a post-complement (Gorgin & Jaberipur, 2016).

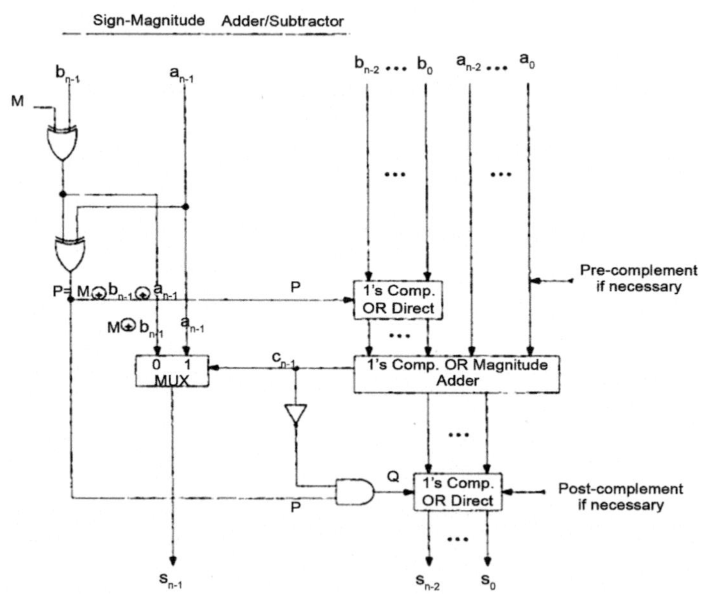

Figure 5.9. Block diagram of sign-magnitude addition/subtraction.

The activation of the post-complement operation is facilitated by the equation Q = PC,-l. In instances of case 1, as indicated in the table mentioned earlier, the value of P is zero, thereby rendering the post-complement unnecessary. In Case 2 instances, where P equals 1, the post-complement is solely required in the event that IBI 2 [A] is present. It is important to note that the adder which utilizes (n – 1)-bit 1's complement performs the operation of (A1 + (–1BI) by 1Al+ (2n–1 – 1 – IBI). When subtracting a larger number from and adding an equal or smaller number to 2n–1 – 1 in IBI 2 / A, the resulting number will be less than 5 2n–1 – 1. This implies that Cn-l is equal to zero. Therefore, in the scenario where P equals 1 and C,-l equals 0, the assertion of Q takes place, and a post-complement operation is subsequently executed (Orts et al., 2019).

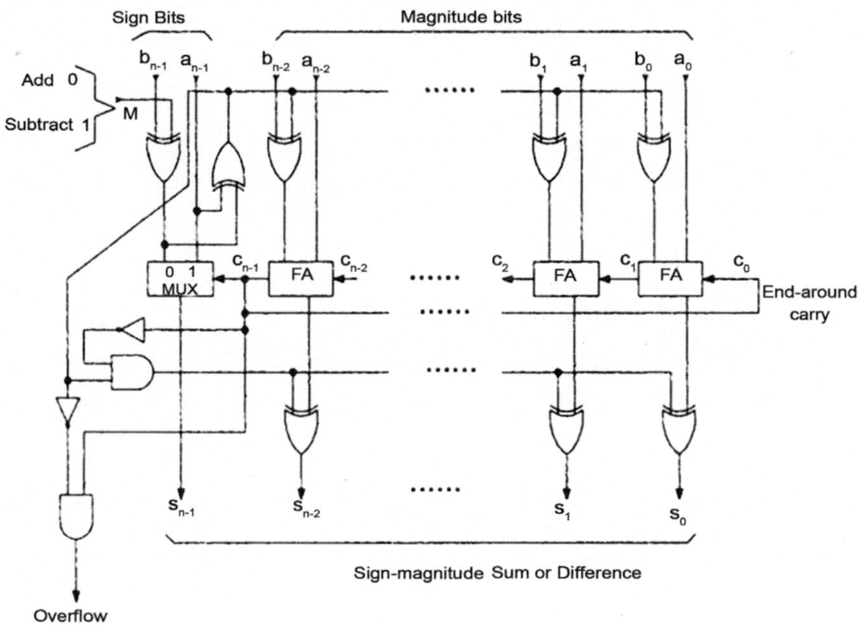

Figure 5.10. Sign-magnitude addition/subtraction.

5.6. HIGH-SPEED ADDERS

5.6.1. Conditional-Sum Addition

The ripple-carry adder is a subject of study wherein the primary focus is on the delay caused by carry propagation. This delay is a significant factor in enhancing the speed of addition operations involving two numbers. The delay time of an n-bit ripple-carry adder exhibits a linear relationship concerning n. It should be noted that when performing the addition operation on two numerical values in the following manner (Sklansky, 1960):

$$\begin{array}{rr} & a_i \\ & b_i \\ +) & c_i \\ \hline c_{i+1} & s_i \end{array}$$

$$\begin{array}{rr} & a_i \\ & b_i \\ +) & 0 \\ \hline c^0_{i+1} & s^0_i \end{array} \quad \text{or} \quad \begin{array}{rr} & a_i \\ & b_i \\ +) & 1 \\ \hline c^1_{i+1} & s^1_i \end{array} .$$

The superscript denotes the assumed carry-in value, while the subscript pertains to the bit index. Given the premise that the carry-in value is 0, the values of s and c R 1 can be readily determined through the following method (Suzuki et al., 1993):

$$\begin{aligned} s^0_i &= a_i\bar{b}_i + \bar{a}_i b_i = a_i \oplus b_i \\ c^0_{i+1} &= a_i b_i . \end{aligned}$$

$$\begin{aligned} s^1_i &= a_i b_i + \bar{a}_i\bar{b}_i = a_i \odot b_i \\ c^1_{i+1} &= a_i + b_i , \end{aligned}$$

Based on the reasoning mentioned above, a conditional-sum adder is constructed. The Conditional Sum (CS) cell is equipped with two sets of circuits that are capable of executing additions based on two distinct carry-in values. Simultaneous preparation of two sets of outputs is possible, and the selection of one out of the two can be made once the carry-in value is determined (Martin & Hufnagel, 1980).

The merging process involves the simultaneous merging of two adjacent groups, doubling the group size at each step. The initial bit is allocated to a group, followed by two and four. During the k-th step, a group of bits consisting of 2k–1 elements is formed. The carry-in value to the least significant bit (LSB) or group is consistently zero, thereby negating alternative assumptions and validating the output of this particular group (Kruy, 1965).

The binary values of A and B are A = (01101.10)2 and B = (1101101)2, respectively. The process of conditional sum addition is depicted in Figure 3.1 for explanatory purposes. The presence of a superscript 0 or 1 in a numerical representation denotes the assumption of a carry 0 or carry 1 into each group, respectively. The groups exhibit isolation from one another, as the carry-out produced within a group of lower order does not propagate to a group of higher order. In the given step of merging groups, arrows indicate the direction from the right group toward the left group. The right group's carry-out indicates a selection made in the left group in the opposite direction. If the carry value is zero, it indicates the uppermost data set within the left group. The lower data set is referenced if the carry is equal to 1 (Haixia et al., 2011).

As the circle exemplifies, the sole group in which carry-out has a known value is the least significant. As the box demonstrates, the sum acquired by this carry-out group contributes to the ultimate outcome. Alternatively, two arrows emanate from each group on the right, indicating the involvement of two carry-out signals in the selection process. At present, all values are assumed, and the true carry value remains unknown to all. The individuals chosen within the left group of candidates may or may not comprise the outcome. The circuit provides the pathway for the signals, and subsequently, a distinct dataset will be chosen upon integration into the least significant cluster during a subsequent phase. Certain groups on the figure's rightmost side exhibit an incomplete size configuration. The scenario where n is not a power of 2 only includes the residual bit positions. Figure 3.2 depicts the schematic circuit of a conditional-sum adder utilized to add the aforementioned 7-bit numerical values. The adder's routed data is displayed in scenario (b) with respect to the given inputs (Saleem & Al-Khalili, 1998).

Step	i	6	5	4	3	2	1	0
	a_i	0	1	1	0	1	1	0
	b_i	1	1	0	1	1	0	1
1	S^0_i	1	0	1	1	0	1	1
	C^0_{i+1}	0	1	0	0	1	0	0
	S^1_i	0	1	0	0	1	0	
	C^1_{i+1}	1	1	1	1	1	1	
2	S^0_i	0	0	1	1	0	1	1
	C^0_{i+1}	1		0		1		0
	S^1_i	0	1	0	0	1	0	
	C^1_{i+1}	1		1		1		
3	S^0_i	0	0	1	1	0	1	1
	C^0_{i+1}	1				1		
	S^1_i	0	1	0	0			
	C^1_{i+1}	1						
Result	S	0	1	0	0	0	1	1
	C_{out}	1						

Figure 5.11. Conditional-sum addition.

5.6.2. Addition with Carry-Completion Sensing

Since carry is propagated from the least significant bit location to the most significant bit position, the delay time of ripple-carry adders is linear. In the event of the full adder is in the most significant bit position, the maximum duration required for it to generate the accurate sum and carry-out is referred to as the worst-case waiting time. It should be noted that when a finite automaton (FA) is combined with a combinatorial circuit, it can generate an output based on the data on its input lines. The output is subject to change in accordance with potential alterations to the input signal. Until the worst-case delay time is attained, it is impossible to ensure the output's accuracy, and it is not appropriate to assert the conclusion of the addition process (Gadamsetti & Singh, 2010).

This section presents the introduction of a carry-completion sensing adder (CCSA). The system permits the independent and simultaneous propagation of multiple carriers and detects the result of all such propagation. On average, the stabilization time for the output is shorter in comparison to the conventional ripple-carry adder, rendering it a faster option (Chong et al., 2004).

The present study outlines two distinct categories of carry, namely independent carry and dependent carry. It should be noted that every form of carry can be instigated at all bit positions concurrently, without the need to wait for the transmitted carries from the previous bit positions.

$$\left.\begin{array}{l} a_i = 0 \\ b_i = 0 \end{array}\right\} IC_{i+1} = 0$$

$$\left.\begin{array}{l} a_i = 1 \\ b_i = 1 \end{array}\right\} IC_{i+1} = 1$$

$$\left.\begin{array}{l} a_i = 0 \\ b_i = 1 \\ or \\ a_i = 1 \\ b_i = 0 \end{array}\right\} DC_{i+1} = \begin{cases} DC_i & \text{if it exists} \\ IC_i & \text{otherwise} \end{cases}$$

The process of multiple carry propagation can be initiated from the independent carries. Carry propagation durations vary depending on the bit position immediately above the independent carry, with some longer and others shorter. Please consult the numerical illustration depicted in Figure 3.3, which displays the independent and dependent carries, as well as the carry propagation. The position of the blocked bit has the potential to produce a carry (Rao & Nowrouzian, 1995).

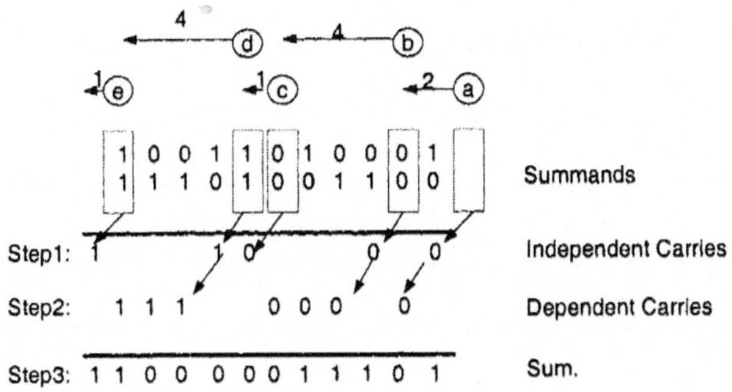

Figure 5.12. Generation and transmission of carries.

The initial step involves identifying the presence of autonomous carriers for a given column by examining the equivalence of the two bits that constitute the summand in the previous column. Subsequently, these self-reliant carriers are assigned the value as specified earlier.

During the second step, the dependent carries are produced by equating the right member of each pair of independent carries to all the carries between them. During the third step, each column's carry and summand bits are subjected to a module-2 addition (Lu & Ercegovac, 1991).

In Figure 5.13, assuming that aibi equals 11, it can be inferred that the output of gate 1 will be asserted, and the carry-out ci+l will be equal to 1. If aibi equals 00, it can be inferred that gate 2 will produce an asserted output, and the carry-out Ei+1 will be equal to 1.

The two aforementioned cases are mutually exclusive, whereby gate 1 or gate 2 output can only be 1. This implies that in cases where ci+l equals 1, Ci+l must be 0, and when t?i+l equals 1, ci+l must also be 0. The carry produced in both of these instances is referred to as an independent carry. Subsequently, based on the carry-in variable (ci) and Ei, gate 4 will produce a value of 1, and gate 5 will produce a value of 0, or conversely. The aforementioned signals shall be conveyed via gates 6 and 7 towards the outputs denoted as c * + ~an d ~?i+.b~e, representing the carry-out signals. These signals are reliant on the carry. It should be noted that the present case and the two preceding cases are incompatible, indicating that solely one of them can transpire at every bit position (Fleischer et al., 2009).

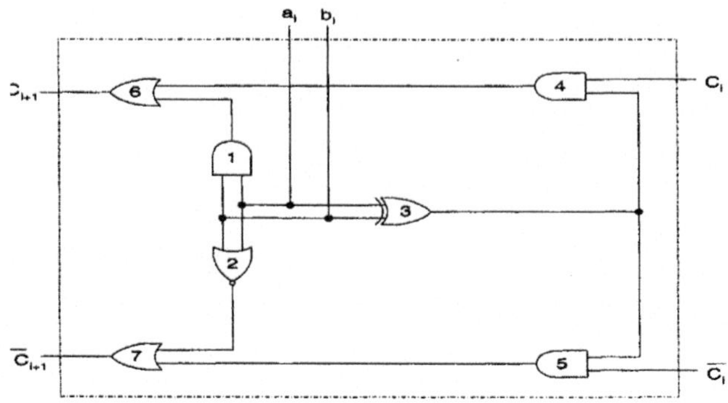

Figure 5.13. Carry transmission unit.

The CT cell operates such that when the two summand bits ai and bi are equal in a given bit position, an independent carry, denoted as carry 1 or 0, is immediately propagated. To indicate that the carry-transmission has been completed in bit position i, one of the outputs, ci+1 or Ei+1, must be high. These outputs are then ORed together and sent to an n-input AND gate, which serves as a carry-completion sensing gate. The output of this gate is high only if all inputs are 1, depicting that carry generation and propagation have been completed in all bit positions (Cheng et al., 2000). In summary, the CT cell's logic can be expressed as

$$c_{i+1} = a_i \cdot b_i + (a_i \oplus b_i) \cdot c_i$$
$$\bar{c}_{i+1} = \bar{a}_i \cdot \bar{b}_i + (a_i \oplus b_i) \cdot \bar{c}_i$$

The variable "co" represents the initial independent carry that is carried into the least significant bit (LSB) position. It should be noted that the term c,+1 in the aforementioned equation is comprised of two distinct components, namely the production of the autonomous carry and the production and transmission of the reliant carry.

The temporal complexity of this adder is comprised of three primary constituents, which may exhibit overlap:

1. The duration required for the generation of all independent carries.
2. It is now time to generate dependent carries.
3. The subsequent step involves the final piecewise summation to obtain the ultimate solution (Chandel et al., 2010).

Please refer to the numerical illustration depicted in Figure 5.13, where the value of n is equal to 11, and the circuit is illustrated in the accompanying Figure. Upon inputting the summand bits ai and bi, gates 1, 2, and 3 can produce their respective outputs in a maximum time of 2A during the CT of all bit positions. Subsequently, for the range of bits spanning from ci to ci+l, a total of 4A units are required to facilitate the carry propagation process. Additionally, the [Zogzn] bit positions must be taken into account based on the mean propagation distance. The circuit in question operates asynchronously. The Full Adder (FA) consistently generates an output with a value present on the carry-in (ci), albeit potentially incorrect. The adoption of the outputs of the Fas for further utilization is contingent upon the transmission of a signal from the AND gate to the control circuitry, which indicates the completion of all carry generation and propagation. Utilizing the upper limit value, we obtain (Rahman et al., 2014):

$$\begin{aligned}\Delta_{CCSA} &= \Delta_{CT} + \Delta_{OR} + \Delta_{AND} \\ &= (2\,\Delta_g + (\lceil log_2 n \rceil) \cdot 4\Delta_g) + 2\,\Delta_g + 2\,\Delta_g \\ &= (6 + 4\lceil log_2 n \rceil)\,\Delta_g\,.\end{aligned}$$

$$\begin{aligned}A_{CCSA} &= n(A_{FA} + A_{CT} + A_{OR}) + A_{AND} \\ &= n[A_{FA} + (A_{XOR} + 3A_{AND} + 2A_{OR} + A_{NOR}) + A_{OR}] \\ &\quad + A_{AND} \\ &= \{n[10 + (3 + 6 + 4 + 1) + 2] + 2\}A_g \\ &= (2 + 26n)A_g.\end{aligned}$$

5.7. CARRY-LOOK AHEAD ADDITION

The ripple-carry adder sequentially generates carries across various bit positions. The value of *Ci+l* is contingent upon Ci, and the determination of Ci necessitates prior knowledge of Ci–1 (Thapliyal et al., 2013).

5.7.1. Carry-Lookahead Adder

Consider two binary numbers A = (An–1 . . . A1 Ao) and B = (Bn–1 . . . B1 Bo). Let Ci denote the carry into bit position i. The carry into the least significant bit (LSB) is commonly referred to as Co. The carry generation function is defined to explore the scenario where a carry can be produced in bit position i, while disregarding the carry-in Ci (Kao et al., 2006).

Gi = A. Bi.

Pi = Ai @ Bi.

$$
\begin{aligned}
S_i &= (A \oplus B) \oplus C_i \\
&= P_i \oplus C_i
\end{aligned}
$$

Once more, the objective at hand is to accelerate the process of carry propagation. The values of Pi and Gi, where i ranges from n–1 to l and eventually to 0, can be concurrently produced based on the initial availability of Ais and Bis at the onset of the addition process, as depicted in part (a) of Figure 3.5.

By iteratively utilizing the equation above, it iś possible to generate all subsequent Ci+l values by relying on the initial values of Gi, Pi, and Co (Javali et al., 2014).

$$
\begin{aligned}
C_{i+1} &= A_i \cdot B_i + (A \oplus B) \cdot C_i \\
&= G_i + P_i \cdot C_i.
\end{aligned}
$$

The electronic configuration responsible for producing Ci+ls is referred to as the carry-look ahead unit, as illustrated in the segment (b) of the diagram. The ultimate value of S can be calculated upon obtaining the values of Cis, where i ranges from 1 to n, inclusively. Please provide more context or information about the text you want me to rewrite. The latency of the carry propagation. The calculation of a look-ahead adder can be expressed as follows (Lynch & Swartzlander, 1992):

$$
\Delta_T = \Delta_{carry\ gener./prop.\ unit} + \Delta_{CLA} + \Delta_{SUM}
$$

$$
\begin{aligned}
C_1 &= G_0 + C_0 P_0 \\
C_2 &= G_1 + C_1 P_1 \\
&= G_1 + G_0 P_1 + C_0 P_0 P_1 \\
C_3 &= G_2 + C_2 P_2 \\
&= G_2 + G_1 P_2 + G_0 P_1 P_2 + C_0 P_0 P_1 P_2 \cdots\cdots \\
C_{i+1} &= G_i + G_{i-1} P_i + G_{i-2} P_{i-1} P_i + \cdots + G_0 P_1 P_2 \cdots P_i \\
&\quad + C_0 P_0 P_1 \cdots P_i \cdots\cdots \\
C_n &= G_{n-1} + G_{n-2} P_{n-1} + \cdots\cdots \\
&\quad + G_0 P_1 P_2 \cdots P_{n-1} + C_0 P_0 P_1 \cdots P_{n-1}.
\end{aligned}
$$

It is evident that the number of terms in the OR function in Equation is equivalent to n + 1, while the number of variables in the AND function in the final term is also *n + 1*. The adoption of carry-look ahead may pose a challenge in terms of fan-in and fan-out as the value of n, representing the number of bits, increases. Conversely, the consecutive production of each *Ci+l* exhibits a sluggish pace. The block carry-lookahead adder (BCLA) is a viable option that combines the aforementioned approaches, whereby parallel generation of group(s) of carries is implemented (Zlatanovici et al., 2009).

5.7.2. Block Carry Look Ahead Adder

Carry generation and propagation variables Pis and Gis are again created simultaneously for $i = 0, 1, \ldots, n\text{–}1$ in a block carry look ahead adder (BCLA). Divide the n bits into two blocks of m bits each. We give the following definitions for the block carry generate function G* and the block carry propagate function P*, both of which apply to m-bit blocks (Desoete & De Vos, 2002).

$$
\begin{aligned}
P^* &= P_0 P_1 \cdots P_{m-1} \\
G^* &= G_{m-1} + G_{m-2}P_{m-1} + G_{m-3}P_{m-2}P_{m-1} + \cdots \\
&\quad + G_1 P_2 P_3 \cdots P_{m-1} + G_0 P_1 P_2 P_3 \cdots P_{m-1}.
\end{aligned}
$$

Figure 3.6(a) depicts the circuit diagram for a 4-bit BCLA unit. As long as Pis and Gis are accessible, we can calculate each block's P* and G*. Next, we discuss how to ensure each block has access to such carry-in.

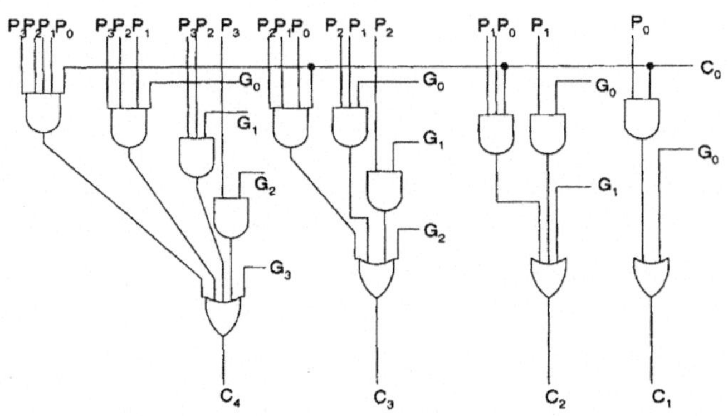

Figure 5.14. Carry-lookahead unit.

An additional level of carry lookahead is required. By utilizing G, s, and Pis, it is possible to simultaneously determine the carry-out Ci+ls for the i-th bit position. In a similar vein, by utilizing block carry propagation

P*s and block carry generation G*s, it is possible to concurrently determine the carry-out for each block, including C4, Cg,…, Cis, where m = 4. The expression Cm(k+l)k, where k ranges from 0 to 2 – 1, denotes the carry-out of block k, which can be utilized as the carry-in of the block (k + 1). It is generally observed that Cm(k+l)k equals zero or one. Upon feeding it back to BCLA, the (k + 1) of the first level carry look ahead can generate C4(k+1)+1C, (4k+l)+2, and C4(k+1)+3c in a parallel manner (Kumar & Dahiya, 2013).

There exist two levels of carry lookahead. The m carries originating from a single block are concurrently produced, while the carry-in signals to $ blocks are also concurrently generated. Initially, the carry digits denoted by the symbol $ are computed, and subsequently, the m carries are produced for each of these digits. Successive carriers are produced sequentially, with one type following the other. The 16-bit addition process is demonstrated in Figure 3.6(b) through the utilization of a block carry-lookahead adder. The substitution of the boxes present in the BCLA and CLA Unit levels with the circuit depicted in (a) is a viable option. The upper level of the circuit receives input from *Pis* and *Gis*, while the lower level receives input from *P*s* and *G*s* (Jamal et al., 2012).

It is important to remember that.

$$\begin{aligned} S_i &= P_i \oplus C_i \\ &= (A_i \oplus B_i) \oplus C_i. \end{aligned}$$

The delay time is:

$$\begin{aligned} \Delta_T &= \Delta_{carry\ gener./prop.\ unit} + \Delta_{BCLA^1} + \Delta_{4-bit\ CLAU} + \Delta_{BCLA^2} + \Delta_{SUM} \\ &= 3\Delta_g + 2\Delta_g + 2\Delta_g + 2\Delta_g + 2\Delta_g = 11\Delta_g \end{aligned}$$

If the AND-OR function is transformed into a NAND-NAND implementation. It should be noted that the analysis has taken into account the utilization of two BCLA delay passes.

Each iteration involves a distinct pathway for the data, while the duration of the routing process may remain constant. The initial BCLA' pass occurs between *PislGis* and *P*slG*s*, while the subsequent BCLA' pass takes place between *CQk* and *C41~+3*. This concept can be expanded to incorporate multiple levels of Binary Coded Decimal (BCD) adders into a single adder circuit. Including supplementary carry-lookahead levels increases 4Ag delay time, with 2Ag attributed to both BCLA' and BCLA2 (Balasubramanian & Maskell, 2019).

5.8. CARRY-SAVE ADDERS

The adders that have been previously mentioned are limited to the addition of solely two numbers. Multi-operand addition is a common occurrence in array processing, as well as in multiplication and division. There is a need for more robust adders that are capable of performing the addition of multiple numbers as opposed to just two. This section presents the design of a high-speed multi operand adder, commonly known as a carry-save adder (CSA). The proposed approach involves overlapping the carry propagation of the initial addition with the computation of the subsequent addition, rather than waiting for the former to complete before commencing the latter. This strategy is particularly advantageous when a multi operand adder executes multiple additions (Piestrak, 1994).

The schematic diagram depicted in Figure 5.15 illustrates an n-bit carry-save adder (CSA) that is comprised of n full adders.

Registers are employed to temporarily buffer the outputs of the full adders prior to their transmission to the input lines of the adders. The carry-save register is the nomenclature used to refer to this particular type of register (Kim et al., 1998).

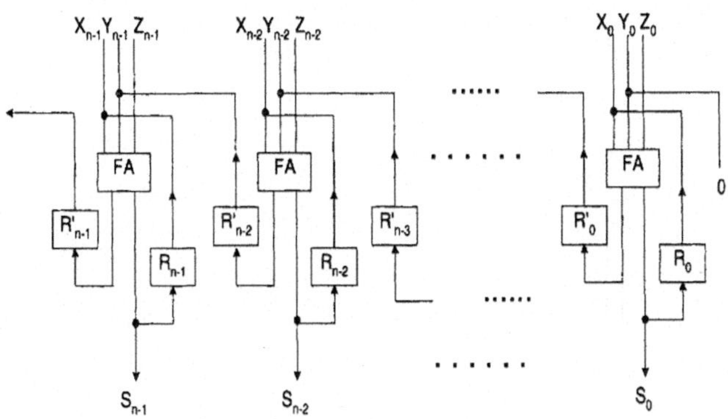

Figure 5.15. n-bit carry-save adder.

Consider a set of k summands, denoted as *F1, F2, …, Fk*, to be aggregated. Additionally, let X, Y, and Z represent the three inputs of the carry-save adder. Initially, input numerical values *F1*, *F2*, and *F3* into the adder and perform the addition operation. Subsequently, the outcomes denoted as S and C are transmitted in a loop to X and Y, respectively, while

F4 is initialized into 2. The partial sum obtained from the previous addition is combined with the saved carry and added to F4. Subsequent iterations of the operation will involve the selection of a novel addend until the final addend, *Fk*, is reached. Let there be a set of k numbers to be summed. The procedures pertaining to every complete adder in the *i-th* bit position are outlined as follows (Gustafsson et al., 2004).

1. Apply the inputs *f:, fz, and f:* to the full adder and perform addition. Assign the value of the result *si* to *Ri* and the value of *ci+l* to *Ri*.
2. The second step requires feeding the current value of si stored in the register back to the full adder as the first input. In addition, the entire adder, bit position *(i + I)*, should receive the register value *ci+l*. To conduct an addition operation, the complete adder at the current bit position takes the "f" from the new summand as its third input and the carry-in from the $(i-1)^{th}$ bit position as its additional input. The result *Si* should be written to register *Ri*, while *Ci+l* should be written to register *R*.
3. In the *jth* iteration, instead of utilizing *f* as in Step 2, employ *fjf3* for the third step.
4. Iterate Step 3 while setting the third input of the full adder to 0 until the addition process is performed for all registers up to the point where *j* equals *Ic*. The variables *Rk-l* through *Rb* are observed to possess a value of zero (Hormigo et al., 2009).

During the first three steps of the process, it is crucial to perform (*k*–*2*) additions in order to add *k* numbers. This is due to the fact that the first cycle allows for the addition of three numbers, while the remaining (*k-3*) numbers require (*k*–*3*) additional cycles to be added. Subsequent to the execution of Step 3, the carry propagation process is initiated. The final summation value, represented as (*Sn–1* – *SO*), can be obtained within a maximum of *n–1* cycles, along with the *k–2* cycles previously specified. Let *t* denote the total number of cycles required for the addition of k n-bit numbers.

$$k-2 \leq t \leq n+k-3.$$

The delay time is:

$$\Delta_{CSA} = t \times f(\Delta_{FA}, \Delta_{FF}).$$

The area complexity of an n-bit CSA is:

$$A_{CSA} = n \times f(A_{FA}, A_{FF})$$

In instances where the value of the word length n is extensive, the performance of CSA may be notably impaired by the ripple carry transmission that occurs in the final stage. In order to expedite the execution of Step 4, it is possible to employ a carry propagate adder (CPA). In Step 4 of the process, it is required to add only two vectors, namely the sum vector and the carry vector. Therefore, the high-speed two-operand adder to be used in the CPA can be selected from the options described in the preceding sections of this chapter. An instance of a CLA may be implemented. In such an instance, the necessary quantity of iterations to finalize the summation of k numerical values shall be determined ((Erniyazov & Jeon, 2019).

$t = k - \mathbf{2} + 1 = (k - 1)$ cycles.

The CSA that has been previously described is a unilevel structure. It is important to note that in Step 2, only a single number can be added. Sequential addition is performed on *N4*, *N5*, …, *Nk*. It is possible to link various Carry Select Adders (CSAs) tiers in a hierarchical structure, enabling the concurrent addition of k quantities, where k is equivalent to 4, 5, 6, or 7.

It should be noted that every line for input or output denotes n individual single-bit lines. Each block in the CSA architecture comprises a set of n full adders that do not incorporate any flip-flops. The carry output lines are denoted by left-pointing arrows, which signify that the carries undergo a leftward shift by one-bit position before being transmitted to the subsequent stage. Additionally, a 0 is introduced into the least significant bit position. Adding the sum vector and carry vector is necessary for a Certified Public Accountant (CPA) to perform at the base of the tree. In cases where the quantity of inputs is a multiple of three, it is possible to present an alternative tree structure. The summing of k numbers necessitates the utilization of *(k – 2)* carry-save adders (CSAs), with the number of CSAs increasing by one for each supplementary input operand. Therefore, the area complexity of the CSA tree is.

$$\Delta_{CSA\ Tree} = 2l\Delta_g + \Delta_{CPA},$$

The delay incurred by a CSA tree is a function of its depth (Mahalakshmi & Sasilatha, 2013). The propagation delay, which refers to the delay time of a full adder, is contributed by 2A at each level of CSAs. The given configuration of a CSA involves three inputs and two outputs. It follows that the product of the number of outputs and the number of times they are utilized will yield the number of inputs present in the upper level of the system. In cases where the quantity of outputs is not divisible by 2, the modulo 2 operation denotes the quantity of additional outputs present at the higher level. Therefore, X(1) may be defined recursively as follows:

$$\lambda(l) = \left\lfloor \frac{\lambda(l-1)}{2} \right\rfloor \times 3 + \lambda(l-1)\ mod\ 2.$$

The maximum number of input operands that a CSA tree can add varies for distinct values of 1. There exist two distinct methods for performing multi-operand addition. One approach involves the simultaneous processing of all bits within an operand, with operands being processed sequentially. The alternate approach involves the addition of corresponding bits in the operands' identical positions. The examination sequentially evaluates each bit position. The symbol "x" denotes a singular unit of binary information, commonly called a bit. The carry-save addition, which has been previously introduced, pertains to the first method. The subsequent section presents an augmentation utilizing the second technique, bit partitioned addition. The carry-save adders execute multi-operand addition sequentially. In contrast, the forthcoming bit-partitioned adders discussed in this section adopt a column-wise methodology to add k numbers (Singh et al., 2009).

5.9. BIT-PARTITIONED MULTIPLE ADDITION

The bit-partitioned multiple addition method involves the addition of numbers in a column-wise manner, with each adder processing a single bit at a time. The binary representation of the tally of "1"s in a specific column is obtained by performing a binary addition operation, wherein each binary digit is shifted to one position relative to its adjacent digit. The length of the partial sum can be expressed as *rlogk*, where k represents the quantity of multiple operands to be added (Kondo & Nakamura, 2005). The process of designing bit-partitioned adders is demonstrated by adding seven 4-bit numbers, as depicted in Figure 5.15. The register contains seven numerical values that undergo a leftward shift of one-bit position per iteration. The seven numerical values are sequentially inputted into a 7-input columnar register (CA) in a column-wise manner, starting from the leftmost column. It has been observed that the highest possible sum resulting from a 7-bit addition is 7. This value can be effectively represented by 3 bits. Therefore, in order to accommodate this, three output lines have been designated for the Carry-Out Adder (CA) (Farooqui et al., 1999).

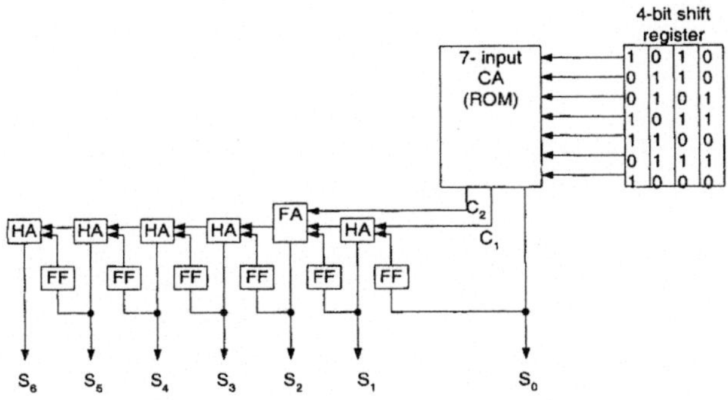

Figure 5.16. Bit-partitioned adder.

The sequential addition of distinct bit-slices will be performed. A carry-save adder is employed for this objective. It is important to consider assigning varying weights to the results of the cellular automata (CA) that are produced for distinct bit-slices. In order to add the (*i–1*) bit slice, it is necessary to shift the partial sum resulting from the addition of the *i* bit slice one-bit position to the left. Therefore, it is evident that rather than directing the previous sum bit to the identical bit position observed in a conventional carry save adder, it is preserved and subsequently transmitted to the adjacent bit position in the succeeding cycle. The utilization of half-adders is feasible in substituting full adders in cases where certain bit positions involve solely two input bits for summation (Ghodrati et al., 2020). Given that the adjacent groups exhibit a positional offset of 4 bits, it is possible to concatenate every 4 bits from the corresponding positions of each group to generate a complete numerical value. The procedure involves the allocation of the lower order 4 bits produced by each group to register A, while the higher order 3 bits from each group are assigned to register B. Subsequently, a two-operand addition, A + B, is executed. Adopting a Carry Look-Ahead (CLA) adder, a high-speed two-operand adder performs the addition operation. It should be noted that in cases where the least significant bit (LSB) and the most significant bit (MSB) of number B are positioned four bits higher than those of number A, the process of lineup involves appending four zeros to the least significant bit positions of the addend and four zeros to the most significant bit positions of the augend.

The delay time is:

$$\Delta_T = m\ cycles + \Delta_{CLA} = (m+1)\ cycles$$

when; m is the 3; ΔT is the 4 cycles (Yoon et al., 2015).

5.10. SUMMARY

The fundamental operations in computer arithmetic are addition and subtraction. The multiplication and division operations are founded upon the principles of addition and subtraction. Efficient adders and subtractors are highly advantageous in expediting basic arithmetic operations and hastening the multiplication and division processes that necessitate extensive addition and subtraction. The ripple-carry adder sequentially generates carries across various bit positions. The value of C_{i+1} is contingent upon the value of C_i, and the determination of C_i necessitates prior knowledge of C_{i-1}. This section presents an adder capable of producing all carries in parallel. The absence of carry propagation is not a contributing factor to delay.

REFERENCES

1. An, H., Chen, Y., Fan, Z., Zhang, Q., Abillama, P., Kim, H. S., & Sylvester, D., (2023). 29.3 An 8.09 TOPS/W neural engine leveraging bit-sparsified sign-magnitude multiplications and dual adder trees. In: *2023 IEEE International Solid-State Circuits Conference (ISSCC)* (Vol. 2, pp. 422–424). IEEE.
2. Andréasson, J., Pischel, U., Straight, S. D., Moore, T. A., Moore, A. L., & Gust, D., (2011). All-photonic multifunctional molecular logic device. *Journal of the American Chemical Society, 133*(30), 11641–11648.
3. Balasubramanian, P., & Maskell, D. L., (2019). Factorized carry lookahead adders. In: *2019 International Symposium on Signals, Circuits and Systems (ISSCS)* (Vol. 2, pp. 1–4). IEEE.
4. Blair, G. M., (1998). The equivalence of twos-complement addition and the conversion of redundant-binary to twos-complement numbers. *IEEE Transactions on Circuits and Systems I: Fundamental Theory and Applications*, *45*(6), 669–671.
5. Bogoni, A., Wu, X., Fazal, I., & Willner, A., (2008). All-optical 160Gb/s half-addition half-subtraction and AND/OR function exploiting pump depletion and nonlinearities in a PPLN waveguide. In: *2008 34th European Conference on Optical Communication* (Vol. 1, pp. 1–2). IEEE.
6. Carpenter, T. P., & Moser, J. M., (1984). The acquisition of addition and subtraction concepts in grades one through three. *Journal for Research in Mathematics Education, 15*(3), 179–202.
7. Chandel, R., Singh, D. P., Banta, R., Karan, R., & Bhatt, P., (2010). A comparative analysis of voltage-scaled two operand binary adders. *Journal of Active & Passive Electronic Devices*, *5*, 987–990.
8. Cheng, F. C., Unger, S. H., & Theobald, M., (2000). Self-timed carry-lookahead adders. *IEEE Transactions on Computers*, *49*(7), 659–672.
9. Chong, K. S., Gwee, B. H., & Chang, J. S., (2004). A robust low voltage low energy asynchronous carry-completion sensing adder for biomedical applications. In: *IEEE International Workshop on Biomedical Circuits and Systems, 2004* (Vol. 2, pp. 1–2). IEEE.
10. Cilardo, A., (2009). A new speculative addition architecture suitable for two's complement operations. In: *2009 Design, Automation & Test in Europe Conference & Exhibition* (Vol. 6, pp. 664–669). IEEE.
11. Desoete, B., & De Vos, A., (2002). A reversible carry-look-ahead adder using control gates. *Integration*, *33*(1–2), 89–104.

12. Erniyazov, S., & Jeon, J. C., (2019). Carry save adder and carry look ahead adder using inverter chain based coplanar QCA full adder for low energy dissipation. *Microelectronic Engineering, 211*, 37–43.
13. Farooqui, A. A., Oklobdzija, V. G., & Chechrazi, F., (1999). Multiplexer based adder for media signal processing. In: *1999 International Symposium on VLSI Technology, Systems, and Applications. Proceedings of Technical Papers (Cat. No. 99TH8453)* (Vol. 3, pp. 100–103). IEEE.
14. Fisher, P., Comber, A. J., & Wadsworth, R., (2005). Land use and land cover: contradiction or complement. *Re-Presenting GIS*, 7, *85*, 98.
15. Fleischer, D. L., Naitzat, G., & Prokupets, L., (2009). An RSA processor for near real-time operation. In: *2009 IEEE International Conference on Microwaves, Communications, Antennas and Electronics Systems* (Vol. 3, pp. 1–4). IEEE.
16. Gadamsetti, B., & Singh, A. D., (2010). Current sensing completion detection for high speed and area efficient arithmetic. In: *2010 IEEE Asia Pacific Conference on Circuits and Systems* (Vol. 3, pp. 240–243). IEEE.
17. Garner., (1978). Theory of computer addition and overflows. *IEEE Transactions on Computers, 100*(4), 297–301.
18. Ghodrati, S., Sharma, H., Kinzer, S., Yazdanbakhsh, A., Park, J., Kim, N. S., & Esmaeilzadeh, H., (2020). Mixed-signal charge-domain acceleration of deep neural networks through interleaved bit-partitioned arithmetic. In: *Proceedings of the ACM International Conference on Parallel Architectures and Compilation Techniques* (Vol. 2, pp. 399–411).
19. González, C., Noda, A., Bruno, A., Moreno, L., & Muñoz, V., (2015). Learning subtraction and addition through digital boards: A down syndrome case. *Universal Access in the Information Society, 14*, 29–44.
20. Gorgin, S., & Jaberipur, G., (2016). Sign-magnitude encoding for efficient VLSI realization of decimal multiplication. *IEEE Transactions on Very Large-Scale Integration (VLSI) Systems, 25*(1), 75–86.
21. Gustafsson, O., Dempster, A. G., & Wanhammar, L., (2004). Multiplier blocks using carry-save adders. In: *2004 IEEE International Symposium on Circuits and Systems (IEEE Cat. No. 04CH37512)* (Vol. 2, pp. 450–473). IEEE.
22. Haixia, W., Shunan, Z., Xiaonan, Q., Qianbin, X., & Yueyang, C., (2011). Design of a conditional sum adder based on multiple-valued logic. In: *2011 International Conference on Electronics, Communications and Control (ICECC)* (Vol. 2, pp. 810–813). IEEE.
23. Hashemian, R., (1996). A new method for conversion of a 2's complement to canonic signed digit number system and its representation. In:

Conference Record of the Thirtieth Asilomar Conference on Signals, Systems and Computers (Vol. 3, pp. 904–907). IEEE.

24. Hoffmann, E. M., & Houle, J. J., (1995). Contradictory roles for antibody and complement in the interaction of Brucella abortus with its host. *Critical Reviews in Microbiology*, *21*(3), 153–163.
25. Hoover, D. R., (1990). Subset complement addition upper bounds-an improved inclusion-exclusion method. *Journal of Statistical Planning and Inference*, *24*(2), 195–202.
26. Hormigo, J., Ortiz, M., Quiles, F., Jaime, F. J., Villalba, J., & Zapata, E. L., (2009). Efficient implementation of carry-save adders in FPGAs. In: *2009 20th IEEE International Conference on Application-Specific Systems, Architectures and Processors* (Vol. 2, pp. 207–210). IEEE.
27. Hwang, S., Yeo, S., & Son, T., (2021). A comparative analysis of fraction addition and subtraction contents in the mathematics textbooks in the US and South Korea. *International Electronic Journal of Elementary Education*, *13*(4).
28. Jamal, L., Shamsujjoha, M., & Babu, H. H., (2012). Design of optimal reversible carry lookahead adder with optimal garbage and quantum cost. *International Journal of Engineering and Technology*, *2*(1), 44–50.
29. Javali, R. A., Nayak, R. J., Mhetar, A. M., & Lakkannavar, M. C., (2014). Design of high-speed carry save adder using carry lookahead adder. In: *International Conference on Circuits, Communication, Control and Computing* (Vol. 2, pp. 33–36). IEEE.
30. Kao, S., Zlatanovici, R., & Nikolic, B., (2006). A 240ps 64b carry-lookahead adder in 90 nm CMOS. In: *2006 IEEE International Solid State Circuits Conference-Digest of Technical Papers* (Vol. 2, pp. 1735–1744). IEEE.
31. Kianpour, M., Sabbaghi-Nadooshan, R., & Navi, K., (2014). A novel design of 8-bit adder/subtractor by quantum-dot cellular automata. *Journal of Computer and System Sciences*, *80*(7), 1404–1414.
32. Kim, T., Jao, W., & Tjiang, S., (1998). Arithmetic optimization using carry-save-adders. In: *Proceedings of the 35th Annual Design Automation Conference* (Vol. 1, pp. 433–438).
33. Kondo, M., & Nakamura, H., (2005). A small, fast, and low-power register file by bit-partitioning. In: *11th International Symposium on High-Performance Computer Architecture* (Vol. 3, pp. 40–49). IEEE.
34. Kruy, J. F., (1965). A fast conditional sum adder using carry bypass logic. In: *Proceedings of the Fall Joint Computer Conference, Part I* (Vol. 2, pp. 695–703).

35. Kumar, R., & Dahiya, S., (2013). Performance analysis of different bit carry look ahead adder using vhdl environment. *International Journal of Engineering Science and Innovative Technology (IJESIT)*, *2*(4), 80–88.
36. Lewandowski Jr, G. W., & Bizzoco, N. M., (2007). Addition through subtraction: Growth following the dissolution of a low-quality relationship. *The Journal of Positive Psychology*, *2*(1), 40–54.
37. Li, G., Qian, F., Ruan, H., & Liu, L., (1999). Compact parallel optical modified-signed-digit arithmetic-logic array processor with electron-trapping device. *Applied Optics*, *38*(23), 5039–5045.
38. Lorenz, R., Buess, P., Macuvele, J., Friedli, T., & Netland, T. H., (2019). Lean and digitalization—contradictions or complements? In: *Advances in Production Management Systems. Production Management for the Factory of the Future: Proceedings IFIP WG 5.7 International Conference, APMS 2019, Austin, TX, USA.* Springer International Publishing. *Part I* (Vol. 2, pp. 77–84).
39. Lu, S. L., & Ercegovac, M. D., (1991). Evaluation of two-summand adders implemented in ECDL CMOS differential logic. *IEEE Journal of Solid-State Circuits*, *26*(8), 1152–1160.
40. Lynch, T., & Swartzlander Jr, E. E., (1992). A spanning tree carry lookahead adder. *IEEE Transactions on Computers*, *41*(08), 931–939.
41. Lyon, R., (1976). Two's complement pipeline multipliers. *IEEE Transactions on Communications*, *24*(4), 418–425.
42. Mahalakshmi, R., & Sasilatha, T., (2013). A power efficient carry save adder and modified carry save adder using CMOS technology. In: *2013 IEEE International Conference on Computational Intelligence and Computing Research.* IEEE. (Vol. 2, pp. 1–5).
43. Mak, K. Y., Xia, J., Zhang, X. C., Li, L., Fattouhi, M., Ezawa, M., & Zhou, Y., (2022). Single-bit full adder and logic gate based on synthetic antiferromagnetic bilayer skyrmions. *Rare Metals*, *41*(7), 2249–2258.
44. Martin, N. M., & Hufnagel, S. P., (1980). Conditional-sum early completion adder logic. *IEEE Transactions on Computers*, *29*(08), 753–756.
45. Maweu, J. M., (2011). Indigenous ecological knowledge and modern western ecological knowledge: Complementary, not contradictory. *Thought and Practice*, *3*(2), 35–47.
46. Miller, G. A., (1922). Contradictions in the literature of group theory. *The American Mathematical Monthly*, *29*(9), 319–328.
47. Nesher, P., & Katriel, T., (1977). A semantic analysis of addition and subtraction word problems in arithmetic. *Educational Studies in Mathematics*, 251–269.

48. Orts, F., Ortega, G., & Garzón, E. M., (2019). An optimized quantum circuit for converting from sign–magnitude to two's complement. *Quantum Information Processing*, *18*, 1–14.
49. Pai, P. D., & Tran, A., (1992). Overflow detection in multioperand addition. *International Journal of Electronics*, *73*(3), 461–469.
50. Pekmestzi, K., & Efstathiou, C., (2016). Design of efficient 1's complement modified booth multiplier. In: *2016 Euromicro Conference on Digital System Design (DSD)* (Vol. 3, pp. 238–243). IEEE.
51. Piestrak, S. J., (1994). Design of residue generators and multioperand modular adders using carry-save adders. *IEEE Transactions on Computers*, *43*(1), 68–77.
52. Qingkun, M., Shameng, W., Chao, F., & Chaojing, T., (2016). Predicting integer overflow through static integer operation attributes. In: *2016 5th International Conference on Computer Science and Network Technology (ICCSNT)* (Vol. 2, pp. 177–181). IEEE.
53. Rahman, M. Z., Kleeman, L., & Habib, M. A., (2014). Recursive approach to the design of a parallel self-timed adder. *IEEE Transactions on Very Large Scale Integration (VLSI) Systems*, *23*(1), 213–217.
54. Rao, V. M., & Nowrouzian, B., (1995). Design and implementation of asynchronous parallel multiply-accumulate arithmetic architectures. In: *38th Midwest Symposium on Circuits and Systems. Proceedings* (Vol. 2, pp. 761–764). IEEE.
55. Rysin, A., Nikiforov, I., & Boykachev, V., (2021). The paradoxes of mathematics in the laws physics and solution of contradictions between SRT and GRT of Einstein. *Sciences of Europe*, *84–1*, 41–53.
56. Saleem, D., & Al-Khalili, D., (1998). Low power conditional sum adder using pass logic topology. In: *Conference Proceedings; IEEE Canadian Conference on Electrical and Computer Engineering (Cat. No. 98TH8341)* (Vol. 1, pp. 9–12). IEEE.
57. Salomon, O., Green, J. M., & Klar, H., (1995). General algorithms for a simplified addition of 2's complement numbers. *IEEE Journal of Solid-State Circuits*, *30*(7), 839–844.
58. Samuel, B., & Herbert, G., (2020). Democracy and capitalism: [Contradiction, Accommodation, and Instability]. In: *Classes and Elites in Democracy and Democratization* (Vol. 3, pp. 111–119). Routledge.
59. Singh, R. P. P., Kumar, P., & Singh, B., (2009). Performance analysis of 32-bit array multiplier with a carry save adder and with a carry-look-ahead adder. *International Journal of Recent Trends in Engineering*, *2*(6), 83.

60. Sklansky, J., (1960). Conditional-sum addition logic. *IRE Transactions on Electronic Computers*, (2), 226–231.
61. Sterling, S., (2014). Contradiction or complement: Can higher education be deeper education? In: *Intergenerational Learning and Transformative Leadership for Sustainable Futures* (Vol. 2, pp. 55–74). Wageningen Academic Publishers.
62. Suzuki, M., Ohkubo, N., Shinbo, T., Yamanaka, T., Shimizu, A., Sasaki, K., & Nakagome, Y., (1993). A 1.5-ns 32-b CMOS ALU in double pass-transistor logic. *IEEE Journal of Solid-State Circuits*, *28*(11), 1145–1151.
63. Thapliyal, H., Jayashree, H. V., Nagamani, A. N., & Arabnia, H. R., (2013). Progress in reversible processor design: A novel methodology for reversible carry look-ahead adder. *Transactions on Computational Science XVII*, 4(45), 73–97.
64. Thompson, I., (1999). Mental calculation strategies for addition and subtraction. Part 1. *Mathematics in School*, *28*(5), 2–4.
65. Tsang, E. W., (2004). Superstition and decision-making: Contradiction or complement? *Academy of Management Perspectives*, *18*(4), 92–104.
66. Vassiliadis, S., Lemon, D. S., & Putrino, M., (1989). S/370 sign-magnitude floating-point adder. *IEEE Journal of Solid-State Circuits*, *24*(4), 1062–1070.
67. Wang, G., & Tull, M. P., (2004). A new redundant binary number to 2's-complement number converter. In: *Region 5 Conference: Annual Technical and Leadership Workshop, 2004* (Vol. 3, pp. 141–143). IEEE.
68. Warren Jr, H. S., (1977). Functions realizable with word-parallel logical and two's-complement addition instructions. *Communications of the ACM*, *20*(6), 439–441.
69. Woranetsudathip, N., Yuenyong, C., & Nguyen, T. T., (2021). The innovative lesson study for enhancing students' mathematical ideas about addition and subtraction through open approach. In: *Journal of Physics: Conference Series* (Vol. 1835, pp. 012061). IOP Publishing.
70. Yoon, H. S., Park, J. K., & Kim, J. T., (2015). An efficient error detection technique for 3D bit-partitioned SRAM devices. *Journal of Semiconductor Technology and Science*, *15*(5), 445–454.
71. Zaranis, N., (2017). Does the use of information and communication technology through the use of realistic mathematics education help kindergarten students to enhance their effectiveness in addition and subtraction? *Preschool and Primary Education*, *5*(1), 46–62.

72. Zhakatayev, A., Lee, S., Sim, H., & Lee, J., (2018). Sign-magnitude SC: getting 10x accuracy for free in stochastic computing for deep neural networks. In: *Proceedings of the 55th Annual Design Automation Conference* (Vol. 5, pp. 1–6).
73. Zlatanovici, R., Kao, S., & Nikolic, B., (2009). Energy–delay optimization of 64-bit carry-lookahead adders with a 240 ps 90 nm CMOS design example. *IEEE Journal of Solid-State Circuits*, *44*(2), 569–583.
74. Zou, J., Xu, L., Yang, M., Zhang, X., & Yang, D., (2017). Towards comprehending the non-functional requirements through developers' eyes: An exploration of stack overflow using topic analysis. *Information and Software Technology*, *84*, 19–32.

CHAPTER

6 Multiplication

Contents

The operation of multiplication holds significant importance in computer arithmetic operations. It is imperative to develop efficient algorithms & high-speed hardware to accomplish multiplication promptly and effectively. The algorithms for sequential multiplication presented in this chapter are founded upon an approach that involves adding and shifting. A comprehensive exposition on the intricate design of various types of multipliers shall be presented. The present discourse will expound upon the multiplication of signed numbers through indirect schemes and Robertson's approach. Furthermore, this paper will elucidate the utilization of recoding techniques & Booth's algorithm, which enhance multiplication efficiency through multi-bit scanning (Mitchell, 1962).

Consider two unsigned numbers, A and B, each consisting of n bits, where A is the multiplicand and B is the multiplier. The multiplication

$P = A \times B$

The process will result in the generation of a product P that consists of 2n bits. In the scenario where A & B are signed numbers, each number contains n–1 bits, not including the sign bit. Consequently, the total number of bits in the product, including sign bit, will be 2n – 1, where n represents the value of (n – 1) in the expression 2(n – 1) + 1. To achieve a standardized depiction, a supplementary bit is inserted between sign bit & highest significant bit, resulting in a cumulative count of 2n bits. The value of the dummy bit is contingent upon sign-magnitude representation or 1's or 2's complement representation of the signed numbers. The product can be represented as either 0 or a duplication of the sign bit (Chang et al., 2008). This chapter will cover two distinct forms of multiplication:

1. Sequential multiplication; and
2. Parallel multiplication.

Initially, we will address the concept of sequential multiplication.

6.1. ADD-AND-SHIFT APPROACH

Using paper & pencil, conventional method of multiplication involves systematically examining individual bits in a multiplier, one at a time. Process of multiplication involves generating partial products by multiplying the multiplicand with different digits of the multiplier, which are then summed up to obtain the final product of the two numerical values. If the bit under consideration holds a value of 1, multiplying the multiplicand by 1 is executed, resulting in the multiplicand serving as the partial product. If the bit under examination is determined to be 0, the resulting partial product will be zero (Bernstein, 2001). As an illustration,

$$\begin{array}{cccccccc}
 & & & & 1 & 1 & 0 & 1 \\
 & \times &) & & 1 & 0 & 1 & 1 \\
\hline
 & & & & 1 & 1 & 0 & 1 \\
 & & & 1 & 1 & 0 & 1 & \\
 & & 0 & 0 & 0 & 0 & & \\
 & 1 & 1 & 0 & 1 & & & \\
\hline
1 & 0 & 0 & 0 & 1 & 1 & 1 & 1.
\end{array}$$

AND gates can generate the partial product because any value ANDed with 1 will yield itself, while any value ANDed with 0 will result in 0. Rather than producing all partial products beforehand and subsequently summing them, we add each partial product to the running total as soon as it is computed. It is recommended to position each partial product one bit to left of preceding one, considering that each bit examined is located one bit higher than previous one.

Alternatively, one may maintain a constant position for the partial product while shifting the accumulated sum one bit to right during each iteration. Therefore, this multiplication method is commonly called an add-and-shift approach (Farsiu et al., 2003).

Figure 6.1 illustrates that an indirect multiply unit typically comprises multiple functional devices. The utilization of three distinct registers, namely Multiplier Register (MR), Accumulator (AC), & Auxiliary Register (AX), is required. Every item has a length of n bits and can load in parallel. Values of A & B are stored in variables A & B.

When a signature is not present, the registers are filled with a value of zero. The intermediate result is augmented with an n-bit adder to perform the addition operation with partial product. Utilization of a control counter (CTR) is necessary to monitor and record quantity of iterations performed & to signal conclusion of multiplication process (Koc et al., 1996).

The present discourse outlines a conventional method for indirect multiplication:

1. $MR \leftarrow B;$
   $AX \leftarrow A;$
   $AC \leftarrow 0;$
   $CTR \leftarrow 0.$

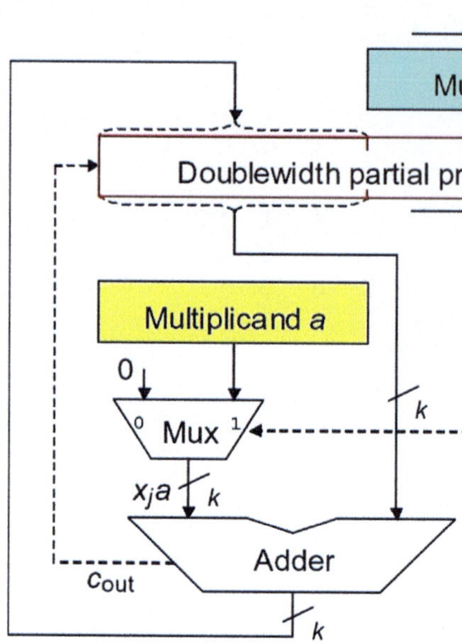

Figure 6.1. Hardware for sequential multiplication.

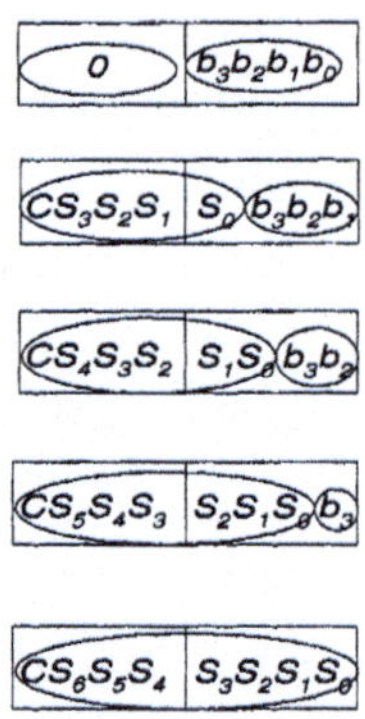

Figure 6.2. Register occupation.

2. $AX \wedge MR_0$.
3. $C_{out} \cdot AC \leftarrow AC + (AX \wedge MR_0)$.
4. $AC \cdot MR \leftarrow C_{out} \cdot (AC_{n-1} \cdots AC_0) \cdot (MR_{n-1} \cdots MR_1)$.
5. $CTR \leftarrow CTR + 1$. If $CTR \neq n$, go to 2.

A certain degree of evaluation is assigned to the procedure mentioned above. Initially, the value of A is stored in AX register, while a value of B is stored in the MR register. The air conditioning system should be cleaned to restore intermediate result's initial zero states. In Step 2, the partial product is obtained by performing a logical AND operation between the vector AX & least significant bit of M R, MRo. The adder will be provided with either a replica of the multiplicand A or a vector of zeroes, depending on whether M& is equal to 1 or 0 (Gwee et al., 2008).

During the third step, partial product derived from the second step will be incorporated into AC, that contains upper n-bit of current intermediate result. During the process of addition, a carry-out Gout can be produced.

Step 4 involves performing right shift operation on sum before concatenating it with content in register M R. Cout is transferred to the AC register, while M& is transferred out of the M register and into the R register.

In Step 5, the counter is incremented, and a check is performed to determine if the number of iterations executed equals n, at which point the procedure will terminate.

The procedure above necessitates iteration n times, whereby each of the n bits in the multiplier is scrutinized individually. Upon completion of procedure, the n-bit multiplier denoted as B will be displaced towards the right end of M R. Subsequently, the 2n-bit product, represented as P, is expected to manifest within the cascaded register AC. MR. When multiplying signed numbers, the sign of the result can be found in AC,-1. Figure 6.2 illustrates the contents of AC and M R after each iteration, providing an example of 4-bit multiplication. The observed phenomenon pertains to the expansion of the partial product's length and the concurrent contraction of the multiplier fragment.

The temporal latency of the indirect multiplication module is currently under consideration (Hancock, 2007).

$$\Delta_T = \Delta_{SETUP} + n\Delta_{ADD-SHIFT} + \Delta_{STORE}.$$

Here,

$$\Delta_{ADD-SHIFT} = \Delta_{AND} + \Delta_{ADD} + \Delta_{LATCH},$$

When the value of n is sufficiently large, the add-shift operation experiences a delay that surpasses that of other operations.

6.2. INDIRECT MULTIPLICATION SCHEMES

This section pertains to the multiplication of signed numbers. This paper will present four conventional methods for performing indirect multiplication.

The four types of number multiplication that can be distinguished are (1) multiplication of unsigned numbers, (2) multiplication of sign-magnitude numbers, (3) multiplication of one's complement numbers, & (4) multiplication of 2 complement numbers (Huang & Lu, 1994).

6.2.1. Unsigned Number Multiplication

Process of multiplying two unsigned numbers with n bits is delineated by flow chart depicted in Figure 6.3. The procedure above is executed within n plus one iteration. Loading data into the appropriate registers necessitates a single cycle, denoted as CO. The loop for multiplication must be iterated n times within cycles C1, C2, ..., Cn (Rajput & Swamy, 2012).

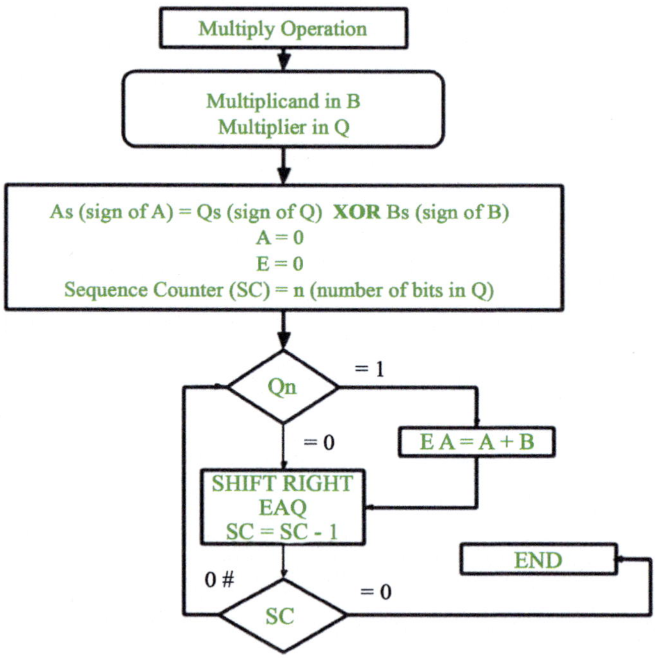

Figure 6.3. Multiplication of unsigned numbers.

6.2.2. Sign-Magnitude Number Multiplication

It can be observed that in multiplying two sign-magnitude numbers, magnitude of either multiplicand or multiplier comprises only n – 1 bits. Therefore, it is necessary to utilize n – 1 cycles to execute the multiplication loop. Flip-flops A & B in Co are loaded with sign bits of A & B, namely an-l & bn–1, respectively. At outset, most significant bit (MSB) of register AX and MR are initialized to zero. The determination of the sign of the product can be accomplished after the multiplication process through the execution of A, and B, and subsequently storing the result in position ACn-l, while ensuring that position ACn–2 retains a value of 0. Figure 6.4 depicts the flow chart utilized for the multiplication of sign-magnitude numbers (Gorgin & Jaberipur, 2016).

6.2.3. One's Complement Number Multiplication

Multiplication method above illustrates that the magnitude of a product is obtained by multiplying the magnitudes of two given operands. In the event that the input operands are expressed in complement form, it is imperative to transform those that denote negative numerical values into sign-magnitude form prior to entering the multiplication loop. Moreover, if resultant output is negative, converting it into its complement form is imperative. The multiplication procedure encompasses both pre-complements and post-complements, thereby earning the nomenclature of "indirect multiplication" for the method under discussion (Sait et al., 1995). In the case of 1's complement numbers, the precomplement or post-complement can be achieved solely through bitwise negation. A single additional cycle for each is adequate.

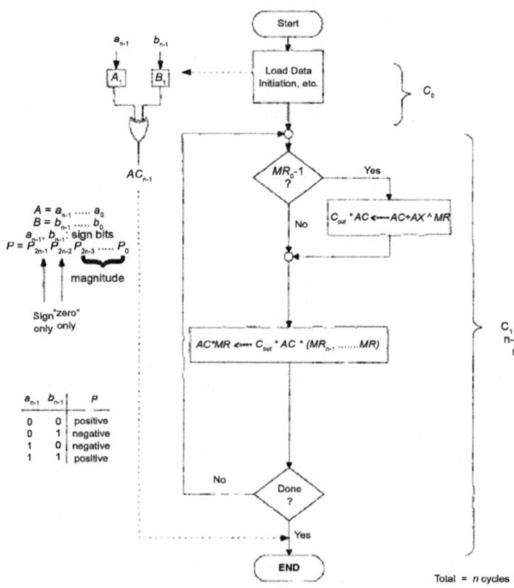

Figure 6.4. Sign-magnitude number multiplication.

The initial configuration in C_O involves pre-complement, while the subsequent n – 1 cycles, spanning from Cz to *C,* pertain to multiplication loop. Additionally, the post-complement necessitates the use of C_{n+1}.

The flow chart for multiplication of 1's-complement numbers is depicted in Figure 6.5. According to the mathematical computation, multiplying two n-bit 1's complement numbers necessitates a total of n + 2 cycles (Rubinfield, 1975).

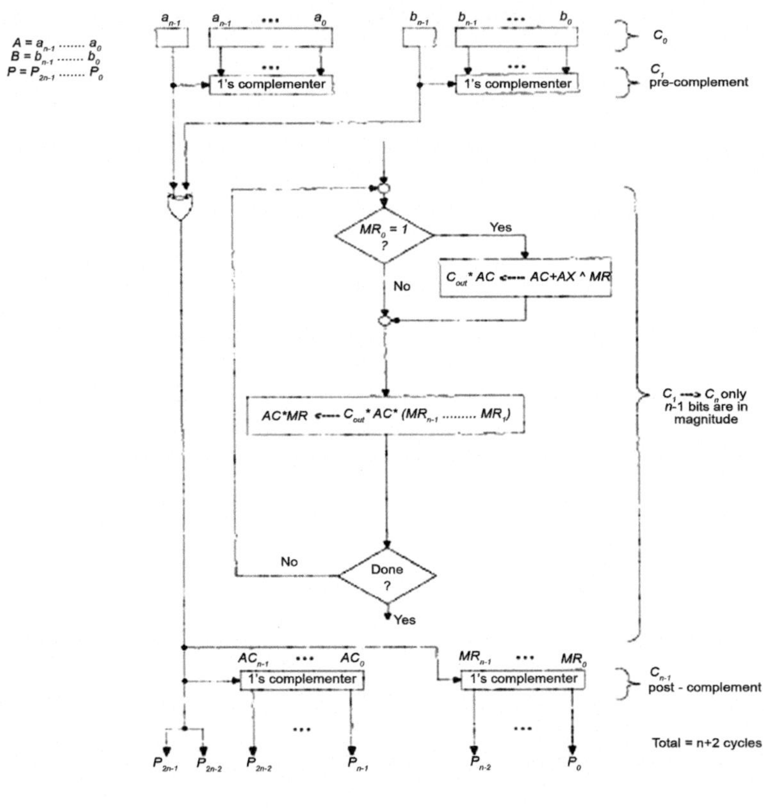

Figure 6.5. Multiplication of one's complement numbers.

6.2.4. Two's Complement Number Multiplication

Performing a 2's complement operation involves initially executing a 1's complement operation, followed by adding a 1 to least significant bit position. The pre-complement or post-complement necessitates a minimum of two cycles. After the setup cycle Co, the pre-complement operation is carried out in cycles C1 & C2. On other hand, the post-complement operation is performed using Cnf2 and Cn+ cycles, following the execution of the multiply loop from cycle *C* to *C,+l.* The process of post-complement operation entails the retention of a 2n-bit result in AC or MR, as illustrated in Figure 6.6. This operation aims to determine the 2's complement of this extensive numerical value. The process involves the generation of a signal denoted as "Zero MR" or *ZMR*, which is achieved by performing a NOR operation on all the bits contained in the MR register. Subsequently, performing the one's complement of *ZMR* and adding it to the accumulator (*AC*) is to be carried out (Bocker et al., 1983).

It is important to note that in obtaining 2's complement of a number, the leftmost bit to the right of the rightmost 1 is negated, while every bit to its left is negated. If the rightmost digit with a value of 1 is located in the MR position, then the value of ZMR will be equal to zero. The negation of each bit in the AC can be achieved by executing the operation of performing (1's complement + 0). If the rightmost digit, "1," is located in the AC position, then ZMR will be equal to 1. Subsequently, executing the 2's complement operation on the AC is necessary by adding 1's complement and 1 (Li et al., 1995).

If the MR register consists entirely of binary digits with a value of zero, performing a one's complement operation would yield a sequence of binary digits with a value of one. The addition of "l" to a binary number, represented as MR, results in propagation of carry from the least significant bit of MR to the accumulator (AC) through all the intervening bits. The reason for this is that the AC currently holds the rightmost 0, which is the sole bit capable of terminating the carry propagation, as it is the rightmost 1 prior to the 1's complement operation. Through this mechanism, it is possible to anticipate adding or carrying 1 into the bit position n without waiting for carry propagation. This results in a reduction of the carry propagation length from 2n to n. It is important to note that in 2's complement operation, bit negation occurs when there's a presence of at least one 1 to the right of it. When ZMR equals zero, the "if" condition is satisfied for each bit executed in AC. This is applicable when AC's content is the 1's complement (Lyon, 1976).

$$AC \leftarrow (\overline{AC})$$

$$MR \leftarrow (\overline{MR}) + 1$$

The value of ZMR is equivalent to 1 if all bits within MR are represented as 0s. The computation of M R t (M R) + 1 yield an identical MR and induces a carry into AC within the given context. The following task is to be executed:

$$MR = MR$$

$$AC \leftarrow (\overline{AC}) + 1,$$

The addition of ZMR = 1 to the least significant bit (LSB) position of AC can be performed immediately without waiting for the carry-in to propagate from MR. Complement operation is executed during the cycle denoted as Cn+2, while increment operation is carried out during the cycle Cn+3. To multiply a 2's-complement number consisting of n bits, a total of n+4 cycles are required. The procedure undertaken is depicted in the flow chart presented in Figure 4.6. The algorithms that were previously outlined can be combined to create a flexible multiplier that is capable of performing any of the four types of multiplication (Kang & Gaudiot, 2006).

6.3. ROBERTSON'S SIGNED NUMBER MULTIPLICATION

Although the concept is straightforward, pre-& post-complement discussed in subsections 4.2.3 & 4.2.4 are known to be time-consuming. Efforts should be made to explore a more effective procedure (Li & Liu, 1994).

Robertson's Signed Number Multiplication discusses two cases as follows:

- **Case 1:** The proposition has been put forth that if solely multiplicand holds a negative value while multiplier remains positive, one may execute methodology expounded upon in Section 4.1. It is possible to perform addition of the multiplicand to accumulator without need for a pre-complement operation, even in instances where the multiplicand is expressed in the 2's complement representation. In the event of a partial product shift to the right, the introduction of a 0 occurs when the leftmost bit is also 0. If the most significant bit holds a value of 1, a 1 is introduced through shifting. The process under discussion is called an arithmetic shift, which differs from a logic shift that consistently shifts in a 0. The numerical illustration of 4-bit signed number multiplication for this particular scenario is presented in Figure (Carter & Robertson, 1990).

- **Case 2:** If the multiplier is negative, it is imperative to execute a distinct correction step while implementing the procedure above. In other words, performing a subtraction of the multiplicand rather than an addition during the final step.

Consider the negative multiplicand B, which is represented in 2's complement form as 1bn–2... bo. The sign bit bn-l is equal to 1 (Carter & Robertson, 1990) . Then

$$\begin{aligned} |B| &= 2^n - B \\ &= 1(00\cdots0) - (1b_{n-2}\cdots b_0) \\ &= 1(00\cdots0) - (10\cdots0) - (b_{n-2}\cdots b_0) \\ &= (10\cdots0) - (b_{n-2}\cdots b_0) \\ &= 2^{n-1} - \sum_0^{n-2} b_i \cdot 2^i, \end{aligned}$$

Hence,

Equation 6.1

$$B = -|B| = -2^{n-1} + \sum_0^{n-2} b_i \cdot 2^i.$$

When implementing the procedure described in Case 1 for the multiplication of A and B, the bit scan spanning from b_0 to bn–2 is precise, as it corresponds to the outcome of the product between A and the second factor in Equation (6.1). In 2's complement notation of B, bit bn-l is assigned value of 1. Upon scanning, the add A operation will be executed following the Case 1 procedure.

The addition of A x 2n–1 results from the bit position shift. In contrast to the initial term presented in Equation (6.1), performing a subtraction of A x Z n – l is necessary. The final step of the Case 1 procedure necessitates a correction wherein the deduction of A is required for instances where the multiplier is negative. The procedure depicted in Figure 4.8 has been specifically devised for Case 2. The operation of subtracting A can be performed by adding the 2's complement of A (Robertson, 1958).

6.4. RECODING TECHNIQUE

Typically, delay times in indirect multiplication schemes exhibit a proportionality to n cycles, where n denotes the length of the input operands.

Adopting the multiple-bit scanning approach can expedite the multiplication process by reducing the delay time by incorporating supplementary hardware (Swartz, 1998).

6.4.1. Non-Overlapped Multiple-Bit Scanning

The previously mentioned multiplication methods entail the sequential examination of individual bits. The addition and shifting operations of the multiplicand A and intermediate result are contingent upon value of least significant bit (LSB) of MR, whereby if the LSB is 1, The addition and subsequent shift both involve multiplicand A & intermediate product. In contrast, if LSB is 0, only the intermediate result is shifted. Currently, the analysis of the least significant bit (LSB) of MR has been expanded to include the scanning of two bits simultaneously (Swain, 2018).

After this, the intermediate outcome may be augmented by 0, A, 2A, or 3A, contingent upon the values of least significant two bits in MR, which may be 00, 01, 10, or 11. Obtaining 2A can be achieved through a simple operation of shifting A one-bit position to the left. The value of 3A can be derived from the sum of A and 2A. In this instance, the addition operation involves the summation of three operands, including the intermediate result. The request being made is for a multi-operand adder.

It should be noted that in scanning a single bit, the delay duration is directly proportional to the number of cycles, with each cycle's duration being linked to the delay of a 2-operand adder.

The current delay duration exhibits a direct correlation with a factor of 5 cycles, with each duration contingent upon the delay of the 3-operand adder. Typically, when scanning m bits at a time, the overall delay duration exhibits a direct correlation with 2 cycles, whereby each cycle duration is associated with the delay of a (m + 1)-operand adder (Li et al., 2020).

6.4.2. Overlapped Multiple Bit Scanning

During each scan of the rn-bit, the non-overlapped multiple-bit scanning algorithm adds m multiples of multiplicand to the intermediate result. The expression can be represented as the sum of a geometric series, where each term is obtained by multiplying the previous term by a common ratio of 2. The first term is 2OA, and the last is 2”-l A. The forthcoming overlapped multiple-bit scanning algorithm will demonstrate that the addition of only one multiple of A is necessary (Yin et al., 2019).

Integer number systems with a "conventional radix" are examined first, as their "string property" is analyzed.

$$2i+k-22 = 2\ i + k - 1 + 2i+k-2 + \ldots\ldots + 2i+1 + 2\ i.$$

The utilization of the property above for recoding purposes is exemplified in Figure 6.6. The contiguous sequence of ones in a numerical value's binary notation shall hereafter be referred to as the "string of Is" or simply "string" for brevity. Assuming a right-to-left bit scanning approach. Designate the 1 at the rightmost end of the string as the "start of a string." The digit 1 at the far left position of a sequence is denoted as the "leftmost 1," and a numerical value of 0 located to its immediate left is commonly called "end of string." The process of replacing a long sequence of 1s with a 0 on its left involves the insertion of a 1 in the initial position of the string, a 1 in the terminal position of the string, and the population of all other positions with 0s. The signed-digital representation utilizes a specific notation to indicate the numerical value of negative one (Meher & Mehling, 1990). That is,

$$\begin{aligned} & 0|0111111|00000|01111|0 \\ = \ & 0|100000\bar{1}|00000|1000\bar{1}|0. \end{aligned}$$

Utilizing a specific technique allows it to streamline the process of multiplying a given number, denoted as B. This involves substituting a series of successive additions of multiples of the multiplicand with a single subtraction at the outset of the sequence, followed by a solitary addition after the sequence.

In practical implementation, the duration of each scan is constant. Assuming the discovery of a sequence of contiguous bits, including their least significant bit, during a scan, all set to 1.

The precise location of the LSB within a given string remains undetermined, as it is uncertain whether it is positioned at the string's outset or within its interior. The implementation of overlapped scanning is deemed necessary. In other words, allow for overlapping the least significant bit in the current scan with the most significant bit in the preceding scan. Stated differently, that particular segment is subjected to two scans.

The second scan employs the reference bit solely to indicate the function of the bit situated to its left. Table 6.1 provides a comprehensive recoding and explanation for each triplet and a corresponding list of operations (Macwan, 2007).

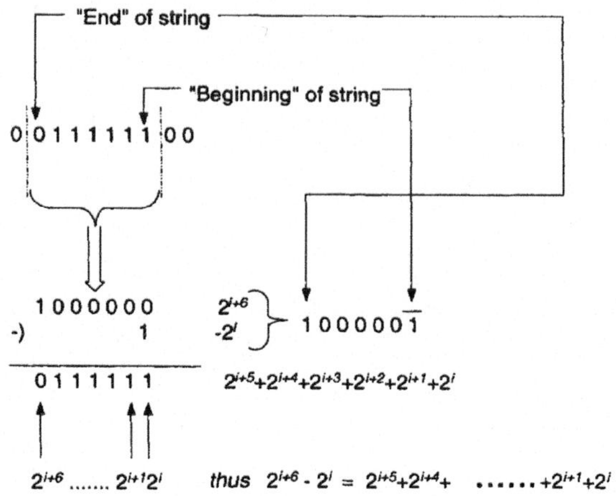

Figure 6.6. String property.

The visual representation depicted in Figure 6.1 illustrates the utilization of a 3-bit overlapped scan, which differs from the implementation of a 2-bit non-overlapped scan when applied to a 16-bit numerical value. It should be noted that a zero placeholder is appended to the least significant bit (LSB) position. This is done to facilitate the identification of the case where the LSB is one, which corresponds to the beginning of string or isolated one scenario. Additionally, the algorithm enables bidirectional scanning, allowing for both left-to-right and right-to-left scanning. Furthermore, it is possible to scan each triplet simultaneously, indicating the potential use of a parallel scanning framework (Broggi, 1994).

Table 6.1. Recoding the Triplets

		2^2	2^1	2^0			
		Scanned bits					
	X_{i+3}	X_{i+2}	X_{i+1}	X_i	X_{i-1}	Multiples of 0, 2A or 4A	String position
	d	0	0	0	d	⇒ 0	No string of "1"
	d	0	0	1	d		
=	*d*	*0*	*1*	*0*	*d*	⇒ $+2A$	End of string
	d	0	1	0	d	⇒ $+2A$	Isolated "1"
	d	0	1	1	d		
=	*d*	*1*	*0*	*0*	*d*	⇒ $+4A$	End of string
	d	1	0	0	d		
=	*d*	$\bar{1}$	*0*	*0*	*d*	⇒ $-4A$	Beginning of string
	d	1	0	1	d		
=	*d*	$\bar{1}$	*1*	*0*	*d*	⇒ $-2A$	Beginning and end of string
	d	1	1	0	d		
=	*d*	*0*	$\bar{1}$	*0*	*d*	⇒ $-2A$	Beginning of string
	d	1	1	1	d		
=	*d*	*0*	*0*	*0*	*d*	⇒ 0	Middle of string

6.4.3. Booth's Algorithm

The multiplier B can be recoded as D based on the string property outlined earlier. According to the scheme, this can be achieved by identifying a bit di for every two bits bib_{i-1}.

b_i	b_{i-1}	d_i	
0	0	0	no string
0	1	1	end of string
1	0	$\bar{1}$	beginning of string
1	1	0	center of string

Booth's Algorithm has following operation designed accordingly:

$$d_i = \begin{cases} 0, & \text{if } b_i = b_{i-1} \\ 1, & \text{if } b_i < b_{i-1} \\ \bar{1}, & \text{if } b_i > b_{i-1} \end{cases}.$$

It is important to note that the initiation of a string is denoted by a 0 on the right side. A non-significant 0 is appended to right of least significant bit to ensure proper alignment. Scanning may be executed by identifying consecutive ones within the encoding table. The consistency of outcomes should be maintained irrespective of the direction of the operation, whether it is executed from right to left, left to right, or in parallel (Bonatto & Olkobdzija 1995).

Given,

$A = a_{n-1} \cdots a_1 a_0$ *multiplicand*

$B = b_{n-1} \cdots b_1 b_0$ *multiplier*,

the Booth's Algorithm can be described as follows:

Initialize $b_{-1} = 0$, and $i = 0$.
Add A to partial product and shift right if $b_i < b_{i-1}$.
Add $-A$ to partial product and shift right if $b_i > b_{i-1}$.
Shift right if $b_i = b_{i-1}$.
Increment i, go to 2 if $i < n$.

The Booth multiplication algorithm is capable of performing direct multiplication of two 2's complement numbers, without necessitating any specific consideration for the signs of the operands. Therefore, it can be deduced that the utilization of pre-complement and post-complement is superfluous and direct multiplication is adequate. It should be noted that the shift being referred to is an arithmetic shift. If most significant bit (MSB) holds a value of 1, a 1 is to be shifted in. Conversely, if the MSB holds a value of 0, a 0 will be shifted in (Elguibaly, 2000).

Figure illustrates the application of Booth's Algorithm to multiply 5 by (–6). The correctness of the procedure above can be determined by calculating the value of **P**, which is obtained by multiplying 5 and –6, resulting in **P = –30**. Notably, the two most significant bits hold sign of product. The binary value (11100010)2 also denotes 2's complement form of negative 30. This approach is appealing for values of B which comprise extended sequences of ones. The efficiency of the process may be compromised in cases where there are numerous isolated instances of the digit 1, as the resulting recoded output D may exhibit a higher count of non-zero bits compared to the initial input **B** (Shanbhag & Juneja, 1988). The investigation of higher radix string recoding has been undertaken to address this limitation. Instead of examining the radix-2 string recoding presented in the previous table, performing a similar analysis on a radix-4 string recoding is possible. The system receives a three-bit input consisting of bi, bi–1, and bi–2 and produces a two-bit output comprising d and di–1. Notably, the two most significant bits hold the sign of the product (Madrid et al., 1993). The binary value (11100010)2 also denotes the 2's complement form of –30. This approach is appealing for values of B that comprise extensive sequences of ones. The efficiency of the process may be compromised when a significant number of isolated 1s are present, as the resulting recoded D may exhibit a higher number of non-zero bits than original B (Seo & Kim, 2009). To address this limitation, scholars have researched the implementation of higher radix string recoding. Instead of examining the radix-2 string recoding as presented in the table, performing a similar analysis on a radix-4 string recoding is possible. Input consists of 3 binary digits: bi, ***bi–1***, and ***bi–2***. On other hand, the output is composed of two binary digits, denoted as d and ***di–1*** (Asef et al., 2017).

b_i	b_{i-1}	b_{i-2}	d_i	d_{i-1}
0	0	0	0	0
0	0	1	0	1
0	1	0	0	1
0	1	1	1	0
1	0	0	$\bar{1}$	0
1	0	1	$\bar{1}$	1
1	1	0	0	$\bar{1}$
1	1	1	0	0

6.4.4. Canonical Multiplier Recoding

The employment of signed-digit (SD) representation is utilized in this particular recoding method. Notably, a minimal SD vector is characterized by having the least possible number of non-zero digits. The canonical signed-digit vector is defined herein for a specific category of minimal SD vectors.

A vector D containing the minimal standard deviation and no consecutive non-zero digits is referred to as a canonical signed-digit vector. It can be observed that the product of di and di-l is equal to zero, where i is an integer within the range of 1 to *n–1*.

A canonical SD vector, indicated by (OOOlOT), is present in the above representations, although (000011)2 does not. Empirical evidence has demonstrated that for any *D = d,-ld,-z* with constant value & length, a "distinct" canonical SD configuration can be attained provided that *d,-l* x d,-z # 1. By selecting a specific value for the nth digit, denoted as d and with an initial value of z 0, it is always possible to attain this objective. It is assumed that *D = d, d, –l…* dido comprises n + 1 bits and that d, z 0 (Wang et al., 2007).

Upon obtaining canonical signed-digit representation of given number, specifically the multiplier B that is of interest, it can be inferred that the canonical form is comprised of non-zero digits or bits. In the context of multiplier design, only enabling the addition of A or its negation (-A) is recommended.

It should be noted that 0s result in shifts rather than additions, affecting the delay time (Wang et al., 2007). In the following section, we shall examine the process of converting a given (n + 1)-bit numerical value, represented as (Ob, –l. –. b_0), into an (n + 1)-bit canonical SD number, denoted as *D = d, d, –l…* do. It is important to note that the condition b, *x b,-l = 0* must hold during this transformation, and the resulting canonical SD number must satisfy the equation *Cy=ob i x 2i = Cy=odi x 2i* (Ruiz & Manzano, 2001). The algorithm may be delineated subsequently:

Start with LSB, b_0, of B and let $i = 0$ and $c_0 = 0$.
Find $c_{i+1} = b_{i+1} \wedge b_i \vee b_i \wedge c_i \vee b_{i+1} \wedge c_i$.
Find $d_i = b_i + c_i - 2c_{i+1}$.
$i = i + 1$. If $i = n$, stop; else, go to step 2.

Stop: $c_n d_{n-1} d_{n-2} \cdots d_0$ is the $(n+1)$-bit canonical SD.

Based on Step 2 and 3, a table is generated as follows.

Conventional Multiplier Bits b_{i+1}	b_i	Assumed Carry-in c_i	Recoded Bit c_{i+1}	Carry-out d_i
0	0	0	0	0
0	0	1	0	1
0	1	0	0	1
0	1	1	1	0
1	0	0	0	0
1	0	1	1	$\bar{1}$
1	1	0	1	$\bar{1}$
1	1	1	1	0

So, we have D = (1 0 I 0 I 0 I).

Scanning pattern used in 32-bit multiplication with the extended Booth's Algorithm is shown in Figure 4.13(a). A supplementary bit, commonly called a "dummy bit," is appended to the multiplier's least significant bit (LSB) (Hu & Al-Khalili, 2002). The scanning process encompasses a total of 33 bits. The scanning process is performed sequentially, comprising eight iterations. Five bits are inspected during each iteration, with one bit being overlapped. The initial iteration examines a sequence of 5 binary digits. The subsequent seven iterations involve scanning an additional 28 bits, with a rate of 4 new bits per iteration, not including the overlapping bit. Booth's Algorithm handles 5 bits in a single iteration by implementing an overlapped 2-bit scanning technique (Arumugam& Paramasivan, 2021).

Firstly, preparing the multiplicand multiples of A, –A, and 0 is possible. The one's complement of A is calculated, and a "1" is added to it to obtain the A complement. Subsequently, a multiple will be chosen based on the bibi-l bit value for every scanned bit pair. Figure 4.13(b) depicts the diagrammatic representation of a logical circuit that effectively chooses the suitable multiplicand multiples. The output of Gate 4 will obstruct Gate 2 when bi equals *b,-l*. In this scenario, the output of Gate 2 will be 0, which is the appropriate selection (Koc & Hung, 1992). In cases where bi is greater than bi–1, the resulting outcome is the negation of A after it passes through Gate 1, thereby transforming into the 1's complement of A. The signal routing is anticipated to take place via Gate 2, with an additional output of "1" generated by Gate 3. The values mentioned above will be aggregated in forthcoming addition to generate 2's complement of A, which is equivalent to –A. To open Gate 2, bi < bi–1, as per the given case, is necessary. In this scenario, the value of A will remain unaltered after the completion of Gate 1. Furthermore, the chosen multiple is A (Sharma & Ramesh, 2016).

The four distinct multiples, namely Mo, MI, M2, & M3, can be derived by performing four bit-pair scans in conjunction with the duplicated MS cells. Subsequently, the values are to be aggregated. Notably, in a given iteration, one of the multiples is positioned slightly differently than its adjacent multiple. A six-input carry-select adder (CSA) tree is utilized to optimize the operational speed at the cost of increased hardware expenses. The carry and sum values that have been preserved are reintroduced to input side. The vector representing the carry is horizontally displaced to the left in relation to the vector representing sum (Guo & DeBrunner, 2011) The CSA tree is generated through a continuous iteration of four multiples, and the pipeline addition of various groups is feasible. The CSA tree generates two distinct outputs: the sum and the carry. It is necessary to perform addition utilizing a two-operand rapid adder to obtain the outcome. Suppose additional addends are introduced, and the addition process is repeated. In that case, it is possible to retain the carry and utilize the two resulting outputs as input to the CSA tree, where they can be combined with new inputs. A certain number of iterations are necessary to execute an n-bit multiplication utilizing a scan pattern of 5 bits per iteration, whereby 4 new bits are scrutinized at each iteration, excluding overlapped bit. In contrast, utilizing basic hardware necessitates n cycles to scan all n bits (Bhandari & Mamatha, 2018)

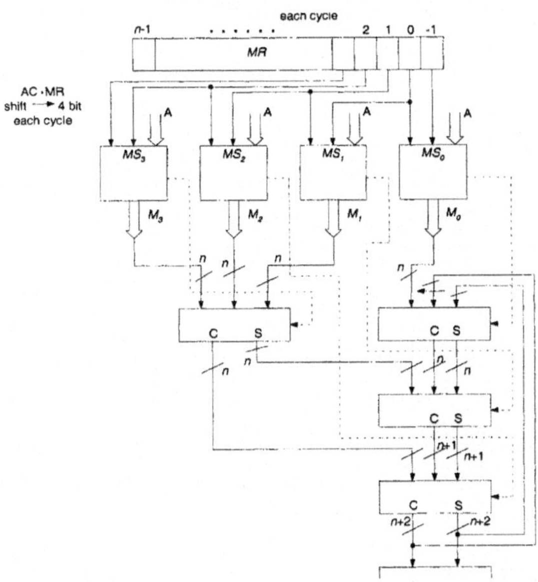

Figure 6.7. Combining the bit-pairs from a parallel CSA tree scan.

In the previous section, a multiplication function was executed in n iterations, where n represents length of the input operand. During each iteration, a fundamental operation involving addition and shifting was executed. The present chapter introduces an Array Multiplier as a solution to the issue of utilizing single-stage hardware repeatedly. This proposed approach involves replicating the single-stage circuit to provide multiple stages of hardware (Koc, 1996). Distinct hardware stages can execute various versions of addition, and each shift operation is implemented through appropriate wiring between the hardware stages. In this instance, it is possible to overlap multiple multiplication operations. The concurrent execution of multiplication functions can reduce the overall time required for their completion, as the second multiplication may commence before the completion of the first. Currently, several iterative array multipliers and cellular array processors possess the capability to perform high-speed multiplication, which is a requirement in scientific computation (Wu et al., 2010).

6.5. WALLACE TREES

The summation of partial products is the most time-intensive aspect of the multiplication procedure. The preceding section discusses the methodology to diminish the quantity of partial products.

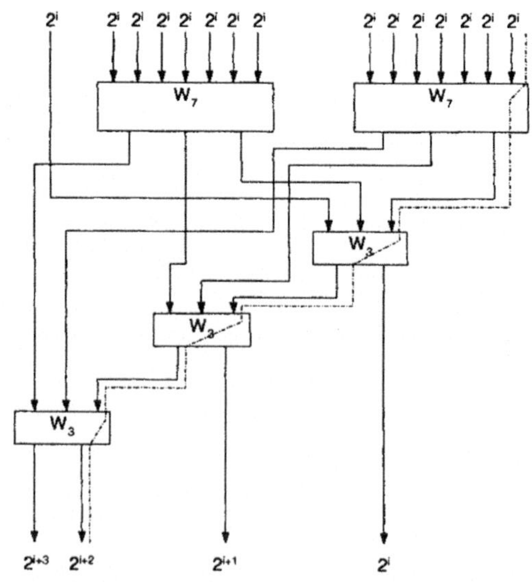

Figure 6.8. Wallace tree.

This paper introduces a hardware implementation for efficiently managing the iterative addition process utilizing the Wallace tree algorithm. The Wallace tree is a type of bit-slice adder that performs addition on all bits located in the same position. The Wallace trees for varying numbers of inputs are presented in Figure 6.8. The present study introduces a 3-bit slice adder denoted as W3, that functions as a carry-save full adder with three inputs and two outputs (Sureka et al., 2013).

It should be noted that delay time on critical path is 3 A F A. Upon the elapse of 2nFA time, the output can be obtained at the 22nd-bit position. The provided information includes a W15 and a Wallace tree consisting of 2 W~S & 3 W3s. Delay duration is observed on the critical path (indicated by the dashed line).

$$\Delta_T = 2\Delta_{FA} + \Delta_{FA} + \Delta_{FA} + \Delta_{FA}$$

A Wallace tree with k inputs is a circuit that performs bit-slice addition and generates the sum of k bits that carry the same weight. Table 5.1 displays combination & delay time for conventional Ic-input Wallace trees. It should be noted that a Wallace tree with k inputs can produce $\log_2(k + 1)$ outputs (Bhardwaj et al., 2014).

6.6. UNSIGNED ARRAY MULTIPLIER

This section presents an implementation of a multiplier for unsigned arrays. Assuming A and B are non-negative integers represented in base 10 and 2, respectively, let P be the product of A and B. P is represented in base 2 as (prn + n–lprn + n–2 –. –plpo). We possess or hold.

$$\begin{aligned}
&= \sum_{i=0}^{m-1} a_i \cdot 2^i \times \sum_{j=0}^{n-1} b_j \cdot 2^j \\
&= \sum_{i=0}^{m-1} \sum_{j=0}^{n-1} (a_i b_j) \cdot 2^{i+j} \\
&= \sum_{k=0}^{m+n-1} p_k \cdot 2^k.
\end{aligned}$$

It should be noted that variable A comprises m bits, while variable B consists of n bits. Furthermore, the resulting product P is composed of m + n bits. The operation above is commonly denoted as m-by-n multiplication in academic discourse. Given that A & B are of equal length, with each containing n bits, P is a 2n-bit long value. The multiplication in question is commonly denoted as n-by-n multiplication or n-bit multiplication. The multiplication of a 5-by-5 matrix is illustrated in Figure 5.2 (Gurumurthy & Prahalad, 2010).

The term "partial product" refers to each ai, bj where 0≤ I, j ≤ n–1. This task necessitates two distinct operations: the production of summands and the subsequent addition of said summands. Parallel generation of the summands is feasible if an array of AND gates with dimensions m x n exists. An array of (m – 1) x n finite automata can be used to summate summands. The addends contained within a designated compartment depicted in Figure 5.2 can be computed via the employment of a full adder (FA). If a box is situated above, the summand is incorporated into the sum produced by a said box. The multiplication of a 5-by-5 unsigned number is demonstrated in Figure 5.3 by utilizing a 4 x 5 array of FAs. The input vector (*a4bj+l, a36j+l, azbj+l, albj+l, aobj+l*) is received from the right of the finite automata in row j (Bajaj et al., 2009).

Two vectors are generated, one for carrying and the other for summing. The carry is propagated to the adjacent position on the left in the subsequent row, combining with the input vector from the right and the sum vector from the row above. If unity is not a concern, a row of half-adders (HAS) can be utilized solely to add the input vector in the top row, comprising of (a4b0, asbo, a2b0, albo, a&) as its components. The carry is propagated from the rightmost bit to the leftmost bit in the lowermost row. As illustrated in Figure 5.2, it is evident that $p_0 = a_0b_0$, and there is no requirement for any supplementary value in the least significant bit position. Hence, it can be inferred that a 4 x 5 array is adequate for executing the multiplication of a 5-by-5 matrix instead of a 5 x 5 array. The duration for generating the summands is equivalent to that of the AND gate (Walter, 1992). Therefore, it can be concluded that A is equivalent to AAND. The delay time required for the summation of summands is not uniform for all bits p j present in the product form simultaneously. It is imperative to sustain the input values sufficiently to attain stable outputs. Identifying the path with the highest possible propagation delay in this scenario is imperative. Commencing from the terminal cell located at the far right of the uppermost row, a delay period of approximately A F A is encountered before arriving at the lowermost row. Furthermore, the time it takes for a signal to travel from the rightmost terminal cell to the leftmost terminal cell in the bottom row is 4 nanoseconds multiplied by the capacitance of the circuit, denoted by F, and the area of the circuit, denoted by A (Di et al., 2006). Thus, the time needed for summands is:

$$\Delta_{ss} = 4\Delta_{FA} + 4\Delta_{FA} = 8\Delta_{FA}.$$

Typically, when conducting multiplication of an m-by-n unsigned numerical value, it is possible to attain a certain level of time complexity.

$$\begin{aligned} \Delta_{US} &= \Delta_{AND} + [(m-1) + (n-1)]\Delta_{FA} \\ &= \Delta_{AND} + (m+n-2)\Delta_{FA}. \end{aligned}$$

Also, we have area complexity.

$$A_{US} = m \times n \times A_{AND} + (m-1) \times n \times A_{FA}.$$

If m=n,

$$\Delta_{US} = \Delta_{AND} + (2n-2)\Delta_{FA},$$

And,

$$A_{US} = n^2 \times A_{AND} + n(n-1)A_{FA}.$$

$\Delta_{AND} = 2\Delta_g$ and $\Delta_{FA} = 2\Delta_g$, we have

$$\Delta_{US} = 2\Delta_g + (2n-2) \cdot 2\Delta_g = (4n-2)\Delta_g.$$

It is possible to substitute the lower row of Full Adders depicted in Figure 5.3 with a Carry Lookahead Adder of a single level. This will eliminate the ripple-carry and render the delay time unaffected by the length of the multiplicand (Costa et al., 2002). Regarding this particular instance,

$$\begin{aligned} \Delta_{US} &= \Delta_{AND} + (n-1)\Delta_{FA} + \Delta_{CLA} \\ &= 2n\Delta_g + \Delta_{CLA} \\ &= (2n+7)\Delta_g. \end{aligned}$$

The potential enhancement of efficiency can be achieved by implementing a pipelining mechanism whereby the insertion of latch registers between the rows of FAs can facilitate this improvement. Multiple multiplication operations can be concurrently executed. The overlapping of the addition of partial products from a previous multiplication with that of a subsequent multiplication is a feasible scenario. Assuming that the carry-lookahead is treated as a single stage, the interval between two latches mustn't be less than the delay duration of any given stage (Valinataj, 2017).

As to the area complexity, with,

$$\begin{aligned} A_{US} &= n^2 A_{AND} + (n(n-1))A_{FA} \\ &= 2n^2 A_g + (n^2 - n) \cdot 10A_g \\ &= (2n^2 + 10n^2 - 10n)A_g \\ &= (12n^2 - 10n)A_g \end{aligned}$$

we have without CLA. In the case that a CLA is used,

$$\begin{aligned} A_{US} &= n^2 A_{AND} + (n-1)(n-1)A_{FA} + A_{CLA} \\ &= (2n^2 + 10n^2 - 20n + 10)A_g + A_{CLA} \\ &= (12n^2 - 20n + 10)A_g + A_{CLA}. \end{aligned}$$

With the LSI or VLSI technology, the above multiplier can be easily implemented on a single chip.

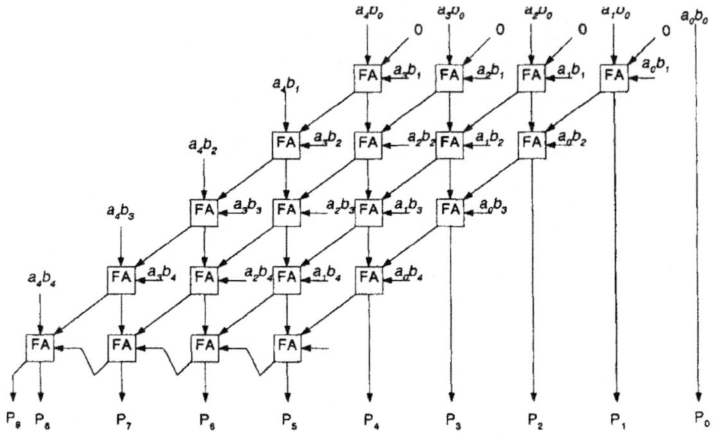

Figure 6.9. 5 × 4 array multiplier performing 5-by-5 multiplication.

The present array is intended to perform multiplication operations on unsigned numerical values (US). To perform multiplication on sign-magnitude (SM), 1's complement (OC), or 2's complement (TC) numbers, it is necessary to utilize both a pre-complementor and a post-complementor (Devi et al., 2011).

It should be noted that both A and B have a length of (n+l) bits, while P has a length of (2n+l). The sign bits for A, B, and P2 are included. It is worth noting that a 1's complement exhibits a delay time of AT = 2A, while a 2's complementor displays a delay time of AT = (2n+2)A. An alternative approach is being pursued to utilize the "indirect" array multiplier (Kornerup, 1994).

6.7. TWO'S COMPLEMENT ARRAY MULTIPLIER

This section presents a multiplication method considered "direct" as it eliminates the need for pre-complement and post-complement operations when multiplying 2's complement numbers.

Utilizing a multiplier can result in a noteworthy speed enhancement in implementing the approach above.

Initially, we explain the mathematical principles that underlie the direct multiplication of 2's complement. Consider a 2's complement number N represented as (a_{n-1}, a_{n-2}, …, a_0), where the sign bit is included. The variable N can be represented as an–1.

$$N = \begin{cases} +(a_{n-2}\cdots a_0)_2 = +(\sum_{i=0}^{n-2} a_i 2^i)_{10} & \text{if } a_{n-1} = 0 \\ -[(\bar{a}_{n-2}\cdots \bar{a}_0) + 1]_2 = -(\sum_{i=0}^{n-2}(1-a_i)2^i + 1)_{10} & \text{if } a_{n-1} = 1. \end{cases}$$

with the first term equal to 0 since *an–1* = 0. For (*N* = l an – 2… *U O*) ~we have,

$$N = \left(+\sum_{i=0}^{n-2} a_i 2^i\right) = -a_{n-1}2^{n-1} + \left(\sum_{i=0}^{n-2} a_i 2^i\right)$$

with the first term equal to 0 since *an–1* = 0. For (*N* = l an – 2… *U O*) ~we have

$$\begin{aligned} N &= -\left(\sum_{i=0}(1-a_i)2^i) + 1\right) \\ &= -\left(\sum_{i=0}^{n-2} 2^i - \sum_{i=0}^{n-2} a_i 2^i + 1\right) \\ &= -\left[\left(\sum_{i=0}^{n-2} 2^i\right) + 1\right] + \sum_{i=0}^{n-2} a_i 2^i \\ &= -(2^{n-1}) + \left(\sum_{i=0}^{n-2} a_i 2^i\right) \\ &= -a_{n-1}2^{n-1} + \left(\sum_{i=0}^{n-2} a_i 2^i\right) \end{aligned}$$

with the first term equal to –2n–1 since *un-l* = 1. Notice that:

$$\begin{aligned} \sum_{i=0}^{n-2} 2^i &= \frac{2^0(2^{n-1}-1)}{2-1} \\ &= 2^{n-1} - 1, \end{aligned}$$

and hence,

$$\sum_{i=0}^{n-2} 2^i + 1 = 2^{n-1}.$$

That is for N,

$$N = -a_{n-1}2^{n-1} + \left(\sum_{i=0}^{n-2} a_i 2^i\right).$$

With the first term equal to 0 since *an–1* = 0. For ***(N*** **= l an – 2…** *U O)* ~we have

$$\begin{array}{ccccc} N = & -a_{n-1}2^{n-1} & +\left[\sum_{i=0}^{n-2} a_i 2^i\right] & +0 \\ \updownarrow & \updownarrow & \updownarrow & \updownarrow \\ -N = & -(1-a_{n-1})2^{n-1} & +\left[\sum_{i=0}^{n-2}(1-a_i)2^i\right] & +1. \end{array}$$

The illustration above demonstrates that the negation of a numerical value can be achieved by negating its constituent bits. Specifically, this involves altering the value of ai to (1 – a_i) and substituting 1 for 0 or vice versa. Designers are motivated to modify a full adder to enable certain inputs and outputs to bear negated weights (Baugh & Wooley, 1973). The construction of various types of adders is depicted in Figure 6.10. The Type I adder is characterized by the absence of negative input. A single negative input characterizes type I1, whereas its modified variant, Type 11,' features two negative inputs. Type I' is a Type I variant with three negative inputs. Additionally, the arithmetic relationships between the inputs and outputs of said adders are provided. By utilizing a specific combination of diverse adders, creating an array that executes direct complement multiplication is feasible (Pekmestzi, 1999).

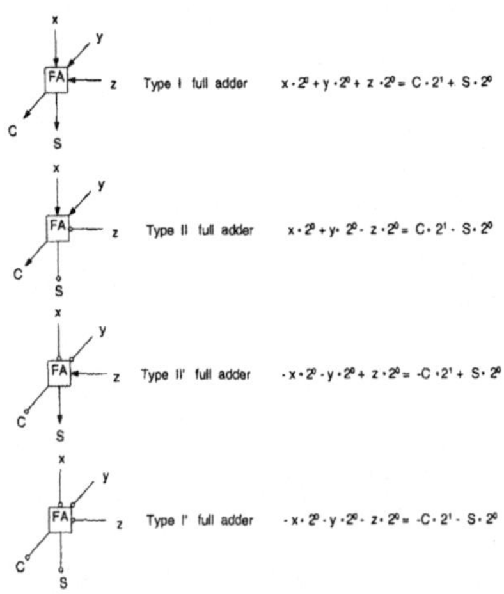

Figure 6.10. Different types of full adders.

6.7.1. Baugh-Wooley Two's Complement Multiplier

Consider two binary numbers, A and B, represented in 2's complement notation with lengths of rn and n, respectively. Let P be the product of A and B, represented in 2's complement notation, and has a length of rn + n bits. From Equation,

Since

$$A = -a_{m-1}2^{m-1} + \left(\sum_{i=0}^{m-2} a_i 2^i\right),$$

$$B = -b_{n-1}2^{n-1} + \left(\sum_{i=0}^{n-2} b_i 2^i\right),$$

$$P = -p_{m+n-1}2^{m+n-1} + \left(\sum_{i=0}^{m+n-2} p_i 2^i\right).$$

$$P = A \times B,$$

$$\begin{aligned} P &= \left(-a_{m-1}2^{m-1} + \sum_{i=0}^{m-2} a_i 2^i\right) \times \left(-b_{n-1}2^{n-1} + \sum_{i=0}^{n-2} b_i 2^i\right) \\ &= +a_{m-1}b_{n-1}2^{m+n-2} + \sum_{i=0}^{m-2}\sum_{j=0}^{n-2} a_i b_j 2^{i+j} \\ &\quad - \sum_{i=0}^{m-2} a_i b_{n-1} 2^{n-1+i} - \sum_{i=0}^{n-2} a_{m-1} b_i 2^{m-1+i}. \end{aligned}$$

The third and fourth terms exhibit a negative value. It is desired that the negative weight be distributed across various bits. It can be demonstrated that the third term (Karuppusamy, 2019).

$$-\sum_{i=0}^{m-2} a_i b_{n-1} 2^{n-1+i} = 2^{n-1}\left(-2^m + 2^{m-1} + \bar{b}_{n-1}2^{m-1} + b_{n-1} + \sum_{i=0}^{m-2} \bar{a}_i b_{n-1} 2^i\right).$$

A type of array that utilizes the algorithm above is commonly known as a Baugh-Wooley array. An illustrative instance of a hardware configuration with m = 6 and n = 4 is presented. The architecture necessitates the provision of input bits in both their original and complemented forms. It is relatively easy to achieve satisfaction, particularly when the bits are stored in flip-flops. One can calculate the delay time of the array.

$$
\begin{aligned}
& \Delta_{NOT} + \Delta_{AND} + [(n-1) + m]\Delta_{FA} \\
= \; & 1 + 2 + (m + n - 1) \times 2\Delta_g \\
= \; & [2(m+n) + 1]\Delta_g .
\end{aligned}
$$

The given problem involves the computation of the product of two numbers, A and B, represented in binary form as (001010)2 and (1101)2 respectively. The result is obtained through the application of the Baugh-Wooley algorithm for 2's complement multiplication, which yields a product P equal to –30. This process is illustrated in Figure 5.7.

Figure 5.8 illustrates a 4-by-4 Baugh-Wooley 2's complement array multiplier in the scenario where m equals n. The calculation of the delay time for such an array can be determined (Sunder et al., 1995).

$$
\begin{aligned}
& \Delta_{NOT} + \Delta_{AND} + [(n-1) + (n+1)]\Delta_{FA} \\
= \; & (1 + 2 + 2n \times 2)\Delta_g \\
= \; & (4n+3)\Delta_g .
\end{aligned}
$$

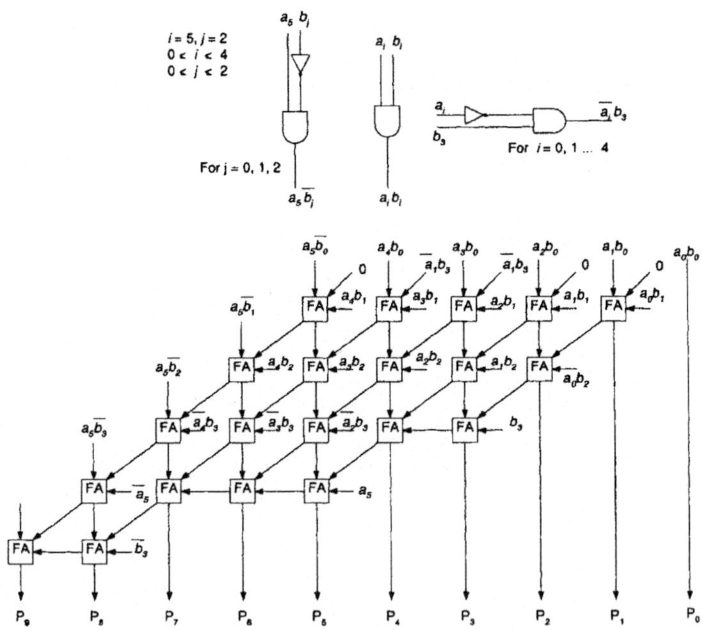

Figure 6.11. Baugh-Wooley array multiplier performing 6-by-4 two's complement.

6.7.2. Pezaris Two's Complement Multipliers

Furthermore, this article presents an alternative form of direct 2's complement array multiplier, the Pezaris array multiplier, its modified iterations, and the Baugh-Wooley 2's complement array multiplier.

Consider two numbers A and B, where A is *a4a3a2ala0*, and B is *b4b3b2blb0*. These numbers are being multiplied.

In the notations above and subsequent content, a bit with negative weight is denoted in bold. Figure 6.12 illustrates the distribution of summands required to multiply matrices A and B. The present study proposes the utilization of a Pezaris array multiplier for the operation above. The said multiplier comprises *Type I, Type 1,' Type I1, and Type 11'* full adders. The schematic logic circuit diagram for a Pezaris array with dimensions of 5-by-5 is depicted in Figure 6.12 (Pezaris 1970).

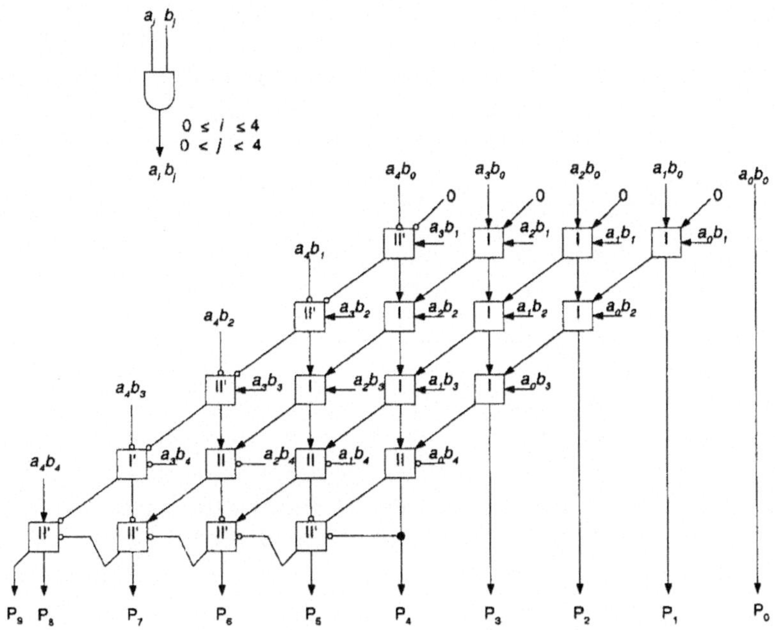

Figure 6.12. 5-by-5 Pezaris array multiplier.

The Type I1 adder at the rightmost position in the second row from the bottom, as depicted in Figure 6.12, possesses unique characteristics. The adder's resultant signal "s" generated is expected to possess a favorable weight as a collective outcome of the entire array. In a conventional Type I1 adder, the expression x + y – z = 2c – s is utilized, wherein the weight of s is negative and serves as a carrier. The equation 2c – s = 2c + s – 2s can be manipulated to yield 2(c – s) + s. This allows for the rightmost Type I1 adder to output an s with positive weight while simultaneously subtracting s at the input of the rightmost Type II adder, which is situated one-bit position higher and thus carries twice the weight (Bandeira et al., 1983). The Type 11 adder utilizes three inputs, namely x, y, and z. Notably, z serves as a negative weight carried input and is thus connected to the s output of the Type I1 adder on its right. When that output is 0, nothing will affect the Type 11’ adder on the left. n(n – 1) full adders in total are required in an n-by-n Pezaris array (Ma & Taylor, 1990). In general, the delay time for an m-by-n Pezaris array is

$$
\begin{aligned}
&= \triangle_{AND} + [(n-1) + (m-1)]\triangle_{FA} \\
&= 2\triangle_g + (m+n-2)2\triangle_g \\
&= [2(m+n)-2]\triangle_g.
\end{aligned}
$$

Figure 6.12 presents a proposed array multiplier incorporating a reduced number of full adder types. The bi-section array multiplier is characterized by its utilization of solely two variants of full adders. The upper section of the circuit contains Type I full adders, while the lower section comprises Type II full adders. The bi-section array multiplier provided is capable of executing a multiplication operation with a 5-by-5 matrix. The delay time of an m-by-n bi-section array multiplier is quantified.

$$
\begin{aligned}
& [n + (m-1)]\triangle_{FA} + \triangle_{AND} \\
&= [2(m+n-1)+2]\triangle_g \\
&= 2(m+n)\triangle_g.
\end{aligned}
$$

The *tri-section array multiplier* is comprised of three distinct sections. One section exclusively comprises Type I full adders, another section comprises only Type I1 adders, and the remaining third section is composed entirely of Type 11’ full adders. The 5-by-5 tri-section array illustrated in Figure 6.13 is demarcated into three distinct sections using dashed lines (Chinbat et al., 2020).

The delay time for an m-by-n tri-section array multiplier can be determined in a broader context.

$$
\begin{aligned}
& [(n-1) + (m-1)]\triangle_{FA} + \triangle_{AND} \\
&= (m+n-2)2\triangle_g + 2\triangle_g \\
&= [2(m+n)-2]\triangle_g.
\end{aligned}
$$

6.8. MODULAR STRUCTURE OF LARGE MULTIPLIER

To perform multiplication on two numbers of significant magnitude, a modular framework is required. This framework should be capable of producing and aggregating sub-products and possess a recursive structure.

6.8.1. Modular Structure

Multiply modules refer to array multipliers capable of efficiently performing multiplication operations on operands of limited or moderate length. In this discourse, we shall explain constructing a substantial 2n–by–2n multiplier using n-by-n multiply modules. The function of concatenation can be denoted by the symbol "o." In the case of a large multiplicand A, it is possible to partition it into two halves of different orders, namely a higher order half (AH) and a lower order half (AL), such that the original multiplicand can be expressed as the concatenation of the two halves, i.e., *A = AH o AL.* Comparably, it is possible to partition multiplier B into two parts, namely BH and BL, such that B is equal to the product of BH and BL, denoted as *B = BH o BL* (Parnas et al., 1985).

Given that A consists of 2n bits, it can be inferred that both AH and AL contain n bits each. The scenario above applies similarly to variable B. Hence, it is feasible to compute the 2n–by–2n multiplication A x B through a series of n-by-n multiplications, with each yielding a sub-product of length 2n bits. When computing the sum of the four sub-products in Equation (5.8), it is crucial to ensure proper alignment. It should be noted that AH is positioned n bits higher than AL (Mitra et al., 2013).

Consequently, the initial sub-product, AH x BH, is n bits higher than the subsequent sub-product, *AL x BH*. Similarly, the third sub-product, *AH x BL*, is n bits higher than the fourth, *AL x BL*. In the interim, it is noteworthy that BH holds a bit position that are n units higher than BL. As a result, the second sub-product, the product of AL and BH, is also positioned n bits higher than the fourth sub-product, which is the product of AL and BL. Consequently, the second sub-product is situated in the same bit position as the third sub-product, which is the product of AH and BL (Frankel & Kim, 1991).

The alignment of the four sub-products is depicted in Figure 6.14. The production of each sub-product can be achieved through the utilization of an n-by-n multiplier module. A total of four of these modules are required to complete the process. If A and B are numerical values consisting of 8 bits, the range of bit positions for the four sub-products can be observed in Figure 6.15, as denoted by their respective weights (Saldana et al., 2018).

To add sub-products, it is necessary to utilize 3-input Wallace trees within the range of bit position n to 3n–1. By interchanging the positions of the initial and secondary sub-products alongside the third and fourth ones, it is possible to arrange the module outputs in a left-right-top-bottom configuration. This is illustrated in Figure 6.16, where each rectangular shape represents a 4-by-4 module utilized to achieve an 8-by-8 multiplier. Moreover, this particular framework has the potential for recursive application.

A 16-by-16 multiplier can be constructed by arranging 8-by-8 multipliers in a left-right-top-bottom orientation. Similarly, a 32-by-32 multiplier can be constructed utilizing a comparable approach, as depicted in Figure 6.16 (Puius et al., 1998).

The selection of Wallace trees is contingent upon the magnitude of the multiplier. The categorization of Wallace trees required for the right portion of the multiplier has been completed. The left side exhibits symmetry with respect to the right side.

The time complexity of the multiply module (MM) can be determined by utilizing the Equation and exemplifying an 8-by-8 multiplication (Sorensen et al., 2013).

$$\begin{aligned}\triangle_{MM4\times4} &= \triangle_{AND} + [(4-1)+(4-1)]\triangle_{FA} \\ &= (2+6\times2)\triangle_g \\ &= 14\triangle_g,\end{aligned}$$

$$\triangle_{W_3} = \triangle_{FA} = 2\triangle_g,$$

hence,

$$\begin{aligned}\triangle_{MM8\times8} &= (14+2)\triangle_g + \triangle_{CPA} \\ &= 16\triangle_g + \triangle_{CPA}.\end{aligned}$$

6.8.2. Additive Multiple Modules

The Additive Multiply Modules (AMM) can accept supplementary addends and incorporate them into the input multiplicand and multiplier product. The preceding subsection has referenced multiple modules that lack the function above, commonly known as non-additive multiply modules. The diagram presented in Figure 6.17 depicts a 4-by-2 Array Multiplier Module (AMM) that is capable of executing arithmetic computations, specifically the operation of P = A x B + C + D. The variables A and B represent a multiplicand of 4 bits and a multiplier of 2 bits, respectively. The product denoted as P comprises six bits, as the sum of four and two equals six. The variable C has a bit length of 4, while the variable D has a bit length of 2 (Valencia et al., 2009).

Let,

$$\begin{aligned} P &= A \times B \\ &= A_H \circ A_L \times B_4 \circ B_3 \circ B_2 \circ B_1 . \end{aligned}$$

If A and B are 8-bit numerical values, the range of bit positions for the four subproducts can be observed in Figure 6.18, as denoted by their respective weights. Figure 6.19 depicts the implementation of the array multiplier through the utilization of 4-by-2 AMMs.

$$\begin{aligned} \Delta_{AMM(4\times 2)} &= 5\Delta_{FA} + \Delta_{AND} \\ &= (10+2)\Delta_g \\ &= 12\Delta_g . \end{aligned}$$

As depicted in Figure 6.17, the maximum delay for a 4-by-2 asynchronous message router is referred to. It should be noted that in cases where only PI and Po are required, waiting for 12A is not essential. A duration of 6A is adequate for this purpose. Therefore, as depicted in Figure 6.19, the two AMMs linked by the dotted lines experience a delay time of (6 + 12 = 18)A. There exist three pairs along the delay path. The cumulative delay time of the modular multiplier for accomplishing 8-by-8 multiplication, encompassing the initial and final AMMs, is calculated as follows (Ugus et al., 2009).

6.8.3. Programmable Multiply Modules

The matrix of summands depicted in Figure 6.20 (a) is to be subjected to observation, partitioning it into two halves horizontally and vertically. The sub-matrices have been partitioned into four distinct regions denoted as (0), (I), (2), and (3). It can be observed that the sub-matrix located in region (0) does not possess any summand with negative weight. The sub-matrix depicted in equation (1) exhibits a configuration in which the summands in the lowermost row are assigned negative weights. Conversely, the sub-matrix illustrated in equation (3) displays a pattern in which the summands along the left border are endowed with negative weights (Daly & Marnane 2002). The sub-matrix in region (2) exhibits characteristics that are common to both matrices in (1) and (3). The notation AMMi refers to the specific Additive Multiply Module required within a given region denoted as i.

According to Figure 6.20 (a), it can be inferred that a multiplier utilizing the 2's complement method can be constructed by utilizing four additive multiply modules, namely *AMMO*, *AMMI*, *AMM2*, and *AMM3*. Moreover, these types of Automated Market Makers (AMMs) can potentially facilitate the creation of even larger multipliers (Ghosh et al., 2011).

The array structure of *AMMi* can be consistently standardized for varying values of i. To generate distinct *AMMs*, it is only necessary to modify the summands entered at the lower and/or left borders. In lieu of consistently utilizing "aibj," it is necessary to incorporate "Tiibj" at the lower section for AMMI, and "ai6j" on the left margin for AM&. Regarding *AMM2,* the input summands specified above are taken by the bottom and left borders, respectively (Leon et al., 1999).

To clarify, by enabling function modes to regulate the generation of summands, it is possible to create distinct *AMMis* through mode switching. The resulting array is denoted as AMMO after generating all the summands under mode 0. If the array is generated under mode 1 for some of the summands at the bottom while the others are generated under mode 0, the resulting array can be denoted as *AMMl.* Moreover, if the addends on the left border are produced under mode 3 while the rest are under mode 0, the resulting array is called *AMMs* (Hwang, 1979).

If the addends on the left are produced using mode 3, and the one at the bottom is produced using mode 1, while the remaining ones are produced using mode 0, the resulting output is AMM2. The programmability of additive multiplication modules is achieved through this approach (Tai et al., 1979). To conform to a specific mode, negating one variable among the summands input to the bottom and the left border is necessary. If this condition is not met, the summands should follow the standard form of aibj. Figure 6.13 illustrates the mode-controlled generation of the summands above. It should be noted that the finite automaton located at the intersection of the bottom row and left border can accept both of the summands transmitted to it from the former and the latter. According to the Baugh-Wooley multiplication method, it is recommended to designate the functional unit on the left-hand side of the FA as the "corner." The various summands provided as input under different modes are enumerated, along with the supplementary summands exclusively input during Mode 2, such as *Tin-l, bn-l,* and a unitary value (Mutlu & Dolen, 2010).

The utilization of AMM(4 x 4)s in creating extended multiplication networks, specifically AMM(8×8), is illustrated in Figure 6.13. It should be noted that AMMo (4×4), AMMl (4×4), AMM2 (4×4), or M3 (4×4) can be derived through the programming of the AMMi (4×4) matrices (Rabaey, 1997). The present iterative approach has the potential to be expanded to devise multipliers of various dimensions, including but not limited to (16 x 16), (32 x 32), and (4k×4k), where k is an integer. Typically, a multiplier with dimensions of (4k×4k) necessitates k 2 AMM(4×4)s. Of these, (/ ~ –1 a) r~e AMh / l o (4 ~ 4), (k – 1) a r eAMM~ (4 ~ 4), (k – l) a r eAM~ ~ (4 ~ 4), and one is AMM2(4×4) (Amanor et al., 2005).

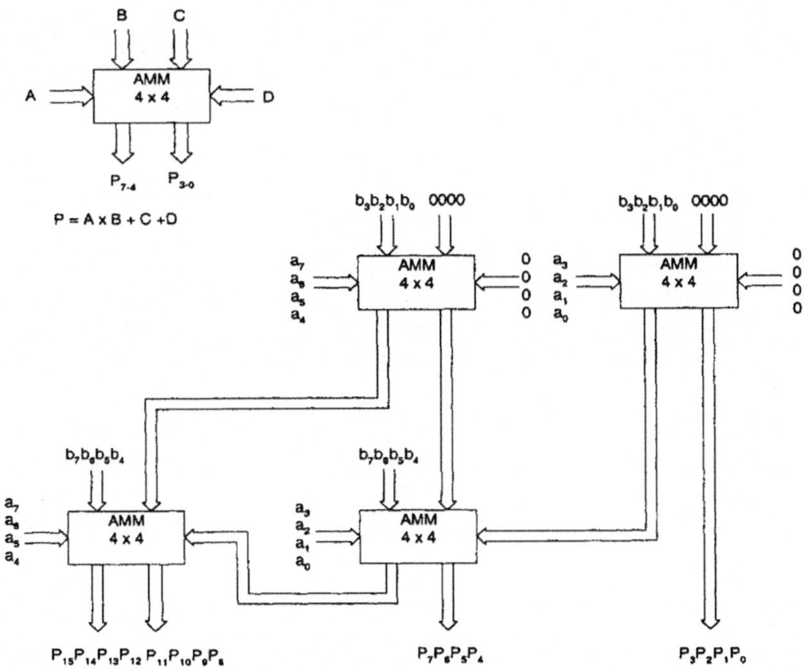

Figure 6.13. AMM (8×8) applying AMM 4×4.

6.9. SUMMARY

The operation of multiplication holds significant importance in the realm of computer arithmetic operations. It is imperative to develop efficient algorithms and high-speed hardware to accomplish multiplication promptly and effectively. The algorithms for sequential multiplication presented in this chapter are founded on an approach that involves adding and shifting. A comprehensive exposition of various types of multipliers will be presented in this study. The present discourse shall delve into multiplication involving signed numbers, particularly emphasizing the indirect schemes and Robertson's approach. In the event that the input operands are articulated in the complement form, it is imperative to transform those that denote negative numbers into the sign-magnitude form prior to commencing the multiplication loop.

Moreover, if the outcome is negative, it is necessary to convert the product back to its complement form. The multiplication procedure encompasses both pre-complements and post-complements, thus earning the nomenclature of "indirect multiplication" for the method under discussion. Currently, the analysis of the least significant bit (LSB) of MR is being expanded to include the scanning of two bits simultaneously.

In the context of two's complement array multiplication, the intermediate result may be augmented by 0, A, 2A, or 3A, contingent upon least significant 2 bits of MR being 00, 01, 10, or 11. Acquiring 2A can be achieved through a simple leftward shift of A by one-bit position. The value of 3A can be derived by adding A and 2A. In this instance, three operands are added, including the intermediate result. The request being made is for a multi-operand adder.

It should be noted that the delay time associated with scanning a single bit is directly proportional to the number of cycles, denoted by 'n,' where each cycle time is correlated with the delay of a 2-operand adder. There is a direct correlation between the current duration of delay and a factor of five cycles. The duration of each cycle is dependent on the delay of the 3-operand adder. Typically, when scanning m bits at a time, the overall delay duration exhibits a direct relationship with 2 cycles, and the duration of each cycle is linked to delay of an adder with (m + 1) operands.

REFERENCES

1. Amanor, D. N., Paar, C., Pelzl, J., Bunimov, V., & Schimmler, M., (2005). Efficient hardware architectures for modular multiplication on FPGAs. In: *International Conference on Field Programmable Logic and Applications, 2005.* (pp. 539–542). IEEE.
2. Ananyi, K., Alrimeih, H., & Rakhmatov, D., (2009). Flexible hardware processor for elliptic curve cryptography over NIST prime fields. *IEEE Transactions on Very Large-Scale Integration (VLSI) Systems*, *17*(8), 1099–1112.
3. Arumugam, N., & Paramasivan, B., (2021). An integrated FIR adaptive filter design by hybridizing canonical signed digit (CSD) and approximate booth recode (ABR) algorithm in DA architecture for the reduction of noise in the sensor nodes. *Multidimensional Systems and Signal Processing*, *32*(4), 1277–1311.
4. Asef, P., Perpina, R. B., Barzegaran, M. R., Lapthorn, A., & Mewes, D., (2017). Multiobjective design optimization using dual-level response surface methodology and booth's algorithm for permanent magnet synchronous generators. *IEEE Transactions on Energy Conversion*, *33*(2), 652–659.
5. Bajaj, R., Chhabra, S., Veeramachaneni, S., & Srinivas, M. B., (2009). A novel, low-power array multiplier architecture. In: *2009 9th International Symposium on Communications and Information Technology* (pp. 119–123). IEEE.
6. Bandeira, N., Vaccaro, K., & Howard, J. A., (1983). A two's complement array multiplier using true values of the operands. *IEEE Transactions on Computers*, *32*(08), 745–747.
7. Baugh, C. R., & Wooley, B. A., (1973). A two's complement parallel array multiplication algorithm. *IEEE Transactions on Computers*, *100*(12), 1045–1047.
8. Bernstein, D. J., (2001). Multidigit multiplication for mathematicians. *Advances in Applied Mathematics*, 1–19.
9. Bhandari, J. K., & Mamatha, B., (*2018*). A novel approach for recoding canonical signed digit. *International Journal of Research in Electronics and Computer Engineering (IJRECE), 6*(2)
10. Bhardwaj, K., Mane, P. S., & Henkel, J., (2014). Power-and area-efficient approximate Wallace tree multiplier for error-resilient systems. In: *15th International Symposium on Quality Electronic Design* (pp. 263–269). IEEE.

11. Bocker, R. P., Clayton, S. R., & Bromley, K., (1983). Electrooptical matrix multiplication using the twos complement arithmetic for improved accuracy. *Applied Optics*, *22*(13), 2019–2021.
12. Bonatto, P., & Oklobdzija, V. G., (1995). Evaluation of Booth's algorithm for implementation in parallel multipliers. In: *Conference Record of the 29th Asilomar Conference on Signals, Systems and Computers* (Vol. 1, pp. 608–610). IEEE.
13. Brickell, E. F., (1983). A fast modular multiplication algorithm with application to two key cryptography. In: *Advances in Cryptology: Proceedings of Crypto 82* (pp. 51–60). Springer US.
14. Broggi, A., (1994). Speeding-up mathematical morphology computations with special-purpose array processors. In: *1994 Proceedings of the 27th Hawaii International Conference on System Sciences* (Vol. 1, pp. 321–330). IEEE.
15. Carter, T. M., & Robertson, J. E., (1990). Radix-16 signed-digit division. *IEEE Transactions on Computers*, *39*(12), 1424–1433.
16. Chang, K. E., Sung, Y. T., Chen, Y. L., & Huang, L. H., (2008). Learning multiplication through computer-assisted learning activities. *Computers in Human Behavior*, *24*(6), 2904–2916.
17. Chinbat, M., Wu, L., Batsukh, A., Khuchit, U., Zhang, X., Mongolyn, B., & Yang, W., (2020). Performance comparison of finite field multipliers for SM2 algorithm based on FPGA implementation. In: *2020 IEEE 14th International Conference on Anti-Counterfeiting, Security, and Identification (ASID)* (pp. 69–72). IEEE.
18. Costa, E., Bampi, S., & Monteiro, J., (2002). A new architecture for signed radix-2/sup m/pure array multipliers. In: *Proceedings. IEEE International Conference on Computer Design: VLSI in Computers and Processors* (pp. 112–117). IEEE.
19. Daly, A., & Marnane, W., (2002). Efficient architectures for implementing montgomery modular multiplication and RSA modular exponentiation on reconfigurable logic. In: *Proceedings of the 2002 ACM/SIGDA 10th International Symposium on Field-Programmable Gate Arrays* (pp. 40–49).
20. Devi, P., Singh, G. P., & Singh, B., (2011). Low power optimized array multiplier with reduced area. In: *High Performance Architecture and Grid Computing: Proceedings International Conference, HPAGC 2011, Chandigarh, India* (pp. 224–232). Springer Berlin Heidelberg.
21. Di, J., Yuan, J. S., & Demara, R., (2006). Improving power-awareness of pipelined array multipliers using two-dimensional pipeline gating and its application on FIR design. *Integration*, *39*(2), 90–112.

22. Eldridge, S. E., & Walter, C. D., (1993). Hardware implementation of Montgomery's modular multiplication algorithm. *IEEE Transactions on Computers, 42*(6), 693–699.

23. Elguibaly, F., (2000). A fast parallel multiplier-accumulator using the modified Booth algorithm. *IEEE Transactions on Circuits and Systems II: Analog and Digital Signal Processing, 47*(9), 902–908.

24. Farsiu, S., Robinson, D., Elad, M., & Milanfar, P., (2003). Robust shift and add approach to superresolution. In: *Applications of Digital Image Processing XXVI* (Vol. 5203, pp. 121–130). SPIE.

25. Frankel, A. D., & Kim, P. S., (1991). Modular structure of transcription factors: Implications for gene regulation. *Cell, 65*(5), 717–719.

26. Ghosh, S., Mukhopadhyay, D., & Roychowdhury, D., (2011). Petrel: Power and timing attack resistant elliptic curve scalar multiplier based on programmable ${\rm GF}(p) $ arithmetic unit. *IEEE Transactions on Circuits and Systems I: Regular Papers, 58*(8), 1798–1812.

27. Gorgin, S., & Jaberipur, G., (2016). Sign-magnitude encoding for efficient VLSI realization of decimal multiplication. *IEEE Transactions on Very Large-Scale Integration (VLSI) Systems, 25*(1), 75–86.

28. Guo, R., & DeBrunner, L. S., (2011). A novel fast canonical-signed-digit conversion technique for multiplication. In: *2011 IEEE International Conference on Acoustics, Speech, and Signal Processing (ICASSP)* (pp. 1637–1640). IEEE.

29. Gurumurthy, K. S., & Prahalad, M. S., (2010). Fast and power efficient 16× 16 Array of Array multiplier using Vedic multiplication. In: *2010 5th International Microsystems Packaging Assembly and Circuits Technology Conference* (pp. 1–4). IEEE.

30. Gwee, B. H., Chang, J. S., Shi, Y., Chua, C. C., & Chong, K. S., (2008). A low-voltage micropower asynchronous multiplier with shift–add multiplication approach. *IEEE Transactions on Circuits and Systems I: Regular Papers, 56*(7), 1349–1359.

31. Hancock, A. M., (2007). When multiplication doesn't equal quick addition: Examining intersectionality as a research paradigm. *Perspectives on Politics, 5*(1), 63–79.

32. Hu, A., & Al-Khalili, A. J., (2002). Comparison of constant coefficient multipliers for CSD and booth recoding. In: *The 14th International Conference on Microelectronics,* (pp. 66–69). IEEE.

33. Huang, H. S., & Lu, C. N., (1994). Efficient storage scheme and algorithms for W-matrix vector multiplication on vector computers. *IEEE Transactions on Power Systems, 9*(2), 1083–1091.

34. Hwang, K., (1979). Global and modular two's complement cellular array multipliers. *IEEE Transactions on Computers, 100*(4), 300–306.

35. Kaihara, M. E., & Takagi, N., (2005). A hardware algorithm for modular multiplication/division. *IEEE Transactions on Computers, 54*(1), 12–21.

36. Kang, J. Y., & Gaudiot, J. L., (2006). A simple high-speed multiplier design. *IEEE Transactions on Computers, 55*(10), 1253–1258.

37. Karuppusamy, P., (2019). Design and analysis of low-power. high-speed Baugh Wooley multiplier. *Journal of Electronics, 1*(02), 60–70.

38. Koç, Ç. K., & Hung, C. Y., (1992). Adaptive m-ARY segmentation and canonical recoding algorithms for multiplication of large binary numbers. *Computers & Mathematics with Applications, 24*(3), 3–12.

39. Koc, C. K., (1996). Parallel canonical recoding. *Electronics Letters, 32*(22), 2063–2065.

40. Koc, C. K., Acar, T., & Kaliski, B. S., (1996). Analyzing and comparing Montgomery multiplication algorithms. *IEEE Micro, 16*(3), 26–33.

41. Kornerup, P., (1994). A systolic, linear-array multiplier for a class of right-shift algorithms. *IEEE Transactions on Computers, 43*(8), 892–898.

42. Leon, M. A., Castro, A. R., & Ascencio, R. L., (1999). An artificial neural network on a field programmable gate array as a virtual sensor. In: *Proceedings of the Third International Workshop on Design of Mixed-Mode Integrated Circuits and Applications (Cat. No. 99EX303)* (pp. 114–117). IEEE.

43. Li, F., Yu, Z., & Qin, C., (2020). Constructive texture steganography based on compression mapping of secret messages. *CMES-Computer Modeling in Engineering & Sciences, 124*(1).

44. Li, G., & Liu, L., (1994). Complex-valued matrix-vector multiplication using twos complement representation. *Optics Communications, 105*(3–4), 161–166.

45. Li, G., Liu, L., Shao, L., & Yin, Y., (1995). Modified direct twos-complement parallel array multiplication algorithm for complex matrix operation. *Applied Optics, 34*(8), 1321–1328.

46. Lyon, R., (1976). Two's complement pipeline multipliers. *IEEE Transactions on Communications, 24*(4), 418–425.

47. Ma, G. K., & Taylor, F. J., (1990). Multiplier policies for digital signal processing. *IEEE ASSP Magazine, 7*(1), 6–20.

48. Macwan, A., (2007). *Design, Synthesis and Simulation of a 64-bit Fast Multiplier Using Verilog HDL.* Doctoral dissertation, California State University, Northridge

49. Madrid, P. E., Millar, B., & Swartzlander, E. E., (1993). Modified Booth algorithm for high radix fixed-point multiplication. *IEEE Transactions on Very Large-Scale Integration (VLSI) Systems*, *1*(2), 164–167.
50. Meyer, R., & Mehling, R., (1990). Architecture and performance of a new arithmetic unit for the computation of elementary functions. In: *International Conference on Acoustics, Speech, and Signal Processing* (pp. 1783–1786). IEEE.
51. Mitchell, J. N., (1962). Computer multiplication and division using binary logarithms. *IRE Transactions on Electronic Computers*, (4), 512–517.
52. Mitra, K., Carvunis, A. R., Ramesh, S. K., & Ideker, T., (2013). Integrative approaches for finding modular structure in biological networks. *Nature Reviews Genetics*, *14*(10), 719–732.
53. Mutlu, B. R., & Dolen, M., (2010). Implementations of state-space controllers using field programmable gate arrays. In: *SPEEDAM 2010* (pp. 1436–1441). IEEE.
54. Parnas, D. L., Clements, P. C., & Weiss, D. M., (1985). The modular structure of complex systems. *IEEE Transactions on Software Engineering*, (3), 259–266.
55. Pekmestzi, K. Z., (1999). Multiplexer-based array multipliers. *IEEE Transactions on Computers*, *48*(1), 15–23.
56. Pezaris, S. D., (1971). A 40-ns 17-bit by 17-bit array multiplier. *IEEE Transactions on Computers*, *100*(4), 442–447.
57. Puius, Y. A., Mahoney, N. M., & Almo, S. C., (1998). The modular structure of actin-regulatory proteins. *Current Opinion in Cell Biology*, *10*(1), 23–34.
58. Rabaey, J. M., (1997). Reconfigurable processing: The solution to low-power programmable DSP. In: *1997 IEEE International Conference on Acoustics, Speech, and Signal Processing* (Vol. 1, pp. 275–278). IEEE.
59. Rajput, R. P., & Swamy, M. S., (2012). High speed modified booth encoder multiplier for signed and unsigned numbers. In: *2012 UKSim 14th International Conference on Computer Modelling and Simulation* (pp. 649–654). IEEE.
60. Robertson, J. E., (1958). A new class of digital division methods. *IRE Transactions on Electronic Computers*, (3), 218–222.
61. Rodríguez-Borbón, J. M., Kalantar, A., Yamijala, S. S., Oviedo, M. B., Najjar, W., & Wong, B. M., (2020). Field programmable gate arrays for enhancing the speed and energy efficiency of quantum dynamics simulations. *Journal of Chemical Theory and Computation*, *16*(4), 2085–

2098.

62. Rubinfield, L. P., (1975). A proof of the modified Booth's algorithm for multiplication. *IEEE Transactions on Computers*, *100*(10), 1014–1015.
63. Ruiz, G. A., & Manzano, M. A., (2001). Self-timed multiplier based on canonical signed-digit recoding. *IEE Proceedings-Circuits, Devices and Systems*, *148*(5), 235–241.
64. Sait, S. M., Farooqui, A. A., & Beckhoff, G. F., (1995). A novel technique for fast multiplication. In: *Proceedings International Phoenix Conference on Computers and Communications* (pp. 109–114). IEEE.
65. Saldana, D., Gabrich, B., Li, G., Yim, M., & Kumar, V., (2018). Modquad: The flying modular structure that self-assembles in midair. In: *2018 IEEE International Conference on Robotics and Automation (ICRA)* (pp. 691–698). IEEE.
66. Shanbhag, N. R., & Juneja, P., (1988). Parallel implementation of a 4* 4-bit multiplier using a modified Booth's algorithm. *IEEE Journal of Solid-State Circuits*, *23*(4), 1010–1013.
67. Sharma, D. H., & Ramesh, A. P., (2016). Floating point multiplier using canonical signed digit. *Int. J. Adv. Res. Electron Commun. Eng. (IJARECE)*, *2*(11), 99–110.
68. Sørensen, P., Andresen, B., Fortmann, J., & Pourbeik, P., (2013). Modular structure of wind turbine models in IEC 61400-27-1. In: *2013 IEEE Power & Energy Society General Meeting* (pp. 1–5). IEEE.
69. Sunder, S., El-Guibaly, F., & Antoniou, A., (1995). Two's-complement fast serial-parallel multiplier. *IEE Proceedings-Circuits, Devices and Systems*, *142*(1), 41–44.
70. Sureka, N., Porselvi, R., & Kumuthapriya, K., (2013). An efficient high speed Wallace tree multiplier. In: *2013 International Conference on Information Communication and Embedded Systems (ICICES)* (pp. 1023–1026). IEEE.
71. Swain, G., (2018). Adaptive and non-adaptive PVD steganography using overlapped pixel blocks. *Arabian Journal for Science and Engineering*, *43*(12), 7549–7562.
72. Swartz, B. E., (1998). The advantages of digital over analog recording techniques. *Electroencephalography and Clinical Neurophysiology*, *106*(2), 113–117.
73. Tai, A., Cindrich, I., Fienup, J. R., & Aleksoff, C. C., (1979). Optical residue arithmetic computer with programmable computation modules. *Applied Optics*, *18*(16), 2812–2823.

74. Ugus, O., Westhoff, D., Laue, R., Shoufan, A., & Huss, S. A., (2009). Optimized implementation of elliptic curve based additive homomorphic encryption for wireless sensor networks. *arXiv Preprint arXiv:0903.3900.*

75. Valencia, M., Pastor, M. A., Fernández-Seara, M. A., Artieda, J., Martinerie, J., & Chavez, M., (2009). Complex modular structure of large-scale brain networks. *Chaos: An Interdisciplinary Journal of Nonlinear Science, 19*(2), 023119.

76. Valinataj, M., (2017). Novel parity-preserving reversible logic array multipliers. *The Journal of Supercomputing, 73*(11), 4843–4867.

77. Walter, C. D., (1992). Faster modular multiplication by operand scaling. In: *Advances in Cryptology—CRYPTO'91: Proceedings 11* (pp. 313–323). Springer Berlin Heidelberg.

78. Wang, Y., DeBrunner, L. S., Zhou, D., & DeBrunner, V. E., (2007). A multiplier structure based on a novel real-time CSD recoding. In: *2007 IEEE International Symposium on Circuits and Systems* (pp. 3195–3198). IEEE.

79. Wu, C. L., Lou, D. C., & Chang, T. J., (2010). Fast modular multiplication based on complement representation and canonical recoding. *International Journal of Computer Mathematics, 87*(13), 2871–2879.

80. Yin, Z., Xiang, Y., & Zhang, X., (2019). Reversible data hiding in encrypted images based on multi-MSB prediction and Huffman coding. *IEEE Transactions on Multimedia, 22*(4), 874–884.

CHAPTER

7 Division

Contents

In contrast to adding, subtracting, and multiplying, division typically does not yield a precise outcome due to the possibility of the dividends not being a multiple of the divisor. The subsequent sections of this chapter will expound upon several division algorithms (Obermann et al., 1997).

7.1. SUBTRACT-AND-SHIFT APPROACH

An illustration depicting the process of pencil-and-paper division is presented in Figure 7.1. The numerical value of 2746 is denoted as the Dividend, while 32 represents the Divisor. The Quotient is represented by the numerical value of 85, and the Remainder is indicated by the numerical value of 26. Upon completion of the initial step involving the arithmetic operation of subtracting 256 from 274, a partial remainder of 18 is derived (Nikmehr et al, 2006; Tustin, 1947). The value of 18 increases to 180 by means of a six-fold increase, achieved by subtracting six from the initial value. In the realm of digital computing, a significant proportion of division operations are executed through a recursive procedure that can be denoted by the subsequent formula:

$$R^{(j+1)} = r \times R^{(j)} - q_{j+1} \times D,$$

The recursion index, denoted by j = 0,1, …, n–1, and the fractional remainder within the jth repetition, represented by R(j), are related in the given context. The dividend is equivalent to the original partial remainder R (0), while the last remainder is represented by R(“). The recurrent procedure determines the quotient digit by digit, where the (j+1)th quotient number is represented by qj+l. The variable D represents the divisor, while T denotes the radix. In the instance, the value of T is 10.

The recurrence formula yields the following result

For $j = 0$: $R^{(1)} = r \times R^{(0)} - q_1 \times D,$

For $j = 1$: $R^{(2)} = r \times R^{(1)} - q_2 \times D$

$$= r \times (r \times R^{(0)} - q_1 \times D) - q_2 \times D$$

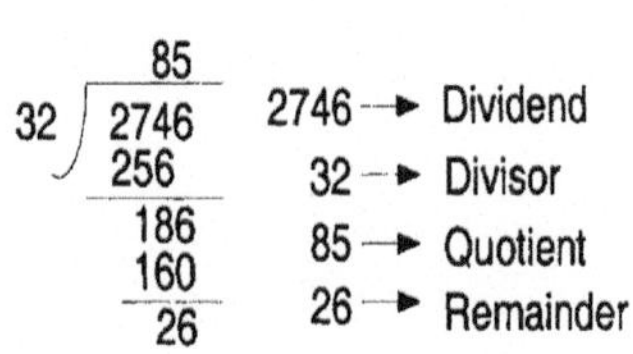

Figure 7.1. Pencil-and-paper division (Hickendorff et al., 2010).

$$= r^2 \times R^{(0)} - r \times q_1 \times D - q_2 \times D$$
$$= r^2 \times R^{(0)} - (r \times q_1 + q_2) \times D,$$
$$\text{For } j = n-1: \; R^{(n)} = r \times R^{(n-1)} - q_n \times D$$
$$\vdots$$
$$= r^n \times R^{(0)} - (r^{n-1} \times q_1 + \cdots + r \times q_{n-1} + q_n) \times D.$$

The following analysis outlines the sequential process by which the quotient number q j is ascertained in the aforementioned manual technique. During the initial stage, an approximation was made to determine the number of times 32 can be divided into 274 while remaining below it. It has been determined that the most likely number is 8, as the product of 9 and 32 exceeds 280 as well as 274 is insufficient to perform the subtraction. In contrast to a human's ability to make estimations based on initial observations, a machine is limited to executing tasks according to its programmed instructions. The iterative process of subtracting 32 from 274 can be employed until the residual difference is less than or equal to 32. The quotient number qj may be determined by keeping a record of the effective subtractions. Following the shifting of the partial remainder, the subsequent step involves initiating the trial procedure for the succeeding quotient digit (MacSorley, 1961). The majority of operations are necessary to involve subtraction and shifting, with division being achievable through the implementation of the subtract-and-shift methodology. The outcome of 2746 divided by 32 is not conclusively 85, as indicated in the aforementioned instance. Instead

$$\frac{R^{(0)}}{D} = Q + \frac{R^{(n)}}{D},$$

$$Q = \sum_{j=1}^{n} r^j \times q_j.$$

Typically, the length of the dividends is 2 times n bits, while the divisor seems n bits in size. The dimension of the quotient has become n, indicating the termination point of the recursion procedure (Gellert et al, 2012; Erle et al, 2002).

$$R^{(0)} = r_0.r_1r_2\cdots,$$

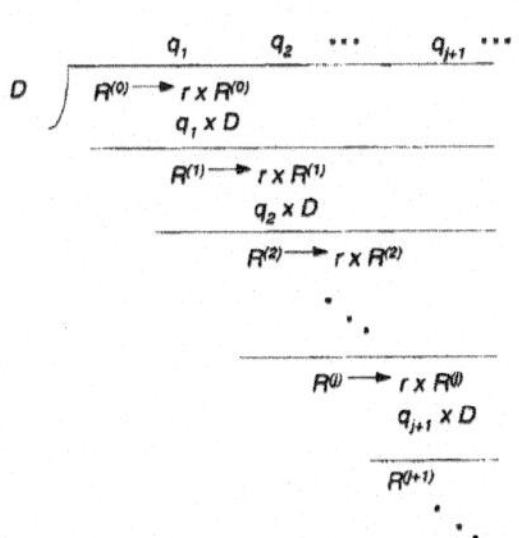

Figure 7.2. Long division form (Hickendorff et al., 2019).

$$D = d_0.d_1d_2\cdots,$$

The symbols located to the right of the values ro as well as do are known as radix points, while the symbols TO as well as do represent signs.

The quotient Q can be defined as a fractional value

$Q = q_0.q_1q_2\cdots q_{n-1}q_n,$

The symbol qo is equivalent to the combination of ro and do. It is postulated that the value of R(O) is less than that of D, and that D is a non-zero positive numerical quantity (Atkins, 1968; Mitchell, 1962; Tanaka et al., 2009). These assumptions are made solely for the purpose of elucidation. In this context, Q is assumed to be less than 1, and if the value of R(O) is twice that of D, it results in a quotient overflow. The procedures depicted in Figure 6.3 are executed in the subsequent manner:

$$\begin{aligned} R^{(1)} &= r \times R^{(0)} - q_1 \times D \\ 0.48 &= 6.08 - 5.60 \end{aligned}$$

$$\begin{aligned} R^{(2)} &= r \times R^{(1)} - q_2 \times D \\ 0.6 &= 4.8 - 4.2. \end{aligned}$$

In the binary numeral system, the sole permissible digits are 0 as well as 1 (Schwemmer et al., 2010). It will be demonstrated subsequently that various arithmetic conditions can significantly streamline the method of selecting quotient digits qj, where j ranges from 1 to n and R(n–1) is the range of possible values, based on distinct processes that utilize R(0), R(1), and so on. By defining R(j+l) as the partial remainder, it follows that:

- Restoring division: 0 5 *R(j+l)* < D;
- Nonrestoring division: I *R(j+l)* 151 *D* I.

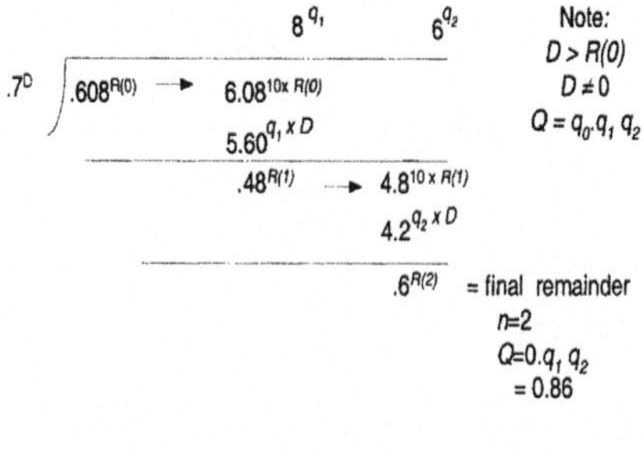

Figure 7.3. Example of long division.

7.2. BINARY RESTORING DIVISION

In the context of conventional recovering division, it can be stated that the value of 0 5 R(j+l) is less than D. The selection of the quotient number q j + l, where j ranges from 0 to n–1, is achieved through a series of shifts as well as subtractions (Qian et al., 2000; Horton, 1976; Sharma & Thakre, 2018).

The partial remaining T x R (j) is repeatedly reduced by the value of D until a negative result is obtained. Subsequently, the negative variance is subjected to a restoring process whereby D is reintroduced. The final subtraction operation is negated by the subsequent addition operation in this context. The quotient digit can be determined based on the count of subtractions, where qj+l = (the number for subtractions –1). Typically, in the most extreme case, it necessitates qj+l + 1 subtraction as well as 1 addition to determine qj+l (Qian et al., 2001; Shah et al., 2015). The provided illustration, denoted as Figure 6.4, serves as an exemplar. In a binary numeral system where the base value is T = 2, there exists the potential for significant enhancement in the extreme case.

$$R^{(j+1)} = r \times R^{(j)} - q_{j+1} \times D$$

With **qj+i** E (0, 1}, 0 *5 R(j+ ')* < D. The digit of the quotient is able to be ascertained in the following manner:

$$q_{j+1} = \begin{cases} 0 & \text{if } 2R^{(j)} < D \\ 1 & \text{if } 2R^{(j)} \geq D. \end{cases}$$

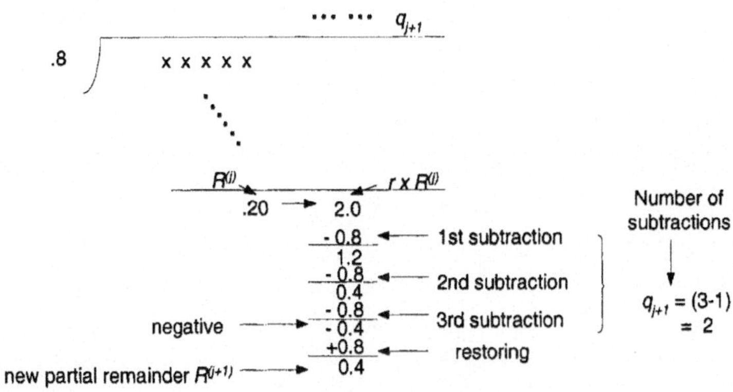

Figure 7.4. Example of restoring procedure.

The partial remainder may be acquired through a single left shift of R(j), while the test procedure can be executed via a single subtraction:

$$R^{(j+1)} = 2R^{(j)} - D.$$

Subsequently, the sign of R(j+l) is verified. In the event that the value is affirmative, the equation qj+l = 1 holds true. Conversely, if the value is negative, the equation qj+l = 0 is applicable and necessitates the execution of a restoring addition (Khosropour et al., 2011; Kaur et al., 2013).

The binary recovering division algorithm necessitates a maximum of one subtraction along with one addition operation for the computation of a single quotient digit. The inclusion of an additional component is necessary in order to rectify the accurate partial remainder:

$$R^{(j+1)} = R^{(j+1)} + D = 2R^{(j)}.$$

Figure 6.5 depicts the hardware execution of the binary recovering division.

The system comprises 3 registers, each consisting of n bits:

1. Accumulator (AC);
2. Auxiliary register (AX); and
3. Quotient-multiplier register (QM).

The storage mechanism for the multiplier within multiplication, as discussed earlier, as well as the container for the ultimate quotient within division activities, are currently being examined.

The initial storage of the 2n-bit dividend occurs in registers AC by combining QM (Jun et al., 2012; Andersen et al., 1994; Robertson, 1958). The AX register holds the divisor of n bits. It is possible to perform a left shift within the concatenation of AC and QM.

The digit qj+l of the quotient is able to be conveniently introduced from the rightmost position, while the bit that is shifted away from the leftmost terminus of AC may be temporarily held in a buffered register denoted as T.

It is evident that the hardware utilized for multiplication may be adapted for division, with the exception of certain modifications made to address the following concerns. In multiplying, the register shift guidelines are towards the right, while for division, it is towards the left. Furthermore, it should be noted that the adder currently executes a subtraction operation by adding the 2's complement representation of the divisor. Figure 6.5 depicts the input AX is situated on the right-hand side within the Adder.

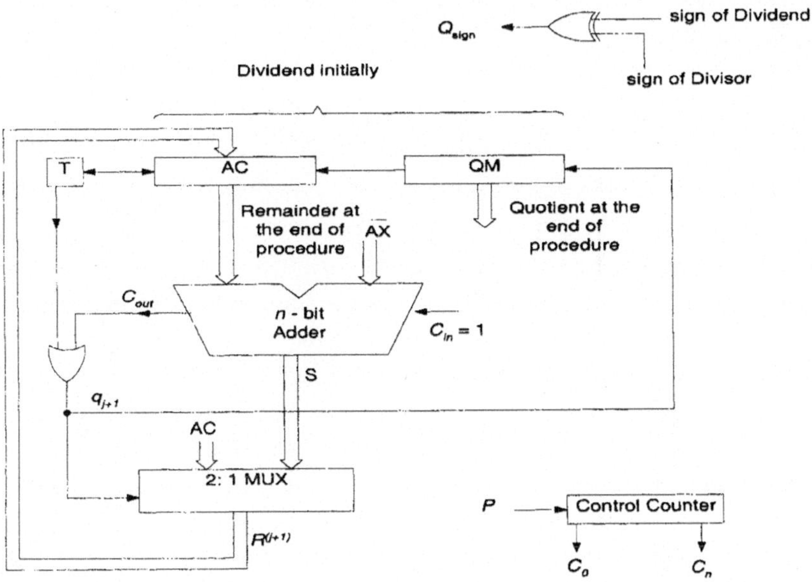

Figure 7.5. Hardware for restoring division (Cui et al., 2014).

The additional component represents the dividend in the 1's complement system. By setting Ci equal to 1, we can observe that AC + AX + 1 is equivalent to AC – AX. This allows us to examine whether 2R(j) is less than either D or 2D (Jain et al., 2014; Schwarz et al., 2007; Lehman, 1958). The term "Cout" refers to the carrying out of a mathematical operation. The quotient number q_{j+1} is derived through a specific process.

$$q_{j+1} = T \vee C_{out},$$

The aforementioned can be elucidated in the following manner. Assuming n to get 4, for the purpose of illustration. At time T = 1, it is true that for any given digit "x," the subsequent statement holds

```
   1 xxxx    ← 2R(j)
–) 1010      ← D, for example
```

It is evident that 2R(j) 2 D, thus it is imperative to establish qj+l = 1. At the point where T equals zero, we obtain the following result. Assuming that Gout is equal to 1, the expression 2R(j) + (2n – D) * 2 * 2n can be simplified to 2R(j) * 2D. Therefore, it is advisable to assign the value of qj+l as 1. The equation qj+l = 1 holds true when either T equals 1 or Gout equals 1. A restoring operation takes place when the value of D is less than 2 times the value of R(j). Addition cancels out subtraction, while the partial remainder remains unaltered. The equation qj+l = 0 holds true in this particular scenario. In lieu of the process of deducting D and subsequently reintroducing it, a 2-to-1 multiplexer is employed. This multiplexer has the capability to choose the unaltered partial remainder as well as direct it through if the command signal qj+1 equals zero. When qj+1 equals 1, the MUX selects the variance for 2R(j) – D as its additional input data.

As the fractional remainder is successively shifted away from the leftmost bit sets for record AC o Q M, additional bit positions become accessible on the right side of the register for the quotient (Kaur et al., 2013; Jun & Swartzlander, 2012). The allotted space to accommodate the partial remainder has been decreased from its initial size of 2n bits towards n bits, while the space allocated for the quotient has been expanded to n bits. The ultimate residue denoted as R (“) shall be situated within the range of To AC1ACZ. Acn–l, representing its corresponding numerical value. It is necessary to iterate the compare-and-shift functioning n times, as well as the process of loading the provided operands requires a single cycle. The binary recovering division algorithm necessitates an additional cycle, resulting in a total of twice the number of cycles (Andersen et al., 1994; Sasamal et al., 2016).

7.3. BINARY NON-RESTORING DIVISION

The binary non-restoring dividing method represents an enhanced approach to the division that eliminates the requirement for the previously discussed “restoring addition.” It is assumed that D is greater than zero and the absolute value of IR(j+1) is less than D.

These assumptions remain constant while the fractional remainder, R(j+1), is permitted to take on positive or negative values (Nair et al., 2006; Sayedsalehi et al., 2015; Ercegovac et al., 1994). The arithmetic procedure to be executed is contingent upon the partial remainder and may consist of either subtraction or just addition. Insufficient information to provide an academic rewrite. Please provide more context or the full text for me to work with,

$$R^{(j+1)} = \begin{cases} 2R^{(j)} - D & \text{if } 2R^{(j)} > 0 \\ 2R^{(j)} + D & \text{if } 2R^{(j)} < 0. \end{cases}$$

Thus, it can be inferred that the digit of the quotient must be either a positive one or a negative one, excluding zero. In other words, qi+l belongs to the set of {1, –1}. The process of selecting the quotient number is explicated as follows:

$$q_{(j+1)} = \begin{cases} 1 & \text{if } 0 < 2R^{(j)} < D \\ -1 & \text{if } -D < 2R^{(j)} < 0. \end{cases}$$

The process is able to be ended when the value of 2R(j) equals zero. Consequently, the quotient Q is denoted by a signed-digit code that does not comprise any zeros. The numeral 1 is represented as the symbol "1." In the process of restoring division, it is observed that if the value of 2R(j) – D is less than zero, then the remainder will be regenerated to 2R(j). Upon performing a shift and subsequent subtraction of D, the resulting expression is 4R(j) – D. In the context of non-restoring division, while the difference between 2 times the remainder at iteration j along with the divisor is negative, the negative disparity is retained and rectified by adding the divisor in the subsequent iteration. By utilizing the equation 2(2R(j) – D) + D = 4R(j) – D, it is possible to derive the identical outcome as previously mentioned. In the context of division algorithms, it has been observed that when the digits qj and qj+1 in the quotient sequence are consecutive and equal to 01 in the restored division, they are represented as li within the non-restoring divisions (Tan, 1978; Cortadella et al., 1994).

Evidently, the numerical value 01 corresponds to the chemical element lithium (Li) in the periodic table.

Figure 6.6(a) illustrates the execution of binary non-restoring division (B.N.D.) on the sum of 0.001011 and 0.01, while (b) depicts the binary restoring division (B.R.D.) for the same operation.

The BND method eliminates the need for restoration, thereby enabling the elimination of the MUX depicted in Figure 6.5. As a result, the duration of cell division is enhanced. Noticing That

$$\begin{aligned} \Delta_T(B.N.D) \quad &\alpha \quad n \times (\text{subtraction or addition}) \\ \Delta_T(B.R.D) \quad &\alpha \quad n \times (\text{subtraction} + \text{restoration}), \end{aligned}$$

We have:

$$\Delta_T(B.R.D.) > \Delta_T(B.N.D.).$$

In the context of signed digit representations, it may be necessary to alter the quotient into a format that is compatible with additional operands, including 2's complement form (Ercegovac et al., 1993; Schwarz et al., 1991). This conversion can be executed with ease by following the following steps. Given the total of weights for all positive digits as Q+ and the total of weights for all negative digits as Q-, we can derive the following equation

$$Q{+}{+}Q{-} = Q$$

$Q+\text{-}Q - 1 - 2^{-n}$

Given that any position in Q+ that contains a 0 is accompanied by a corresponding 1 in Q-, it follows that the difference between Q+ and Q– is equal to 0.11… By summing Equation (6.1) as well as Equation (6.2), we obtain the following result.

$2Q+ = Q + 1 - 2\text{-}n$

or

$Q = 2Q + -1 + 2\text{-}.''$

The value of 2Q+ can be derived through a process of left-shifting Q+ via one-bit position. A value of –1 indicates that the sign should be inverted following the shift, while a value of +2-n signifies the insertion of a 1 in the least significant bit position that becomes available after the shift. The variable Q is not taken into consideration in this context (Montuschi & Lang, 2001; Chen et al., 2018).

If a partial remainder becomes zero during the process of division, it indicates that all subsequent digits in the quotient will also be zero. It is possible to devise a circuitry for detecting a 0 remainder, which would enable the algorithm to promptly terminate upon encountering such a value.

Traditionally, it is customary for the ultimate remainder to possess the identical sign to be the dividend. In the event that the sum of 7 and 4 yields a quotient of 2 with a remainder of –1, it is necessary to perform an appropriate adjustment. Specifically, the quotient should be modified to 1 by subtracting 1 from the original quotient of 2. Additionally, the remainder should be adjusted to 3 by adding 4 to the original remainder of –1. In the context of binary non-restoring division, it can be observed that when the dividend along with divisor share the same sign, then the quotient (Q) can be computed as Q = Q – 2-n, while the remainder (R) can be computed as R = R + D. In cases where the dividend along with divisor possess opposite signs, the necessary adjustment is able to be executed through the application of the formula Q = Q + 2-n as well as R = R – D.

The two, restoring division along with non-restoring division algorithms require a significant number of shifts that are directly proportional to the input size n, as well as the time complexity T. The adoption of high-radix divisions might act as a means to enhance lightning-fast division operations. The methodology pertaining to this matter will be deliberated upon in the subsequent section.

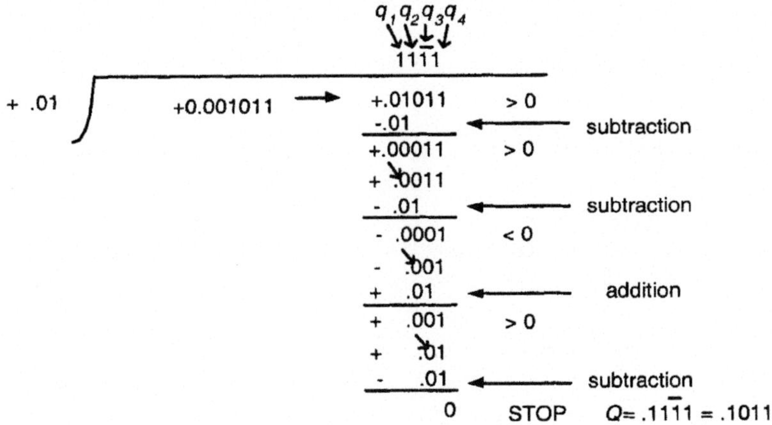

Figure 7.6. Binary non-restoring division (Lang & Montuschi, 1995).

7.4. HIGH-RADIX DIVISION

The division techniques that were previously delineated are based on radix 2, where the value of radix r is 2, and the digit set E is comprised of l-bit strings within the range of (0, l}. The radix 4 division has been defined by a value of r equal to 4, and a digit set consisting of 2-bit strings {00, 01, 10, 11}.

The process of division within radix 8 involves a radix value of 8 as well as a digit set denoted by E, which comprises 3-bit strings including 000, 001, 010, 011, 100, 101, 110, as well as 111. In the context of mathematical computations, when the value of r is equal to 2, the corresponding scenario is commonly known as high-radix division. As previously stated, the utilization of high-radix division results in expedited execution time due to the decreased number of repetitions required for a dividend of a specific size. Nonetheless, the subsequent subsections will elucidate that the aforementioned augmented velocity is accompanied by amplified hardware costs (Schwarz & Flynn, 1993; Bashagha & Ibrahim, 1995; Stine & Hill, 2020).

7.4.1. High-Radix Non-Restoring Division

It is important to note that with binary non-restoring divisions, the set of quotient numbers is {–1, 1}, excluding 0. In the context of high-radix non-restoring divisions, the set of quotient numbers is defined as {-(r-l), …, –1,

1, …, (r–l)}, where r represents the radix (Krishnamoorthy & Tekumalla, 2013). An illustration of radix-4 non-restoring division can be demonstrated by considering a quotient number set E that comprises {–3, –2, –1, 1, 2, 3}, given that r = 4. Once more, it can be observed that –0 is less than Rj which is less than 0, indicating that –40 is less than 4R(j) which is less than 40, as previously stated (Wang et al., 2012; Sutter & Deschamps, 2009). There are several options available for gj+l:

$$q_{j+1} = \begin{cases} -3 & \text{if } -4D < 4R^{(j)} < -3D \\ -3 \text{ or } -2 & \text{if } -3D < 4R^{(j)} < -2D \\ -2 \text{ or } -1 & \text{if } -2D < 4R^{(j)} < -D \\ -1 & \text{if } -D < 4R^{(j)} < 0 \\ +1 & \text{if } 0 < 4R^{(j)} < D \\ +1 \text{ or } +2 & \text{if } D < 4R^{(j)} < 2D \\ +2 \text{ or } +3 & \text{if } 2D < 4R^{(j)} < 3D \\ +3 & \text{if } 3D < 4R^{(j)} < 4D. \end{cases}$$

It should be noted that the result obtained through the non-restoring division constitutes a signed-digit code within radix-r,

$$Q = .q_1 q_2 \cdots q_n$$

For every value of q within the set of integers ranging from negative (r-l) to positive (r-l), inclusive. Hence, it may be necessary to convert a radix-r signed-digit number into an ordinary radix-complement shape, for instance,

$$Q = q_0.q'_1 q'_2 \cdots q'_n$$

with each *q:* **E** (0, 1,…, (T – 1)) &

$$q_0 = \begin{cases} 0 & \text{for a positive number} \\ 1 & \text{for a negative number.} \end{cases}$$

7.4.2. SRT Division

The acronym SRT is derived from the surnames of its creators, namely Sweeney, Robertson, along with Tocher. Simultaneously and autonomously, D. W. Sweeney from IBM, J. E. Robertson from the University of Illinois, as well as K. D. Tocher from Imperial College, London, devised a novel technique for performing binary division. The method assumes that the divisor represents an adjusted fraction within the form 0.14…d, where 1 < ID1 < 1. It is also postulated that 1 – < (2R(j)I < 1,2, thereby implying that the entire partial dividends are expressed as normalized sections (Juang et al., 2008; Harris et al., 1997). It is important to note that the partial dividends are generally equal to T times the partial remainder. In contrast to the non-restoring dividing algorithm, *qj.+l* E **{–1,** 1},

$q_{j+1} \in \{-1, 0, 1\}$

The task at hand is to choose from the set of integers {–1, 0, 1}. In this case, the divisor is either moved, added alongside, or minus from the selective dividend

$$R^{j+1} = \begin{cases} 2R^{(j)} + D, & \text{if } 2R^{(j)} < -D, \\ 2R^{(j)}, & \text{if } -D \leq 2R^{(j)} \leq D, \\ 2R^{(j)} - D, & \text{if } 2R^{(j)} > D. \end{cases}$$

The procedure for determining the quotient number qj+l can be described as follows:

$$q_{j+1} = \begin{cases} -1 & \text{if } 2R^{(j)} < -D, \\ 0 & \text{if } -D \leq 2R^{(j)} \leq D, \end{cases}$$

It is noteworthy that the divisor, denoted as D, and the portion of the dividend, represented as 2R(j)a, are expressed as normalized fractions, where f < (DI < 1 as well as $ < 12R(j)I < 1. The utilization of the identifier results in a reduction of the comparison

$$R^{j+1} = \begin{cases} 2R^{(j)} + D, & \text{if } 2R^{(j)} \leq -\frac{1}{2}, \\ 2R^{(j)}, & \text{if } -\frac{1}{2} < 2R^{(j)} \leq \frac{1}{2}, \\ 2R^{(j)} - D, & \text{if } 2R^{(j)} \geq \frac{1}{2}, \end{cases}$$

The quotient selecting rule may be simplified as such:

$$q_{j+1} = \begin{cases} -1, & \text{if } |2R^{(j)}| > \frac{1}{2}, \text{ and sign of } 2R^{(j)} \text{ is negative}, \\ 0, & \text{if } |2R^{(j)}| \leq \frac{1}{2}, \\ +1, & \text{if } |2R^{(j)}| > \frac{1}{2}, \text{ and sign of } 2R^{(j)} \text{ is positive}. \end{cases}$$

The utilization of this novel set of regulations for ascertaining R(j+l) and qj+l offers a distinct advantage as solely comparing the value of 2R(j) with the constant f or –f is necessary (Kornerup, 2005).

7.4.3. Modified SRT Division

Wilson and Ledley have presented a revised variant of the SRT algorithm, aimed at minimizing the number of subtracting and adding operations involved in the division process. The present methodology operates under the assumption that the divisor D represents a positive, adjusted fraction, while the dividend N seems either normalized or contains a maximum of one zero following the binary point (Rueß et al., 1996; McQuillan et al., 1993; Clarke et al., 1996). The inequality N < D remains valid as previously stated. The flow chart depicted in Figure outlines the algorithm. The repeated procedure is initiated by the user:

N(s) = N(s–1) – *D.*

If there are zeros to the right for the binary point within the partial remainder N('), Y quotient digits may be identified in a single iteration. In the event that N (s) is less than zero, as is the case during the initial iteration as per the aforementioned assumption, the newly created quotient digit qi is to be assigned a value of zero, and subsequently appended with (a – 1) ones to its right. The forthcoming iterative procedure will execute NS = MS – 1 + D. In the case where N(') is equal to zero, assign the value of one to qi and append a sequence of (a – 1) zeros to its right. The subsequent iterative procedure will execute N(') = N('-l) – D. The index for each quotient number gets raised by the sum of LY in every iteration. Upon reaching the target number of bits within the quotient, the procedure terminates. The numerical example presented in Figure serves as a means of verifying the procedure. The result yielded by this approach will be in a reduced form, albeit not necessarily in canonical form, when normalized divisors are employed (Wey & Wang, 1999; Burgess & Williams, 1995; McCann & Pippenger, 2005).

7.4.4. Robertson's High-Radix Division

The present discourse aims to provide a generalized version of the SRT division algorithm, as initially introduced by Robertson. This generalization involves the incorporation of an arbitrary radix, denoted as "r," as well as a quotient number set, represented by "qj+1" and comprising elements from the set {-m, ..., –1, 0, 1, –*., m}. It is worth noting that the condition (r – 1) I m 5 r – 1 holds true in this context. The process of selecting successive quotient numbers must adhere to the recursive formula, which involves the addition of the quotient digit (j) and the divisor digit (l) to obtain the product (r) that is then multiplied by the divisor (Pan et al., 1995; Clarke et al., 1999; McQuillan et al., 1993). This results in a partial remaining one that must always be subtracted from the dividend to continue the process.

qj+l x D, JR(jfl)I 5 k x JDJ,

Given a constant k, where k is less than or equal to 1. There are specific discrete values of k within a particular range for which division methods are applicable

1 – 2 < –*k* < *l.*

In the case where k equals 1, the division method utilized is the non-restoring division, as previously discussed in section 6.2. A comprehensive examination of all potential scenarios indicates that

4j+l I *k* (*r* – 1).

The division approach known as Robertson's method comprises a sequence of three distinct steps:

- In the first step, the fractional remainder R(j) undergoes a left shift by one digital setting.
- In the second step, a suitable arithmetic procedure is chosen from a set of permissible methods. The chosen procedure aims to decrease the maximum total value of rlR(j)I through a quantity of l h (Ibrahem et al., 2003). It should be noted that as a result of disparities in various aspects, such as socioeconomic status, there exists inequality,

TIR(j)I 5 TklDI.

IR(j+l)[5 k x *[DI.*

Due to identical reasons, the subsequent partial remainder R(j+1) fulfills the condition. In accordance with the chosen arithmetic method, a digit representing the quotient is produced. This constitutes the third step.

The execution of the arithmetic method is crucial in achieving the reduction stated in Step 2. The objective is to identify a suitable value for qj+l in the equation R(jfl) = T x R(j) – qj+l x D, which can transform T+ into ~(jflL)e.t. The range of qj+l is – rn,..., –2, –1, 0, +1, +2,..., m, where IT] r – 1 < m < (T – 1).

The objective is to plot R(j+l) against r R(j) on a Cartesian coordinate system. When the sum of qj and l equals zero, R(j+l) corresponds to a line with a slope of 45° passing through the origin. A set of discrete figures for q corresponds to an assortment of lines alongside a constant slope, commonly known as q-lines (Burgess, 1991; Kornerup, 2005). According to the inequality (6.3), the value of Rj+' must be limited by kl DI, while the value of rR(j) must be limited by rkJDI. It should be noted that in the given equation, f equals 5 and k equals 1. Thus, it is possible to construct a rectangle alongside vertices (rklDI, klDI), (rklDI, –klDl), (–rklDl, –klDI), as well as (-rklDl, k/DI), within which the q-lines are constrained. The diagram depicted in the figure is commonly known as Robertson's schematic. It is advisable to reduce the number of q-lines in order to decrease the number of divisor multiples that require preparation. Maximizing the overlapping of estimates of the q-lines is necessary to ensure precision. The two stipulations conflict with one another (McQuillan et al., 1994; Wang et al., 1996). Given that the q-line up on the right front of the rectangle must pass via the vertex located in the top right corner, the coordinates (rklDI, klDI) are substituted into the equation.

$$R^{(j+1)} = r \times R^{(j)} - m \times |D|$$

To determine the value of k, and ascertain its solution

$$k = \frac{m}{r-1}.$$

Since $k >$ _ $, we have

, we have

$$m \geq \frac{r-1}{2}.$$

Conversely, it can be observed that q3 is equal to 3T–1, and one of the potential values of qj is rn where r is greater than or equal to 3 and less than or equal to r – 1. The range has been limited for rn

$$\frac{r-1}{2} \leq m \leq r-1.$$

7.5. CONVERGENCE DIVISION

The division computations expounded in the aforementioned sections are founded upon the technique of successive subtraction as well as shift. This section presents an alternative methodology (Tan, 1978; Bashagha et al., 1995; Parhami, 2003).

The envisioned quotient can be generated through the execution of iterative multiplications. Hence, the identical hardware that is employed for multiplication may additionally be utilized for division. The suggested approach involves treating the dividend as well as the divisor to be the numerators and denominators, respectively, of a fraction. The fraction's value stays constant as it is subjected to multiplication by an identical sequence of convergent factors. As the denominator approaches a value of 1, the resulting quotient is achieved by the corresponding increase within the numerator.

7.5.1. Convergence Division Methodologies

The division functioning can be represented as Q = N/D, when Q denotes the quotient or just fraction, N represents the numerator or just dividend, alongside D stands for the denominator or just divisor. The repeated procedure of the integration division approach involves multiplying the numerator as well as the denominator through a fixed factor, R, for a specified number of iterations, denoted by i = 0, I,..., m. This results in the denominator, D. (n: Ri), converging to 1 at an exponential rate, as shown below. Consequently, the numerator, N. (n:z," Ri), also converges towards the intended quotient Q at an exponential rate (Parhami, 2001; Fenwick, 1996). That is,

$$\frac{N}{D} = Q$$

$$\frac{N \times R_0 \times R_1 \times \cdots \times R_m}{D \times R_0 \times R_1 \times \cdots R_m} = Q.$$

When m is of a significant magnitude,

$$D \times R_0 \times R_1 \times \cdots \times R_m \longrightarrow 1$$

$$N \times R_0 \times R_1 \times \cdots \times R_m \longrightarrow Q.$$

The operations performed are devoid of division, similar to binary SRT divisions. Insufficient information to provide an academic rewrite. Please provide more context or the full text,

$$D_i \rightarrow 1.0,$$

It is assumed that N along with D are binary portions that have been normalized as well as are positive

$$\frac{1}{2} \leq N < 1$$

$$\frac{1}{2} \leq D < 1.$$

A commonly accepted guideline for selecting the consecutive multipliers Ri, where i ranges from 0 to m, is as follows:

$$D < D_0 < D_1 < D_2 \cdots < D_i$$

$$\begin{cases} D_0 = D \times R_0 \\ D_1 = D_0 \times R_1 = D \times R_0 \times R_1 \\ D_2 = D_1 \times R_2 = D \times R_0 \times R_1 \times R_2 \\ \vdots \\ D_i = D_{i-1} \times R_i = D \times R_0 \times \cdots\cdots \times R_i. \end{cases}$$

Ultimately, when the value of i equals m,

$$D_i \rightarrow 1.0,$$

That is.

$$D_m = D \times R_0 \times \cdots \times R_m \rightarrow 1.0.$$

There exist multiple methods for selecting the factor R is; however, our focus is on methods that are exponential or in greater order. It is worth noting that the expression (1 + zn)(l – zn) is equivalent to 1 – x2n. As hypothesized, the inequality \$5D < 1\$ holds, where \$D\$ is an adjusted fraction. Consequently, there exists a pair of normalized fractions \$D\$ and \$E\$ such that their sum is equal to 1, i.e., \$D + E = 1\$. It is evident that,

$$\varepsilon > 0 \quad \text{since} \quad D < 1$$

Since,

$$\varepsilon \leq \frac{1}{2} \quad \text{since} \quad D \geq \frac{1}{2},$$

And,

$$0 < \varepsilon \leq \frac{1}{2}.$$

Since,

$$D = 1 - \varepsilon$$

Let us now select the initial factor for multiplication,

$$R_0 = 1 + \varepsilon.$$

Hence,

$$\begin{aligned} D_0 &= D \times R_0 \\ &= D \times (1 + \varepsilon) \\ &= (1 - \varepsilon) \times (1 + \varepsilon) \\ &= 1 - \varepsilon^2 (= 1 - \varepsilon^{2^1}). \end{aligned}$$

Thus,

$D_1 = D_0 \times R_1 \quad (D_i = D_{i-1} \times R_i)$. Hence,

$$\begin{aligned} R_1 &= 1 + \varepsilon^2, \\ D = 1 - \varepsilon &< D_0 = 1 - \varepsilon^2. \end{aligned}$$

The expression denotes the complementary pair of Di-1, which is equivalent to the product of D, Ro, R1, and so on up to Ri-1. The value of Ri can be derived by computing the two-digit complement for Di-1, which is calculated from the preceding iteration (Schwarz & Flynn, 1991; Arrighi et al., 2003).

7.5.2. Divider Implementing Convergence Division Algorithm

The algorithm for the division of convergence, originally delineated, has been executed in various commercial computing systems, like the IBM 360.

The IBM 360 system represents D as an adjusted floating-point portion with 56 bits adhering to the binary point, where x is multiplied by 0.1,

$$\frac{1}{2} \leq D < 1$$

$$\varepsilon = 1 - D \leq \frac{1}{2}$$

The variable "yield" is a string. The value 1.0 appears as 0.11…1 with an accuracy of 56 bits. As per the information provided by the source,

$$1.00 \cdots 0\bar{1} = 1 - 2^{-56}.$$

It is highly probable that a discrepancy of 2–56 may occur. It is important to remember that

$$1 - D_m \leq 2^{-56}.$$

$$\left(\frac{1}{2}\right)^{2^{(m+1)}} \leq 2^{-56}.$$

7.6. DIVISION BY DIVISOR RECIPROCATION

This section introduces an alternative technique over division by two that utilizes multiplication proximity (Arrighi et al., 2003). This technique can be executed iteratively with uncomplicated logic circuits. Let us demonstrate the division operation in the following manner:

$$\begin{aligned} -2^{(m+1)} &\leq -56 \\ 2^{(m+1)} &\geq 56 \\ m &\geq log_2 56 - 1 \\ m &= \lceil 5.8 - 1 \rceil = 5. \end{aligned}$$

The inverse of D is denoted by D in academic discourse. Let us consider the assumption that D has become a positive as well as an adjusted fraction,

$$D > 0,$$

$$\frac{1}{2} \leq D < 1,$$

$$2 \geq \frac{1}{D} > 1.$$

$$\frac{1}{r} \leq N$$

is assumed.

The determination of the value of D cannot be achieved through the utilization of the reciprocal of D, as this would result in a circular argument that returns to the initial division problem (Thorogood et al., 2001). Another technique involves utilizing a convergence method to iteratively determine and finalize the division through the reciprocation for the divisor. Initially, it is recommended to obtain an estimated value of the variable $ through the use of table lookup or just combinational circuits. A Read-Only Memory (ROM) can be utilized for this particular objective. Let us consider a variable p, denoted by $, and let po indicate the starting proximity of p. Initially, a PO is chosen and subsequently refined iteratively to approach p.

Suppose that

$$D = 0.1d_2d_3 \cdots d_n$$

$$\frac{1}{2} \leq D < 1;$$

$$(0.10 \cdots 0)_2 \leq D < 1.$$

The set of 2j figures is denoted as 0.1.d2d3.+ dj+l, can be utilized in order to divide the spectrum of D, spanning from (0.10...0)2 towards 1, into 2j sub-ranges. The size of any given sub-range is equal to f / 2 j, which can be expressed as 2-(j+l). Let "s" denote the indexes of the aforementioned sub-ranges. The variable D must be assigned to a specific sub-range. In the event that j equals 2, there exist four sub-ranges, namely [0.1@, 0.101), [O.lOl, 0.1 lo), [O.llO, 0.1 11), and [O.lU, 1.000). Upon analysis of the binary representation of D = 0.1 10 11111, it can be inferred that the value of D lies within the third sub-interval, where the value of s is equal to 3, based on the examination of the jth bit, where j is equal to 2. Upon obtaining the value of D within the sth sub-range, where s is a positive integer ranging from 1 to 2j, the midpoint within said sub-range is determined (Kyriakidou et al., 2011). The beginning value, indicated as Po, is determined by taking the reciprocal corresponding to the middle point value. The aforementioned methodology may be executed through the utilization of a read-only memory (ROM) table. The j bits have the potential to serve as the input for the Read-Only Memory (ROM). The ROM chart can accommodate a total of 23 entries, with each entry related to a specific sub-range as previously indicated. The ROM generates starting reciprocal proximity by listing the reciprocal measurement of the middle point value for a sub-range PO to be output. If a restricted quantity of bits, denoted as k bits, is employed for representing it, the ROM table encompasses Ic outputs. Due to the relatively smaller sizes of j and Ic in comparison to n, the use of ROM seems a cost-effective approach.

It should be noted that, based on the given equation, where 1 is less than 5, we can conclude that the value of wj is an integer of 1. As a result, there is no requirement for storing the radix point within ROM. The presented data in Table 6.1 exhibits a Read-Only Memory (ROM) alongside an input number of j = 2 as well as an output size of k = 4. It is noteworthy that the value 2122×324 solely represents the fractional component of the variable po. The calculation of PO, which must be computed prior to its storage in ROM, is able to be achieved using the formula presented below, where j and s are given.

$$p_0(s) = \frac{2^{j+1}}{2^j + s - \frac{1}{2}}.$$

This is due to the subsequent factors. According to the principle of 1/2, if the value of D is situated within the sub-range denoted as s, the addition of s numerous of the total length for the sub-range, along with the subtraction of 50% of the sub-range size, yields the values of the center,

$$\frac{1}{2} + s \times 2^{-(j+1)} - \frac{1}{2} \times 2^{-(j+1)}.$$

7.7. FAST ARRAY DIVIDERS

This chapter delves into the design along with the construction of diverse high-speed recursive cellular arrays that facilitate parallel divisions (Shinn, 2000; Kong & Swartzlander, 2009). The suggested array dividers employ a significant number of duplicated units to facilitate the comparability of the limited remainder as well as a divisor, while the shift operation is implemented through physical wiring. The introduction of three distinct categories of array dividers is forthcoming.

1. The restoration of array dividers;
2. The non-restoration of array dividers; and
3. The carry-lookahead array dividers.

Furthermore, an analysis of their performance as well as cost-effectiveness is required.

7.7.1. Restoring Cellular Array Divider

It is founded on the Repairing Division Algorithm. Please refer to Figure for the circuit diagram illustrating the divider that utilizes the restoring division approach. The register is utilized to retain partial remainders, which are subsequently subjected to subtractions using a two-operand adder. The MUX is responsible for executing restorations. The hardware utilized for this methodology is rudimentary in nature, albeit lacking in speed and efficiency (Ito et al., 1995). The implementation of the cell-based array divider for restoration purposes, as demonstrated below, can significantly enhance the speed of execution.

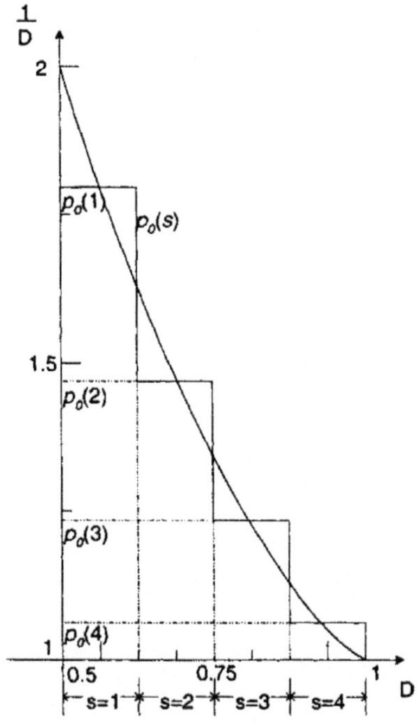

Figure 7.7. Stepwise approximation of the reciprocal of divisor (Park et al., 2015).

Consider the dividend A represented as.a102.–+a2nd.iv and divisor D represented as.dld2…d, with quotient Q represented as.qlq2… qn. The schematic logic representation of a regaining array divider alongside dimensions n-by-n and n = 4 is depicted in Figure 7.1. The illustrated component is a regulated subtracter cell that executes a subtraction operation between an as well as d when mode P equals 0. This operation determines the discrepancy within the divisor as well as the preceding partial remainder. The borrow signal

$$c_{out} = \bar{a}d + \bar{a}c_{in} + dc_{in},$$

and the variation

$$s = aP + ad\bar{c}_{in} + adc_{in} + \bar{a}d\bar{c}_{in}\bar{P} + \bar{a}\bar{d}c_{in}\bar{P},$$

That is,

$$s = \begin{cases} a \oplus d \oplus c_{in} & \text{if } P = 0 \text{ (subtract)}, \\ a & \text{if } P = 1 \text{ (no operation)}. \end{cases}$$

Instead of left-shifting the partial remaining ones to form rR(j), a comparable approach involves keeping the rest of the number fixed along with right-shifting the divisor in tandem with the diagonals. Quantum information states (QIS) are acquired from the left-hand side of every row (Sergeyev, 1998).

$$q_i = a_i + \bar{c}_{out},$$

The variable "ai" represents the bit that has been shifted out during the $(i - 1)^{th}$ repetition. The subtraction operation is deemed successful while the value of ai is equal to 1, indicating that rR(j) is greater than D. In the event that c' denotes the borrow-out signal located within the leftmost place of every row and E' equals 1, a value of c' equaling 0, indicating no borrow, results in an efficient subtraction (Kyriakidou et al., 2011). The control signal is denoted by the symbol P.

$$P = \begin{cases} 0 & \text{if performing subtraction}, \\ 1 & \text{no operation}. \end{cases}$$

Here,

$$P = \bar{q}_i.$$

The values of P = 0 and qi = 1 correspond to instances where the subtraction operation is successful. Conversely, the values of P = 1 and qi = 0 correspond to instances where no operation is performed. It should be noted that during the process of restoring division, it is necessary to add the fractional part back in the event of an ineffective subtraction. The 2 operations exhibited a mutual nullification, resulting in the absence of any further operation to be executed. In the aforementioned example, the ultimate residual value is denoted as O.OOOOrgrgr7r8. Typically, a restoring binary cell-based array divider of size n x n is designed to accept a dividend of 2n bits and a divisor of n bits and subsequently generates an n-bit quotient as well as a 2n-bit remaining ones that contains n leading zeros (Kyriakidou et al., 2009).

It should be noted that the AND-OR logical relationship is able to be implemented through the use of NAND-NAND gates. Additionally, it is possible to execute the corresponding logical function for a time frame of 30 units. An array with dimensions of n x n must be used for division involving n bits.

The propagation of signals via providing information to results out within a CS cell requires a duration of 30-time units, given the availability of ci. Parallel transmission can be accomplished for all of the CS cells within a given row. The transmission of the signal that goes from the source pin towards the resultant cOvt requires a duration of 2 0. The lag times of all cells in a given row, with the exception of the rightmost cell where overlap alongside the lag from a till cOvt is possible, are cumulative for the remaining (n–1) cells. The expression denotes a cumulative delay of 2 multiplied by the difference between the number of nodes (n) and the number of links (l), multiplied by the propagation delay (Ag). For c' to be looped again into P off the left-hand side of each row, a total of four zero operations are required. The attainment of output s, which represents the parallel lag period between all cells in a given row, necessitates the utilization of 30 units subsequent to the preparation of P (Kazaura et et al., 2010). Therefore, with regard to the initial row, the cumulative duration of the delay is determined

$$[3 + 2(n - 1) + 4 + 3]\Delta_g = (2n + 8)\Delta_g.$$

In subsequent rows, specifically the 2nd and all subsequent ones, the final cell on the right-hand side is independent of the variable "s" from the preceding row. The signal of the tout within the aforementioned cell has the potential to be prepared in advance, resulting in a temporal overlap alongside the delay period necessary for the processes in the top row. A parallel tardiness time of 30 is necessary for the signal to be transmitted from the source (s) or input (a) to the output (cou) for the cell located second from the right as well as the (n–2) cells that are to the left. Subsequently, a delay time of 2(n – 2)A must be accumulated over the transmission of cin to tout towards the left part of the row. The inclusion of the 4A to provide feedback to D, along with the utilization of 30 over P towards s propagation, are noteworthy aspects to consider,

$$[3+2(n-2)+4+3]\Delta_g=2n+6\Delta_g$$

A certain amount of time is necessary for the completion of each row, with the exception of the initial row. The number of rows that meet the given criteria is (n – 1). Therefore, the cumulative delay for these rows is:

$[(2n+6)\times(n-1)]\Delta_{g=2n}{}^{2}+4n-6\Delta_{g.}$

Incorporating the delay of the initial row, the cumulative delay duration of the restorative cell-based array divider is expressed as follows:

$$[(2n+8)+(2n^2+4n-6)]\Delta_g = 2n^2+6n+2\Delta_g.$$

The requisite quantity of controlled subtracters (CS) is equivalent to n_2. Around 14 gates are observed in every CS cell. Upon considering the presence of a single OR gate as well as two NOT gates located at the far-left end of each row, it can be observed that an additional count for 3n yields is incurred (Waller et al., 1990). The total gate measure of the reestablishing array divider can be calculated by summing the number of gates utilized in the circuit.

$$14n^{2}+3n.$$

The area complexities of the reestablishing array divider can be calculated by utilizing NAND-NAND gates in order to perform the AND-OR operation, with each gate that requires a volume of 1 A:

$$\begin{aligned} & 14(n\times n)A_g + (A_{OR}+2A_{NOT})\times n \\ = \; & 14n\times nA_G + (2+2)nA_g \\ = \; & (14n^2+4n)A_g. \end{aligned}$$

7.8. NON-RESTORING CELLULAR ARRAY DIVIDER

It should be noted that within the non-restoring divisions, there is no need for restoration. The sole mathematical operation available is limited to either subtracting or adding. Partial leftovers are obtained by subtracting or adding repeatedly right-shifted kinds of divisors that constitute the dividend.

The determination to use the quotient bit along with the decision to add or just subtract the relocated divisor within the subsequent cycle are contingent upon the sign for the fractional remainder. It should be noted that the utilization of 2's complement computations enables the facile handling and implementation of addition and subtraction through hardware (Freixas et al., 2021).

Consider dividend A represented as a product of its digits a_0, a_1, a_2, ..., a_{2n}. Similarly, let divisor D be represented as d_0, d_1, d_2, ..., d_n. The quotient

Q can be expressed as q_0, q_1, q_2, …, q_n. It presumes that the variables being used are positive as well as adjusted fractions, where a_0 and do are both equal to zero, as well as a_1 and d_1 are both equal to one. Given that $ 5 (A, D) < 1, it follows that Amin/D, <Q < Amas/Dmin, and therefore f < Q < 2. In order to execute the n-bit perpendicular non-restoring divisions, it is necessary to utilize a non-restoring array divider with dimensions of (n + 1)-by-(n + 1). The illustrated logic representation of a 5-by-5 non-restoring set divider is depicted in Figure 7.2. The division being performed is a 4-bit division, eliminating bit 0, where n + 1 equals 5. It should be noted that the variables q_0, a_0, as well as do are implicated in the current operation. Whereas the restoring array divider that was previously described does not utilize them for computational purposes. Furthermore, it can be observed that in the context of the array divider delineated in this particular section, the variable Q no longer retains its status as a signed-digit value. The given number is represented in 2's complement notation (Squillero & Tonda, 2016).

The non-restoring array division algorithm is comprised of multiple rows of carry-propagate additives. Every logic cell within the array is composed of a full adder as well as an exclusive OR gate. The limited remainder remains constant while the divisor undergoes a rightward bit-by-bit shift. The XOR gate regulates the divisor input that is fed into the entire adder. The command signal denoted by P is utilized to determine the arithmetic operation to be executed, either subtracting or adding. The process of subtraction is executed in 2's complement representation by generating the 1's complement corresponding to the divisor after which introducing a carry through the least significant bit.

The signal indicating carry-out from the leftmost cell serves as an indicator of the partial remainder's sign. The value of the quotient digit, qi, is contingent upon a certain factor. In the event that the limited remainder is less than zero, the value of qi shall be assigned as zero. In cases where the portion of the remainder is greater than zero, the quotient qi is assigned a value of one. The quotient bit derived from the preceding iteration, as depicted in the top row, serves as the controlling signal P over the selection of subtracting or adding in the subsequent iteration, as illustrated in the bottom row. In the event that P equals zero, a summation operation is to be executed. In the event that P equals 1, a subtraction operation is executed by means of adding a 2's complement value. It should be noted that due to the opposite characteristics of the limited remainder as well as multiples divisor, both operands for the full adder within the leftmost cell generally result in a sum of 1. The value of tout is equal to 1 solely when the 3rd operand possesses a value of 1. In such a scenario, the sum evaluates to 0, thereby signifying that the updated partial remainder possesses a positive sign (Kowalski, 2022).

The limited remainder may be derived by computing the sum within the following manner:

$$\begin{aligned} s_i &= a_i \oplus (d_i \oplus P) \oplus c_i \\ &= \bar{a}_i d_i c_i P + a_i \bar{d}_i c_i P + a_i d_i \bar{c}_i P + a_i d_i c_i \bar{P} + a_i \bar{d}_i \bar{c}_i \bar{P} + \bar{a}_i d_i \bar{c}_i \bar{P} \\ &\quad + \bar{a}_i \bar{d}_i c_i \bar{P} + \bar{a}_i \bar{d}_i \bar{c}_i P. \end{aligned}$$

In the case of 3-level gates, a lag period of 3A is necessary,

$$c_{i+1} = (a_i + c_i)(d_i \oplus P) + a_i c_i$$

7.9. CARRY-LOOKAHEAD CELLULAR ARRAY DIVIDER

The dividers that were previously discussed entail carrying transmission throughout the row. The relationship between the size of a row, as well as the number of bits, is directly proportional, and as the row length increases, the delay period becomes significantly pronounced (Aljedani et al., 2021). The signal bit for the limited remainder, which affects the quotient bit along with the add/subtract functioning within the following row, is contingent upon the carry-out for each respective row. Incorporating carry-lookahead wiring can optimize the solution in terms of speed. Figure 7.3 displays the array along with its corresponding inputs:

$$A = A_0.A_1A_2 \cdots A_n,$$

$$D = D_0.D_1D_2 \cdots D_n,$$

$$Q = Q_0.Q_1Q_2 \cdots Q_n.$$

The array comprises A cells, S cells, as well as CLA cells. The dividend, denoted as Ajs, is received from the upper portion of the system, while the divisor, represented by the supported Djs, is received by means of the intersecting lines. The A cells are subject to the same rules as the non-restoring division method, wherein subtracting or adding is to be executed. It is important to note that an S cell must be present at the leftmost position of each row. Every individual cell function as a regulated carry-save adder or maybe subtractor, with the objective of producing two distinct outputs:

a sum as well as a carry. The variable "Sf" represents the total value of the bit produced within the jth cell of the ith row. Additionally, "Cj" and "Cf-l" denote the carry-in as well as carry-out values of that same position, accordingly The two resultant outputs obtained from the top row are utilized as inputs for the subsequent row. The vectors serve as a representation for them

$$
\begin{array}{rcllllllll}
S^{i-1} & = & S_0^{i-1}. & S_1^{i-1} & S_2^{i-1} & \cdots & S_{n-1}^{i-1} & A_{n+i} & \text{sum vector} \\
C^{i-1} & = & C_0^{i-1}. & C_1^{i-1} & C_2^{i-1} & \cdots & 0 & Q_{i-1} & \text{carry vector} \\
\pm D & = & D_0. & D_1 & D_2 & \cdots & D_{n-1} & D_n & \\
\hline
S^i & = & S_0^i. & S_1^i & S_2^i & \cdots & S_{n-1}^i & S_n^i & \\
C^i & = & C_0^i. & C_1^i & C_2^i & \cdots & C_{n-1}^i & 0. &
\end{array}
$$

The Carry-Lookahead (CLA) cells are utilized for the purpose of carry propagation in digital circuits. Let

$$
\begin{aligned}
G_j^i &= C_j^i S_j^i \\
P_j^i &= C_j^i \oplus S_j^i.
\end{aligned}
$$

The result for carry-lookahead is

$$\hat{C}^i = G_1^i + P_1^i G_2^i + P_1^i P_2^i G_3^i + \cdots$$

$$+P_1^i P_2^i \ldots\ldots\ldots P_{n-2}^i G_{n-1}^i.$$

The command signal denoted by "K i" propagates in a unidirectional manner via the left towards the right within the i-th row, without any noticeable delay.

Due to the preservation of the carry, there is no need to await its propagation through the rightmost cell towards the left side cell (Obermann& Flynn, 1997). The process performed in this context is agnostic to the overall length of the given word, denoted as n. Consequently, the duration of the lag for the carry-lookahead set divider is

$$\Delta_{CLA} = (n+1) \times \Delta_{row} + \Delta_{not}.$$

It can be observed that the overall delay time exhibits a time complexity of O(n). Stated differently, the complexity is proportional to n. It is worth noting that both restoring as well as non-restoring division methods require a time of 0(n') for completion.

All operations within A cells are executed concurrently, with a lag that commences upon the readiness of K,

$$\Delta_{XOR} + \Delta_{FA} = (2+2)\Delta_g = 4\Delta_g.$$

Subsequently, the acquisition of Gi and Pj necessitates the inclusion of two additional A, which may be superimposed with the latency for the XOR gate within the S cell. Subsequently, the NAND-NAND operation necessitates the utilization of 2A to acquire di within the Carry Lookahead Adder (CLA). In a time span of two additional A, Ka may be supplied to the subsequent row. So,

$$\Delta_{row} = 4 + 2 + 2 + 2 = 10\Delta_g.$$

Given that the array comprises (n + 1) rows and an additional inverter in the last row, the aggregate time of delaying the array can be determined

$$\begin{aligned}\Delta_{array} &= (n+1)\times\Delta_{row} + \Delta_{not} \\ &= ((n+1)\times 10 + 1)\Delta_g \\ &= (10n+11)\Delta_g.\end{aligned}$$

The analysis of the area complexities of the carry-lookahead set divider is as follows. The execution of an n-bit dividing operation necessitates the utilization of n(n + 1) A cells, (n + 1) S cells, (n + 1) CLA circuits, as well (n + 1) XOR gates, and a solitary inverter (Patankar, U. S., & Koel, 2021; Gallagher et al., 2021). The operational procedure executed by the carry-lookahead set divider is outlined below:

Initialization:
$S^{-1} = A(dividend)$; $C^{-1} = 00\cdots 1$, and $Q_{-1} = 1$
Do for $i = 0$ to n.
Step 1. Generate the two-vectors, carry and partial remainder:
  if $Q_{i-1} = 1$, $C^i \circ S^i \leftarrow S^{i-1} + C^{i-1} - D$;
  if $Q_{i-1} = 0$, $C^i \circ S^i \leftarrow S^{i-1} + C^{i-1} + D$.
Step 2. Lookahead: $\hat{C}^i = G_1^i + P_1^i G_2^i + P_1^i P_2^i G_3^i + \cdots + P_1^i \cdots P_{n-2}^i G_{n-1}^i$
  where $G_j^i = S_j^i C_j^i$ and $P_j^i = S_j^i \oplus C_j^i$.
Step 3. Decide the sign for partial remainder:
  $R_0 = S_0^i \oplus C_0^i \oplus \hat{C}^i$, and quotient bit $Q_i = \bar{R}_0$.
Step 4. Shift partial remainder: $C \circ S = 2(C^i \circ S^i)$.
Step 5. If $i > n$, End. Otherwise, $i = i + 1$, go to *Step 1*.

In short, the table below presents the gate count along with the delay period for all 3 set divider kinds in relation to the quotient of words n along with the measurement of the gate delaying ΔA,

Table 7.1. Types of Array Dividers

Type of Array Divider	Gate Count	Divide Time
Restoring	$14n^2 + 4n$	$(2n^2 + 6n + 2)\Delta_g$
Non-restoring	$15(n+1)^2$	$(2n^2 + 6n + 4)\Delta_g$
Non-restoring with CLA	$18n^2 + 27n + 10$	$(10n + 11)\Delta_g$

It is noteworthy that the gate measure isn't the sole factor to be taken into account when considering area complexity. In contemporary electronic systems, a single component has the potential to comprise a vast number of gates, with each gate occupying a limited amount of physical area. For these gates to function collaboratively, intercommunication is required. Interconnectivity necessitates the use of wires, which can occasionally occupy a significant portion of the space. The presented illustration, Figure 7.8, depicts a circuit utilizing the routed data encryption standard, wherein the wires' area holds considerable importance.

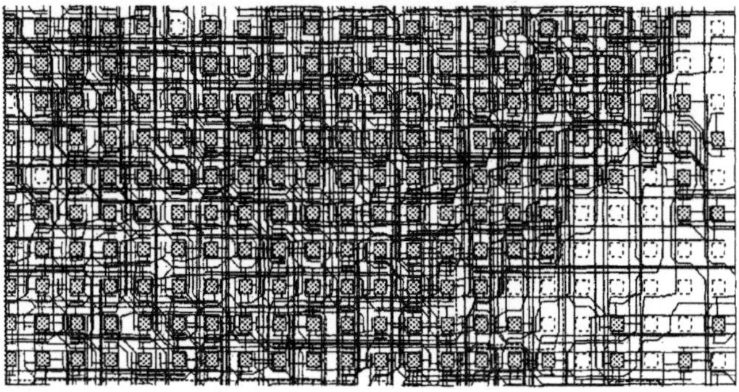

Figure 7.8. Wires can take up significant space.

7.10. SUMMARY

In contrast to subtracting, adding, and multiplying, division typically does not yield a precise outcome due to the fact that the dividend might not represent a multiple based on the divisor. The forthcoming section of this chapter will explicate a range of division computations. The binary non-restoring dividing method is an enhanced approach that eliminates the requirement for the aforementioned "restoring addition." It is assumed that D is greater than zero along with the absolute value of IR(j+1) is less than D. These assumptions remain constant while the fractional remainder, R(j+1), is permitted to take on positive or negative values. The arithmetic procedure to be executed is contingent upon the fractional remainder and may consist of either subtraction or just addition. The division computations expounded in the antecedent sections are founded on the method of successive subtraction as well as shift. This section presents an alternative methodology. The envisioned quotient can be generated through the execution of iterative multiplications. Thus, the identical hardware that is utilized for multiplication can also be employed for division. The suggested approach involves the consideration of the dividend along with the divisor to be the denominator as well as the numerator for a fraction. The fraction's value stays constant as it is multiplied by an identical sequence of integration factors. This chapter delves into the discourse surrounding the development and assembly of diverse high-velocity iterative cell-based arrays that facilitate parallel divides. The proposed set dividers employ a significant number of duplicated units to facilitate the analysis of the limited remainder as well as the divisor. Additionally, the shift operation is implemented through physical wiring. The text introduces three distinct categories of array separators.

REFERENCES

1. Aljedani, S. S., Liban, T. J., Tran, K., Phad, G., Singh, S., Dubrovskaya, V., & Pancera, M., (2021). Structurally related but genetically unrelated antibody lineages converge on an immunodominant HIV-1 Env neutralizing determinant following trimer immunization. *PLoS Pathogens, 17*(9), e1009543.
2. Andersen, J. B., Nielsen, A. F., & Olsen, O., (1994). A systolic ON-LINE non-restoring division scheme. In: *1994 Proceedings of the 27th Hawaii International Conference on System Sciences* (Vol. 1, pp. 339–348). IEEE.
3. Arrighi, G., Silver, B. J., & Brewer, B. D., (2003). Industrial convergence, globalization, and the persistence of the North-South divide. *Studies in Comparative International Development, 38*, 3–31.
4. Atkins, D. E., (1968). Higher-radix division using estimates of the divisor and partial remainders. *IEEE Transactions on computers, 100*(10), 925–934.
5. Bashagha, A. E., & Ibrahim, M. K., (1995). A new high radix non-restoring divider architecture. *International Journal of Electronics, 79*(4), 455–470.
6. Bashagha, A. E., & Ibrahim, M. K., (1997). Two's complement high radix division. In: *1997 IEEE International Symposium on Circuits and Systems (ISCAS)* (Vol. 3, pp. 2088–2091). IEEE.
7. Burgess, N., & Williams, T., (1995). Choices of operand truncation in the SRT division algorithm. *IEEE Transactions on Computers, 44*(7), 933–938.
8. Burgess, N., (1991). Radix-2 SRT division algorithm with simple quotient digit selection. *Electronics Letters, 21*(27), 1910–1911.
9. Burgess, N., (2001). Efficient RNS-to-binary conversion using high-radix SRT division. *IEE Proceedings-Computers and Digital Techniques, 148*(1), 49–52.
10. Cappa, M., & Hamacher, V. C., (1973). An augmented iterative array for high-speed binary division. *IEEE Transactions on Computers, 100*(2), 172–175.
11. Chen, L., Han, J., Liu, W., Montuschi, P., & Lombardi, F., (2018). Design, evaluation, and application of approximate high-radix dividers. *IEEE Transactions on Multi-Scale Computing Systems, 4*(3), 299–312.
12. Clarke, E. M., German, S. M., & Zhao, X., (1996). Verifying the SRT division algorithm using theorem proving techniques. In: *Computer Aided Verification: Proceedings 8th International Conference, CAV'96 New Brunswick, NJ, USA* (pp. 111–122). Springer Berlin Heidelberg.

13. Clarke, E. M., German, S. M., & Zhao, X., (1999). Verifying the SRT division algorithm using theorem proving techniques. *Formal Methods in System Design, 14*, 7–44.

14. Cortadella, J., & Lang, T., (1994). High-radix division and square-root with speculation. *IEEE Transactions on Computers, 43*(8), 919–931.

15. Cui, H., Cai, L., Yang, X., Feng, C., & Qin, T., (2014). Design of non-restoring binary array divider in quantum-dot cellular automata. *Micro & Nano Letters, 9*(7), 464–467.

16. Deverell, J., (1975). Pipeline iterative arithmetic arrays. *IEEE Transactions on Computers, 100*(3), 317–322.

17. Ercegovac, M. D., Lang, T., & Montuschi, P., (1993). Very high radix division with selection by rounding and prescaling. In: *Proceedings of IEEE 11th Symposium on Computer Arithmetic* (pp. 112–119). IEEE.

18. Ercegovac, M. D., Lang, T., & Montuschi, P., (1994). Very-high radix division with prescaling and selection by rounding. *IEEE Transactions on Computers, 43*(8), 909–918.

19. Erle, M. A., Schulte, M. J., & Linebarger, J. M., (2002). Potential speedup using decimal floating-point hardware. In: *Conference Record of the 36th Asilomar Conference on Signals, Systems and Computers, 2002* (Vol. 2, pp. 1073–1077). IEEE.

20. Fenwick, P., (1996). High-radix division with approximate quotient-digit estimation. *The Journal of Universal Computer Science (J. UCS): Annual Print and CD-ROM Archive Edition, 1*, 2–22.

21. Flynn, M. J., (1970). On division by functional iteration. *IEEE Transactions on Computers, 100*(8), 702–706.

22. Freixas, V. M., White, A. J., Nelson, T., Song, H., Makhov, D. V., Shalashilin, D., & Tretiak, S., (2021). Nonadiabatic excited-state molecular dynamics methodologies: Comparison and convergence. *The Journal of Physical Chemistry Letters, 12*(11), 2970–2982.

23. Gallagher, W. L., & Swartzlander, E. E., (2000). Fault-tolerant Newton-Raphson and Goldschmidt dividers using time shared TMR. *IEEE Transactions on Computers, 49*(6), 588–595.

24. Gardiner, A. B., (1971). Asynchronous binary restoring divider array. *Electronics Letters, 18*(7), 542–544.

25. Gardiner, A. B., (1971). Fast economical binary divider. *Electronics Letters, 7*(23), 691–692.

26. Gellert, W., Hellwich, M., Kästner, H., & Küstner, H., (2012). *The VNR Concise Encyclopedia of Mathematics*. Springer Science & Business Media.

27. Harris, D. L., Oberman, S. F., & Horowitz, M. A., (1997). SRT division architectures and implementations. In: *Proceedings 13th IEEE Symposium on Computer Arithmetic* (pp. 18–25). IEEE.
28. Hickendorff, M., Torbeyns, J., & Verschaffel, L., (2019). Multi-digit addition, subtraction, multiplication, and division strategies. *International Handbook of Mathematical Learning Difficulties: From the Laboratory to the Classroom*, 543–560.
29. Hickendorff, M., van Putten, C. M., Verhelst, N. D., & Heiser, W. J., (2010). Individual differences in strategy use on division problems: Mental versus written computation. *Journal of Educational Psychology, 102*(2), 438.
30. Horton, J. W., (1976). Walsh functions for digital impedance relaying of power lines. *IBM Journal of Research and Development, 20*(6), 530–541.
31. Ibrahem, A., Elsimary, H., & Salama, A. E., (2003). FPGA implementation of modified radix 2 SRT division algorithm. In: *2003 46th Midwest Symposium on Circuits and Systems* (Vol. 3, pp. 1419–1422). IEEE.
32. Ito, M., Takagi, N., & Yajima, S., (1995). Efficient initial approximation and fast converging methods for division and square root. In: *Proceedings of the 12th Symposium on Computer Arithmetic* (pp. 2–9). IEEE.
33. Jacobsohn, D. H., (1973). A combinatoric division algorithm for fixed-integer divisors. *IEEE Transactions on Computers, 100*(6), 608–610.
34. Jain, S., Pancholi, M., Garg, H., & Saini, S., (2014). Binary division algorithm and high-speed deconvolution algorithm (based on ancient Indian Vedic mathematics). In: *2014 11th International Conference on Electrical Engineering/Electronics, Computer, Telecommunications, and Information Technology (ECTI-CON)* (pp. 1–5). IEEE.
35. Jiang, H., Lombardi, F., & Han, J., (2019). Low-power unsigned divider and square root circuit designs using adaptive approximation. *IEEE Transactions on Computers, 68*(11), 1635–1646.
36. Juang, T. B., Chen, S. H., & Li, S. M., (2008). A novel VLSI iterative divider architecture for fast quotient generation. In: *2008 IEEE International Symposium on Circuits and Systems (ISCAS)* (pp. 3358–3361). IEEE.
37. Jun, K., & Swartzlander, E. E., (2012). Modified non-restoring division algorithm with improved delay profile and error correction. In: *2012 Conference Record of the 46th Asilomar Conference on Signals, Systems and Computers (ASILOMAR)* (pp. 1460–1464). IEEE.
38. Kaur, S., Singh, M., & Agarwal, R., (2013). Vhdl implementation of non-restoring division algorithm using high speed adder/subtractor. *International Journal of Advanced Research in Electrical, Electronics and Instrumentation Engineering, 2*(7), 3317–3324.

39. Kazaura, K., Wakamori, K., Matsumoto, M., Higashino, T., Tsukamoto, K., & Komaki, S., (2010). RoFSO: a universal platform for convergence of fiber and free-space optical communication networks. *IEEE Communications Magazine, 48*(2), 130–137.

40. Khosropour, A., Aghababa, H., & Forouzandeh, B., (2011). Quantum division circuit based on restoring division algorithm. In: *2011 Eighth International Conference on Information Technology: New Generations* (pp. 1037–1040). IEEE.

41. Kong, I., & Swartzlander, E. E., (2009). A Goldschmidt division method with faster than quadratic convergence. *IEEE Transactions on Very Large-Scale Integration (VLSI) Systems, 19*(4), 696–700.

42. Kornerup, P., (2005). Digit selection for SRT division and square root. *IEEE Transactions on Computers, 54*(3), 294–303.

43. Kowalski, A. M., (2022). Innovation divide in the world economy: China's convergence towards the Triad. *Technological and Economic Development of Economy, 28*(5), 1350–1367.

44. Krishnamoorthy, P., & Tekumalla, R., (2013). Quotient prediction for low power division. In: *2013 IEEE International SOC Conference* (pp. 273–277). IEEE.

45. Kyriakidou, V., Michalakelis, C., & Sphicopoulos, T., (2011). Digital divide gap convergence in Europe. *Technology in Society, 33*(3–4), 265–270.

46. Kyriakidou, V., Michalakelis, C., Varoutas, D., Panepistimioupolis, I., & Athens, G. R. E. E. C. E., (2009). Estimating digital divide convergence. In: *Good, the Bad and the Challenging: The User and the Future of Information and Communication Technologies: A Transdisciplinary Conference Organized by COST Action* (Vol. 298).

47. Lang, T., & Montuschi, P., (1995). Very-high radix combined division and square root with prescaling and selection by rounding. In: *Proceedings of the 12th Symposium on Computer Arithmetic* (pp. 124–131). IEEE.

48. Lang, T., & Montuschi, P., (1999). Very high radix square root with prescaling and rounding and a combined division/square root unit. *IEEE Transactions on Computers, 48*(8), 827–841.

49. Lehman, M., (1958). Short-cut multiplication and division in automatic binary digital computers, with special reference to a new multiplication process. *Proceedings of the IEE-Part B: Radio and Electronic Engineering, 105*(23), 496–504.

50. MacSorley, O. L., (1961). High-speed arithmetic in binary computers. *Proceedings of the IRE, 49*(1), 67–91.

51. McCann, M., & Pippenger, N., (2005). SRT division algorithms as dynamical systems. *SIAM Journal on Computing, 34*(6), 1279–1301.
52. McQuillan, S. E., & McCanny, J. V., (1994). Fast VLSI algorithms for division and square root. *Journal of VLSI Signal Processing Systems for Signal, Image, and Video Technology, 8*(2), 151–168.
53. McQuillan, S. E., McCanny, J. V., & Hamill, R., (1993). New algorithms and VLSI architectures for SRT division and square root. In: *Proceedings of IEEE 11th Symposium on Computer Arithmetic* (pp. 80–86). IEEE.
54. Metze, G., (1962). A class of binary divisions yielding minimally represented quotients. *IRE Transactions on Electronic Computers, 6*, 761–764.
55. Mitchell, J. N., (1962). Computer multiplication and division using binary logarithms. *IRE Transactions on Electronic Computers, 4*, 512–517.
56. Montuschi, P., & Lang, T., (2001). Boosting very-high radix division with prescaling and selection by rounding. *IEEE Transactions on Computers, 50*(1), 13–27.
57. Nair, P., Kudithipudi, D., & John, E., (2006). Design and implementation of a CMOS non-restoring divider. In: *2006 IEEE Region 5 Conference* (pp. 211–217). IEEE.
58. Nenadic, N. M., & Mladenovic, S. B., (2005). Fast division on fixed-point DSP processors using Newton-Raphson method. In: *EUROCON 2005–The International Conference on" Computer as a Tool"* (Vol. 1, pp. 705–708). IEEE.
59. Nikmehr, H., Phillips, B., & Lim, C. C., (2006). Fast decimal floating-point division. *IEEE Transactions on Very Large-Scale Integration (VLSI) Systems, 14*(9), 951–961.
60. Obermann, S. F., & Flynn, M. J., (1997). Division algorithms and implementations. *IEEE Transactions on Computers, 46*(8), 833–854.
61. Pan, T. H., Kay, H. S., Chun, Y., & Wey, C. L., (1995). High-radix SRT division with speculation of quotient digits. In: *Proceedings of ICCD'95 International Conference on Computer Design. VLSI in Computers and Processors* (pp. 479–484). IEEE.
62. Parashar, A., Aggarwal, G., Dang, R., Dalmia, P., & Pandey, N., (2017). Fast combinational architecture for a Vedic divider. In: *2017 14th IEEE India Council International Conference (INDICON)* (pp. 1–5). IEEE.
63. Parhami, B., (2001). Precision requirements for quotient digit selection in high-radix division. In: *Conference Record of 35th Asilomar Conference on Signals, Systems and Computers (Cat. No. 01CH37256)* (Vol. 2, pp. 1670–1673). IEEE.

64. Parhami, B., (2003). Tight upper bounds on the minimum precision required of the divisor and the partial remainder in high-radix division. *IEEE Transactions on Computers, 52*(11), 1509–1514.
65. Park, S. R., Choi, D. Y., & Hong, P., (2015). Club convergence and factors of digital divide across countries. *Technological Forecasting and Social Change, 96*, 92–100.
66. Patankar, U. S., & Koel, A., (2021). Review of basic classes of dividers based on division algorithm. *IEEE Access, 9*, 23035–23069.
67. Prabhu, J. A., & Zyner, G. B., (1995). 167 MHz radix-8 divide and square root using overlapped radix-2 stages. In: *Proceedings of the 12th Symposium on Computer Arithmetic* (pp. 155–162). IEEE.
68. Qian, F., Li, G., & Alam, M. S., (2000). Quotient-selected modified signed-digit division algorithm and its optoelectronic implementations. In: *Photonic Devices and Algorithms for Computing II* (Vol. 4114, pp. 129–139). SPIE.
69. Qian, F., Li, G., & Alam, M. S., (2001). Optoelectronic quotient-selected modified signed-digit division. *Optical Engineering, 40*(2), 275–282.
70. Robertson, J. E., (1958). A new class of digital division methods. *IRE Transactions on Electronic Computers, 3*, 218–222.
71. Rueß, H., Shankar, N., & Srivas, M. K., (1996). Modular verification of SRT division. In: *Computer Aided Verification: Proceedings 8th International Conference, CAV'96 New Brunswick, NJ, USA* (pp. 123–134). Springer Berlin Heidelberg.
72. Sasamal, T. N., Singh, A. K., & Ghanekar, U., (2016). Design of non - restoring binary array divider in majority logic - based QCA. *Electronics Letters, 52*(24), 2001–2003.
73. Sayedsalehi, S., Azghadi, M. R., Angizi, S., & Navi, K., (2015). Restoring and non-restoring array divider designs in quantum-dot cellular automata. *Information Sciences, 311*, 86–101.
74. Schwarz, E. M., & Carlough, S. R., (2007). Power6 decimal divide. In: *2007 IEEE International Conf. on Application-Specific Systems, Architectures and Processors (ASAP)* (pp. 128–133). IEEE.
75. Schwarz, E. M., & Flynn, M. J., (1991). Cost-efficient high-radix division. *Journal of VLSI Signal Processing Systems for Signal, Image, and Video Technology, 3*, 293–305.
76. Schwarz, E. M., & Flynn, M. J., (1993). Parallel high radix nonrestoring division. *IEEE Transactions on Computers, 42*(10), 1234–1246.
77. Schwemmer, C., Prümmer, M., Daum, V., & Hornegger, J., (2010). High-

density object removal from projection images using low-frequency-based object masking. In: *Bildverarbeitung für die Medizin* (pp. 365–369).

78. Sergeyev, Y. D., (1998). On convergence of "divide the best" global optimization algorithms. *Optimization, 44*(3), 303–325.
79. Shah, S., Dave, P., & Gupta, M. K., (2015). Computing real numbers using DNA self-assembly. *arXiv Preprint arXiv:1502.05552*.
80. Sharma, R., & Thakre, P., (2018). A CORDIC architecture implementation for rectangular to polar conversion. In: *International Journal of Scientific Research in Science and Technology (IJSRST)* (Vol. 4, No. 8, pp. 389–395).
81. Shinn, T., (2000). Formes de division du travail scientifique et convergence intellectuelle: La recherche technico-instrumentale. *Revue Française de sociologie,* 447–473.
82. Squillero, G., & Tonda, A., (2016). Divergence of character and premature convergence: A survey of methodologies for promoting diversity in evolutionary optimization. *Information Sciences, 329*, 782–799.
83. Srinivas, H. R., & Parhi, K. K., (1995). A fast radix-4 division algorithm and its architecture. *IEEE Transactions on Computers, 44*(6), 826–831.
84. Stine, J. E., & Hill, K., (2020). An efficient implementation of radix-4 integer division using scaling. In: *2020 IEEE 63rd International Midwest Symposium on Circuits and Systems (MWSCAS)* (pp. 1092–1095). IEEE.
85. Sutter, G., & Deschamps, J. P., (2009). High-speed fixed-point dividers for FPGAs. In: *2009 International Conference on Field Programmable Logic and Applications* (pp. 448–452). IEEE.
86. Swartzlander, E. E., Cho, H., Kong, I., & Kim, S. W., (2010). Computer arithmetic implemented with QCA: A progress report. In: *2010 Conference Record of the 44th Asilomar Conference on Signals, Systems and Computers* (pp. 1392–1398). IEEE.
87. Tan, K. G., (1978). The theory and implementations of high-radix division. In: *1978 IEEE 4th Symposium on Computer Arithmetic (ARITH)* (pp. 154–163). IEEE.
88. Tanaka, M., Obata, K., Takagi, K., Takagi, N., Fujimaki, A., & Yoshikawa, N., (2009). A high-throughput single-flux quantum floating-point serial divider using the signed-digit representation. *IEEE Transactions on Applied Superconductivity, 19*(3), 653–656.
89. Thorogood, C. J., Teixeira - Costa, L., Ceccantini, G., Davis, C., & Hiscock, S. J., (2021). Endoparasitic plants and fungi show evolutionary convergence across phylogenetic divisions. *New Phytologist, 232*(3), 1159–1167.

90. Tustin, A., (1947). A method of analyzing the behavior of linear systems in terms of time series. *Journal of the Institution of Electrical Engineers-Part IIA: Automatic Regulators and Servo Mechanisms, 94*(1), 130–142.
91. Vemula, R., & Chari, K. M., (2018). A review on various divider circuit designs in VLSI. In: *2018 Conference on Signal Processing and Communication Engineering Systems (SPACES)* (pp. 206–209). IEEE.
92. Waller, W., & Jennings, A., (1990). On the possibility of a feminist economics: The convergence of institutional and feminist methodology. *Journal of Economic Issues, 24*(2), 613–622.
93. Wang, J. S., & Wey, C. L., (1999). A 12-bit 100-ns/bit 1.9-mW CMOS switched-current cyclic A/D converter. *IEEE Transactions on Circuits and Systems II: Analog and Digital Signal Processing, 46*(5), 507–516.
94. Wang, Z., Han, L., & Ko, S. B., (2012). Design and implementation of a Radix-100 division unit. In: *2012 IEEE International Symposium on Circuits and Systems (ISCAS)* (pp. 1239–1242). IEEE.
95. Wey, C. L., & Wang, C. P., (1999). Design of a fast radix-4 SRT divider and its VLSI implementation. *IEE Proceedings-Computers and Digital Techniques, 146*(4), 205–210.
96. Williams, J., & Hamacher, V. C., (1981). A linear-time divider array. *Canadian Electrical Engineering Journal, 6*(4), 14–20.

CHAPTER

8 The FFT and Modular Arithmetic

Contents

The focus of this chapter pertains to modular arithmetic, which involves the efficient computation of values within a given integer N. Typically, the modulus N remains constant across various applications. Moreover, specific algorithms designed for this purpose leverage pre-computations dependent solely on N. These pre-computations facilitate faster arithmetic operations performed modulo N (De et al., 2008). This section assumes that a modulus of N takes up n words within the word base β until otherwise specified. Specifically, this means that βn–1 N is less than βn (Negre & Plantard, 2008).

8.1. REPRESENTATION

This section examines the various potential representations of residues concerning N. Similar to the preceding sections, one focus primarily pertains to compact representations (Meng & Johnson, 2013).

8.1.1. Classical Representation

In the classical approach, a residue (class) denoted by 'a' is stored as an integer satisfying the condition $0 \leq a < N$. The residues are consistently in a fully reduced state, also known as the canonical form. An alternative approach that avoids redundancy involves selecting a symmetric representation, where the range of values for the variable is given by $-N/2 \leq a < N/2$. This form can potentially reduce the number of additions or subtractions required (Negre & Plantard, 2008). Negative values can be stored using a distinct sign or a two's match representation. Given that N is represented by n words within base β, a redundant illustration can be adopted as an alternative by selecting a residue class to be represented by $0 \leq a < \beta n$. If the fundamental arithmetic operations are based on language, there will be no decrease in speed compared to the standard form. One benefit of utilizing this particular representation is that it is adequate to compare the total with βn when adding a pair of residues. The outcome of this comparison can be easily determined by examining the carry bit for the addition rather than having to compare the total with N (Kalach & David, 2005).

8.1.2. Montgomery's Form

The Montgomery form is a frequently employed representation in cases where multiple modular operations, such as additions, subtractions, and modular multiplications, must be executed modulo a common integer N (Okeya et al., 2000). The conversion between the classical illustration and Montgomery's representation may incur a minor overhead, but this can be outweighed by the acceleration achieved in the modular multiplying process. The central concept involves the representation of a residue and as a′ = aR modification N, where R is equal to βn and N is comprised of n words within base β. Montgomery focuses not on the physical manifestation of an inherited class but on the connotation attributed to a specific physical manifestation (Cohen & Montgomery, 1984). Thus, it can be inferred that the various options outlined previously for the physical manifestation are all viable. The operations of addition and subtraction remain unaltered. However, modular multiplication is subject to a distinct algorithm that is notably less complex (Plantard, 2021). In numerous applications that utilize Montgomery's form, the initial step involves the conversion of all inputs for Montgomery's form, which is achieved by computing a′ = aR mod N. Subsequently, all computations are executed in Montgomery's form, and ultimately, if necessary, all outputs are reconverted to the classical form by computing a = a′/R mod N. It is necessary to assume that the (R, N) is 1, which is equivalent to (β, N) = 1, to guarantee that it exists 1/R mod N. Typically, this circumstance does not pose a challenge as β is a binary exponent or N can be presumed to be an odd value (Tenca & Koç, 2003).

8.1.3. Residue Number Systems

The Residue Number System (RNS) is a mathematical system in which a residue, denoted as a, is expressed as a sequence of residues 'ai' modulo 'Ni.' Notably, the moduli 'Ni' are mutually prime, and the result is equivalent to 'N' (Posch & Posch, 1995). The computation of the integers ai can be executed efficiently by utilizing a remainder tree. Moreover, the distinctive integers $0 \leq a < N = N_1N_2 \cdots$ can be derived from the air using a Clear Chinese Remainder Theorem. The residual number system (RNS) is a mathematical technique representing integers by their remainders modulo a pairwise relatively prime integer (Brönnimannet al., 1999).

Table 8.1. Equivalence between LSB and MSB

Classical (MSB)	***p*-adic (LSB)**
Euclidean division Svoboda's algorithm Euclidean GCD Newton's method	Hensel division, Montgomery reduction Montgomery-Svoboda binary GCD Hensel lifting

This is intriguing as parallel computation of multiplication and addition can be executed on individual residues ai. Nevertheless, this particular representation necessitates the factorization of N into moduli N_1, N_2, and so on, which may only sometimes be feasible (Chervyakov et al., 2014).

8.1.4. MSB vs. LSB Algorithms

Numerous classical algorithms can be transformed into their p-adic counterparts, where the least significant bit (LSB) is processed first, as opposed to the most significant bit (MSB) in the former (Akinola & Olatidoye, 2015). Several algorithms discussed in the following section are variations of the Least Significant Bit (LSB) algorithm.

8.1.5. Link with Polynomials

A robust relationship exists between modular arithmetic and arithmetic operations performed on polynomials. A common method for implementing finite fields Fq, where q = pn, involves the utilization of polynomials in Fp[x] (Marin & Wagner, 2013). These polynomials are reduced using a monic indestructible polynomial f(x) ¥ Fp[x] for degree n. Modular reduction occurs in this particular instance, in both the coefficient level, specifically in Fp, and at the polynomial's level, which is modulo f(x). Certain algorithms operate within the ring (Z/nZ)[x], where n represents a composite integer. Schönage-Strassen's multiplication algorithm is a significant case in computational mathematics, particularly when n is expressed in the form of 2ℓ + 1 (Traldi, 1989). Efficient application of the Kronecker-Schönage trick is possible in both Fp[x] and (Z/nZ)[x]. The efficiency of the segmentation process is notable due to the established bounds of the coefficients, which are limited by p and n and therefore possess a constant magnitude. When the degree of polynomials is d, and their coefficients are limited to n, the number of operations required can be reduced to O(M (d log n)) as opposed to M (d)M (log n) in the conventional method. Furthermore, the implementation process is less complex as it requires the execution of efficient arithmetic operations for large integers, as opposed to efficient arithmetic operations at the two different polynomial and coefficient levels solely (Jones, 1987).

8.2. ADDITION AND SUBTRACTION

The process of adding two residues in traditional representation is executed in the following manner (Montgomery, 1985):

```
1 Algorithm BarrettDivRem.
2 Input: integers A, B with 0 ≤ A < β², β/2 < B < β.
3 Output: quotient Q and remainder R of A divided by B.
4 I ← ⌊β²/B⌋ [precomputation]
5 Q ← ⌊A₁I/β⌋ where A = A₁β + A₀ with 0 ≤ A₀ < β
6 R ← A − QB
7 while R ≥ B do
8     (Q, R) ← (Q + 1, R − B)
9 Return (Q, R).
```

Figure 8.1. Algorithm Barrett div rem is correct, and step 8 is performed at most 3 times.

Given that both an and b have equal distributions within the range [0, N–1], the probability of subtracting c from N is (1–1/N)/2. By employing a symmetric representation within the interval [N/2, N/2), the likelihood of requiring an addition or subtraction of N diminishes to 1/4 + O(1/N 2), albeit with the inclusion of an extra test (Großschädl et al., 2005). The additional examination may incur high costs for a limited sample size, such as one or two words. However, it would be comparatively economical for larger sample sizes, such as those consisting of a dozen words.

8.3. MULTIPLICATION

The process of modular multiplication involves the computation of A · B mod N, in which A and B represent residues modulo N, and the number system used has n words in base β (Eldridge & Walter, 1993). It is posited within this context that both A and B possess a maximum of n words, while in certain instances, they are completely reduced, signifying that 0 ≤ A, B < N. The initial approach involves the computation of C = AB using the naive algorithm, which has a maximum of 2n words. Subsequently, the resulting C is subjected to a modulo N reduction. The optimal algorithms are currently known once the modulus of N is variable. In this context, we examine superior algorithms that derive advantages from an unchanging modulus (Tenca & Koç, 2003). These algorithms are permitted to conduct precomputations based solely on the value of N. The pre-computation expenses are not factored in, as they are deemed insignificant for numerous modular reductions. It is assumed that the quantity of pre-computed data utilizes solely linear space, specifically O(log N) memory.

Algorithms that involve precomputations encompass Barrett's algorithm, which calculates an estimation of the opposite of the modulus, thereby replacing division with multiplication (Gu & Li, 2018). Montgomery's algorithm resembles Hensel's dividing with the remainder; its subquadratic variation constitutes the MSB variant of Barrett's algorithm. Lastly, Mihailescu's algorithm is also included.

8.3.1. Barrett's Algorithm

The algorithm proposed by Barrett (6) is noteworthy in situations where repetitive divisions with a constant divisor are required, particularly in computations performed under the modulo of a predetermined integer (Barrett et al., 2011). The concept involves the precomputation of a rough estimate of the inverse of the divisor. Thus, a single multiplication yields an estimate of the quotient, while a subsequent multiplication produces the corresponding remainder. It is possible to transform those estimations into precise numerical values by making a few adjustments. For the purpose of facilitating comprehension, Barrett's algorithm is presented in base β. Nonetheless, it is worth noting that β can be substituted by any integer, including but not limited to 2n or βn (Lim et al., 2006).

Algorithm Barrett Div Rem.

2 Input: I n t e g e r s A, B with $0 \leq A < \beta$, $\beta/2 < B < \beta$.

3 Output: q uot, i.e., nt Q and remainder R o f A *divided* by B.

2

4 $I \leftarrow \lfloor \beta / B \rfloor$ [precomputation]

5 $Q \leftarrow \lfloor A_1 I/\beta \rfloor$ where $A = A_1\beta + A_0$ with $0 \leq A_0 < \beta$

6 $R \leftarrow A - QB$

7 while $R \geq B$ do

8 $(Q, R) \leftarrow (Q + 1, R - B)$

9 Return (Q, R).

\z

- **Theorem 8.3.1:** The Barrett algorithm is a computational method used for modular reduction in cryptography. The accuracy of DivRem is confirmed, and it can be observed that step 8 is executed a maximum of three times (Barrett & Britter, 2009).
- **Proof:** Given that the equation A = QB+R remains constant throughout the algorithm, it suffices to demonstrate that the inequality 0 ≤ R < B holds upon completion. The values of Q and R are initially evaluated before the execution of the while-

loop (Barrett & Britter, 2008). Given the inequality β/2 < B < β, it follows that β < β2/B < 2β. Therefore, we can conclude that β is less than or equal to I, which is less than 2β. The inequality Q ≤ A1I/β ≤ A1β/B ≤ A/B holds. This condition guarantees that the value of R is greater than or equal to zero (Yao et al., 2012). The current equation follows: "Now, the value of I is greater than β2/B – 1."

$IB > \beta^2 - B.$ (8.1)

Similarly, $Q > A_1 I/\beta - 1$ gives:

$\beta Q > A_1 I - \beta.$ (8.2)

The resulting inequality is βQB > A1IB–βB > A1(β2–B)–βB equals β(A–A0)–B(β+A1) > βA – 4βB, given that A0 < β < 2B and A1 < β. Based on our analysis, it can be inferred that A is less than B multiplied by the sum of Q and 4. Therefore, it can be deduced that a maximum of three corrections will be required. The upper limit of three corrections is stringent and can be demonstrated by considering the values of A = 1980, B equals 36, and n = 6. In this instance, the values are as follows: I equals 113, A1 equals 30, Q equals 52, and R equals 108, equivalent to 3B. It is possible to substitute the multiplications performed in steps 5 and 6 with short products. Specifically, the multiplication at step 5 can be replaced with a high shorter product, while multiplying at step 6 can be substituted with a tiny product (Ghosh & Fowler, 2015).

8.3.2. Complexity of Barrett's Algorithm

When executing Barrett's algorithm with a divide of size n and performing multiplication at steps five and six employing full products, the computational cost incurred is 2M(n) (Wurman et al., 2022). The total expense in the FFT range can be reduced to 1.5M (n) by utilizing the "wrap-around trick" described in section 3.4.1. Additionally, if the forward converts of I and B are saved, the cost can be further reduced to M (n), assuming that one FFT is equivalent to three transforms (Barret et al., 2008).

8.3.3. Montgomery's Multiplication

The efficiency of Montgomery's algorithm in performing modular arithmetic concerning a fixed modulus N is noteworthy (Koc et al., 1996). The primary concept involves the substitution of a residue A modulo N with A′ = λA modulo N, where A′ denotes the Montgomery form corresponding to the original residue A. The addition and subtraction operations remain unaltered, as the number of holds is the relationship between λA + λB ≡ λ(A + B) mod N. The product of two residues within the Montgomery representation does not yield the desired outcome, as expressed by the equation (λA)(λB) corresponds to λ(AB) mod N (Bajard et al., 1998). The strategy involves substituting the conventional modular multiplication with "Montgomery's multiplication":

$$\textbf{Montgomery Mul}(A',B') = \frac{A'B'}{\lambda} \bmod N.$$

Montgomery multiplication of A' and B' may be easily computed for certain values of λ. Specifically, λ = βn, in which N is represented in n words within base β. In this context, Figure 2.2 illustrates a quadratic algorithm denoted as REDC, which is utilized for computing MontgomeryMul(A,' B'). Additionally, Figure 8.3 provides a subquadratic reduction known as FastREDC. An alternative perspective on Montgomery's algorithm for λ corresponds to βn is conceptualizing it as calculating the residual value resulting from Hensel's division (Huang et al., 2010).

```
1 Algorithm REDC.
2 Input: 0 ≤ C < β^{2n}, N < β^n, μ ← −N^{-1} mod β, (β,N) = 1
3 Output: 0 ≤ R < β^n such that R = Cβ^{-n} mod N
4 for i from 0 to n − 1 do
5     q_i ← μc_i mod β
6     C ← C + q_i N β^i
7 R ← Cβ^{-n}
8 if R ≥ β^n then return R − N else return R.
```

Figure 8.2. Montgomery multiplication (quadratic non-interleaved version).

The ci coefficients are defined as the base-β breakdown of C, where C is expressed as P2n–1 0 ciβi.

- **Proof:** Initially, one establishes the proof that the R Cβ–n modification N: C undergoes modification solely in line 6. This modification does not alter C mod N. Therefore, in line 7, one can infer that R Cβ–n modification N holds, which remains valid in the final line. Let us consider the scenario where, for a given value of I, C is congruent to 0 modulo βi upon reaching step 5. Subsequently, given that qi is equivalent to ci divided by N modulo β, it follows that at the subsequent stage, C plus qi multiplied by N multiplied by βi is congruent to 0 modulo βi+1 (Kawamura et al., 200). Therefore, ci is equal to 0. Consequently, upon exiting the for-loop, it can be inferred that C is various of βn, concluding that R represents an integer during step 7. At present, we are currently in the seventh step of the process:

$C < \beta^{2n} + (\beta - 1)N(1 + \beta + \cdots + \beta^{n-1}) = \beta^{2n} + N(\beta^n - 1)$ thus $R < \beta^n + N$, and $R - N < \beta^n$.

In contrast to the classical division method known as Algorithm BasecaseDivRem (1.4.1), Montgomery's algorithm offers two notable benefits. Firstly, the quotient selection is executed through a multiplication operation modulo the word or base β, making it more efficient than the division operation performed by BasecaseDivRem using the most important word bn–1 for the divisor (López & Dahab, 1999). Secondly, unlike BasecaseDivRem, Montgomery's algorithm does not require a repair step within the for-loop but only one after the loop. Given that the inputs of C correspond to 766970544842443844, N = 862664913, and β = 1000, the algorithm produces the following results. REDC precomputes μ = 23, then we have $q_0 = 412$, which yields $C = C + 412N = 766970900260388000$; then $q_1 = 924$, which yields $C = C + 924N\beta = 767768002640000000$; then $q_2 = 720$, which yields $C = C + 720N\beta^2 = 1388886740000000000$. At step 7, $R = 1388886740$, and

since $R \geq \beta^3$, one returns $R - N = 526221827$.

Montgomery's algorithm, known as Hensel's division with the rest only, may be considered a least significant bit (LSB) version of the traditional division. This observation is in line with Svoboda's findings (Huang, et al., 2008).

```
Algorithm FastREDC.
Input: 0 ≤ C < β², N < β, μ ← −1/N mod β
Output: 0 ≤ R < β such that R = C/β mod N
Q ← μC mod β
R ← (C + QN)/β
if R ≥ β then return R − N else return R.
```

Figure 8.3. Subquadratic montgomery multiplication.

The application of divisor preconditioning extends to the least significant bit (LSB) context. To be more precise, the objective of Algorithm REDC is to alter the divisor N in such a way that the "quotient selection" q μci mod β during step 5 can be simplified. An optimal selection would be to set the value of μ to 1, equivalent to N being congruent to 1 modulo β. The parameter μ within REDC is the multiplier k in the Svoboda division (Huang et al., 2010). The algorithm obtained by Montgomery-Svoboda operates in the following manner:

1. first compute $N' = \mu N$, with $N' < \beta^{n+1}$;
2. Then perform the n 1 first loops of REDC, replacing μ by 1 and N by N';

3. Perform a last classical loop with μ and N, and the last steps from REDC.

Selecting the quotient using Montgomery-Svoboda's algorithm involves retrieving the term of weight βi from the divisor C. In the instance above, the value of N′ is determined to be 19841292999. The least essential word of C, denoted as q_0, is found to be 844. Consequently, C is updated to C + 844N′, resulting in the value 766987290893735000 (Kalach & David, 2005). Subsequently, q_1 is computed as 735, and C is updated to C + 735N′β, resulting in the value 781570641248000000. Finally, q_2 is computed as 704, and C is updated to C + 704Nβ2, resulting in the value 1388886740000000000. This value is identical to the one obtained earlier after the for-loop.

8.3.4. Subquadratic Montgomery Reduction

A variant of REDC that exhibits subquadratic behavior can be derived by setting n to 1 in the REDC algorithm and treating β as a "giant base" (or as an alternative, substituting β with βn in the subsequent steps) (Lee et al., 2014).

The statement above pertains to the 2-adic equivalent of Barrett's subquadratic algorithm, wherein the execution of steps 4–5 involves utilizing a low short product along with a high short product, respectively. The reduction process necessitates 2 multiplication operations of size n when combined with Karatsuba's multiplication, provided steps 4–5 outcomes are complete. In other words, 6 multiplication operations of size n/2 (where n represents the size of N and β is a giant base) are required (Bajard et al., 2010). Given supplementary precomputation, executing the reduction utilizing 5 multiplications of magnitude n/2 is plausible because n is an even number (Giorg et al., 2021). The algorithm employed here is Montgomery-Svoboda's, where the parameter N is represented in base βn/2 using two significant words:

```
1 Algorithm MontgomerySvoboda2.
2 Input: 0 ≤ C < β^{2n}, N < β^n, μ ← −1/N mod β^{n/2}, N′ = μN
3 Output: 0 ≤ R < β^n such that R = C/β^n mod N
4 q0 ← C mod β^{n/2}
5 C ← (C + q0 N′)/β^{n/2}
6 q1 ← μC mod β^{n/2}
7 R ← (C + q1 N)/β^{n/2}
8 if R ≥ β^n then return R − N else return R.
```

Figure 8.4. Algorithm Montgomery Svoboda.

The computational expense of the power source algorithm is denoted by M (n, n/2) for the computation of q_0N' (even if N' theoretically consists of 3n/2 words, it is known that N' = Hβn/2 1 alongside H < βn, hence multiplying q_0 by H is sufficient). Additionally, M (n/2) is required to determine μC mod βn/2, and another M (n, n/2) is necessary to compute q_1N. Therefore, the total computational cost is 5M (n/2) if every n×(n/2) product is executed through two (n/2) × (n/2) outcomes. The algorithm resembles the one expounded in the concluding section 1.4.6, wherein the expense amounted to 3M (n/2) + D(n/2) over a division operation involving 2n divided by n with only the remainder being considered (Bajard et al., 2005). The primary distinction lies in utilizing Montgomery's form, which replaces Svoboda's algorithm's final classical division D(n/2) with multiplications for the total expense of 2M (n/2). This approach is typically more efficient.

The MontgomerySvoboda2 algorithm can be expanded in the following manner. The resultant value C, ascertained in the fifth step, comprises a surplus of n/2 words, totaling 3n/2 words. Instead of utilizing the REDC method for reducing the excess, one could opt for Svoboda's technique, which involves setting μ' as 1 divided by N modulo βn/4 and N" as the product of μ' and N (Hars, 2006). The proposed approach aims to decrease the occurrence of low n/4 words in C, albeit at the expense of M (n, n/4). To address the remaining excess of n/4, a final REDC step is employed, resulting in D(2n, n) = M (n, n/2) + M (n, n/4) + M (n/4) + M (n, n/4). The process of "folding" can be extended to D(2n, n) by utilizing the formula M (n, n/2) + · · · + M (n, n/2k) + M (n/2k) + M (n, n/2k).

Table 8.2. Theoretical Complexity of Sub-Quadratic REDC with 1-, 2-, and 3-Folding for Different Multiplication Algorithm

Algorithm	**Karatsuba**	**Toom-Cook 3-Way**	**Toom-Cook 4-Way**
$D(n)$	$2M(n)$	$2.63M(n)$	$3.10M(n)$
1-folding	$1.67M(n)$	$1.81M(n)$	$1.89M(n)$
2-folding	$1.67M(n)$	$1.91M(n)$	$2.04M(n)$
3-folding	$1.74M(n)$	$2.06M(n)$	$2.25M(n)$

$M(n, n/2^k)$ reduces to $2^k M(n/2^k)$, this gives:

The formula presented is D(n) = 2M (n/2) + 4M (n/4) +…+ 2k–1M (n/2k–1) + (2k+1 + 1)M (n/2k), where M represents a certain operation and n is the input size.

Regrettably, the products obtained exhibit increasing levels of imbalance. Additionally, it is necessary to retain k pre-computed multiples of N, denoted as N′, N″,…, each necessitating a minimum of n words for storage (unless the lower portion of these constants, all of which are equivalent to –1, is not retained) (Lee et al., 2014). According to Figure 2.4, it can be observed that the technique known as the single-folding algorithm exhibits superior performance compared to other algorithms. The discourse delves into additional enhancements to Montgomery-Svoboda's algorithm, resulting in D(n) = 1.58M(n) when Karatsuba multiplication is employed (Chen et al., 2015).

8.3.5. Mihailescu's Algorithm

Mihailescu's algorithm postulates the ability to execute rapid multiplication within the constraints of modulo 2n – 1 alongside 2n + 1 for a satisfactory number of n values (Mahmood et al., 2020). The veracity of this assumption is exemplified by the Schönage-Strassen algorithm. The initial iteration of this algorithm involves the multiplication of two integers modulo 2n + 1. However, if the "twist" operations are omitted before and following the Fourier transforms, the resulting product is computed modulo 2n 1. (This operation is performed at the upper level only: both cases involve the computation of n′ modulo 2 + 1 using recursive methods.) Mihailescu's algorithm centers around executing a Montgomery reduction AB/R, where R is not equivalent to a power βn for the word base but is equal to βn – 1. Efficient convolution to operate can be achieved through FFT, subject to the value mentioned earlier being taken into account (Avanzi & Mihăilescu, 2004).

The present text pertains to Algorithm Theorem 2.3.3. MultiplyMihailescu accurately calculates ABβ–n mod N in 1.5M (n) operations, assuming that multiplication multiplied by 2n 1 incurs a 1 M (n) cost (Titu et al., 2022).

```
Algorithm MultiplyMihailescu.
Input: A, B with 0 ≤ A, B < N < β^n
Output: AB/(2^n − 1) mod N
Assumes: μ = N^{-1} mod (2^n − 1) is precomputed
c ← AB mod (2^n − 1)
d ← AB mod (2^n + 1)
γ ← cμ mod (2^n − 1)
δ ← γN mod (2^n + 1)
Return (δ − d)/2 mod (2^n + 1)
```

Figure 8.5. Algorithm multiply Mihailescu.

- **Proof:** The equation AB = h(2n–1)+ℓ is presented. The desired outcome is to obtain the equation AB/(2n–1) = h+ℓ/(2n–1) mod N. Subsequently, in step 5, the value of c is equated to ℓ, while in step 6, the computation of d is performed by taking the modulus of (2n+1) of the difference between ℓ and twice the value of h (Mihailescn & Teo, 2010). The equation $\gamma = \ell/N \bmod (2n-1)$ implies that $\gamma N = \ell + (2n-1)\tau$ for $\tau \geq 0$. This can be simplified to $\tau \equiv -\ell/(2n-1) \bmod N$. The equation above produces the value of δ as $\ell - 2\tau$. Subsequently, the expression $(\delta - d)/2$ is equivalent to $h - \tau$. The primary expense associated with the algorithm pertains to the four convolutions, namely AB mod (2n 1), cμ mod (2n 1), and γN mod (2n +1), which collectively amount to a cost of 4 M (n). In the context of cμ mod (2n 1) along with γN mod (2n + 1), it is noteworthy that the operands μ and N remain constant, thereby rendering their Fourier transform amenable to precomputation (Mihailescu et al., 2007). This precomputation leads to a reduction of 1 M (n) in computational costs. An additional economy of 1 M (n) can be achieved through the retention of d and δ within Fourier space during steps 6 and 8, the execution of the d – δ subtraction in Fourier space, and the implementation of a solitary inverse transform over step 9. The expression (2 – 1/3 – 1/6) M (n) is equivalent to 1.5M (n) as a result of the given calculation).

The cost of Mihailescu's algorithm, amounting to 1.5 million (n), is remarkable as it implies that the swiftness of modular multiplication surpasses that of two multiplication. Stated differently, modular multiplication can be conceptualized as a multiplication operation succeeded by a division operation (Mihailescu & Teo, 2010). Consequently, the division operation can be executed with the expenditure of only half a multiplication operation!

8.3.6. Special Moduli

There may exist faster methods for special moduli N. The ideal can be expressed as $N = \beta n \pm 1$ in academic discourse (Cao et al., 2007). The modulus above is the exact type employed in the Schönage-Strassen algorithm, which relies on utilizing the fast Fourier transform (FFT).

Within the FFT spectrum, multiplying two integers with a maximum of n/2 words is executed through a modulo $\beta n \pm 1$ operation (Wang, 2000). The cost of this operation is $M(n/2) \leq 1\ M(n)$. In most applications, the selection of the modulus is not feasible since there is no compelling rationale for it to possess a distinctive structure. Further information regarding special moduli can be found in section 2.8.

8.3.7. Fast Multiplication Over GF(2)[x]

There may exist faster methods for special moduli N. The ideal can be expressed as N = βn±1 in academic discourse (Brent et al., 2008). The modulus above is the exact type employed in the Schönage-Strassen algorithm, which relies on utilizing the fast Fourier transform (FFT). Within the FFT spectrum, multiplying two integers with a maximum of n/2 words is executed through a modulo βn ± 1 operation. The cost of this operation is M (n/2) ≤ 1 M (n). In most applications, the selection of the modulus is not feasible since there is no compelling rationale for it to possess a distinctive structure. Further information regarding special moduli can be found in section 2.8:

$$A = \sum_{i=0}^{d-1} a_i x^i,$$

The element ai, which belongs to the Galois Field GF(2), can be expressed as a binary digit, taking on the value of 0 or 1 (López & Dahab, 1999; Silverman, 1999). The digital depiction of a binary form polynomial with a degree of d – 1 resembles that of a single integer consisting of d bits. It is a legitimate inquiry to inquire about the speed at which binary polynomials can be multiplied. The multiplication operation in GF(2)[x] can be viewed as analogous to integer multiplication, albeit without carrying operations. As such, the computational efficiency of multiplying two binary polynomials of degree d is expected to surpass that of multiplying a pair of d-bit integers. In practical terms, the assertion, as mentioned above, is invalid due to the absence of a multiplication instruction for GF(2)[x] during the word level in contemporary processors. This paper presents expeditious multiplication techniques for GF(2)[x]. Specifically, we discuss a fundamental algorithm, a Toom-Cook 3-way variation, and a Schönage algorithm that utilizes the Fast Fourier Transform (Scott et al., 1986; Itoh & Tsujii, 1988).

8.3.7.1. The Base Case

If the processor does not offer multiplication across GF(2)[x] at the linguistic level, executing it via software implementation is necessary (De Win et al., 1996; López & Dahab, 1999). Let us consider a computer with a 64-bit architecture as an illustrative example. A prescribed procedure is necessary to multiply two 64-bit words, construed as each binary polynomial with a maximum degree of 63. The outcome of this operation should be two 64-bit words representing both the upper and lower halves of the product. This paper demonstrates a proficient approach to implementing the abovementioned procedure through word-level operations. Let i be an integer. We denote the binary polynomial corresponding to me as π(i). Similarly, for a polynomial with the value p, we denote the integer related to p as v(p). As an illustration, the values of π for various inputs are as follows: π(0) equals 0, π(1) equals 1, π(2) equals x, π(3) equals x + 1, π(4) equals x2. Additionally, it is known that v(x4 + 1) equals 17.,

```
1  Algorithm GF2MulBaseCase.
2  Input: nonnegative integers 0 ≤ a,b < 2^w = β (word base).
3  Output: nonnegative integers ℓ,h with π(a)π(b) = π(h)x^w + π(ℓ).
4  Parameter: a slice size k, and n = ⌈w/k⌉.
5  Compute A_s = ν(π(a)π(s) mod x^w) for all 0 ≤ s < 2^k.
6  Write b in base 2^k: b = b_0 + b_1 2^k + ··· + b_{n-1} 2^{(n-1)k} where 0 ≤ b_j < 2^k.
7  h ← 0, ℓ ← A_{b_{n-1}}
8  for i from n − 2 downto 0 do
9      h2^w + ℓ ← (h2^w + ℓ) ≪ k
10     ℓ ← ℓ ⊕ A_{b_i}
11 u = b, m ← (2^{k-1} − 1)(2^{nk} − 1)/(2^k − 1) mod 2^w
12 for j from 1 to k − 1 do { repair step }
13     u ← (u ≫ 1) ∧ m
14     if bit w − j of a is set, then h ← h ⊕ u
```

Figure 8.6. Algorithm GF2 base case.

According to line 9, the sum of h2w and ℓ is subjected to a leftward shift by k bits, whereby the lower w bits are retained in ℓ while the remaining bits are kept in h. An illustrative case is the multiplication of two binary numbers, a = (110010110)2, representing a polynomial of x8 + x7 + x4 + x2 + x, and b = (100000101), without loss of generality. Compute the value of polynomial 2, denoted by x8 + x2 + 1, when w equals 9 and k equals 3. In Step 5, the values of A_0 and A_1 will be calculated, where A_0 equals 0, and A_1 equals the binary number a, which is represented as (110010110). In this context, one can observe that A_2 is equivalent to the result of the mathematical operation xa mod x9, which can be expressed as the sum of x8, x5, x3, and x2. Additionally, A3 can be represented as the product of x and (1+1). The given expressions can be represented as follows: mod(x9, x7+x5+x4+x3+x), A4(x6+x4+x3), A5(x8+x7+x6+x3+x2+x), A6(x8+x6+x5+x4+x2), and A7(x7+x6+x5+x). In step 6 of the process, the value of b was decomposed into its constituent parts, resulting in the values b0 equals 5, b1 equals 0, and b2 = 4. Therefore, it can be observed that the values of n, h, and ℓ are 3, (000000000)2, and A4 (001011000), respectively. Upon completion of step 9 where i = 1, the values of h and ℓ are (000000001)2 and (011000000)2, respectively. Subsequently, in step 10, the value of ℓ remains unaltered because b1 is equal to 0 and A0 is also equal to 0. Upon completion of step 9 with i = 0, the values of h and ℓ are (000001011)2 and (000000000)2, respectively. Subsequently, after executing step 10, the value of ℓ is A5, equivalent to (111001110)2.

Steps 12 through 14 constitute a reparative cycle. This is deemed necessary due to the discarding of certain upper bits from variable a during the process of generating table A. In the context of the given scenario, it can be observed that bit w – j of an is eliminated in As when the condition w – j + deg(π(s)) ≥ w is satisfied, indicating that deg(π(s)) ≥ j. The example above demonstrates that the bit with the greatest importance of an is eliminated in A2 to A7, while the next is discarded in A4 to A7. If bit w j of an is activated, it is necessary to include the bit corresponding to the product for every monomial tx in a given π(s) where t j, or for every set of bit 2t in a given bi. The parallel execution of the operation on all relevant components of b can be achieved by utilizing a binary mask.

In Step 11, the values of u and m are calculated as (100000101)2 and (011011011), respectively.2. The utilization of a mask, denoted as m, serves to impede the transmission of bits belonging to a specific set of k successive bits to the subsequent set. At step 13, when j equals 1, the binary value of you is (010000010)2. Given that the eighth bit of variable a was previously assigned a value, the value of h is updated to h ⊕ u = (010001001)2. When j equals 2, the u value is (001000001) in binary format. Additionally, due to the activation of bit 7 in variable a, the resulting value of h is (011001000) when multiplied by u. The aforementioned equation accurately represents the product of π(a) and π(b), which is equivalent to x16 + x15 + x12 + x8 + x7 + x6 + x3 + x2 + x. The utilization of double-length registers could potentially prevent the complexity of repair procedures, albeit at the cost of considerably reduced speed (Mastrovito, 1988; Großschädl & Savaş, 2004; Zimmermann, 2007; Chung et al., 2007).

8.3.7.2. Toom-Cook 3-Way

The Karatsuba algorithm utilizes minimal evaluation points, typically selecting 0 and 1 for 3 points. The requirement of five evaluation points for Toom-Cook 3-way may initially suggest that obtaining several such points in GF(2) is unfeasible. One potential strategy for addressing this challenge involves utilizing the transcendental variable x, as well as various combinations thereof, as a means of assessing the situation (Larasati et al., 2021; Umer et al., 2022; Putranto et al., 2023). An illustrative instance is presented in the GF2ToomCook3 Algorithm. The equation C equals $c_0 + c_1X + c_2X^2 + c_3X^3 + c_4X^4$ is utilized to determine $v_1 = A(1)B(1) = C(1)$, where C(1) is equivalent to $c_0 + c_1 + c_2 + c_3 + c_4$. Consequently, the value of w_1 is obtained by summing c_1, c_2, and c_3. In a similar vein, the equation vx equals $c_0 + c_1x + c_2x^2 + c_3x^3 + c_4x^4$ can be observed, leading to $wx = c_1 + c_2x + c_3x^2$. Consequently, w_1/x can be expressed as $c_1x^2 + c_2x + c_3$. The equation for t is expressed as the sum of c_1 and c_3,

Algorithm GF2ToomCook3.
Input: binary polynomials $A = \sum_{i=0}^{n-1} a_i x^i$, $B = \sum_{i=0}^{n-1} b_i x^i$
Output: $C = AB = c_0 + c_1X + c_2X^2 + c_3X^3 + c_4X^4$
Let $X = x^k$ where $k = \lceil n/3 \rceil$
Write $A = a_0 + a_1X + a_2X^2$, $B = b_0 + b_1X + b_2X^2$, $\deg(a_i), \deg(b_i) < k$
$c_0 \leftarrow a_0b_0$
$c_4 \leftarrow a_2b_2$
$v_1 \leftarrow (a_0 + a_1 + a_2)(b_0 + b_1 + b_2)$
$v_x \leftarrow (a_0 + a_1x + a_2x^2)(b_0 + b_1x + b_2x^2)$
$v_{1/x} \leftarrow (a_0x^2 + a_1x + a_2)(b_0x^2 + b_1x + b_2)$
$w_1 \leftarrow v_1 - c_0 - c_4$
$w_x \leftarrow (v_x - c_0 - c_4x^4)/x$
$w_{1/x} \leftarrow (v_{1/x} - c_0x^4 - c_4)/x$
$t \leftarrow (w_x + w_{1/x})/(1 + x^2)$
$c_2 \leftarrow w_1 + t$
$c_1 \leftarrow (w_{1/x} + c_2x + t)/(1 + x^2)$
$c_3 \leftarrow t + c_1$

Figure 8.7. Algorithm GF2Tom Cook3.

The expression for c_2 is obtained by adding w_1 and t. Substituting $(w_1/x + c_2x + t)/(1 + x^2)$ yields c_1, and adding t and c_1 results in c_3. Hensel's division can efficiently implement the precise divisions by $1 + x^2$, given that the remaining amount is zero. To be more precise, if T (x) possesses a degree that is less than n, the application of Hensel's division results in.:

$$T(x) = Q(x)(1 + x^2) + R(x)x^n \qquad (8.3)$$

The function Q(x) with a degree that is lower than n is uniquely defined as Q(x) = T(x)/(1 + x^2) mod xn, where R(x) has a degree that is less than 2. The division process can be executed sequentially, analyzing each word of

T (x) in ascending order of significance (Imran et al., 2021; Zimmermann, 2007; Robert & Véron, 2022). Let us consider a scenario where the variable w represents the number of bits contained in a word, which is a power of 2. For instance, we can assume that w equals 32.

One uses the identity:

$$\frac{1}{1+x^2} = (1-x^2)(1-x^4)(1-x^8)(1-x^{16}) \bmod x^{32}.$$

It is worth noting that the identity above can be substituted with "+" signs if the fundamental field is GF(2). Subsequently, one will utilize this notation moving forward. The process of dividing the word t(x) of T(x) by 1 + x^2, as proposed by Hensel, is expressed as follows:

$$t(x) = q(x)(1 + x^2) + r(x)x^w \quad (8.4)$$

In cases where the degree of q is less than w, and the degree of r is less than 2, the polynomial t(x) can be expressed as the remainder of q(x) divided by xw, where t(x) is equal to the product of (1 + x^2), (1 + x^4), (1 + x^8), and (1 + x^{16}). The remainder r(x) can be formed by extracting the two most important q bits (x). This is because the division of (2.4) by xw results in q(x) div xw–2 equals r(x). Subsequently, the remainder mentioned above is appended to the subsequent term of T (x), so it is established that the ultimate remainder is of a null value.

8.3.7.3. Using the Fast Fourier Transform

This section presents an algorithm that utilizes the Fast Fourier Transform (FFT) to multiply a pair of polynomials of n degrees each from GF(2)[x] (Pollard, 1971; Fedorenko & Trifonov, 2002; Trifonov & Fedorenko, 2003). The time complexity of this algorithm is O(n log n log log n). The conventional Fast Fourier Transform (FFT) algorithm necessitates the use of 2k-the origins of unity, rendering it inapplicable in GF(2)[x] due to the non-existence of these roots for unity in this field. The proposed resolution entails substituting exponents of 2 with exponents of 3 (Robinson & Ninowski, 2003; Guo et al., 1998). Suppose that the objective is to perform polynomial multiplication on two elements of GF(2)[x]/(xN +1), in which N is equal to KM and K is a power of 3. Formulate the polynomials a and b, both possessing a degree lower than N, which will be subjected to multiplication in the following manner:

$$a = \sum_{i=0}^{K=1} a_i x^{iM}, \quad b = \sum_{i=0}^{K-1} b_i x^{iM},$$

The variables ai, and bi denotes polynomials with a lower degree than M. The present study involves the examination of ai as constituents of RN′ = GF(2)[x]/(x2N′ + xN′ + 1), where N′ = KM′/3, to gain further insight. Let us consider a vector ω defined as xM′ and belongs to the N-dimensional Euclidean space RN′. The equation 1+ωK/3+ω2K/3 = 0 holds, with ωK equaling 1 in RN′. The Fourier transform of a sequence (a_0, a_1, …, a_{K-1}) is represented by (ˆa_0, ˆa_1, …, ˆa_{K-1}). Similarly, the Fourier transform of another sequence (b_0, b_1, …, b_{K-1}) is also represented similarly. The resulting vector ($c^\wedge_0$, …, $c^\wedge_{K-1}$) is obtained through the pointwise multiplication of the vectors ($a^\wedge_0$, …, $a^\wedge_{K-1}$) and (ˆb_0, …, ˆb_{K-1}).

$$a = \sum_{j=0}^{K=1} \omega^{ij} a_j,$$

$$\hat{c}_i = \left(\sum_{j=0}^{K-1} \omega^{ij} a_j\right)\left(\sum_{k=0}^{K-1} \omega^{ij} b_k\right)$$

Now the inverse transform of ($c^\wedge_0$, …, $c^\wedge_{K-1}$) is defined as (c_0, …, c_{K-1}) where:

$$cl = \sum_{i=0}^{K=1} \omega^{-li} \hat{c}_i$$

It is noteworthy that given ωK = 1, it follows that ω–λ equals ω–λ mod K, or equivalently, ω–1 equals ωK–1 =xM′(K–1). Insight into the topic at hand and provides a better understanding of the subject matter:

$$cl = \sum_{i=0}^{K=1} \omega^{-li} \left(\sum_{j=0}^{K-1} \omega^{-li} a_j\right)\left(\sum_{k=0}^{K-1} \omega^{-li} b_j\right)$$

$$= \sum_{j=0}^{K=1}\sum_{k=0}^{K=1} a_j b_k \sum_{i=0}^{K-1} \omega^{i(j+k-l)}$$

The mathematical expression t equals the sum of j and k, subtracted by the value of ℓ. If t is not congruent to 0 modulo K, the summation of ωit from I equals 0 to K–1 is equivalent to ωKt+1, which equals 0. This is because ωK equals 1, while ωt does not equal 1. Given that t is congruent to 0 modulo K, the value of ωit equals 1 (Yan et al., 2003; Roncero et al., 2009). Additionally, the inequality –K is less than the summation of j+k-ℓ, which in turn is less than 2K. This phenomenon occurs solely when the sum of j, k, and negative ℓ belongs to the set containing 0 and K. The summation is equivalent to K, where K represents a factor of 3 and is congruent to 1 modulo 2. Therefore, the range of ℓ is from 0 to K – 1. Like Schönage-

Strassen's algorithm for integer multiplication, the present algorithm is amenable to recursive application. The pointwise products modulo x2N′ + xN′ + 1 exhibit the property of being reducible modulo x3N′ + 1. Consequently, the multiplication modulo xN + 1 operation can be simplified to approximately K products modulo x3N/K + 1, assuming that N′ equals M. As mentioned above, the expression denotes the asymptotic complexity, which is of the order of O(N log N). Typically, the algorithm is employed singularly in practice. Specifically, the multiplication of two polynomials of degree N/2 can be executed utilizing K products of polynomials with a degree of approximately 2N/K (Guo & Wang, 1998; Mason et al., 2013; Robinson et al., 2012).

- **Example:** Consider $N = 3 \cdot 5$, with $K = 3$, $M = 5$, $N' = 5$, $M' = 5$, $a = x^{14} + x^{13} + x^{12} + x^{11} + x^{10} + x^8 + x^6 + x^5 + x^4 + x^3 + x^2 + 1$, $b = x^{13} + x^{11} + x^8 + x^7 + x^6 + x^2$.

We have $(a_0, a_1, a_2) = (x^4 + x^3 + x^2 + 1, x^3 + x + 1, x^4 + x^3 + x^2 + x + 1)$, $(b_0, b_1, b_2) = (x^2, x^3 + x^2 + x, x^3 + x)$. In the Fourier domain, we perform computations modulo $x^{10} + x^5 + 1$, and $\omega = x^5$, which gives

$(\hat{a}_0, \hat{a}_1, \hat{a}_2) = (x^3 + 1, x^9 + x^7 + x, x^9 + x^7 + x^4 + x^2 + x)$,

$(\hat{b}_0, \hat{b}_1, \hat{b}_2) = (0, x^7 + x^3 + x^2 + x, x^7 + x^3 + x)$,

$(\hat{c}_0, \hat{c}_1, \hat{c}_2) = (0, x^7 + x^6 + x^3, x^6 + x^3)$,

$(c_0, c_1, c_2) = (x^7, x^6 + x^3 + x^2, x^7 + x^6 + x^3 + x^2)$

and

$c_0 + x^M c_1 + x^{2M} c_2 = x^{13} + x^{12} + x^{11} + x^8 + x^2 + x \bmod (x^{15} + 1)$.

The mathematical expression t equals the sum of j and k, subtracted by the value of ℓ. If t is not congruent to 0 modulo K, the summation of ωit from I equals 0 to K–1 is equivalent to ωKt+1, which equals 0. The methodology utilized in executing the rapid Fourier transform is explicated. Efficient computation is our objective.

where; K = 3k. Define FFT(ω, (a_0, …, a_{K-1})) = (ˆa_0, …, ˆa_{K-1}). For 0 ≤ ℓ < K/3 we define

a′ = FFT(ω_3, (a_0, a_3, …, aK/3–3)),

a″ = FFT(ω_3, (a_1, a_4, …, aK/3–2)),

a‴ = FFT(ω_3, (a_2, a_5, …, aK/3–1)),

Thus, we have for 0 ≤ ℓ < K/3:

ˆaℓ = a′ℓ + ωℓa″ℓ + ω2ℓa‴ℓ,

$$\hat{a}_{\ell+K/3} = a'_\ell + \omega^{\ell+K/3} a''_\ell + \omega^{2\ell+2K/3} a'''_\ell,$$

$$\hat{a}_{\ell+2K/3} = a'_\ell + \omega^{\ell+2K/3} a''_\ell + \omega^{2\ell+4K/3} a'''_\ell.$$

This set of operations corresponds to the "butterfly" operation (where a ← + b, b ← a + ωb) found in classical FFT.

8.4. DIVISION AND INVERSION

As demonstrated previously, modular multiplication can be simplified to integer division. Specifically, when calculating ab mod N using the traditional approach, the computation involves dividing ab by N, resulting in ab = qN + r (Palmer et al., 1987; Coyne et al., 1993). Consequently, ab ≡ r mod N. Modular division can be expressed as an integer (extended) greatest common divisor. Typically, the computation of the product of a/b mod N involves the modular multiplication of a and the modular inverse of b mod N, indicating that a modular multiplication follows a modular inverse. This section is focused on the topic of modular inversion. Previous observations that there is evidence to support the notion that… As demonstrated in Chapter 1, computation of an extended greatest common divisor (gcd) is costly. This is true for small sizes, where it typically requires multiple multiplications, and for larger sizes, it has a time complexity of O(M(n) log n). Hence, it is advisable to circumvent modular inversions whenever feasible. In the concluding part of this section, we will elucidate the methods to achieve this (Dixon et al., 1991; Desai et al., 2002; Seoighe et al., 2000).

Algorithm Modular Inverse, as presented in Figure 8.4, is essentially Algorithm ExtendedGcd (as described in Section 1.6.2), with the input parameters (a, b) being replaced by (b, N), and with the lines that calculate the cofactors of N being excluded.

```
Algorithm ModularInverse.
Input: integers b and N, b prime to N.
Output: integer u = 1/b mod N.
(u, w) ← (1, 0), c ← N
while c ≠ 0 do
    (q, r) ← DivRem(b, c)
    (b, c) ← (c, r)
    (u, w) ← (w, u − qw)
Return u.
```

Figure 8.8. Algorithm modular inverse.

Algorithm the modular inverse algorithm represents a basic implementation of flexible inversion, with a computational complexity of $O(n_2)$ if N comprises n words within base β. The algorithm that operates in O(M(n) log n) time complexity is subquadratic and relies on the HalfGcd method as its foundation (Albrecht-Buehler, 2006; Dobzhansky, T., & Sturtevant, 1999). In cases where the modulus N exhibits a specific structure, it is possible that more efficient algorithms can be employed. Specifically, O (M(n)) algorithms that utilize Hensel's lifting exist for N equal to pk. This method can be viewed as the p-adic version of Newton's method (4.2). The computation of 1/b mod N involves the process of iteration:

$$x_{j+1} = x_j + x_j(1 - bx_j) \bmod p^k.$$

Let xj be an approximation of 1/b with "p-adic precision" ℓ, meaning that bxj equals 1 + εpℓ. Subsequently, the value of bxj+1 can be expressed as the product of bxj and (2-bxj), which can be further simplified as (1 + εpℓ)(1 − εpℓ) resulting in 1 − ε2p2ℓ. Consequently, the value of xk+1 can be considered a double precision approximation of 1/b in the p-adic sense (Palmer et al., 1987; Beresnev, 2003; Gordon, 1998). For illustration, let us consider the computation of the modular inverse of a number that is odd b modulo 232. The value of $x_0 = 1$ is deemed satisfactory as it satisfies x_0 equals 1/b mod 2. Therefore, it is determined that a total of five iterations will suffice. The initial step involves the computation of x_1, which is obtained by applying the formula $x_1 \leftarrow x_0 + x_0(1 - bx_0)$ mod 22. By substituting $x_0 = 1$, the expression can be simplified to $x_1 \leftarrow 2 - b$ mod 4. Whether b is congruent to 1 modulo 4 or b is congruent to 3 modulo 4, it follows that 2 minus b is congruent to b modulo 4 (Dimitrov et al., 1998; Miller, 1994). Therefore, one may proceed directly to the second iteration by setting x_1 equal to:

$x_2 \leftarrow b(2 - b^2) \bmod 2^4$

$x_3 \leftarrow x_2(2 - bx_2) \bmod$

$2^8\ x_4 \leftarrow x_3(2 - bx_3) \bmod$

$2^{16}\ x_5 \leftarrow x_4(2 - bx_4) \bmod 2^{32}$

An illustrative instance to contemplate is when b equals 17. The algorithm presented above produces the values $x_2 = 1$, x_3 equals 241, $x_4 = 61681$, and x_5 equals 4042322161. Naturally, it is possible to perform computations modulo pk over k ≥ ℓ, including computations modulo pℓ (Brickell et al., 1992; Nedjah et al., 2002; Moreno & Hasan, 2011).

The operation is to be executed under the modulus of 232. Arithmetic operations on fundamental integer types are typically modulo 232 on a 32-bit computer. Consequently, the reduction is inherently incorporated, and it is customary to utilize unsigned variables when coding in the C programming language):

$$x_2 = b * (2 - b * b); \quad x_3 = x_2 * (2 - b * x_2); x_4 = x_3 * (2 - b * x_3); x_5 = x_4 * (2 - b * x_4)$$

Hensel's division is an alternative method for executing modular division in cases where the modulus exhibits a distinctive structure (Ha & Moon, 1998; Zerguine et al., 2020; Paillier, 1999). In the context of a modulus, N equals βn; it is possible to compute the quotient Q and remainder R when dividing two integers A and B.

$$A = QB + R\beta^n$$

Consequently, it can be stated that A/B is congruent to Q modulo βn. Montgomery's modular multiplication algorithm utilizes solely the remainder R obtained from Hensel's division. In contrast, the modular division requires the quotient Q. Therefore, Hensel's division is crucial in calculating modulo βn (Fit-Florea et al., 2005; Gordon, 1998; Quijano, 2000).

8.4.1. Several Inversions at Once

The computational cost of a modular inverting, which can be simplified to an extended greatest common divisor calculation, is typically higher than that of a multiplication operation. This assertion holds validity not solely within the FFT range, in which the computation of the greatest common divisor (gcd) requires a time complexity of Θ(M (n) log n), yet additionally for comparatively smaller numerical values (O'Connor, 1999; Phillips & Burgess, 2000). In cases where multiple inversions need to be executed modulo a common number, it is typically more efficient to utilize the following algorithm:

```
Algorithm MultipleInversion.
Input: 0 < x_1,...,x_k < N
Output: y_1 = 1/x_1 mod N,...,y_k = 1/x_k mod N
z_1 ← x_1
for i from 2 to k do
    z_i ← z_{i-1} x_i mod N
q ← 1/z_k mod N
for i from k downto 2 do
    y_i ← q z_{i-1} mod N
    q ← q x_i mod N
y_1 ← q
```

Figure 8.9. Algorithm MultipleInversion.

- **Proof:** At the onset of step i (line 8), we obtain zi ≡ x_1, x_2..., x_i mod N. Consequently, q ≡ (x_1... x_i) mod N. This, in turn, yields y_i ≡ 1/xi mod N (Kim & Aggarwal, 2001; Avanzi, 2000; Okeya et al., 2004).

The algorithm employs a singular modular inversion, three times k, and one modular multiplication. Consequently, if the cost of a modular reverse is more than three times the price of a product, the algorithm is quicker than k inversions. The algorithm's recursive variant is depicted in Figure 2.5, which involves an equal number of modular multiplications. Specifically, each internal node requires one modular multiplication when traversing up the product tree and two modular multiplications when traversing down the remainder tree. The recursive variation of this algorithm can be executed concurrently with k processors in O(log k) operations. However, the overall memory consumption was Θ(k log k) residues, as opposed to O(k) during the linear algorithm. The phenomenon of multiple inversion (Gu et al., 2007; Avanzi, 2005; Emmart et al., 2018).

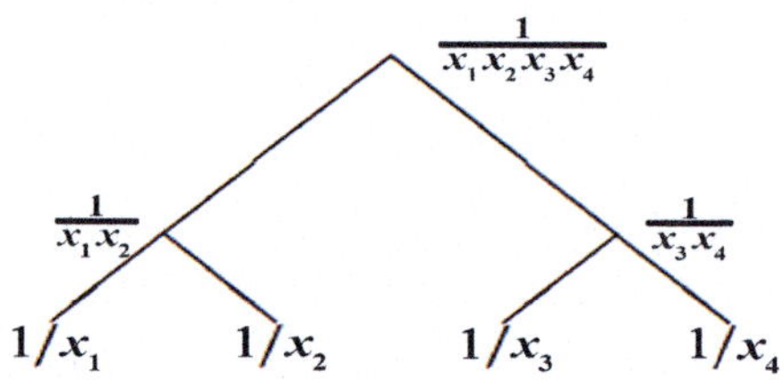

Figure 8.10. A recursive variant of Algorithm MultipleInversion. First, go up the tree, building x_1x_2 mod N from x_1 and x_2 in the left branch, x_3x_4 mod N in the right branch, and $x_1x_2x_3x_4$ mod N at the tree's root. Then invert the root of the tree.

A dual-case scenario arises when multiple moduli exist while the count of elements to be inverted remains constant (O'Connor, 1999; Kondracki, 1997; Wang et al., 2010). Consider the task of computing the modular inverses of x concerning N_1, ..., N_k, i.e., 1/x mod N_1, ..., 1/x mod N_k. A potential algorithm is demonstrated for the scenario where k equals 4. Initially, the computation of N can be achieved by utilizing a product tree, as illustrated in Figure 2.5. Specifically, N_1N_2 and N_3N_4 should be computed, multiplying both results to obtain N, N = (N_1N_2)(N_3N_4). Subsequently, calculate the y value by performing the operation of 1 divided by x modulo N. Proceed to traverse the tree downwards while diminishing the remainder at each node. In the given example, the computation of z equals y mod (N_1N_2) is performed in the left branch. Subsequently, the modulus of z with N_1 results in 1/x mod N_1. A significant contrast between the algorithm under consideration and the algorithm depicted in Figure 2.5 is that in the former, the numerical values increase as one ascends the tree. Therefore, the theoretical relevance of this algorithm may vary depending on the magnitudes of x and Nj (Iftene, 2007; Ekedahl, 1991; Zheng et al., 2007).

8.5. EXPONENTIATION

Modular exponentiation is the most time-consuming mathematical operation in several cryptographic algorithms (Quisquater et al., 2002). The well-known RSA algorithm is based on the fact that computing.

$$c = a^e \bmod N \qquad (8.5)$$

In various cryptographic algorithms, the modular exponentiation method is the mathematical operation that consumes the most time. The RSA algorithm, which is widely recognized, relies on the premise that computation is a relatively straightforward task. In contrast, retrieving the original value of "a" from "c," "e," and "N" is a challenging endeavor, particularly when "N" has a minimum of two prime factors of considerable magnitude. The task at hand is the discrete logarithm problem, which involves the given values of c, a, and N, and the objective is to identify e that satisfies equation (8.5). In cases where an exponent e is predetermined or deemed to be of a small magnitude, it is feasible to precompute an optimal ordering of multiplications and squares (Wang, 1998). This pertains to the classical problem of the addition chain. What is the minimal sequence of additive operations required to obtain the integer e from the number 1? An instance of a potential chain, when e is equal to 15, can be demonstrated as follows:

$$1,\ 1 + 1 = 2,\ 1 + 2 = 3,\ 1 + 3 = 4,\ 3 + 4 = 7,\ 7 + 7 = 14,\ 1 + 14 = 15.$$

The quantification of the extent of a link is established by the numerical value of the summations required for its computation. Therefore, the chain above possesses a length of 6 rather than 7. An addition chain can be easily converted into an exponentiation chain:

$$a,\ a \cdot a = a^2,\ a \cdot a^2 = a^3,\ a \cdot a^3 = a^4,\ a^3 \cdot a^4 = a^7,\ a^7 \cdot a^7 = a^{14},\ a \cdot a^{14} = a^{15}.$$

A shorter chain for $e = 15$ is:

$$1,\ 1 + 1 = 2,\ 2 + 2 = 3,\ 2 + 3 = 5,\ 5 + 5 = 10,\ 5 + 10 = 15.$$

The present chain is the minimal one for e = 15, and it is denoted by σ(15) equals 5, where σ(e) represents the length that is the smallest possible additional chain for e. When the value of e is relatively small, and the shortest possible addition chain of length σ(e) is available for e, a mod N can be computed using σ(e) modular multiplications. In cases where e is sufficiently large and (a, N) = 1, it is possible to perform a reduction of e modulo φ(N), where φ(N) represents Euler's totient function. This function denotes the count of integers within the range of [1, N] roughly equal to N. As mentioned earlier, the statement holds due to Fermat's little theorem, which states that aφ(N) is congruent to 1 modulo N whenever the greatest common divisor of a and N equals 1. Given the prime factorization of N, it is a straightforward task to calculate φ(N) due to the multiplicative nature of the φ function. As an illustration, let us consider the computation of the Euler totient function for the integer 1001. We can express 1001 as the product of its prime factors, namely 7, 11, and 13. Thus, we have φ(1001) equals φ(7 · 11 · 13) equals (7 – 1)(11 – 1)(13 – 1) equals 720. Additionally, we can determine that 2009 is congruent to 569 modulo 720. Consequently, we can conclude that 172009 is congruent to 17569 modulo 1001. Let us assume that the value of e is lesser than that of φ(N). Given that the length of the sum chain for e is bounded below by lg e, the modular exponentiation has a lower bound of (lg e)M(n), where n represents the size of N. In the scenario where e has a size of n, the computational expense of modular exponentiation is O(nM(n)). The algorithms in this section offer a negligible improvement compared to binary exponentiation, only differing by a constant factor.

8.5.1. Binary Exponentiation

As an illustration, the binary exponentiation algorithm is a straightforward and relatively efficient method for modular exponentiation. There are two distinct variants, namely left-to-right and right-to-left (Xiao et al., 2014). The algorithm for Left towards Right Binary Exponentiation is presented while determining the solution is deferred as a practice exercise for the reader.

Using left-to-right binary data exponentiation presents two benefits compared to right-to-left exponential growth.

The proposed method for exponentiation from left to right utilizes a single auxiliary variable, as opposed to the right-to-left method, which requires two variables; one for storing successive values for a_2i and another for storing the final result;

```
1 Algorithm LeftToRightBinaryExp.
2 Input: a,e,N positive integers
3 Output: x = a^e mod N
4 Let (e_ℓ e_{ℓ-1} ... e_1 e_0) be the binary representation of e
5 x ← a
6 for i = ℓ-1 downto 0 do
7     x ← x^2 mod N
8     if e_i = 1 then x ← ax mod N
```

Figure 8.11. Algorithm left to right binary exp.

In scenarios where the value of 'a' is relatively low, the multiplicative operations involving 'a' and 'x' at step 8 consistently entail a diminutive operand. Assuming e is an arbitrary integer consisting of n bits, it can be observed that step 8 is executed approximately n/2 times on average. Consequently, the Algorithm Left To Right Binary Exp is expected to incur an average cost of 3 ℓM (n).

- **Example:** for the exponent $e = 3499211612$, which is:

$(11010000100100011011101101011100)_2$

The Algorithm Left towards Right Binary Exp executes 31 squares and 15 additions and subtractions in binary representation. Each multiplication is performed for every 1-bit, except for the most significant one).

8.5.2. Base 2k Exponentiation

In contrast to binary exponentiation, using base 2k exponentiation results in a decrease in the number of multiplications performed in the ax mod N algorithm (specifically, in step 8 of the LeftToRightBinaryExp algorithm) (Meng et al., 2013). The concept involves the precomputation of minor powers of 'a' modulo 'N': The cost of pre-computation can be expressed as (2k – 2)M (n). Additionally, if the digits ei are uniformly distributed and random within the range of [0, 2k – 1], the probability of step 9 being executed is 1 – 2–k. Assuming that e possesses n bits, the approximate number of loops can be expressed as n/k. Excluding the square roots at step 8 that are dependent on kℓ n, the overall anticipated cost of additions and subtractions modulo N can be determined:

$$2^k - 2 + \underline{n}\,(1 - 2^{-k})$$

The formula above yields n/2 for k = 1, 3n + 2 for k = 2 (which exhibits superior performance for n values greater than or equal to 16), and 7n/8 for k = 3, derived from the k equal 2 formula for n = 48. For sufficiently large values of a variable, the optimum amount of another variable occurs when it is equal to 2 times the logarithm of 2. One of this algorithm's drawbacks is its memory usage, as it necessitates the storage of Θ(2k) precomputed entries.

- **Example:** The exponent e, denoted as 3499211612, is under consideration. The algorithm denoted as BaseKExp executes 31 squaring operations in a k-independent manner, thereby enabling the counting of multiplications exclusively. When k is equal to 2, the value of e is represented by the numerical sequence (3100210123231130).4: The Algorithm BaseKExp executes a single multiplication operation to precompute a_2, followed by 11 multiplication operations for the non-zero numbers of e in base 4, excluding the leading digit. When k equals 3, the value of e is (32044335534)8. The algorithm executes 6 multiplications to precompute a_2, a_3, …, a_7, along with 9 multiplications during step 9. This example presents two pieces of information. Initially, it is not necessary to precompute the powers of an if certain digits, such as 6 and 7, are absent in the base-2k symbol for e. In addition, it is possible to optimize the computation of even digits, such as ei = 2, by reducing the number of required squares. Specifically, instead of performing three squares and multiplying the result by a_2, one can achieve the same outcome by performing two squares, multiplying the result by a, and then performing a final squaring operation. Consequently, the ensuing procedure can be described as follows: The validity of the procedures outlined in steps 9–11 can be deduced from the preceding information:

$$x^{k} a^{m} = (x^{k-m} a)^{m} .$$

In the given example, where k equals 3, the algorithm above executes 4 multiplications for precomputing a_2, followed by a sequence of multiplications for a_3, a_5, a_7, and finally, 9 multiplication operations in step 10.

8.5.3. Sliding Window and Redundant Representation

The algorithm referred to as the "sliding window" is a simple extension of the BaseKExpOdd algorithm. The proposed approach involves partitioning the exponent onto windows instead of fixed kbit segments (Okeya et al., 2000). A contiguous sequence of zero bits may separate these windows. The process of decomposition initiates from the smallest number of bits.

For instance, in the case of e = 3499211612, the binary representation is considered:

`‚1¸x `1‚0¸1x 00 `0‚0¸1x `0‚0¸1x 00 `0‚1¸1x `0‚1¸1x `1‚0¸1x `1‚0¸1x 0 `1‚1¸1x 00

The present configuration comprises a set of 9 windows, denoted by e_8, …, e_0 above. Notably, the algorithm executes 8 multiplicative operations, thus exhibiting an enhancement of one multiplication compared to Algorithm BaseKExpOdd. The sliding opening algorithm typically results in approximately k+1 windows, as opposed to k, when utilizing fixed windows. Exponentiation in base-2.

An additional potential enhancement could be viable in cases where the division operation is feasible and cost-effective within the foundational group. Suppose three consecutive ones are present in the binary form of the mathematical constant e, denoted as 111. In that case, it is possible to substitute certain bits with the value of 1, represented as ¯1, resulting in a modified binary sequence such as 1001¯. Consequently, the procedure above has resulted in substituting three instances of multiplication with a singular instance of multiplication and division, specifically denoted as $x_7 = x_8 \cdot x{-}1$. In the context of our illustrative example, this yields:

e = 110100001001001 00

000¯100¯10¯100¯100,

The numerical value in question exhibits 10 non-zero digits, excluding the initial digit, instead of 15, when restricted to binary digits of 0 and 1. The Booth representation is denoted by the utilization of bits 0, 1, and ¯1 in a redundant manner.

This particular instance pertains to the Avizienis signed-digit redundant notation. Signed-digit notations are present in all numerical bases. The lack of differentiation between the expenses incurred in multiplication and squaring has been observed for the sake of simplicity. However, it is noteworthy that this differentiation holds significance in certain domains, such as elliptic curve cryptography. It should be noted that in groups defined across elliptic curves, where the underlying group operation is typically denoted by additional rather than multiplication, the discourse as mentioned above remains applicable with the substitution of “multiplication” for “addition,” “division” for “subtraction,” and “squaring” for “doubling.”

8.6. CHINESE REMAINDER THEOREM

In scenarios where integers or rational outcomes are anticipated, it can be advantageous to employ a residue number system, as outlined in section 2.1.3, and execute all calculations within the confines of a modular arithmetic framework, utilizing a set of small primes (Zheng et al., 2007). The outcome is retrieved using (CRT) the Chinese Remainder Theorem. In the context of these applications, the expeditious conversion of integers to modular representation and vice versa is of paramount significance. The problem at hand concerns the conversion of an integer to a modular form. This inquiry pertains to the efficient computation of xi, where x is an integer, and mi represents several prime moduli within the range of 1 to n. The objective is to determine the most effective approach to computing xi = x mod mi for each I value within the specified range. This corresponds precisely to the problem of constructing a remainder tree. The converse problem of the Chinese Remainder Theorem reconstruction is defined as follows: Given a set of residues xi and a product $M = m_1, m_2..., m_k$, the task is to efficiently reassemble the distinctive integer x, where $0 \leq x < M$, such that x is congruent to xi modulo mi for $1 \leq I \leq k$. It is adequate to address this issue for the value of k equal to 2 and apply the solution recursively. Let us consider the scenario where x is congruent to a_1 modulo m_1 and x is congruent to a_2 modulo m_2. The equation provided is x equals $\lambda m_1 + \mu m_2$. It follows that μm_2 is congruent to a_1 modulo m_1, and λm_2 is congruent to a_2 modulo m_2. Let us consider the computation of an extended greatest common divisor (gcd) of m_1 or m_2, whereby we possess knowledge of integers u and v such that their product with m_1 and m_2, respectively, sums up to 1. The values of μ and λ are inferred as $\mu \equiv va_1 \bmod m_1$ and $\lambda \equiv ua_2 \bmod m_2$, respectively. The expression $x \leftarrow (ua_2 \bmod m_2)m_1 + (va_1 \bmod m_1)m_2$ is presented. The inequality obtained is $x < 2m_1m_2$. To ensure that the value of x falls within the range of 0 to m_1m_2, it is necessary to set x equal to the difference between x and m_1m_2, provided that x is greater than or equal to m_1m_2 (Xiao et al., 2014; Wang 1998).

8.7. SUMMARY

Modular arithmetic is a crucial component in numerous number-theoretic algorithms, notably those that pertain to integer factorization, such as Pollard's ρ algorithm and the ellipse curve method. Modular arithmetic finds significant application in computer algebra for computing roots for univariate polynomials over a finite field. This necessitates the need for efficient mathematics over Fp[x]. It was stated that residue numeral systems are restricted to cases where N can be factored into N_1N_2... However, it has been demonstrated by Bernstein that modular arithmetic can indeed be carried out using a residual number system, despite this limitation. Steel provides instances of effective utilization of the Kronecker-Schönage technique. The algorithm for multiplication with the base case, as presented in section 2.3.5 under "The Base Case" and incorporating a repair step, is an extension of a previously published algorithm by Shoup in the Number Theory Library (NTL). The algorithm known as Toom-Cook 3-way, described in section 2.3.5, was developed by the second writer in collaboration with Michel Quercia, who suggested the precise division by $1 + x_2$. An implementation of this algorithm using the Number Theory Library (NTL) has been accessible on the second author's website since 2004. The multiplication algorithm utilizing a fast Fourier transform was developed by Schönage.

The initial exposition of Montgomery's Residue Decimation Algorithm (REDC). Currently, it is extensively utilized in various applications. Nonetheless, few authors have considered using a reduction factor that deviates from the conventional form of βn. Notably, McLaughlin, along with Mihailescu, are among those who have explored this approach. The technique of optimizing folding in REDC, as expounded in section 2.3.2 (Subquadratic Montgomery Reduction), constitutes an extension of the algorithm explicated in the context of Barrett's algorithm by Hasenplaugh, Gaubatz, and Gopal, specifically concerning the least significant bit. The algorithm proposed by Mihailescu, as described in section 2.3.3, draws inspiration from David Harvey's work.

REFERENCES

1. Akinola, S. O., & Olatidoye, A. A., (2015). On the image quality and encoding times of LSB, MSB and combined LSB-MSB steganography algorithms using digital images. *International Journal of Computer Science & Information Technology, 7*(4), 79–91.
2. Albrecht-Buehler, G., (2006). Asymptotically increasing compliance of genomes with Chargaff's second parity rules through inversions and inverted transpositions. *Proceedings of the National Academy of Sciences, 103*(47), 17828–17833.
3. Avanzi, R. M., & Mihăilescu, P., (2004). Generic efficient arithmetic algorithms for PAFFs (P rocessor A dequate F inite F ields) and related algebraic structures. In: *Selected Areas in Cryptography: 10th Annual International Workshop, SAC 2003, Ottawa, Canada* (pp. 320–334).
4. Avanzi, R. M., (2002). On multi-exponentiation in cryptography. *Cryptology ePrint Archive*.
5. Avanzi, R. M., (2005). A note on the signed sliding window integer recoding and a left-to-right analogue. In: *Selected Areas in Cryptography: 11th International Workshop, SAC 2004, Waterloo, Canada* (pp. 130–143). Springer Berlin Heidelberg.
6. Bajard, J. C., Didier, L. S., & Kornerup, P., (1998). An RNS Montgomery modular multiplication algorithm. *IEEE Transactions on Computers, 47*(7), 766–776.
7. Bajard, J. C., Imbert, L., & Jullien, G. A., (2005). Parallel Montgomery multiplication in GF (2/sup k/) using trinomial residue arithmetic. In: *17th IEEE Symposium on Computer Arithmetic (ARITH'05)* (pp. 164–171).
8. Bajard, J. C., Negre, C., & Plantard, T., (2010). Subquadratic space complexity binary field multiplier using double polynomial representation. *IEEE Transactions on Computers, 59*(12), 1585–1597.
9. Baktir, S., & Sunar, B., (2006). Achieving efficient polynomial multiplication in Fermat fields using the fast fourier transform. In: *Proceedings of the 44th Annual Southeast Regional Conference* (pp. 549–554).
10. Barrett, C., Bisset, K., Holzer, M., Konjevod, G., Marathe, M., & Wagner, D., (2008). Engineering label-constrained shortest-path algorithms. In: *Algorithmic Aspects in Information and Management: Proceedings 4th International Conference, AAIM 2008, Shanghai, China* (pp. 27–37).
11. Barrett, S. R., & Britter, R. E., (2008). Development of algorithms and approximations for rapid operational air quality modelling. *Atmospheric*

Environment, 42(34), 8105–8111.

12. Barrett, S. R., & Britter, R. E., (2009). Algorithms and analytical solutions for rapidly approximating long-term dispersion from line and area sources. *Atmospheric Environment, 43*(20), 3249–3258.
13. Barrett, S., Stone, P., & Kraus, S., (2011). Empirical evaluation of ad hoc teamwork in the pursuit domain. In: *The 10th International Conference on Autonomous Agents and Multiagent Systems* (Vol. 2, pp. 567–574).
14. Beresnev, I. A., (2003). Uncertainties in finite-fault slip inversions: to what extent to believe? (a critical review). *Bulletin of the Seismological Society of America, 93*(6), 2445–2458.
15. Brent, R. P., Gaudry, P., Thomé, E., & Zimmermann, P., (2008). Faster multiplication in GF (2)[x]. In: *Algorithmic Number Theory: Proceedings 8th International Symposium, ANTS-VIII Banff, Canada* (pp. 153–166). Springer Berlin Heidelberg.
16. Brickell, E. F., Gordon, D. M., McCurley, K. S., & Wilson, D. B., (1992). Fast exponentiation with precomputation. In: *Workshop on the Theory and Application of Cryptographic Techniques* (pp. 200–207). Berlin, Heidelberg: Springer Berlin Heidelberg.
17. Brönnimann, H., Emiris, I. Z., Pan, V. Y., & Pion, S., (1999). Sign determination in residue number systems. *Theoretical Computer Science, 210*(1), 173–197.
18. Cao, B., Chang, C. H., & Srikanthan, T., (2007). A residue-to-binary converter for a new five-moduli set. *IEEE Transactions on Circuits and Systems I: Regular Papers, 54*(5), 1041–1049.
19. Chen, D. D., Yao, G. X., Cheung, R. C., Pao, D., & Koç, C. K., (2015). Parameter space for the architecture of FFT-based Montgomery modular multiplication. *IEEE Transactions on Computers, 65*(1), 147–160.
20. Chervyakov, N. I., Lyakhov, P. A., & Babenko, M. G., (2014). Digital filtering of images in a residue number system using finite-field wavelets. *Automatic Control and Computer Sciences, 48*, 180–189.
21. Chung, J., & Hasan, M. A., (2007). Asymmetric squaring formulae. In: *18th IEEE Symposium on Computer Arithmetic (ARITH'07)* (pp. 113–122). IEEE.
22. Cohen, M., & Montgomery, S., (1984). Group-graded rings, smash products, and group actions. *Transactions of the American Mathematical Society, 282*(1), 237–258.
23. Coyne, J. A., Meyers, W., Crittenden, A. P., & Sniegowski, P., (1993). The fertility effects of pericentric inversions in Drosophila melanogaster. *Genetics, 134*(2), 487–496.

24. De Win, E., Bosselaers, A., Vandenberghe, S., De Gersem, P., & Vandewalle, J., (1996). A fast software implementation for arithmetic operations in GF (2 n). In: *Advances in Cryptology—ASIACRYPT'96: Proceedings International Conference on the Theory and Applications of Cryptology and Information Security Kyongju, Korea* (pp. 65–76). Springer Berlin Heidelberg.
25. De, A., Kurur, P. P., Saha, C., & Saptharishi, R., (2008). Fast integer multiplication using modular arithmetic. In: *Proceedings of the 40th Annual ACM Symposium on Theory of Computing* (Vol. 1, pp. 499–506).
26. Desai, M. A., & Hines Jr. J. R., (2002). Expectations and expatriations: Tracing the causes and consequences of corporate inversions. *National Tax Journal, 55*(3), 409–440.
27. Dimitrov, V. S., Jullien, G. A., & Miller, W. C., (1998). An algorithm for modular exponentiation. *Information Processing Letters, 66*(3), 155–159.
28. Dixon, W. T., Sardashti, M., Castillo, M., & Stomp, G. P., (1991). Multiple inversion recovery reduces static tissue signal in angiograms. *Magnetic Resonance in Medicine, 18*(2), 257–268.
29. Dobzhansky, T., & Sturtevant, A. H., (1999). Inversions in the chromosomes of Drosophila pseudoobscura. *Genetics, 23*(1), 28.
30. Ekedahl, T., (1991). An infinite version of the Chinese remainder theorem. *Rikkyo Daigaku Sugaku Zasshi, 40*(1), 53–59.
31. Eldridge, S. E., & Walter, C. D., (1993). Hardware implementation of Montgomery's modular multiplication algorithm. *IEEE Transactions on Computers, 42*(6), 693–699.
32. Emmart, N., Zheng, F., & Weems, C., (2018). Faster modular exponentiation using double precision floating point arithmetic on the GPU. In: *2018 IEEE 25th Symposium on Computer Arithmetic (ARITH)* (pp. 130–137). IEEE.
33. Fedorenko, S., & Trifonov, P., (2002). On computing the fast Fourier transform over finite fields. In: *Proc. 8th Int. Workshop on Algebraic and Combinatorial Coding Theory, Tsarskoe Selo, Russia* (pp. 108–111).
34. Fit-Florea, A., Matula, D. W., & Thornton, M. A., (2005). Addition-based exponentiation modulo 2k. *Electronics Letters, 41*(2), 56–57.
35. Ghosh, J., & Fowler, A. G., (2015). Leakage-resilient approach to fault-tolerant quantum computing with superconducting elements. *Physical Review A, 91*(2), 020302.
36. Giorgi, P., Negre, C., & Plantard, T., (2007). Subquadratic binary field multiplier in double polynomial system. In: *SECRYPT'2007: International*

Conference on Security and Cryptography (Vol. 1, pp. 229–236)

37. Gordon, D. M., (1998). A survey of fast exponentiation methods. *Journal of Algorithms, 27*(1), 129–146.
38. Großschädl, J., & Savaş, E., (2004). Instruction set extensions for fast arithmetic in finite fields GF (p) and GF (2 m). In: *Cryptographic Hardware and Embedded Systems-CHES 2004: Proceedings 6th International Workshop Cambridge, MA, USA* (pp. 133–147). Springer Berlin Heidelberg.
39. Großschädl, J., Avanzi, R. M., Savaş, E., & Tillich, S., (2005). Energy-efficient software implementation of long integer modular arithmetic. In: *Cryptographic Hardware and Embedded Systems–CHES 2005: Proceedings 7th International Workshop, Edinburgh, UK* (pp. 75–90).
40. Gu, I. Y. H., & Bollen, M. H., (2007). Estimating interharmonics by using sliding-window ESPRIT. *IEEE Transactions on Power Delivery, 23*(1), 13–23.
41. Gu, Z., & Li, S., (2018). A division-free Toom–Cook multiplication-based Montgomery modular multiplication. *IEEE Transactions on Circuits and Systems II: Express Briefs, 66*(8), 1401–1405.
42. Guo, J. H., & Wang, C. L., (1998). Hardware-efficient systolic architecture for inversion and division in GF (2m). *IEE Proceedings-Computers and Digital Techniques, 145*(4), 272–278.
43. Ha, J. C., & Moon, S. J., (1998). A common-multiplicand method to the Montgomery algorithm for speeding up exponentiation. *Information Processing Letters, 66*(2), 105–107.
44. Hars, L., (2006). Applications of fast truncated multiplication in cryptography. *EURASIP Journal on Embedded Systems, 2007*(1), 061721.
45. Huang, M., Gaj, K., & El-Ghazawi, T., (2010). New hardware architectures for Montgomery modular multiplication algorithm. *IEEE Transactions on Computers, 60*(7), 923–936.
46. Huang, M., Gaj, K., Kwon, S., & El-Ghazawi, T., (2008). An optimized hardware architecture for the Montgomery multiplication algorithm. In: *Public Key Cryptography–PKC 2008: Proceedings 11th International Workshop on Practice and Theory in Public-Key Cryptography, Barcelona, Spain* (pp. 214–228).
47. Iftene, S., (2007). General secret sharing based on the Chinese remainder theorem with applications in e-voting. *Electronic Notes in Theoretical Computer Science, 186*, 67–84.
48. Imran, M., Abideen, Z. U., & Pagliarini, S., (2021). An open-source

library of large integer polynomial multipliers. In: *2021 24th International Symposium on Design and Diagnostics of Electronic Circuits & Systems (DDECS)* (pp. 145–150). IEEE.

49. Itoh, T., & Tsujii, S., (1988). A fast algorithm for computing multiplicative inverses in GF (2m) using normal bases. *Information and Computation, 78*(3), 171–177.
50. Jones, V. F., (1987). Hecke algebra representations of braid groups and link polynomials. In: *New Developments in the Theory of Knots* (pp. 20–73).
51. Kalach, K., & David, J. P., (2005). Hardware implementation of large number multiplication by FFT with modular arithmetic. In: *The 3rd International IEEE-NEWCAS Conference* (Vol. 1, pp. 267–270).
52. Kawamura, S., Koike, M., Sano, F., & Shimbo, A., (2000). Cox-rower architecture for fast parallel montgomery multiplication. In: *Advances in Cryptology—EUROCRYPT 2000: Proceedings 19th International Conference on the Theory and Application of Cryptographic Techniques Bruges, Belgium* (pp. 523–538).
53. Kim, C. H., & Aggarwal, R., (2001). Wavelet transforms in power systems. Part II – Examples of application to actual power system transients. *Power Engineering Journal, 15*(4), 193–202.
54. Koc, C. K., Acar, T., & Kaliski, B. S., (1996). Analyzing and comparing Montgomery multiplication algorithms. *IEEE Micro, 16*(3), 26–33.
55. Kondracki, A., (1997). The Chinese remainder theorem. *Formalized Mathematics, 6*(4), 573–577.
56. Larasati, H. T., Awaludin, A. M., Ji, J., & Kim, H., (2021). Quantum circuit design of Toom 3-way multiplication. *Applied Sciences, 11*(9), 3752.
57. Lee, C. Y., Meher, P. K., & Chang, C. P., (2014). Efficient $ M $-ARY exponentiation over $ GF (2^{m}) $ using subquadratic KA-based three-operand Montgomery multiplier. *IEEE Transactions on Circuits and Systems I: Regular Papers, 61*(11), 3125–3134.
58. Lee, C. Y., Yang, C. S., Meher, B. K., Meher, P. K., & Pan, J. S., (2014). Low-complexity digit-serial and scalable SPB/GPB multipliers over large binary extension fields using (b,2)-way Karatsuba decomposition. *IEEE Transactions on Circuits and Systems I: Regular Papers, 61*(11), 3115–3124.
59. Lim, Y. L., Barrett, S. D., Beige, A., Kok, P., & Kwek, L. C., (2006). Repeat-until-success quantum computing using stationary and flying qubits. *Physical Review A, 73*(1), 012304.
60. López, J., & Dahab, R., (1999). Fast multiplication on elliptic curves over GF (2 m) without precomputation. In: *Cryptographic Hardware and*

Embedded Systems: Proceedings 1st International Workshop, CHES'99 Worcester, MA, USA (pp. 316–327). Springer Berlin Heidelberg.

61. Mahmood, M. A., Visan, A. I., Ristoscu, C., & Mihailescu, I. N., (2020). Artificial neural network algorithms for 3D printing. *Materials, 14*(1), 163.
62. Marin, I., & Wagner, E., (2013). A cubic defining algebra for the Links–Gould polynomial. *Advances in Mathematics, 248*, 1332–1365.
63. Mason, G. S., Shuman, T. R., & Cook, K. E., (2013). Comparing the effectiveness of an inverted classroom to a traditional classroom in an upper-division engineering course. *IEEE Transactions on Education, 56*(4), 430–435.
64. Mastrovito, E. D., (1988). VLSI designs for multiplication over finite fields GF (2m). In: *International Conference on Applied Algebra, Algebraic Algorithms, and Error-Correcting Codes* (pp. 297–309). Berlin, Heidelberg: Springer Berlin Heidelberg.
65. Meng, L., & Johnson, J., (2013). Automatic parallel library generation for general-size modular FFT algorithms. In: *Computer Algebra in Scientific Computing: Proceedings 15th International Workshop, CASC 2013, Berlin, Germany* (pp. 243–256).
66. Mihailescu, M., & Teo, Y. M., (2010). On economic and computational-efficient resource pricing in large distributed systems. In: *2010 10th IEEE/ACM International Conference on Cluster, Cloud and Grid Computing* (pp. 838–843)
67. Mihailescu, M., & Teo, Y. M., (2010). Strategy-proof dynamic resource pricing of multiple resource types on federated clouds. In: *ICA3PP* (Vol. 1, pp. 337–350).
68. Mihailescu, P., Morain, F., & Schost, É., (2007). Computing the eigenvalue in the Schoof-Elkies-Atkin algorithm using Abelian lifts. In: *Proceedings of the 2007 International Symposium on Symbolic and Algebraic Computation* (pp. 285–292).
69. Miller, C., (1994). Exponentiation is hard to avoid. *Proceedings of the American Mathematical Society, 122*(1), 257–259.
70. Montgomery, P. L., (1985). Modular multiplication without trial division. *Mathematics of Computation, 44*(170), 519–521.
71. Moreno, C., & Hasan, M. A., (2011). SPA-resistant binary exponentiation with optimal execution time. *Journal of Cryptographic Engineering, 1*(2), 87.
72. Nedjah, N., & de Macedo Mourelle, L., (2002). Reconfigurable hardware

implementation of Montgomery modular multiplication and parallel binary exponentiation. In: *Proceedings Euromicro Symposium on Digital System Design: Architectures, Methods and Tools* (pp. 226–233). IEEE.

73. Negre, C., & Plantard, T., (2008). Efficient modular arithmetic in adapted modular number system using lagrange representation. In: *Information Security and Privacy: Proceedings 13th Australasian Conference, ACISP 2008, Wollongong, Australia* (pp. 463–477).
74. O'Connor, L., (1999). An analysis of exponentiation based on formal languages. In: *Advances in Cryptology—EUROCRYPT'99: Proceedings International Conference on the Theory and Application of Cryptographic Techniques Prague, Czech Republic* (pp. 375–388). Berlin, Heidelberg: Springer Berlin Heidelberg.
75. Okeya, K., Kurumatani, H., & Sakurai, K., (2000). Elliptic curves with the Montgomery-form and their cryptographic applications. In: *Public Key Cryptography* (Vol. 1751, pp. 238–257).
76. Okeya, K., Schmidt-Samoa, K., Spahn, C., & Takagi, T., (2004). Signed binary representations revisited. In: *CRYPTO* (Vol. 2004, pp. 23–139).
77. Paillier, P., (1999). Low-cost double-size modular exponentiation or how to stretch your cryptoprocessor. In: *Public Key Cryptography: Proceedings 2nd International Workshop on Practice and Theory in Public Key Cryptography, PKC'99 Kamakura, Japan* (pp. 223–234). Berlin, Heidelberg: Springer Berlin Heidelberg.
78. Palmer, J. D., Nugent, J. M., & Herbon, L. A., (1987). Unusual structure of geranium chloroplast DNA: a triple-sized inverted repeat, extensive gene duplications, multiple inversions, and two repeat families. *Proceedings of the National Academy of Sciences, 84*(3), 769–773.
79. Palmer, J. D., Osorio, B., Aldrich, J., & Thompson, W. F., (1987). Chloroplast DNA evolution among legumes: loss of a large, inverted repeat occurred prior to other sequence rearrangements. *Current Genetics, 11*, 275–286.
80. Phillips, B., & Burgess, N., (2000). Optimized squaring with sliding windows. In: *Conference Record of the 34th Asilomar Conference on Signals, Systems and Computers* (Cat. No. 00CH37154) (Vol. 1, pp. 130–133). IEEE.
81. Plantard, T., (2021). Efficient word size modular arithmetic. *IEEE Transactions on Emerging Topics in Computing, 9*(3), 1506–1518.
82. Pollard, J. M., (1971). The fast Fourier transform in a finite field. *Mathematics of Computation, 25*(114), 365–374.
83. Posch, K. C., & Posch, R., (1995). Modulo reduction in residue number

systems. *IEEE Transactions on Parallel and Distributed Systems, 6*(5), 449–454.

84. Putranto, D. S. C., Wardhani, R. W., Larasati, H. T., & Kim, H., (2023). Space and time-efficient quantum multiplier in post quantum cryptography era. *IEEE Access, 11*, 21848–21862.
85. Quijano, A., (2000). Coloniality of power and Eurocentrism in Latin America. *International Sociology, 15*(2), 215–232.
86. Quisquater, M., Preneel, B., & Vandewalle, J., (2002). On the security of the threshold scheme based on the Chinese remainder theorem. In: *Public Key Cryptography: Proceedings 5th International Workshop on Practice and Theory in Public Key Cryptosystems, PKC 2002 Paris, France* (pp. 199–210). Springer Berlin Heidelberg.
87. Robert, J. M., & Véron, P., (2022). Faster multiplication over F _2 X F 2 X using AVX512 instruction set and VPCLMULQDQ instruction. *Journal of Cryptographic Engineering*, 1–19.
88. Robinson, K. M., & LeFevre, J. A., (2012). The inverse relation between multiplication and division: Concepts, procedures, and a cognitive framework. *Educational Studies in Mathematics, 79*(3), 409–428.
89. Robinson, K. M., & Ninowski, J. E., (2003). Adults' understanding of inversion concepts: how does performance on addition and subtraction inversion problems compare to performance on multiplication and division inversion problems? *Canadian Journal of Experimental Psychology/Revue canadienne de psychologie expérimentale, 57*(4), 321.
90. Roncero, O., Zanchet, A., Villarreal, P., & Aguado, A., (2009). A density-division embedding potential inversion technique. *The Journal of Chemical Physics, 131*(23), 234110.
91. Schindler, W., (2000). A timing attack against RSA with the Chinese remainder theorem. In: *Cryptographic Hardware and Embedded Systems—CHES 2000: Proceedings 2nd International Workshop Worcester, MA, USA* (pp. 109–124). Springer Berlin Heidelberg.
92. Scott, P., Tavares, S. E., & Peppard, L., (1986). A fast VLSI multiplier for GF (2 m). *IEEE Journal on Selected Areas in Communications, 4*(1), 62–66.
93. Seoighe, C., Federspiel, N., Jones, T., Hansen, N., Bivolarovic, V., Surzycki, R., & Wolfe, K. H., (2000). Prevalence of small inversions in yeast gene order evolution. *Proceedings of the National Academy of Sciences, 97*(26), 14433–14437.
94. Silverman, J. H., (1999). Fast multiplication in finite fields GF (2 N). In: *Cryptographic Hardware and Embedded Systems: Proceedings 1st*

International Workshop, CHES'99 Worcester, MA, USA (pp. 122–134). Springer Berlin Heidelberg.

95. Tenca, A. F., & Koç, Ç. K., (2003). A scalable architecture for modular multiplication based on Montgomery's algorithm. *IEEE Transactions on Computers, 52*(9), 1215–1221.
96. Titu, A. M., Boroiu, A. A., Mihailescu, S., Pop, A. B., & Boroiu, A., (2022). Assessment of road noise pollution in urban residential areas – A case study in Piteşti, Romania. *Applied Sciences, 12*(8), 4053.
97. Traldi, L., (1989). A dichromatic polynomial for weighted graphs and link polynomials. *Proceedings of the American Mathematical Society, 106*(1), 279–286.
98. Trifonov, P. V., & Fedorenko, S. V., (2003). A method for fast computation of the Fourier transform over a finite field. *Problems of Information Transmission, 39*(3), 231–238.
99. Umer, U., Rashid, M., Alharbi, A. R., Alhomoud, A., Kumar, H., & Jafri, A. R., (2022). An efficient crypto processor architecture for side-channel resistant binary huff curves on FPGA. *Electronics, 11*(7), 1131.
100. Wang, W., & Xia, X. G., (2010). A closed-form robust Chinese remainder theorem and its performance analysis. *IEEE Transactions on Signal Processing, 58*(11), 5655–5666.
101. Wang, Y., (1998). New Chinese remainder theorems. In: *Conference Record of 32nd Asilomar Conference on Signals, Systems and Computers* (Cat. No. 98CH36284) (Vol. 1, pp. 165–171). IEEE.
102. Wang, Y., (2000). Residue-to-binary converters based on new Chinese remainder theorems. *IEEE Transactions on Circuits and Systems II: Analog and Digital Signal Processing, 47*(3), 197–205.
103. Wurman, P. R., Barrett, S., Kawamoto, K., MacGlashan, J., Subramanian, K., Walsh, T. J., & Kitano, H., (2022). Outracing champion Gran Turismo drivers with deep reinforcement learning. *Nature, 602*(7896), 223–228.
104. Xiao, L., Xia, X. G., & Wang, W., (2014). Multi-stage robust Chinese remainder theorem. *IEEE Transactions on Signal Processing, 62*(18), 4772–4785.
105. Yan, Z., & Sarwate, D. V., (2003). New systolic architectures for inversion and division in GF (2/sup m/). *IEEE Transactions on Computers, 52*(11), 1514–1519.
106. Yao, X. C., Wang, T. X., Chen, H. Z., Gao, W. B., Fowler, A. G., Raussendorf, R., & Pan, J. W., (2012). Experimental demonstration of topological error correction. *Nature, 482*(7386), 489–494.

107. Zerguine, N., Aliouat, Z., Mostefai, M., & Harous, S., (2020). M-BEB: enhanced and fair binary exponential backoff. In: *2020 14th International Conference on Innovations in Information Technology (IIT)* (pp. 142–147). IEEE.

108. Zheng, X., Huang, C. T., & Matthews, M., (2007). Chinese remainder theorem-based group key management. In: *Proceedings of the 45th Annual Southeast Regional Conference* (pp. 266–271).

109. Zimmermann, P., (2007). How fast can we multiply over gf (2)[x]? In: *Proceedings of Conference on Algorithmic Number Theory 2007* (pp. 165–170).

INDEX